STUDIES IN ISLAMIC LAW AND SOCIETY

EDITED BY

RUUD PETERS AND BERNARD WEISS

VOLUME 4

THE FORMATION OF THE S
9th-10th CEN

THE FORMATION OF THE SUNNI SCHOOLS OF LAW, 9th-10th CENTURIES C.E.

BY

CHRISTOPHER MELCHERT

BRILL
LEIDEN · NEW YORK · KÖLN
1997

This book is printed on acid-free paper.

Library of Congress Cataloging-in-Publication Data

Melchert, Christopher.
The formation of the Sunni schools of law, 9th-10th centuries C.E. / by Christopher Melchert
p. cm. — (Studies in Islamic law and society, ISSN 1384–1130 ; v. 4)
Includes bibliographical references and index.
ISBN 9004109528 (cloth : alk. paper)
1. Islamic law—Study and teaching—History. I. Title. II. Series: Studies in Islamic law and society ; v. 4.
LAW <ISLAM 7 Melc 1997
340.5'9—dc21 97-40209
CIP

Die Deutsche Bibliothek - CIP-Einheitsaufnahme
Melchert, Christopher:
The formation of the sunni schools of law : 9th-10th centuries C.E. / by Christopher Melchert. – Leiden ; New York ; Köln : Brill, 1997
(Studies in Islamic law and society ; Vol. 4)
ISBN 90-04-10952-8

ISSN 1384–1130
ISBN 90 04 10952 8

PRINTED IN THE NETHERLANDS

To my parents, Jim & Mary Ann Melchert

Some of the research behind this book was made possible
by a Fulbright country fellowship (1989-90) and
by a Charlotte Newcombe dissertation fellowship (1990-91).

TABLE OF CONTENTS

TRANSLITERATION AND DATES

My transliteration of Arabic follows the system that the Library of Congress recommends.[1] It distinguishes between *alif* and *alif maqṣūrah* (e.g., *mā*, *'alá*) but not between *alif-lām* before sun and *alif-lām* before moon letters (e.g., al-Shāfi'ī, al-Bājūrī). In alphabetical lists, *al-* is ignored at the beginning of a name (e.g., al-'Abbādī precedes 'Abd Allāh) but not in the middle (e.g., Ibn al-Ṣalāḥ precedes Ibn Ḥajar). I do anglicize adjectives to the extent of omitting the macron over a final *i* (e.g., al-Shāfi'ī, the Shāfi'i school).

I give years first according to the Hijri calendar, then according to the Christian; e.g., 204/820, the year al-Shāfi'ī died. Often, our sources tell us the Hijri year in which something took place but not the month, or the month but not the day, so that one cannot tell in just which Christian year it took place. In such cases, I use a hyphen to indicate that the event took place during a period of 354 or 355 days overlapping those two Christian years; e.g., 150/767-768, the year al-Shāfi'ī was born. Centuries I give only by the common era, except where I expressly indicate otherwise; e.g., "the ninth century" means A.D. 801-900 (roughly A.H. 184-288).

Major place names I write without diacritics. "Old Cairo" indicates what is usually just *Miṣr* in the sources, occasionally *al-Fusṭāṭ*. "Africa" indicates medieval *Ifrīqiyā/Ifrīqīyah*, roughly the area of modern Tunisia. Partly for the sake of euphony, I commonly use Classical Arabic forms for bodies of men; e.g., "the Shāfi'īyah" rather than "the Shāfi'is." The party of 'Alī presents special difficulty. I normally designate an individual adherent by "Shī'i," the body of adherents by "Shī'ah." "Shias" and similar forms seem to have established themselves in South Asian English, but this Arabist cannot bring himself to use them. I have tried to identify correctly the short vowels of names written in Arabic, wherever possible following the advice of Ibn Ḥajar, Carl Brockelmann, and Fuat Sezgin. In the few places where I have found no evidence and dared not guess, I supply asterisks in place of the unwritten vowels.

---

[1] *V. ALA-LC Romanization Tables*, ed. Randall K. Barry (Washington, DC: Library of Congress Cataloging Distribution Service, 1991).

INTRODUCTION

ISLAMIC LAW AND THE *MADHHAB*

This study concerns the formation of schools of law in Sunni Islam. Law is central to Islamic piety. The Qur'an continually relates faith in God to obedience. "He who believes in God and does good works," "Those who believe and give alms"—again and again such phrases recur. An expression of the centrality of law to Islam is that Muslim men of religion, the *'ulamā'*, are jurisprudents, trained to give juridical opinions. Even the great medieval mystics were usually trained jurisprudents; for example, 'Abd al-Qādir al-Jīlānī (d. Baghdad, 561/1166), to whom goes back the earliest Sufi order, was also a jurisprudent of the Ḥanbali school, while Ibn al-'Arabī (d. Damascus, 638/1240), the great master of theosophical Sufism, gave juridical opinions and wrote books on legal duties. Contrast Western figures such as Bernard of Clairvaux and Meister Eckhart, normally discussed without the least reference to their knowledge of canon law.

A Muslim finds out what the law is by asking a jurisprudent to give his opinion. The jurisprudent has been taught the basic evidence of what God wants, mainly the Qur'an and Sunnah (in effect, selected reports of the words and deeds of Muḥammad), and how to derive practical answers from that evidence. He goes over the evidence in his mind, comes to a conclusion, tells it, and at this point there appears Islamic law. The notion of Islamic law as a code to be applied by public authority is modern: classically, Islamic law is much nearer to a process than a code.[1]

Although Islamic law is classically deduced anew every time a question is raised, answers are to some degree predictable. In the first place, most basic points are covered by a consensus among the scholars; for example, that one should pray five times a day, which all Muslims accept as the rule even though neither the Qur'an nor any

[1] For a splendid discussion of Arabic *shar'* and *sharī'ah*, stressing communication between heaven and earth, see Wilfred Cantwell Smith, "The Concept of *Sharī'a* Among Some *Mutakallimūn*," pp. 581-602 in *Arabic and Islamic Studies in Honor of Hamilton A. R. Gibb*, ed. George Makdisi (Leiden: E. J. Brill, 1965), esp. 598f.

prophetic hadith report expressly requires it. In the second place, jurisprudents always adhere to one or another school of law, each with its own answer to many questions, or its own range of answers. In practice, jurisprudents almost never depart from the range of answers preferred by their schools.

The Arabic word I translate as "school" is *madhhab* (pl. *madhāhib*). It means literally the way one goes. As such, it is sometimes used interchangeably with *ṭarīqah*. For example, the Baghdadi Mu'tazili Muḥammad ibn Zayd al-Wāsiṭī (d. 307/921-922) is quoted as jeering, "Whoever wants to go to the utmost in ignorance, let him read *kalām* (dialectical theology) according to the *ṭarīqah* of al-Bāsī, jurisprudence according to the *ṭarīqah* of Dāwūd, and grammar according to the *ṭarīqah* of Nifṭawayh." The later biographer Ibn Ḥajar explains that Nifṭawayh (d. 323/935) practiced *kalām* according to the *ṭarīqah* of "al-Bāsī", jurisprudence according to the *madhhab* of Dāwūd.[2]

Ibn Ḥajar's preference for *ṭarīqah* in grammar, *madhhab* in law, agrees with later convention. Similarly, Ibn Abī al-Wafā' will refer to someone as Ḥanafi of *madhhab* (i.e., as to the rules of jurisprudence), Mu'tazili of *kalām*.[3] Earlier, just as Muḥammad ibn Zayd al-Wāsiṭī would apply *ṭarīqah* to a body of teaching in jurisprudence, so *madhhab* would be applied to schools of theology; hence, for example, al-Khʷārizmī (*fl.* 365/975) speaks of the seven *madhāhib* of the Muslims: Mu'tazilah, Kharijites, *aṣḥāb al-ḥadīth*, Mujbirah, Mushabbihah, Murji'ah, and Shī'ah.[4] Similarly, his contemporary al-Maqdisī (*fl.* 375/985) divides the Muslims among 24 *madhāhib*, of which four concern jurisprudence, four *kalām*, four both jurisprudence and *kalām*, and so on.[5] For this reason, I speak of "schools of law," not simply "schools."

The term *madhhab* most often refers to doctrine. At its simplest,

---

[2] Ibn Ḥajar, *Lisān "al-Mīzān,"* 7 vols. (Hyderabad: Maṭba'at Majlis Dā'irat al-Ma'ārif, 1329-31), 5:173. "Al-Bāsī" is probably a corruption of al-Nāshi' (d. 292/904-905), on whom *v. Lisān* 3:334.

[3] Ibn Abī al-Wafā', *al-Jawāhir al-muḍīyah*, 2 vols. (Hyderabad: Majlis Dā'irat al-Ma'ārif al-Niẓāmīyah, 1332), 2:245.

[4] Al-Khʷārizmī, *Liber Mafâtîh al-olûm*, ed. G. van Vloten (Leiden: E. J. Brill, 1895), 24-31.

[5] Al-Muqaddasī (i.e., al-Maqdisī), *Descriptio imperii moslemici*, ed. M. J. de Goeje, Bibliotheca geographorum Arabicorum 3, 2nd edn. (Leiden: E. J. Brill, 1906), 37.

this means a particular tenet. For example, Ibn al-Nadīm (*fl.* 377/987) accuses the Sufi al-Ḥallāj of espousing the *madhāhib* of the Shī'ah before kings, the *madhāhib* of the Sufis before the general.[6] Here, *madhhab* has no special reference to law.

In the field of law, *madhhab* may similarly refer to a jurisprudent's opinion concerning a particular case. Indeed, this is its most common meaning when one comes across it in a juridical text. For example, Ibn Qudāmah al-Maqdisī (d. Damascus, 620/1223), discussing whether someone's hand is to be amputated for stealing the clothes of a negligent bather, says that it is the *madhhab* of al-Shāfi'ī not to do so, "and the apparent meaning (*ẓāhir*) of the *madhhab* of Aḥmad."[7] If a *madhhab* can have an apparent meaning but also, implicitly, a hidden one, then it must be practically equivalent to the very words that the jurisprudent has used. On the next page, indeed, Ibn Qudāmah uses *madhhab* interchangeably with *qawl*, literally "saying," contrasting the *madhhab* of al-Shāfi'ī, Ibn al-Qāsim, Abū Thawr, and Ibn al-Mundhir to the *qawl* of *aṣḥāb al-ra'y* (adherents of opinion), with which latter Aḥmad ibn Ḥanbal happens to have agreed.[8]

Often, though, *madhhab* as an opinion concerning a particular case has a collective reference. Hence, for example, a Ḥanafi jurisprudent is said to have held that a threefold ritual ablution was absolutely required in a certain case, whereas "the *madhhab*" is that only the first pass is absolutely required, the second and third just highly recommended or that only the second is highly recommended, the third supererogatory.[9] Here, *madhhab* means the doctrine of the school concerning this question, from which it is unusual for an adherent of that school to depart. (In this particular case, the man is said to have been the only Ḥanafi to take up this position.)

As the doctrine of a school, *madhhab* very often appears without reference to any particular case at all. Hence, for example, the Sufi Ibn Ṭāhir al-Maqdisī (d. 507/1113) is said to have been "Dāwūdi of *madhhab*"[10]; that is, his juridical practice was generally that of Dā-

---

[6] Ibn al-Nadīm, *Kitâb al-Fihrist*, ed. Gustav Flügel w. Johannes Roediger & August Mueller (Leipzig: F. C. W. Vogel, 1871), 190 = *fann* 5, *maqalah* 5.

[7] Ibn Qudāmah al-Maqdisī, *al-Mughnī*, ed. Ṭāhā Muḥammad al-Zaynī, 10 vols. (Cairo: Maktabat al-Qāhirah, 1388-90), 9:113.

[8] Ibn Qudāmah, *al-Mughnī* 9:114.

[9] Ibn Abī al-Wafā', *al-Jawāhir* 2 (Hyd.):239.

[10] Al-Sam'ānī, *apud* Ibn Ḥajar, *Lisān* 5:209.

wūd al-Ẓāhirī (d. 270/884) and his followers. Ibn al-Nadīm associates one man after another with the *madhhab* of Mālik, of the Iraqis, of al-Shāfi'ī, and so on (*'alá madhhab Mālik*), alternatively identifying men as Māliki, Iraqi, Shāfi'i, and so on. Here, *madhhab* refers to a range of doctrines concerning many particular cases, within which a jurisprudent was expected to answer questions. *Madhhab* may occur with this meaning more often than any other.

Finally, *madhhab* will refer to a school of law, a body of jurisprudents who somehow follow the teaching of one leader, mainly the jurisprudent for whom the school is named. Hence Ibn al-Nadīm refers to al-Iṣṭakhrī (d. 328/940) as a chief (*ra's*) in the *madhhab* of al-Shāfi'i.[11] It is with this sense of *madhhab*, the school as a body of jurisprudents, that I am here chiefly concerned. More particularly, it is with the *madhhab* as a body of jurisprudents with a regular method of reproducing itself—of training new jurisprudents. The famous Shāfi'i jurisprudent al-Māwardī (d. Baghdad, 450/1058) refers to a colleague who holds that a qadi known for adhering to one school may no longer rule according to the doctrine of any other, "since the settling of the schools and the distinction of those qualified in them (*ba'da istiqrār al-madhāhib wa-tamayyuz ahlihā*)."[12] There were no fully formed schools until there were clear means to distinguish those qualified from those not qualified, first to give authoritative opinions, then to teach jurisprudence.

The history of any early *madhhab* as a particular juridical opinion is almost surely beyond our reach, at present. So is the history of any early *madhhab* as a collection of juridical opinions. Although new editions appear every year, too many early sources remain unpublished or poorly edited. Moreover, the historian of legal doctrine should probably have had a thorough Islamic training in jurisprudence as well as a Western training in history. For one without the Islamic training, it is difficult to tell the significance of any departure from the usual. I know of no one who has mastered both disciplines. One day, a history of Islamic jurisprudence (*fiqh*) itself will emerge. What I offer is another modest preliminary. I believe that on the basis of the biographical sources now available, it is not overambitious to study the *madhāhib* as bodies of jurisprudents; i.e., schools of law. I set out

---

[11] Ibn al-Nadīm, *al-Fihrist*, 213 = *f*. 3, *q*. 6.

[12] Al-Māwardī, *Adab al-qāḍī*, ed. Muḥyī Hilāl al-Sirḥān, Iḥyā' al-turāth al-islāmī 4, 2 vols. (Baghdad: Dīwān al-Awqāf, 1972), 1:185.

here to determine at what point in time each school came to be.

George Makdisi has recently argued that we should no longer talk of "schools of law" (except in the pre-classical period, before the tenth century) but rather "guilds." Indeed, neither "school" nor "guild" literally translates *madhhab*. "Guild" has the positive advantage of implying something about the *madhhab*'s structure and function. Furthermore, the term "guild" suggests parallels with later institutions of higher learning in the Latin West, starting with the Inns of Court, which Makdisi believes were directly influenced by Islamic precedents, transmitted especially through Norman Sicily and the Crusader states. I have continued to translate "*madhhab*" by the conventional "school," not "guild," because it does better fit the other common meanings of *madhhab*, because it applies to the pre-classical schools as well as the classical, and because European parallels are outside the range of this study. This said, let me add that Makdisi's case seems strong, and that I look forward to when Europeanists seriously take up his challenge.

THE FORMATION OF SCHOOLS OF LAW: PREVIOUS STUDIES

There is no easy way to tell when the schools of law came to be. None of the schools of law is associated with anything like a datable charter. Neither is any of the Sufi orders or other institutions of Islam: the Muslims recognize no authority that might issue such charters, beyond the consensus of the community. The literature of jurisprudence is very large, but Muslim writers have seldom directly addressed the question of how and when the schools began. After all, it is something of an embarrassment that the schools began at all, and did not go back to the beginning. The disciples of al-Shāfiʿī did not present him as the inventor of an epochal compromise theory of jurisprudence, as an admiring Western historian might do, but as the renewer of his age, acting in the tradition of a revered caliph from a century before.[13]

Ibn Khaldūn (d. Cairo, 806/1408) is a notable exception, devoting a chapter of his prolegomena to the origins of the various schools of law. Treatments by modern scholars often bear the impress of his dis-

[13] Ella Landau-Tasseron, "The 'Cyclical Reform': A Study of the Mudjaddid Tradition," *Studia Islamica*, no. 70 (1989), 99.

cussion. He begins with the jurisprudents of Iraq and the Hijaz, the former skillful at analogy (*qiyās*), the latter knowing much hadith. The foremost of the Iraqis was Abū Ḥanīfah: on him and on his disciples the school became fixed (*istaqarra*). Similarly, the foremost of the Hijazis was Mālik.[14] This is very close to Joseph Schacht's explanation of how the old regional schools became personalized, as the followers of Abū Ḥanīfah, chiefly by their literary activity, made themselves the sole surviving fraction of the Kufans, while the followers of Mālik similarly transformed themselves into the whole of the Hijazi school.[15] Later, says Ibn Khaldūn, al-Shāfiʿī blended the doctrine of the Hijazis (*mazaja ṭarīqat ahl al-Ḥijāz*) with that of the Iraqis to produce his own school.[16] Implicitly, for Ibn Khaldūn, the distinguishing feature of a school was a body of distinctive juridical opinions. A school was formed when a body of opinions was collected and ascribed to a particular teacher.

The mechanism by which there came to be four schools, not more or fewer, was *taqlīd*, speaking on someone else's authority, whereby one does not search the sources for one's own answer to a question (*ijtihād*) but merely repeats the opinion of a former jurisprudent. "*Taqlīd* in the great centers came to rest on these four; those who spoke on the authority of others died out."[17] This is very close to the recent explanation of George Makdisi, stressing that a school died out at the point when advocates for it were no longer to be found.[18] Ibn Khaldūn goes on to explain that jurisprudents stopped trying to come up with their own solutions "when the ramification of technical terms became too great; when it became difficult to reach the rank of *ijtihād*; and when they began to fear to depend on the unqualified and untrustworthy."[19] This is very close to Joseph Schacht's account of why the formation of new schools came to a halt: that after about

---

[14] Ibn Khaldūn, *al-Muqaddimah* (Beirut: al-Maṭbaʿah al-Adabīyah, 1900; repr. Beirut: Dār al-Qalam, 1978), 446 = M. Quatremère, ed., *Notices et extraits des manuscrits de la Bibliotheque impériale et autres bibliothèques* 16-18: *Prolégomènes d'Ebn-Khaldoun*, 3 vols. (Paris: Didot Frères, Fils, &al., 1858), 3:2f.

[15] Joseph Schacht, "The Schools of Law and Later Developments of Jurisprudence," *Law in the Middle East*, ed. Majid Khadduri & Herbert J. Liebesny (Washington, DC: The Middle East Institute, 1955), 63.

[16] Ibn Khaldūn, *al-Muqaddimah*, 448 = Quatremère, ed., 3:5f.

[17] Ibn Khaldūn, *al-Muqaddimah*, 448 = Quatremère, ed., 3:6.

[18] George Makdisi, *The Rise of Colleges* (Edinburgh: Univ. Press, 1981), 4f.

[19] Ibn Khaldūn, *al-Muqaddimah*, 448 = Quatremère, ed., 3:6.

A.D. 900, all the essential problems had been solved and nothing was left to do but to elaborate the minutiae.[20]

Still, although eminently worthy of the attention it used to receive from Orientalists, Ibn Khaldūn's analysis does have its shortcomings. Above all, it suffers from a definite Māliki bias, for which modern scholars have not always made sufficient allowance; more subtly, from a disinclination to dwell on sharp conflicts within the community (a disinclination common to most Muslims, usually indeed stronger than Ibn Khaldūn's). The Māliki bias is evident in Ibn Khaldūn's equation of *ahl al-ḥadīth*, the traditionalist party, with *ahl al-Ḥijāz*, the Hijazi party of which Mālik was the most prominent representative.[21] The equation re-appears in the twentieth century, as when S. G. Vesey-Fitzgerald refers to Mālik as "founder of the *ahl ul-hadith*."[22] The equation makes a puzzle of where Iraqi traditionalism came from. By Ibn Khaldūn's own account, Mālik related only 300 hadith reports in his *Muwaṭṭa'*, which included all that he considered sound, whereas Aḥmad ibn Ḥanbal related 30,000 in his *Musnad*.[23] Vesey-Fitzgerald immediately admits that Mālik "does not hesitate on occasion to use *qiyas* or even to propound his own opinion as authoritative." Schacht always emphasizes the similarity of Iraqi and Hijazi attitudes towards *ra'y* and *ḥadīth* but still, like Ibn Khaldūn, offers no account of where and how the traditionalist movement began.[24]

---

[20] Schacht, "Schools of Law," 73. Schacht must also have known such works as Ibn Kamāl Pasha (d. 940/1533), *Ṭabaqāt al-mujtahidīn* (*apud* Ibn Abī al-Wafā', 2:558f), which suggests a similar scheme by ranking jurisprudents according to the degrees of *ijtihād* that they could practice, plainly dwindling with time.

[21] Ibn Khaldūn, *al-Muqaddimah*, 446 = Quatremère, ed., 3:2.

[22] S. G. Vesey-Fitzgerald, *Muhammadan Law* (London: Clarendon Press, 1931), 14.

[23] Ibn Khaldūn, ed. Quatremère, 2:404. The textual tradition is confused: Quatremère, 2:400 has 31,000 for the *Musnad*, a footnote to 2:404 states that two other manuscripts read 40,000, the Beirut edition (444) has 50,000. A Ḥanbali tradition puts the number at 30,000 (al-Khaṭīb al-Baghdādī, *Tārīkh Baghdād*, 14 vols. [Cairo: Maktabat al-Khānjī, 1931], 9:375); Ibn al-Nadīm states 40-odd thousand (*Fihrist*, 229 = *f.* 6, *q.* 6); oddly, N. J. Coulson states that the *Musnad* contains 80,000 traditions (*A History of Islamic Law*, Islamic Surveys 2 [Edinburgh: Univ. Press, 1964], 71). Ibn Khaldūn's figure for the *Muwaṭṭa'* is low: Joseph Schacht quotes commentaries according to which different recensions contained 822 hadith reports from the Prophet, 898 from others, or 429 from the Prophet, 750 from others (*The Origins of Muhammadan Jurisprudence* [Oxford: Clarendon Press, 1950], 22). The point remains that Aḥmad collected far more hadith than Mālik.

[24] *V. Encyclopaedia of Islam*, new edn., s.v. "*Aṣḥāb al-ra'y*," "*Ahl al-ḥadīth*," by

(I suggest in Chapter One that the growth of polemics against *aṣḥāb al-ra'y*, the opponents of traditionalism in law, indicates an Iraqi origin for traditionalism, and that the postulate of a created Qur'an is what precipitated an open break.)

A survey of modern scholarship on the schools of law and their origins reveals much vagueness, some downright error, but few answers more direct than what Ibn Khaldūn provides. Ignaz Goldziher speaks of foundation by disciples, but does not describe in detail the formation of any school.[25] His article on the Ḥanbali movement draws attention to its active enforcement of orthodoxy over several centuries, but concerns itself not with the Ḥanbali school of law.[26]

Duncan Black Macdonald, heavily indebted to Goldziher, at first refers to their eponyms as "founders" of the historic schools.[27] This is impossible: even if we suppose that the operation of a school is signalled by no more than the existence of a body of juridical opinions, we cannot consider Abū Ḥanīfah the founder of the Ḥanafi school, for he left no books. Macdonald acknowledges as much two pages later, then wittily states that Sufyān al-Thawrī "narrowly missed founding a separate school."[28] Implicitly, Macdonald recognizes that the formation of a school was chiefly the work of later men who worked up the eponym's ideas into a body of authoritative doctrine. Still, one finds in his account no dates and few names to characterize that decisive later work of forming schools.

Henri Lammens is ever astute but, on this point, equally sketchy. He briefly defines *madhhab*, then skips ahead to the seventh century of the *hijrah* (13th century C.E.), from which point "the struggles subsided and it was agreed to recognize four schools, all considered equally orthodox." As so often, the passive voice disguises real uncertainty.[29] S. G. Vesey-Fitzgerald seems often just as astute, building on a knowledge of Islamic law as actually practiced in the 20th

---

J. Schacht.

[25] Ignaz Goldziher, *Introduction to Islamic Theology and Law*, trans. Andras & Ruth Hamori, Modern Classics in Near Eastern Studies (Princeton: Univ. Press, 1981), 49.

[26] Ignaz Goldziher, "Zur Geschichte der hanbalitischen Bewegungen," *Zeitschrift für der deutsche morgenländische Gesellschaft* 62 (1908):1-28.

[27] Duncan Black Macdonald, *Development of Muslim Theology, Jurisprudence, and Constitutional Theory* (New York: C. Scribner's Sons, 1903), 94.

[28] Macdonald, *Development*, 96, 97.

[29] Lammens, *Islam*, 84.

tury; however, he goes little beyond the superficial traditional account when it comes to the formation of schools. Implicitly identifying the school with a body of writing, he refers to Abū Ḥanīfah, Abū Yūsuf, and al-Shaybānī as the founders of the Ḥanafi school, Mālik as the founder of the Māliki, and allows only that Aḥmad ibn Ḥanbal could not, with his unreasoning hostility towards jurisprudence, have been the actual founder of the Ḥanbali school. How that school was founded he does not say.[30]

A. S. Tritton evidently wrote without the benefit of Schacht's work. Following the traditional account, he suggests that the Qur'an and Sunnah (Prophetic norm) were the original sources of law, and that reliance on *ra'y* was an innovative departure from them.[31] Like Vesey-Fitzgerald and others, he suggests that the Ḥanafi school was founded by his students Abū Yūsuf and al-Shaybānī, the Māliki school by Mālik, and the Shāfi'i school by al-Shāfi'ī. The opinions of Aḥmad ibn Ḥanbal were set in order by his disciples.[32]

Then Schacht: he knew the legal sources better than any predecessor among Western scholars, and his work on Islamic law, particularly the context and significance of al-Shāfi'ī's work, marks the greatest advance since Goldziher's. Much remains to be done, but for the early period it will be done on the basis of Schacht: witness the pioneering work of G. H. A. Juynboll on the growth of hadith reports, so deeply indebted to Schacht for his analysis of chains of authorities.[33]

Reading Schacht with a view to determining when schools emerged, two limitations become apparent. First, Schacht treats the period after al-Shāfi'ī in none of the depth and detail in which he treats the period that ended with him. Some of his remarks on developments in the third century (A.D. 816-913) are acute indeed. For example, he points out the traditionalization of Ḥanafi doctrine during that time.[34] I shall present more evidence of this traditionalization than

---

[30] Vesey-Fitzgerald, *Muhammadan Law*, 11-16.

[31] A. S. Tritton, *Islam: Belief and Practices* (London: Hutchinson Library, 1951), 59; cf. Ibn Khaldūn, *al-Muqaddimah*, 442 = Quatremère, ed., 2:398.

[32] Tritton, *Islam*, 60f.

[33] A debt that Juynboll freely acknowledges: *Muslim Tradition: Studies in Chronology, Provenance and Authorship of Early* ḥadīth (Cambridge: Univ. Press, 1983).

[34] Joseph Schacht, "Sur la transmission de la doctrine dans les écoles juridiques de l'Islam," *Annales de l'Institut des études orientales* (Algiers) 10 (1952):418f.

Schacht actually offers, but less than one imagines in the forthcoming article Schacht says he will devote exclusively to it.

A second limitation is this: only part of the story of the development of Islamic law is to be found in the legal doctrine that mainly interests Schacht. His remarks on the traditionalists are few and sometimes inaccurate, apparently because they did not produce sophisticated treatises on jurisprudence. Schacht locates the formation of schools at around the middle of the third century (*ca.* 865): this is when the Iraqi school became completely Ḥanafi, when Māliki and Shāfiʿi doctrines were crystallized in the respective handbooks of Abū Muṣʿab and al-Muzanī, and the opinions of Aḥmad ibn Ḥanbal were collected by his disciples.[35] Schacht's precision represents a considerable advance on Macdonald's vagueness, Vesey-Fitzgerald's unconsidered anachronism; however, it presupposes a definition of "school" as a body of doctrine with little reference to a body of adherents and especially to any regular means of transmission. The evidence for these additional components of the classical school of law is to be found mainly outside the strictly legal texts with which Schacht worked.

The most important work on the schools of law since Schacht is that of George Makdisi, my own teacher. In the 1960's, he published important articles on institutions of learning and on Ashʿari theology, closely associated with the Shāfiʿī school.[36] Neither touches directly on schools in the formative period, but both studies indicate better than previous works the nature of the classical schools and what any history of the formative period would have to explain. His work of the '70's culminated in *The Rise of Colleges*, much further sharpening our idea of how the school operated in the High Middle Ages. With Makdisi's work, the school of law as a body of men with a regular procedure for transmitting their doctrines at last receives its due emphasis alongside the school as a body of doctrines.

Other work from the '60's advanced the discussion less far. N. J.

[35] Joseph Schacht, "Sur quelques manuscrits de la bibliothèque de la mosquée d'al-Qarawiyyīn à Fès," *Etudes d'orientalisme dédiées à la mémoire de Lévi-Provençal*, 2 vols. (Paris: G.-P. Maisonneuve & Larose, 1962), 2:274; "Schools of Law," 63, 67.

[36] George Makdisi, "Muslim Institutions of Learning in Eleventh-Century Baghdad," *Bulletin of the School of Oriental and African Studies* 24 (1961):1-56; "Ashʿarī and the Ashʿarites in Islamic Religious History," *Studia Islamica*, no. 17 (1962), 37-80, 18 (1963), 19-39.

Coulson, published *A History of Islamic Law*. Coulson is strong at many points, but disappointing when it comes to the formation of schools.[37] He identifies al-Shaybānī as "the true founder of Ḥanafi law," Ibn al-Qāsim as the comparable figure for Māliki law, implying a very narrow definition ("law" alone) of *madhhab*.[38] Coulson goes on to say (following Schacht) that Shāfi'ism became a school in the generation after al-Shāfi'ī, when only a minority were immediately converted to his views, and (I would call this an outright error) Aḥmad founded the Ḥanbali school by collecting his *Musnad*.[39]

Marshall G. S. Hodgson's *The Venture of Islam* may be taken as a representative textbook of the same period. On the one hand, Hodgson substantially relies on Schacht for the crucial work of al-Shāfi'ī, which puts his ahead of earlier textbooks, and adds his own profound analysis of its religious meaning. On the other hand, although he does not assert that the eponyms of the schools were their founders, avoiding the mistake of earlier historians, he finally says little about the schools of law, probably because they did not seem to express sharply different world views.[40]

More recent textbooks show no further advance. John L. Esposito, like Lammens, entirely avoids the question of how the schools were formed by skipping ahead to the 13th century C.E., when, he says, their number became stabilized at four.[41] Gerhard Endress' tone is more serious, but he, too, avoids the question.[42] Having paid attention to Makdisi, Andrew Rippin succinctly and accurately characterizes the relation of law to Islamic theology. As to the foundation of schools of law, though, he is content to warn that none of the teachers around whom schools formed probably intended to found a school. The only dates he gives are of those teachers, none the less.[43] Fred-

[37] Coulson, *A History of Islamic Law*, Part One. Schacht names some of the strong points in his review, "Modernism and Traditionalism in a History of Islamic Law," *Middle Eastern Studies* 1 (1965):388-400.

[38] Coulson, *History*, 48f.

[39] Coulson, *History*, 70f.

[40] Hodgson, *The Venture of Islam*, 3 vols. (Chicago: Univ. of Chicago Press, 1973), 1, bk. 2, chap. 3, esp. 335.

[41] John L. Esposito, *Islam: The Straight Path* (New York: Oxford Univ. Press, 1988), 86.

[42] Gerhard Endress, *An Introduction to Islam*, trans. Carole Hillenbrand (New York: Columbia Univ. Press, 1988), 66-71.

[43] Andrew Rippin, *Muslims: Their Religious Beliefs and Practices* 1: *The Formative*

Mathewson Denny is good on the spirituality of the ritual law and especially of qur'anic recitation, but repeats old errors concerning the formation of schools of law: the Ḥanafi school was founded by Abū Ḥanīfah, Mālik founded another in the Hijaz, al-Shāfi'ī founded the school that bears his name, and Aḥmad ibn Ḥanbal, extending al-Shāfi'ī's enthusiasm for hadith, founded the fourth and last.[44]

Among recent contributions from specialists, again, Wael B. Hallaq's treatment of the end of *ijtihād* stands out.[45] Perhaps, this forthright article will at last put an end to careless talk of "the closing of the gate of *ijtihād.*" Inasmuch as *ijtihād* means going over the sources in order to answer a juridical problem, that gate cannot close so long as any Muslim jurisprudent delivers opinions.

Hallaq also makes valuable suggestions concerning the formation of schools of law. He locates that formation in the late ninth and early tenth centuries, which subsequent research has confirmed. His characterization of the work of al-Khallāl and other jurisprudents of the time as inventing doctrine and projecting it backwards is too sweeping and weakly documented; however, subsequent research has certainly turned up a great deal of invention and backward projection. A weakness of Hallaq's discussion is his own occasional backward projection. Hence, for example, he assumes from the classical literature of *uṣūl al-fiqh*, mostly from the eleventh and twelfth centuries, and mostly Shāfi'i, that analogy was essential to the practice of Islamic law. He is thus led to misrepresent the possibilities of the Ẓāhiri school: it was not un-Islamic *ab initio*, it merely disagreed with the later orthodoxy.

Meanwhile, Makdisi has gone on in the 1980's to characterize the school of law as a guild. Several historians had declared that guilds were not found in the Islamic world before the late Middle Ages; however, Makdisi shows that their definitions, particularly that of Gabriel Baer, perfectly fit the legal *madhhab*: it regulated a profession, the practice of law (including both the teaching of law and the

---

Period (London: Routledge, 1990), 76.

[44] Frederick Mathewson Denny, *An Introduction to Islam* (New York: Macmillan, 1985), 224-226.

[45] Wael B. Hallaq, "Was the Gate of Ijtihad Closed?" *International Journal of Middle East Studies* 16 (1984):3-41. Hallaq refined his first study two years later with "On the Origins of the Controversy About the Existence of Mujtahids and the Gate of Ijtihad," *Studia Islamica*, no. 63 (1986), 129-141; however, it deals only with the literature of *uṣūl al-fiqh* from the fifth century onwards, after the period of my study.

issue of juridical opinions), was organized city by city, had its local chiefs, and so on.[46] Most recently, Makdisi has identified three stages in the development of schools of law: the regional school, the personal school, and the guild school (what I call the "classical").[47] With this sharpening of definitions, the task of determining when the schools originated becomes much easier.

The most important book of the past decade is Norman Calder, *Studies in Early Islamic Jurisprudence*.[48] Calder examines a series of early texts and redates many of them. He casts serious doubt on attributions to the eponyms of the schools, particularly Abū Ḥanīfah, Mālik, and al-Shāfiʿī. Stressing contradictions in the texts, he finds instead that the books traditionally attributed to the eponyms were evidently worked up over time by informal schools; that is, circles of scholars who debated questions of law. These findings tend to confirm earlier suggestions that the schools of law did not achieve their classical form until the tenth century.

My chief hope for this study is that it will help build a more secure chronological basis for future studies of Islamic law. No more should textbook-writers tell us the eponyms founded their schools, nor specialists admit that they did not found schools but weakly retreat from saying who did. I say where and when the classical schools were formed. In addition, I hope to provide students of Islamic law with characterizations both of the nature of the schools found at any of the major centers and at any point in the ninth century and of the elements that went into each of the classical schools, characterizations of considerably more precision than what has been available hitherto.

---

[46] George Makdisi, "The Guilds of Law in Medieval Legal History: An Inquiry Into the Origins of the Inns of Court," *Zeitschrift für Geschichte der arabisch-islamischen Wissenschaften* 1:233-252, ed. Fuat Sezgin (Frankfurt: Institut für Geschichte der arabisch-islamischen Wissenschaften, 1984); *idem*, "La Corporation à l'époque classique de l'Islam," *Présence de Louis Massignon: Hommages et témoignages* (Paris: Maisonneuve & Larose, 1987), 35-49; *The Rise of Humanism in Classical Islam and the Christian West* (Edinburgh: Univ. Press, 1990), 16-23.

[47] George Makdisi, "*Ṭabaqāt*-Biography: Law and Orthodoxy in Classical Islam," *Islamic Studies* (Islamabad) 32 (1993):371-396.

[48] Norman Calder, *Studies in Early Islamic Jurisprudence* (Oxford: Clarendon Press, 1993).

THE FORMATION OF SCHOOLS OF LAW: THE PLAN OF THIS STUDY

My study falls naturally into two parts: before and after the formation of the classical schools from the late ninth century. Before that time, the chief division among Muslim jurisprudents was between adherents of *ra'y* and adherents of *ḥadīth*. Chapter One treats the staunchest adherents of *ḥadīth*, the traditionalist jurisprudents of Iraq. In particular, I develop on the one hand traditionalist objections to rationalistic jurisprudence, important because the adherents of *ra'y* would largely modify their practice to meet them; on the other hand, the impracticalities of the traditionalists' program, which put a term to pure traditionalism and called forth the efforts of traditionists such as al-Bukhārī and Muslim, jurisprudents such as Ibn Surayj and al-Khallāl, to devise a more manageable system of jurisprudence based on hadith. Chapters Two and Three, then, treat the chief opponents of the traditionalists, the rationalistic Iraqi jurisprudents. As Schacht has stated and my study confirms, they were not yet a functioning Ḥanafi school of law. In Chapter Two, I develop two processes by which they made themselves over into something close to the classical Ḥanafi school: their personalization of the school, moving from identification with the city of Kufa to identification with Abū Ḥanīfah, and their absorption of the rationalistic legal tradition of other cities such as Basra. In Chapter Three, I develop first the traditionalization of the Ḥanafi school, as its adherents rewrote history to make their patron saint more traditionalist and rewrote their books of law to make their doctrines rest more fully on hadith; second, the beginnings of a commentary literature, a clear sign of behavior as a self-conscious school.

Chapter Four briefly treats al-Shāfi'ī himself, locating him as between *ra'y* and *ḥadīth* in law, *kalām* and pure traditionalism in theology. Al-Shāfi'ī professed to be close to the traditionalists in both law and theology, even more the adherents of his school; however, ninth-century Iraqi traditionalists saw him otherwise, with some justice. At greater length I treat the loose, ninth-century Shāfi'i school, which likewise upheld a compromise system I call *semi-rationalist*, inclined to defend traditionalist theological positions by the untraditionalist means of *kalām*.

With Chapter Five, I turn to the earliest guild school, the Shāfi'i school founded in Baghdad by Ibn Surayj. I emphasize his method of teaching, particularly the literary production associated with it; the line of teachers that followed him, which is to say the chiefs of the new guild; and the spread of his students and the students of his students. It is apparently with Ibn Surayj that all these elements of the classical school first came together. Chapter Six treats the formation of the classical Ḥanafi school about the same time. Here, I review the work of leading Ḥanafi teachers that finally culminated in the work of al-Karkhī, the first clear chief of the guild. Chapter Seven treats the foundation of the classical Ḥanbali school by al-Khallāl. Henceforward, scholars should date the classical Shāfi'i, Ḥanafi, and Ḥanbali schools from the time of Ibn Surayj, al-Karkhī, and al-Khallāl; that is, the late 200's/800's and early to mid-300's/900's.

Chapters Eight and Nine treat secondary schools. The Mālikīyah of the West played a catch-up game, gradually modifying their forms to agree with developments in the East. In the later tenth century, where my study leaves off, they still had not developed a method of teaching like that of the eastern schools, but state power prevented the infiltration of eastern schools. The eastern Mālikīyah are to be classified amongst the schools of law that died out over time, of which the most renowned are those of Abū Thawr, Dāwūd al-Ẓāhirī, and al-Ṭabarī. Because they did not survive, these schools are harder to characterize: many of their peculiar doctrines are lost, and no specialized biographical dictionaries survive to describe them. I shall argue, however, that they did have a special and identifiable theological character: like the related ninth-century Shāfi'i school, they were early attempts at compromise between *ra'y* and *ḥadīth*, reason and revelation. It is important to look at them also inasmuch as their failure demonstrates the crucial need for a venerable eponym ("patron saint").

Other scholars have pointed toward some of my findings: the turning point in the late ninth century, the importance of Ibn Surayj for the Shāfi'i school, and a few others. My enumeration of the features of the classical school that first came together with Ibn Surayj is new. Other findings are also new, such as the importance of al-Karkhī for the Ḥanafīyah and the nature of eastern Mālikism and Ẓāhirism.

The quantity of evidence that I bring to bear and the precision of my dating are quite new. Such originality has been possible because I have made use of sources relatively neglected, until now; mainly, the biographical dictionaries we have in such abundance concerning Muslim traditionists and jurisprudents. Many rich sources have been in print for most of this century, but scholars have made relatively little use of them. Writing the history of Islamic theology, for example, scholars have examined the explicitly heresiographical literature with some thoroughness, but the biographical dictionaries only sparingly. The biographical dictionaries have the usual faults of literary sources deliberately designed to inform their readers.[49] Like Ibn Khaldūn (often more so), their authors minimize conflict and change, at least concerning religious affairs. Devoted as their authors are to faithful transmission of received data, though, they also often reproduce material from an earlier age when institutions and practices were less well defined but polemics were sharper.

Norman Calder has recently cast doubt on the use of biographical evidence.[50] If Muslim men of religion invented hadith reports to justify their doctrine, as demonstrated by Goldziher, Schacht, &al., they probably also invented much biographical information. When there is a clear conflict between the appearance of a surviving text and stories of how it came to be, Calder is plainly right to dismiss the stories. But he himself often uses biographical evidence, sometimes well and sometimes carelessly, while often it independently confirms his redatings. As a basic rule of historical investigation, every case should be judged by itself.

Describing the jurisprudents and traditionists who transmitted Islamic learning, the biographers furnish our best image of how the Muslims conceived of themselves: a collection of individuals, differences impossible to conceal, with no clear ranking among them but still constituting, altogether, a community faithful through time to its original charge from God. Close-up and from a distance, the biographical dictionaries are our best source for the history of the Muslim community.

---

[49] Marc Bloch, *The Historian's Craft*, trans. Peter Putnam (New York: Knopf, 1953), 61.

[50] Calder, *Studies*, 1fn., 20, 38, *& passim*.

CHAPTER ONE

THE TRADITIONALISTS OF IRAQ

By the end of the tenth century, Muslim jurisprudents were divided amongst the Shāfiʿi, Ḥanafi, and other schools of law. Two centuries before, however, the principal division among jurisprudents had been that between *aṣḥāb al-ḥadīth* or traditionalists and *aṣḥāb al-ra'y*; that is, between proponents of entirely Scriptural authority in theology and law and more or less rationalistic jurisprudents. The traditionalists had separated out from *aṣḥāb al-ra'y* in the later eighth century. Traditionalism enjoyed a spectacular triumph when the caliph al-Mutawakkil rescinded every last measure of the Inquisition, 237/853, and the intellectual descendants of *aṣḥāb al-ra'y* were able to win themselves a measure of acceptance only by imitating certain of the forms of the traditionalists. Yet it was a sharp struggle, in the later eighth century and through much of the ninth. The form of jurisprudence that finally prevailed was a compromise between the two extremes, regulated by the institution of the guild school of law.

THE SPLIT BETWEEN *AṢḤĀB AL-ḤADĪTH* AND *AṢḤĀB AL-RA'Y*

Hadith reports from earlier authorities are a principal foundation of classical Islamic law. They always come with attached chains of transmitters (*isnād*s), in the form "so-and-so related to me, so-and-so related to me, so-and-so related to me," and so on back to the text (*matn*) itself, a statement of what the Prophet (or sometimes rather a contemporary, called a Companion, or someone from the following generation, a Successor) said or did in a particular situation. From the later eighth century to the beginning of the tenth, there raged fierce controversy between those who would found their jurisprudence exclusively on hadith, *aṣḥāb al-ḥadīth* or traditionalists, and those who reserved a leading place for common sense, *aṣḥāb al-ra'y*. The controversy concerned orthodoxy as well as orthopraxy, and on the theological plane continued through most of the Middle Ages; however, the concern of this chapter is with the juridical controversy.

The term "traditionalist" is admittedly difficult, suggesting as it does some allegiance to the way things had always been. Modern scholarship has shown that the traditionalist program was at many points innovative, opposed to mere tradition.[1] Indeed, the traditionalists expressly rejected "tradition" in the usual, loose sense (*'urf*) whenever a hadith report was available as an alternative guide to action. On the other hand, traditionalists certainly saw themselves not as innovators but as loyal to the way things had always been; for example, when they refused to discuss theological problems not known to have been discussed by the first generations of Muslims.[2] Moreover, their usual term for themselves, *ahl al-sunnah*, expressly suggests dedication to following the path already laid out. ("Sunni" would be an appropriate alternative to "traditionalist" if only it had not later acquired such a strong connotation of opposition to "Shī'i.") Other contemporary terms for them, *ahl al-ḥadīth* or *aṣḥāb al-ḥadīth*, make explicit reference only to hadith (long translated as "tradition" in a special sense), and our calling them "traditionalists" is related to the problematic translation of *ḥadīth* as "tradition." I will continue to call them "traditionalists" because our customary English term so easily gives rise to an adjectival form, but hoping to imply nothing about their actual relation to tradition in the usual sense.

(George Makdisi has made a sensible distinction, which I follow, between "traditionist" and "traditionalist." The former is a *muḥaddith*, one who transmits hadith, the latter one of *ahl al-ḥadīth*, an adherent of Scriptuary authority in dogma as against the claims of *ahl al-kalām*.[3] Unfortunately, although the distinction is easy to apply

---

[1] *V.* Marshall G. S. Hodgson, *The Venture of Islam*, 3 vols. (Chicago: Univ. of Chicago Press, 1973), 1:63-66, 386-389.

[2] "How shall I say what has not been said?" asked Aḥmad: *apud* Ibn Abī Ya'lá, *Ṭabaqāt al-ḥanābilah*, ed. Muḥammad Ḥāmid al-Fiqī, 2 vols. (Cairo: Maṭba'at al-Sunnah al-Muḥammadīyah, 1952), 1:7. Hodgson's critique of the term "traditionalism" has recently been reaffirmed by A. Kevin Reinhart, *Before Revelation*, SUNY Series in Middle Eastern Studies (Albany: State Univ. of New York Press, 1995), 27, 182f. Unfortunately, whereas Reinhart's attention to morality before revelation gives him excellent purchase on the varieties of "rationalist" theology, it precludes his considering the (extreme) traditionalists, who rejected the very question inasmuch as the first generations had not addressed it.

[3] George Makdisi, "Ash'arī and the Ash'arites in Islamic Religious History 1: The Ash'arite Movement and Muslim Orthodoxy," *Studia Islamica*, no. 17 (1962), 49.

from the tenth century onwards, it is difficult to apply in the early period, when adherence to *ḥadīth* in law was contrasted not only with adherence to *kalām* but also to *ra'y*, and traditionists were almost always, in theology, traditionalists as well. Joseph Schacht normally used only "traditionist," and indeed there is little need for a distinction in the early period he studied most thoroughly.)

Joseph Schacht located the emergence of hadith in the second quarter of the eighth century C.E.[4] More recently, G. H. A. Juynboll has pushed back the origins to the last quarter of the first Islamic century, roughly A.D. 700-720.[5] He names many qadis of that time and later who do not appear in chains of transmitters and presumably did not mix hadith with their jurisprudence.[6] A party of jurisprudents distinguished by total reliance on hadith seems to have emerged about the second quarter of the second Islamic century. Such is the evidence of, for example, Ibn al-Nadīm's catalogue of books by traditionalist jurisprudents (*fuqahā' ahl al-ḥadīth*).[7] He names one Kufan who died in 136/753-754,[8] otherwise only men who died 150/767-768 or later. Over half the authors in this section are credited with a book concerning jurisprudence titled *Kitāb al-Sunan*, possibly a hallmark of traditionalism.

Conscious enmity between traditionalists and adherents of *ra'y* seems to date only from the later eighth century. As leading representatives of the two approaches to Islamic law in the mid-eighth century, we might take the Kufans Sufyān al-Thawrī (d. Basra, 161/777-778) and Abū Ḥanīfah (d. Kufa, 150/767). It seems clear that hadith weighed more heavily for al-Thawrī: whereas Abū Ḥanīfah related hadith reports only from a few Kufan shaykhs,[9] al-Thawrī collected hadith reports in Kufa, Basra, and the Hijaz from, it is said, 1,100

---

[4] Joseph Schacht, *The Origins of Muhammadan Jurisprudence* (Oxford: Clarendon Press, 1950), 140-151, esp. 149.

[5] G. H. A. Juynboll, *Muslim Tradition* (Cambridge: Univ. Press, 1983), chap. 1, esp. p. 39. *V.* further G. H. A. Juynboll, "Some Notes on Islam's First *fuqahā'* Distilled From Early *ḥadīṯ* Literature," *Arabica* 39 (1992):287-314.

[6] Juynboll, *Muslim Tradition*, chap. 2.

[7] Ibn al-Nadīm, *Kitâb al-Fihrist*, ed. Gustav Flügel, w/ Johannes Roediger & August Mueller (Leipzig: F. C. W. Vogel, 1872), 225-236 = *fann* 6, *maqālah* 6.

[8] Ibn al-Nadīm, *Fihrist*, 226, ll. 11-13 = *f.* 6, *q.* 6.

[9] *V.* Ibn Ḥajar, *Tahdhīb "al-Tahdhīb,"* 12 vols. (Hyderabad: Majlis Dā'irat al-Ma'ārif al-Niẓāmīyah, 1325-27), 10:449.

different shaykhs.[10] In practice, they nonetheless seem to have agreed. In an early *khilāf* work by Muḥammad ibn Naṣr al-Marwazī (d. Samarqand, 294/907), al-Thawrī is not included with *aṣḥāb al-ra'y*, but his opinion usually agrees with theirs, as opposed to the opinion of al-Shāfi'ī, Isḥāq ibn Rāhawayh, Aḥmad, &al. For example, al-Thawrī and *aṣḥāb al-ra'y* agree that the female apostate should be imprisoned, while Mālik and the Medinese, al-Shāfi'ī, Aḥmad, Isḥāq, and Abū 'Ubayd say that she should be killed.[11]

It will not do to assert that al-Thawrī and Abū Ḥanīfah represented distinct and hostile schools of law, for they had followers in common. For example, consider the religious scholars of Isfahan. Al-Nu'mān ibn 'Abd al-Salām (d. 183/799-800) sat with Abū Ḥanīfah and related hadith reports from him, but was remembered in the tenth century as following the juridical system of al-Thawrī.[12] According to Abū Nu'aym, the first to introduce Kufan jurisprudence to Isfahan was al-Ḥusayn ibn Ḥafṣ (d. 212/827-828?), who enjoyed, there, the judgeship, the giving of juridical opinions, and chieftancy.[13] Among those from whom he related hadith reports was Abū Yūsuf, and the Ḥanafi biographer Ibn Abī al-Wafā' takes this to mean that he was an adherent of that school.[14] Yet al-Ḥusayn, too, was connected with the jurisprudence of al-Thawrī: half the hadith reports he is reported to have transmitted have Sufyān in their chains of authorities,[15] and he patronized special associates of his.[16] It does not appear that the juridical systems of al-Thawrī and Abū Ḥanīfah were sharply distinguished in Isfahan.

That jurisprudents consciously reached similar conclusions by different routes can be loosely documented only from the end of the

[10] Cf. Ibn Ḥajar, *Tahdhīb* 4:111f, 113, l. 9 from bottom.

[11] Al-Marwazī, *K. Ikhtilāf al-fuqahā'*, Yusuf Ağa (Konya) 4820/1, 38b.

[12] Abū al-Shaykh, *Ṭabaqāt al-muḥaddithīn bi-Iṣbahān*, ed. 'Abd al-Ghafūr 'Abd al-Ḥaqq Ḥusayn al-Balūshī, 4 vols. (Beirut: Mu'assasat al-Risālah, 1987-), 2:5.

[13] Abū Nu'aym, *Geschichte Isbahāns*, ed. Sven Dedering (Leiden: E. J. Brill, 1931, 1934), 1:274, but admittedly the identification as first is stronger as quoted by Ibn Ḥajar, *Tahdhīb* 2:337. The earlier Abū al-Shaykh makes al-Ḥusayn the first to transmit jurisprudence and hadith to Isfahan, *Ṭabaqāt* 2:58.

[14] Ibn Abī al-Wafā', *al-Jawāhir al-muḍīyah*, ed. 'Abd al-Fattāḥ Muḥammad al-Ḥulw, 2 vols. (Cairo: 'Īsá al-Ḥalabī, 1978), 2:108. References to this edition unless noted.

[15] Abū al-Shaykh, *Ṭabaqāt* 2:56-58.

[16] Abū al-Shaykh, *Ṭabaqāt* 2:58f; Abū Nu'aym, *Geschichte* 1:274f.

eighth century. Aḥmad ibn Ḥanbal (d. Baghdad, 241/855) would relate how the Basran 'Abd al-Raḥmān ibn Mahdī (d. Basra, 198/814) once led him to al-Ḥusayn ibn al-Walīd al-Naysābūrī (d. 202/817-818?). "When I went in, he had in his hand a book containing the *ra'y* of Abū Ḥanīfah. 'Abd al-Raḥmān told him, 'Ask me concerning every problem (*mas'alah*) in your book, and I shall relate to you a hadith report concerning it.'"[17] The point was not that hadith would give different solutions, rather that it was sufficient. (Aḥmad characterized 'Abd al-Raḥmān as siding sometimes with *ahl al-ḥadīth*, sometimes with the Medinese.[18])

On the other hand, the biographical literature often quotes Sufyān al-Thawrī as condemning Abū Ḥanīfah. One story has it that Sufyān was asked about a hadith report from 'Āṣim (d. 127/745?) concerning the female apostate, and said "As for (hearing that hadith report) from a trustworthy transmitter, no." It was known that Abū Ḥanīfah had related it.[19] More directly, Sufyān is quoted as saying, "Neither trustworthy (*thiqah*) nor reliable (*ma'mūn*),"[20] which at least became, if they were not already in his time, technical terms of *rijāl* criticism. He is the usual source for the accusation that Abū Ḥanīfah was twice asked to repent of asserting that the Qur'an was created.[21] He is even quoted as saying "There has not been born one more harmful to Islam than Abū Ḥanīfah."[22] Both favorable and unfavor-

---

[17] Ibn 'Adī al-Qaṭṭān, *al-Kāmil fī ḍu'afā' al-rijāl*, 6 vols. (Beirut: Dār al-Fikr, 1984), 1:118f. Cf. the question of what to do with the female apostate: al-Thawrī rejected the basis for Abū Ḥanīfah's position, but agreed with the position itself, against Mālik, al-Shāfi'ī, Aḥmad, &al.

[18] Ibn Ḥajar, *Tahdhīb* 6:279.

[19] With different chains of transmitters in al-'Uqaylī, *K. al-Ḍu'afā' al-kabīr*, ed. 'Abd al-Mu'ṭī Amīn Qal'ajī, 4 vols. (Beirut: Dār al-Kutub al-'Ilmīyah, 1984), 4: 284, 285; Ibn 'Abd al-Barr, *al-Intiqā' fī faḍā'il al-thalāthah al-a'immah* (Cairo: al-Qudsī, 1350), 148.

[20] Al-'Uqaylī, *Ḍu'afā'* 4:280f.

[21] Aḥmad ibn Ḥanbal, *K. al-'Ilal wa-ma'rifat al-rijāl*, ed. Waṣī Allāh ibn Muḥammad 'Abbās, 4 vols. (Beirut: al-Maktab al-Islāmī, 1988), 2:545, 3:276; 'Abd Allāh ibn Aḥmad, *K. al-Sunnah*, ed. Muḥammad ibn Sa'īd ibn Sālim al-Qaḥṭānī, 2 vols. (Dammam: Dār Ibn al-Qayyim, 1986), 192-197; al-Khaṭīb al-Baghdādī, *Tārīkh Baghdād*, 14 vols. (Cairo: Maktabat al-Khānjī, 1931), 13:382.

[22] Al-'Uqaylī, *Ḍu'afā'* 4:281. Similar statements attributed to Sufyān ibn 'Uyaynah and Mālik *apud* Ibn 'Abd al-Barr, *Intiqā'*, 149f; to al-Awzā'ī *apud* 'Abd Allāh ibn Aḥmad ibn Ḥanbal, *Sunnah*, 188, 204; to Ḥammād ibn Salamah *apud* Ibn 'Adī, *Kāmil* 2:672.

able comments on Abū Ḥanīfah are quoted from Ibn al-Mubārak (d. Hit, 181/797) and other heroes of later traditionalism, as well.

Much evidence suggests that the adherents of *ra'y* and *ḥadīth* began to quarrel vociferously only at the end of the eighth century, and that condemnations of Abū Ḥanīfah from al-Thawrī and others were merely projected backwards from that time. Aḥmad ibn Ḥanbal related that Isḥāq ibn Rāhawayh (d. Nishapur, 238/853?), a prominent figure among the traditionalists of Khurasan, was originally an adherent of *ra'y*. Before going on the pilgrimage, he went through the books of Ibn al-Mubārak looking for hadith reports that agreed with the *ra'y* of Abū Ḥanīfah, and found three hundred. In Basra, then, he looked up 'Abd al-Raḥmān ibn Mahdī. Isḥāq recited to him a long poem praising various traditionists. 'Abd al-Raḥmān was moved to tears, but angrily stopped the recitation when Isḥāq began to praise Abū Ḥanīfah. Ibn al-Mubārak had made no mistake, said 'Abd al-Raḥmān, save relating hadith of Abū Ḥanīfah. Isḥāq said, "Afterwards, I investigated, and lo, with regard to Abū Ḥanīfah, the people were not of the same opinion as we in Khurasan."[23] This story of Isḥāq and 'Abd al-Raḥmān ibn Mahdī suggests that Ibn al-Mubārak's denunciation of Abū Ḥanīfah was unknown in Khurasan—unknown even in Basra; therefore, it is likely to have been fabricated later to preserve Ibn al-Mubārak for traditionalism and to save him from association with Abū Ḥanīfah. This is not all: it suggests, too, that, in the late eighth century, the split between the adherents of *ḥadīth* and *ra'y* had advanced much further in Iraq than Khurasan. Indeed, it seems likely that the split was transmitted from Iraq to Khurasan by such men as Isḥāq.

The strongest evidence for locating the split between *aṣḥāb al-ḥadīth* and *aṣḥāb al-ra'y* only at the end of the eighth century is the behavior of traditionalists in Baghdad. Aḥmad ibn Ḥanbal would become leader of the most uncompromising Baghdadi traditionalists. When he first began to collect religious knowledge, at 16, he took dictation from Abū Ḥanīfah's prominent disciple Abū Yūsuf, although he would not relate hadith from him later on.[24] Thus we have

---

[23] Aḥmad ibn Ḥanbal, *K. al-Wara'*, ed. Zaynab Ibrāhīm al-Qārūṭ (Beirut: Dār al-Kutub al-'Ilmīyah, 1983), 124.

[24] Al-Khalīlī, *al-Irshād fī ma'rifat 'ulamā' al-ḥadīth*, abr. al-Silafī, Aya Sofya 2951, 93b; Ibn al-Jawzī, *Manāqib al-imām Aḥmad ibn Ḥanbal*, ed. 'Abd Allāh ibn 'Abd al-Muḥsin al-Turkī & 'Alī Muḥammad 'Umar (Cairo: al-Khānjī, 1979), 46.

a rough *terminus ad quem* for the split at the death of Abū Yūsuf in 182/798.

If Abū Yūsuf was an exceptional Ḥanafi, to be sure, there may be reasons for pushing back the date of the split. A leading follower of al-Shāfi'ī's would say that Abū Yūsuf was the one leader of *aṣḥāb al-ra'y* who inclined most towards *aṣḥāb al-ḥadīth*.[25] The great Basran traditionist 'Alī ibn al-Madīnī (d. Samarra, 234/849) would report that when he saw Abū Yūsuf in Basra, in 180, he would dictate ten reports of hadith (presumably statements from the Prophet and his Companions), then ten of *ra'y* (presumably the opinions of Ibn Abī Laylá, Abū Ḥanīfah, and the like).[26] A Basran Ḥanafi tradition would describe Abū Yūsuf as looking down on the crowd of jurisprudents (*fuqahā'*) and traditionists (*muḥaddithūn*) at his door and saying, "I am from both parties (*al-farīqayn*). I do not put one party (*firqah*) before the other."[27] However, Yaḥyá ibn Ma'īn went on to write at the dictation of Abū Ḥanīfah's disciple Muḥammad ibn al-Ḥasan al-Shaybānī, although Aḥmad did not.[28] Abū Khaythamah (d. 234/849) was another Baghdadi traditionist who wrote down hadith reports from the Ḥanafīyah at one time, although he would not relate them later on.[29] We can probably say that the traditionalist party of Baghdad became alarmed some time during this decade, the 180's/796-805.

References to Aḥmad's hearing Abū Yūsuf are found in the earliest Ḥanbali sources; e.g., his recollection of Abū Yūsuf's lisping, *apud* 'Abd Allāh ibn Aḥmad, *al-Jāmi' fī al-'ilal wa-ma'rifat al-rijāl*, ed. Muḥammad Ḥusām Bayḍūn, 2 vols. (Beirut: Mu'assasat al-Kitāb, 1990), 1:237.

[25] Opinion of al-Muzanī, *apud* al-Khaṭīb al-Baghdādī, *Tārīkh* 2:176; but note that al-Muzanī was a former Ḥanafi, himself, and continued to consult Ḥanafi books.

[26] Al-Khaṭīb al-Baghdādī, *Tārīkh* 14:255; but note that 'Alī ibn al-Madīnī was incriminated at the Inquisition not only by his affirming that the Qur'an was created—so Yaḥyá ibn Ma'īn, Abū Khaythamah, and many other prominent traditionalists likewise affirmed—but also by suggesting traditionalist arguments to its chief architect, Ibn Abī Duwād: *v.* al-Khaṭīb al-Baghdādī, 11:466f.

[27] Al-Dhahabī, *Siyar a'lām al-nubalā'* 8 (ed. Nadhīr Ḥamdān, Beirut: Mu'assasat al-Risālah, 1981):472.

[28] Al-Khaṭīb al-Baghdādī, *Tārīkh* 2:175f. Yaḥyá was said to incline towards the Ḥanafīyah in jurisprudence, and contradictory opinions of his are reported concerning Abū Ḥanīfah.

[29] Ibn 'Abd al-Barr, *Intiqā'*, 148.

REASONS FOR THE SPLIT

The historian al-Ṭabarī (d. Baghdad, 310/923) said that many traditionists (*qawm min ahl al-ḥadīth*) avoided the hadith reports of Abū Yūsuf on account of his having been given to *ra'y*; on account of his ramifying questions and legal problems; and on account of his friendship toward rulers and his assumption of the judgeship.[30] He must have referred, though, to traditionists who flourished well after Abū Yūsuf's death. When Aḥmad went to hear hadith reports from him, he had already been chief qadi for five years; therefore, it was probably not on account of their association with the powerful that Aḥmad and the others renounced the Ḥanafīyah. Nor could Aḥmad have been ignorant of Abū Yūsuf's devotion to *ra'y* and his ramifying legal problems.

More likely, it was the doctrine of the created Qur'an that occasioned the split, for this doctrine was promulgated by Ḥanafi jurisprudents in the time of Abū Yūsuf and after his death, above all by his student Bishr al-Marīsī.[31] As chief qadi, Abū Yūsuf enforced a policy of non-discussion.[32] Traditionalists sometimes accused him of confessing the Qur'an created, but more often distinguished between him and other leading Ḥanafīyah to his benefit.[33] On their side, the traditionalists probably did not use the formula "uncreated" (*ghayr makhlūq*) before his time.[34] However, his successor Muḥammad ibn al-Ḥasan al-Shaybānī (d. Ranbuyah, 189/805) seems by nearly all accounts to have professed the Qur'an created.[35] The much-maligned

---

[30] Al-Ṭabarī, *apud* Ibn 'Abd al-Barr, *Intiqā'*, 173.

[31] *Encyclopaedia of Islam*, new edn., s.v. "Miḥna," by M. Hinds. There is a Ḥanafi story, put in the mouth of Aḥmad ibn Ḥanbal, that Abū Yūsuf once had Bishr dragged out of his session by the feet: Ibn Abī al-Wafā', *al-Jawāhir al-muḍīyah*, 2 vols. (Hyderabad: Majlis Dā'irat al-Ma'ārif al-Niẓāmīyah, 1332), 2:221.

[32] Wilferd Madelung, "The Origins of the Controversy Concerning the Creation of the Koran," in J. M. Barral, ed., *Orientalia hispanica: sive studia F. M. Pareja octogenaria dicata* (Leiden: E. J. Brill, 1974), 520.

[33] His accuser is anonymous in al-'Uqaylī, *Ḍu'afā'* 4:444. Cf. testimony collected in Ibn Ḥajar, *Lisān "al-Mīzān,"* 7 vols. (Hyderabad: Majlis Dā'irat al-Ma'ārif, 1329-31), 6:300f, particularly Ibn Ḥibbān: "He was unlike them (his two comrades, mainly Abū Ḥanīfah and al-Shaybānī) with regard to faith (Murji'ism) and the Qur'an (its uncreated nature)."

[34] *V.* Madelung, "Origins," 518f.

[35] Al-'Uqaylī, *Ḍu'afā'* 4:52, 54, 55; Ibn Ḥajar, *Lisān* 5:122.

al-Ḥasan ibn Ziyād al-Lu'lu'ī (d. 204/819-820) may have, as well. I have found no explicit statement of it; however, it must have been for some theological error (it was a regular article of traditionalist creeds that no one might be accused of unbelief on account of his works[36]) that the traditionalist Yazīd ibn Hārūn (d. Wasit, 206/821), asked his opinion of al-Lu'lu'ī, asked in return, "Oh—is he a Muslim?"[37]

Traditionalist jurisprudents found many additional reasons to repudiate *aṣḥāb al-ra'y*: reasons having to do with practice and not just belief. One bitter point of contention was the legal device (*ḥīlah*, pl. *ḥiyal*) by which one might apparently defeat the spirit of the law without disobeying the letter. Abū Yūsuf found his way into the Thousand and One Nights for his skill at inventing such devices.[38] "Whoever uses a legal device (to escape an oath he has taken) is a perjurer," said Aḥmad.[39] Also, "Whoever has *Kitāb al-Ḥiyal* in his home and gives opinions on its basis has covered up (as an unbeliever) what God sent down to Muḥammad," presumably referring to a book on legal devices by Abū Yūsuf or one based on it by al-Shaybānī.[40] The traditionist al-Sājī (d. Basra, 307/919-920) accused Ibn al-Thaljī (d. 266/880) of using legal devices "to nullify hadith from the Messenger of God . . . , to deny it in favor of Abū Ḥanīfah and his *ra'y*."[41]

Traditionalists condemned *qiyās*, the principle of analogy, for a similar tendency, namely that it could evidently be used to evade the

---

[36] Against the Kharijites; e.g., in the creeds of Aḥmad, *apud* Ibn Abī Ya'lá, *Ṭabaqāt* 1:27, 130f, 294, 343.

[37] Al-'Uqaylī, *Ḍu'afā'* 1:227. Yazīd ibn Hārūn is quoted both ways concerning Abū Yūsuf: that he did relate traditions from him and that he forbade it, *apud* Ibn Ḥajar, *Lisān* 6:300f.

[38] *V.* Duncan B. Macdonald, *Development of Muslim Theology, Jurisprudence, and Constitutional Theory*, Semitic Ser. (New York: Charles Scribner's Sons, 1903), 97.

[39] Ibn Abī Ya'lá, *Ṭabaqāt* 1:120.

[40] Ibn Abī Ya'lá, *Ṭabaqāt* 1:218. For *K. al-Ḥiyal*, *v.* Ibn al-Nadīm, *Fihrist*, 204 = *f.* 2, *q.* 6, and *Encyclopaedia of Islam*, new edn., s.v. "Abū Yūsuf," by J. Schacht. Admittedly, traditionalists also quoted Ibn al-Mubārak as attributing a *K. al-Ḥiyal* to Abū Ḥanīfah himself and calling it an act of unbelief to give opinions according to it: al-Khaṭīb al-Baghdādī, *Tārīkh* 13:403f.

[41] Al-Khaṭīb al-Baghdādī, *Tārīkh* 5:351. Muḥammad ibn Shujā' al-Thaljī is usually called "Ibn Shujā'" in Ḥanafi sources, "Ibn al-Thaljī" in traditionalist, but also by Fuat Sezgin, whose convention I normally observe: *Geschichte des arabischen Schrifttums*, 9 vols. (Leiden: E. J. Brill, 1967-), 1:436.

strict requirements indicated by hadith. It was the early Mu'tazili al-Naẓẓām (d. 220-330/835-845), it is true, who declaimed a poem on Abū Yūsuf's grave predicting that, had he lived, he would have made virgins and boys licit with his *qiyās*.[42] But Mālik (d. Medina, 179/795) was remembered as telling his disciples of Abū Ḥanīfah, "If he came to your columns, here, and tried to persuade you with his *qiyās* that they were wood, you would think that they were wood."[43] Ja'far al-Firyābī (d. 301/913) related in 232/846-847 that Muḥammad had warned that the worst of the seventy-odd Islamic sects would be that which used analogy according to *ra'y*, making licit what was forbidden and forbidding what was licit.[44] This hadith report found its way into none of the Six Books, but 30,000 turned out to hear al-Firyābī when he visited Baghdad almost seventy years later: plainly, his low opinion of jurisprudence by *ra'y* did not make him unpopular.[45] Several traditionists also transmitted it from the Egyptian Ibn Wahb (d. Old Cairo, 197/813).[46]

Sometimes, traditionists accused Abū Ḥanīfah and his followers of simply setting aside known hadith reports in favor of personal opinion. From Sufyān ibn 'Uyaynah (d. Mecca, 198/814) is often quoted the story of how Abū Ḥanīfah would make up a hypothetical example in order to dismiss a prophetic hadith report. "He heard that I related of the Prophet . . . that he said, 'The buyer and seller are at option (to annul a sale) so long as they have not parted.' Abū Ḥanīfah said, 'What if they are on a boat: then how can they part?'"[47] On this account, Aḥmad ibn Ḥanbal declared, "There is no *qiyās* in the Sunnah, and examples are not to be made up for it."[48] An important Kufan

---

[42] *Apud* al-Shīrāzī, *al-Alqāb al-ruwāh*, *apud* Ibn Ḥajar, *Lisān* 6:301.

[43] Ibn 'Abd al-Barr, *Intiqā'*, 146f.

[44] Ibn 'Adī, *Kāmil* 3:1264.

[45] Al-Khaṭīb al-Baghdādī, *Tārīkh* 7:199f.

[46] Al-Khaṭīb al-Baghdādī, *Tārīkh* 13:307f.

[47] *Yaḍribu li-ḥadīth rasūl Allāh al-amthāl*: 'Abd Allāh ibn Aḥmad, *Sunnah*, 216; Ibn 'Abd al-Barr, *Intiqā'*, 147-149; cf. 151f, where Bishr ibn al-Faḍl argues with Abū Ḥanīfah over this tradition. The language recalls Q.24.36, *yaḍribu Allāh al-amthāl lil-nās*, commonly taken to mean that God speaks to men in metaphors. Ibn 'Uyaynah's story seems clearly to deal with hypothetical applications, not metaphors; however, the qur'anic echo might insinuate that Abū Ḥanīfah presumed to speak with divine authority.

[48] *Al-sunnah 'indanā āthār rasūl Allāh . . . wa-laysa fī al-sunnah qiyās wa-lā yuḍrabu lahā al-amthāl*: *apud* Ibn Abī Ya'lá, *Ṭabaqāt* 1:241. Same from the later Ḥanbali

transmitter from Sufyān al-Thawrī, Wakī' ibn al-Jarrāḥ (d. Fayd, 197/812), reported, "I have found Abū Ḥanīfah to differ with 200 hadith reports from the Messenger of God."[49] Al-Shāfi'ī looked through 180 folios written by Abū Ḥanīfah and his *aṣḥāb*, and found eighty that differed with the Book and the Sunnah.[50]

More simply, traditionalists might reproach the adherents of *ra'y* with ignorance, specifically with having no sound basis of action. The Basran traditionist al-Shādhakūnī told the story that Muḥammad ibn 'Abd Allāh al-Anṣārī (d. Basra, 215/830?) once received 50,000 dirhams from the caliph al-Ma'mūn to distribute among the jurisconsults of Basra. Hilāl al-Ra'y (d. Basra, 245/859-860) considered that the money should go to his students, but Muḥammad al-Anṣārī insisted it was for his. Finally, Muḥammad challenged Hilāl to give the chain of transmitters on whose authority he pronounced the *shahādah* (his testimony that there was no god but God, and that Muḥammad was the Messenger of God). When he could not, Muḥammad expressed his disgust and distributed the money among his own students.[51]

The traditionalists were bothered, too, by Abū Ḥanīfah's willingness to change his position. They quoted the Khurasani traditionist Abū Ḥamzah al-Sukkarī (d. 167/783-784?) as relating,

> I went to Abū Ḥanīfah and asked him about some questions. I went away for some twenty years, then went to him, and lo, he had gone back on those questions. I had given them to people as my juridical opinions (*aftaytu bi-hā al-nās*). I told him of this. He said, "We see one view (*nará al-ra'y*), the next day we see another and take it back."

Abū Ḥamzah was upset and said, "What a wretched man you are."[52]

---

leader al-Barbahārī, *Sharḥ K. al-Sunnah*, *apud* Ibn Abī Ya'lá, 2:19.

[49] In a book by al-Sājī, *apud* Ibn 'Abd al-Barr, *Intiqā'*, 151. According to Yaḥyá ibn Ma'īn, Wakī' nevertheless gave juridical opinions according to the position of Abū Ḥanīfah: Ibn Ḥajar, *Tahdhīb* 11:126f.

[50] Al-Khaṭīb al-Baghdādī, *Tārīkh* 3:410.

[51] Al-Khaṭīb al-Baghdādī, *Tārīkh* 5:409. Admittedly, Muḥammad al-Anṣārī is probably to be counted an adherent of the Basran school of jurisprudence, so this was an argument within the camp of *ra'y*: only the name of al-Shādhakūnī (d. Isfahan, 236/850-851?) makes it traditionalist, and he was bitterly denounced for lying by Yaḥyá ibn Ma'īn, Aḥmad, and other traditionalist critics (for which *v.* Ibn Ḥajar, *Lisān* 3:84-86). I have not determined the reason for their antagonism.

[52] 'Abd Allāh ibn Aḥmad, *Sunnah*, 220f. Similar stories in al-Khaṭīb al-Baghdādī,

When someone complained that the qadi Ḥafṣ ibn Ghiyāth (d. Kufa, 194/809-810?) was taking too long, he replied, "I saw Abū Ḥanīfah state ten positions, then go back on them: why do you rush me?"[53] The later Ḥanafīyah were bothered, as well, for they related a similar story from Ibn al-Thaljī of someone who had heard Abū Ḥanīfah answer some juridical questions, then returned ten years later to find him giving different answers to the same questions. A friend explained to Ibn al-Thaljī, "This indicates the breadth of his knowledge: if his knowledge were narrow, his answer would be one, but his affair is broad and so he treats it however he likes."[54] Plainly, the Baghdadi traditionalists felt otherwise.

Finally, the traditionalists blamed Abū Ḥanīfah for want of humility. They quoted Sufyān al-Thawrī as saying,

> I have never seen anyone more bold before God than Abū Ḥanīfah. A man of Khurasan came to him and said, "I have come to you with a hundred thousand questions that I should like to ask you about." He said, "Bring them here." Have you seen anyone more bold before God than this?[55]

By contrast, when a man told Mālik he had travelled for six months, charged by the people of his city with asking him a question, Mālik listened to the question but would not give an answer, saying only "I am not good at this."[56] Al-Shāfiʻī was quoted admiringly of Sufyān ibn ʻUyaynah, "I have not seen anyone who more steadfastly refused to give juridical opinions."[57] Baghdadi traditionalists would go so far as to allege that Abū Ḥanīfah had accused the Companion and caliph ʻUmar of being mistaken, or mused that had he met the Prophet, or the Prophet him, the Prophet would have learnt a great deal![58]

Only occasionally did the traditionalists blame *aṣḥāb al-ra'y* for de-

---

Tārīkh 13:402.

[53] ʻAbd Allāh ibn Aḥmad, *Sunnah*, 220.

[54] Ibn Abī al-Wafā', *Jawāhir* 2:285, *s.n.* ʻAbbād ibn Ṣuhayb.

[55] ʻAbd Allāh ibn Aḥmad, *Sunnah*, 215f.

[56] Ibn Abī Ḥātim, *Kitāb al-Jarḥ wa-al-taʻdīl*, 9 vols. (Hyderabad: Jamʻīyat Dā'irat al-Maʻārif al-ʻUthmānīyah, 1360), 1:18.

[57] Al-Khalīlī, *Irshād*, 44b; similarly Ibn ʻAdī, *Kāmil*, 1:108. For further stories of traditionists reluctant to give juridical opinions, *v.* Ibn al-Ṣalāḥ al-Shahrazūrī, *Adab al-muftī wa-al-mustaftī*, ed. Muwaffaq ibn ʻAbd Allāh ibn ʻAbd al-Qādir (Beirut? Maktabat al-ʻUlūm wa-al-Ḥikam, 1986), 74-85.

[58] ʻAbd Allāh ibn Aḥmad, *Sunnah*, 226.

ficiencies in their style of piety. Al-Ḥasan ibn Ziyād al-Lu'lu'ī was harshly criticized for his performance of the ritual prayer: "I have seen no one who prayed in a worse fashion than he," said one traditionist; al-Shāfi'ī accused him of laughing aloud during the prayer and committing slander (a serious offense); someone else reported, "al-Ḥasan ibn Ziyād raised his head before the imam did and prostrated himself before he did."[59] However, practices and traits of an ascetic character are much more often found among the traditionalists than among *aṣḥāb al-ra'y*. I shall briefly treat these practices and traits later on.

THE JURIDICAL PROGRAM OF THE TRADITIONALISTS

The juridical program of *aṣḥāb al-ḥadīth* was just as their name suggests: a program of collecting hadith. Not an organized school in the later sense, they had no separate training in jurisprudence. One can often distinguish traditionalists by the terms used to describe their formation. Biographies of Muslim scholars almost always list their authorities. In biographies of traditionalists, one reads *sami'a min* ("he heard from"), *kataba 'an* ("he wrote from"), and *rawá 'an* ("he related from"), but not *akhadha 'an* ("he learnt from") or, more specifically, *tafaqqaha 'alá* ("he learnt jurisprudence from"): these terms are reserved for practitioners of jurisprudence by *ra'y*.

For example, take the traditionists of whom Abū 'Ubayd stated, "Religious knowledge (*'ilm*—not just hadith) has ended up with four": Abū Bakr Ibn Abī Shaybah (d. Kufa, 235/849), Aḥmad ibn Ḥanbal (d. Baghdad, 241/855), 'Alī ibn al-Madīnī (d. Samarra, 234/849), and Yaḥyá ibn Ma'īn (d. Medina, 233/848).[60] Al-Khaṭīb al-Baghdādī (d. 463/1071) has long and laudatory entries for all four, but none identifies a particular teacher in jurisprudence.[61] Abū Isḥāq al-Shīrāzī (d. 476/1083) includes separate entries for only Aḥmad and 'Alī in his biographical dictionary of jurisprudents, doubtless reflecting his intention to exclude mere traditionists[62]; yet neither entry includes

---

[59] Ibn Ḥajar, *Lisān* 2:208f, with worse to follow.

[60] Ibn Abī Ḥātim, *Jarḥ* 1:293, 315, 319.

[61] Al-Khaṭīb al-Baghdādī, *Tārīkh* 4:412-423, 10:66-71, 11:458-473, 14:177-187.

[62] Although Ibn Abī Shaybah and Yaḥyá ibn Ma'īn certainly took an active interest in jurisprudence: Ibn Abī Shaybah's book of jurisprudence, *Kitāb al-Muṣannaf*, has

the phrase *tafaqqaha 'alá*, naming a particular teacher.[63] In fact, I have found the phrase in no biography of any of them. Contrast four Ḥanafi contemporaries: 'Īsá ibn Abān (d. Basra? 221/835-836), Muḥammad ibn Samā'ah (d. Baghdad, 233/848), Hilāl al-Ra'y (d. Basra, 245/859-860), and Ibn Muqātil al-Rāzī (d. Rayy, 248/862-863): biographers regularly tell us that 'Īsá ibn Abān and Ibn Muqātil learnt jurisprudence from Muḥammad al-Shaybānī, Ibn Samā'ah from Abū Yūsuf and Muḥammad, Hilāl al-Ra'y from Abū Yūsuf and Zufar.[64]

The traditionalists were unininterested in a special juridical training because any separate training would have suggested reposing one's trust in a late teacher more than in the Prophet, his Companions, and the pious ancestors. When contradictory hadith reports were attributed to different Companions, it was Aḥmad's policy to relate them all.[65] As a practical matter, one would have to choose among them; however, Aḥmad would not have his own choice become a new standard, as though he were fit to arbitrate among the Companions.[66]

Individual teachers the traditionalists would not trust: what they wanted was an inspired textual basis for doctrine and practice. Someone asked Aḥmad whether he might investigate *ra'y* for the purpose of argument: Aḥmad recommended the Sunnah instead.[67] When he gave similar advice to someone else, recommending that he write down only the *āthār* and *ḥadīth*, this man protested that Ibn al-Mubārak had likewise copied books of *ra'y*: unmoved, Aḥmad replied, "Ibn al-Mubārak did not descend from heaven. We have been ordered

---

been published in seven volumes (ed. Kamāl Yūsuf al-Ḥūt, Beirut: Dār al-Tāj, 1989), while a number of Yaḥyá ibn Ma'īn's opinions are preserved *apud* al-Dhahabī, *Siyar* 11 (ed. Ṣāliḥ al-Samr, 1982):93f; Ibn Ḥajar, *Tahdhīb* 11:286f.

[63] Abū Isḥāq al-Shīrāzī, *Ṭabaqāt al-fuqahā'*, ed. Iḥsān 'Abbās (Beirut: Dār al-Rā'id al-'Arabī, 1970), 91f, 100, 103f.

[64] Al-Khaṭīb al-Baghdādī, *Tārīkh* 5:342, 11:157; Abū Isḥāq, *Ṭabaqāt*, 137-139; Ibn Abī al-Wafā', *Jawāhir* 2:134.

[65] E.g., the ten opinions on cutting off a thief's hand.

[66] There are a number of reports of Aḥmad's forbidding his followers to write down his own juridical opinions, or expressing disgust when they did. *V.* Ibn al-Jawzī, *Manāqib*, 251. For a more extensive treatment of Aḥmad's juridical practice, *v.* Susan A. Spectorsky, "Aḥmad Ibn Ḥanbal's *Fiqh*," *Journal of the American Oriental Society* 102 (1982):461-465.

[67] Ibn Abī Ya'lá, *Ṭabaqāt* 1:327.

to learn *'ilm* (religious knowledge) only from above."[68] A textual basis from above would not be subject to the vicissitudes evident in systems based on *ra'y*: they should not change in twenty years' time, as the opinions of Abū Ḥanīfah changed, they could not make brick appear to be wood.[69]

As traditionalists did not study jurisprudence separately from hearing hadith, a certain opposition was felt between their hadith and others' jurisprudence; that is, the very term for jurisprudence, *fiqh*, sometimes took on the connotation of irresponsible *ra'y*. Hence, for example, 'Alī ibn al-Madīnī was warned to be very careful—evidently more careful than he had to be as a traditionist—if he looked into *fiqh*.[70] On the other hand, there is much evidence that Aḥmad did value *fiqh* as the discernment of legal applications of the received hadith reports. For example, he went on from praising the traditionist 'Abd al-Razzāq to lamenting, "How little of *fiqh* there is among the traditionists."[71]

The inspired textual basis of the traditionalists did include hadith reports from the Companions and Successors. Al-Shāfi'ī is said to have argued for the overriding authority of hadith reports from the Prophet, as against hadith reports from Companions and Successors, and Joseph Schacht has presented the traditionists as sharing that position; e.g., "The Traditionists . . . preferred not to use any human reasoning in law, and chose, as much as possible, to base every single item in their doctrine on a tradition from the Prophet."[72] This goes too far. The traditionalists may indeed have tried to minimize reliance on human reasoning, but they were plainly satisfied to found their jurisprudence on hadith reports from others than the Prophet. The works

---

[68] Ibn Abī Ya'lá, *Ṭabaqāt* 1:329.

[69] W. Montgomery Watt has proposed that al-Ma'mūn declared the Qur'an created in part so that he might contravene it: *The Formative Period of Islamic Thought* (Edinburgh: University Press, 1973), 179. Martin Hinds finds the suggestion improbable (*EI*², s.v. "Miḥna"), and at the level of positive law it is; however, it surely is true at the level of traditionalist impressions of what was at stake.

[70] Al-Khaṭīb al-Baghdādī, *Tārīkh* 11:461.

[71] Ibn Abī Ya'lá, *Ṭabaqāt* 1:329.

[72] Joseph Schacht, "The Schools of Law," *Law in the Middle East*, ed. Majid Khadduri & Herbert J. Liebesny (Washington, D.C.: Middle East Institute, 1955), 66. Cf. *Encyclopaedia of Islam*, new edn., s.v. "Ahl al-Ḥadīth" by J. Schacht; Schacht, *Origins*, 150: "the insistence of Shāfi'ī and the traditionists on the overriding authority of the traditions from the Prophet."

of al-Shāfi'ī may distinguish between *ḥadīth* from the Prophet and *athar* from later authorities,[73] but Aḥmad uses the terms interchangeably.[74] A discussion in Aḥmad's *Kitāb al-'Ilal* of when to cut off the hand of a thief comprises nine hadith reports, all going back to Companions or Successors, none to the Prophet.[75] (The editor notes that a hadith report to the same effect from the Prophet is found in the collection of al-Nisā'ī [d. 303/915?].) Contrast the section on amputation in the *Mukhtaṣar* of al-Muzanī: al-Shāfi'ī cites two hadith reports from the Prophet and the known practice of one Companion.[76] Gérard Lecomte has suggested that Aḥmad Ibn Ḥanbal's inclusion of opinions from Companions and Successors in the authoritative Sunnah represents a step backward by comparison with the position of al-Shāfi'ī.[77] However, Aḥmad's legal works are no more inclusive than those of 'Abd al-Razzāq (d. Yemen, 211/827)[78] and Ibn Abī Shaybah.[79] We must either conclude that al-Shāfi'ī's arguments for reliance on hadith from the Prophet did not immediately sweep the field or follow Calder in redating the putative works of al-Shāfi'ī to the later ninth century and after.[80]

This may be the place to address the traditionalist position concerning *ijtihād* and *taqlīd*. For far too long, it has been a commonplace among Western students of Islam (and many Muslims, as well) that *ijtihād* at some point ceased; that is, that Muslim jurisprudents at some point lost the capacity to propose their own, original solutions.

---

[73] Schacht, *Origins*, 16.

[74] E.g., 'Abd Allāh ibn Aḥmad, *Sunnah*, 226.

[75] Aḥmad Ibn Ḥanbal, *K. al-'Ilal wa-ma'rifat al-rijāl*, ed. Talât Koçyiğit & İsmail Cerrahoğlu, Ankara Üniversitesi Ilâhiyat Fakültesi Yayınlar 49, 1 vol. published (Ankara: Doğuş Matbaacılık ve Ticaret Matbaası, 1963), 1:157f. Schacht admits that al-Shāfi'ī, too, made considerable use in practice, despite his theory, of hadith from the Companions: *Origins*, 18f.

[76] In margin of al-Shāfi'ī, *K. al-Umm*, 7 vols. (Bulaq: al-Maṭba'ah al-Kubrá al-Amīrīyah, 1902-1906), 5:169, 171.

[77] Gérard Lecomte, "Un exemple d'évolution de la controverse en Islam: de l'*Iḫtilāf al-ḥadīṯ* d'al-Šāfi'ī au *Muḫtalif al-ḥadīṯ* d'Ibn Qutayba," *Studia Islamica*, no. 27 (1967), 14.

[78] 'Abd al-Razzāq's chapter on stoning, for example, comprises about 70 hadith reports from Muḥammad, 100 from other authorities.

[79] Ibn Abī Shaybah's discussion of stoning, for example, comprises three hadith reports from Muḥammad, fourteen from other authorities.

[80] Norman Calder, *Studies in Early Muslim Jurisprudence* (Oxford: Clarendon Press, 1993), chaps. 4, 5, 9.

It never rested on impressive documentation.[81] Wael B. Hallaq's demonstrātion that, before modern times, Muslims have not considered the gate of *ijtihād* to be closed is therefore welcome.[82]

On the other hand, Hallaq's characterization of the traditionalists as opposing *ijtihād* needs qualification. These traditionalists, Hallaq says, "were primarily concerned with the study of transmitted sources and their literal interpretation, while denying human reason any right to be exercised in ijtihad or in the process of legal reasoning."[83] Hallaq's understanding is based partly on his identifying *ijtihād* with *qiyās*.[84] His identification is not baseless, for no less than al-Shāfi'ī identified them. A catechism in the *Risālah* reads so: "'What is *qiyās*? Is it *ijtihād* or are they different?' 'They are two names with one meaning.'"[85] But this was al-Shāfi'ī's personal usage (or, very likely, some follower's): not everyone in the ninth century identified *ijtihād* and *qiyās*. For example, Dāwūd al-Ẓāhirī wrote books against both *taqlīd* and *qiyās*, which he could hardly have done if he had thought *ijtihād* identical to *qiyās*.[86] Aḥmad and his fellow traditionalists of the ninth century expressly condemned the Ḥanafi exercise of *qiyās*, but I have seen no express condemnation of their *ijtihād*.

The *taqlīd* that traditionalists did advocate had to do with the Prophet and his Companions, not the teachings of later jurisprudents. So, for example, when Aḥmad repudiates those who deny *taqlīd*, he has in mind not a party that has come up with new solutions to juridical problems, but one that, to his mind, does not wish to follow the

---

[81] C. Snouck Hurgronje names the year 300 and cites al-Bājūrī (d. 1276/1860), who indeed states that *ijtihād* came to an end (*inqaṭa'a*) about that time, *contra* al-Suyūṭī, but without reference to any gate: *Selected Works*, ed. G.-H. Bousquet & Joseph Schacht (Leiden: E. J. Brill, 1957), 283; *Ḥāshiyat al-Bayjūrī* [*sic*] *'alá Sharḥ Ibn Qāsim al-Ghazzī*, 2 vols. (Cairo: Maṭba'at Wādī al-Nīl al-Miṣrīyah, 1298, repr. Beirut: Dār al-Ma'rifah, 1974), 1:31. "The closing of the gate of *ijtihād*" probably entered Orientalist parlance through Ibn Khaldūn, *al-Muqaddimah*, 448 = Quatremère, ed., 3:6.

[82] Wael B. Hallaq, "Was the Gate of Ijtihad Closed?" *International Journal of Middle East Studies* 16 (1984):3-41.

[83] Hallaq, "Was the Gate?" 7f.

[84] Hallaq, "Was the Gate?" 7.

[85] Al-Shāfi'ī, *Umm* 1:66, l. 3.

[86] Ibn al-Nadīm, *Fihrist*, 217, l. 13 = *f.* 4, *q.* 6. Dāwūd carried on polemics against *qiyās* with a Meccan student of al-Shāfi'ī's, Ibn Abī al-Jārūd: Ibn 'Abd al-Barr, *Intiqā'*, 105.

Prophet and his Companions.[87] His position was certainly that one should not ask theological questions that the pious ancestors were not known to have asked, nor adopt juridical positions contrary to what they were known to have adopted; however, this is not the same as rejecting all use of reason, for new cases must arise, and preferences must be expressed when more than one opinion was reliably reported from the pious ancestors concerning some question. Moreover, the traditionalists did not regard their own solutions as final. To the teachings of Abū Ḥanīfah, for example, which seemed to change over time, they opposed not their own teachings that would not change but rather the unchanging hadith reports of Prophet and Companions.[88] The ninth-century debate over *taqlīd* pitted the Ḥanafīyah and Mālikīyah against moderate traditionalists, and the term should not be applied to the juridical position of the primitive Ḥanābilah.[89]

MUDHĀKARAH

A good illustration of the rigors and comforts of the traditionalist system is the practice of *mudhākarah*, a normally friendly contest to de-

---

[87] Creed I, *apud* Ibn Abī Ya'lá, *Ṭabaqāt* 1:31.

[88] On the freedom of traditionalist jurisprudence, cf. Henri Laoust: "Since primitive Muslim law was a doctrine of essentially oral transmission, which on a common substructure left a wide latitude to individual variations, any systematic codification, such as to impose it in terms of thought of any particular representative or to congeal it by fixation, was to change its inner character" (*Encyclopaedia of Islam*, new edn., s.v. "Aḥmad b. Ḥanbal").

[89] The later Ḥanbali school would remain distinguished for its belief that *ijtihād* never came to an end, even when the other schools had admitted that it might: W. Montgomery Watt, "Closing of the Door of *Iǧtihād*," *Orientalia hispanica: sive studia F. M. Pareja octogenario dicata*, ed. J. M. Barral (Leiden: E. J. Brill, 1974), 671. Hallaq revives the term "Ḥashwīyah" to designate the extreme traditionalist party that upheld *taqlīd*. In the fourth century, he says (i.e., the tenth century C.E.), the Ḥanābilah pulled away from them (9). This is unsatisfactory: on the one hand, Hallaq continues to confound their application of *taqlīd* to the theological tenets of the Companions with the rationalistic jurisprudents' application of *taqlīd* to the jurisprudence of the later eighth century; on the other hand, he presents no evidence that the ninth-century Ḥashwīyah and Ḥanābilah were distinct parties. A. S. Halkin's identification of the Ḥashwīyah with Aḥmad ibn Ḥanbal and his followers remains credible: A. S. Halkin, "The Ḥashwiyya," *Journal of the American Oriental Society* 54 (1934):1-28.

termine who could recite the most hadith reports, or the most chains of authorities for a given text. It contrasts with *munāẓarah*, the formal debate over a point of law or theology practiced by *mutakallimūn* and rationalistic jurisprudents.[90] Its friendly and informal nature is evident in the lower standard of accuracy it required. Isḥāq ibn Rāhawayh (d. 238/853) knew 70,000 hadith reports by heart, but used 100,000 in *mudhākarah.*[91] Ismā'īl al-Daylamī (d. 255/868-869), a Baghdadi ascetic associated with Aḥmad, said he knew 40,000 by heart but was said to use 70,000 in *mudhākarah.*[92] Because its conditions were less stringent, no doubt, Abū Zur'ah al-Rāzī (d. 264/878) would not allow auditors to write down what he said in *mudhākarah.*[93]

Mudhākarah agreed with the traditionalists' conception of the community as a fraternity. It was not always free of ill will; for example, other traditionists blamed al-Shādhakūnī for lying in *mudhākarah.*[94] Yet we have no stories of such rancor as, say, ensued from al-Shāfi'ī's *munāẓarah* with his Māliki opponent Fityān: that Fityān defeated al-Shāfi'ī (in other versions, insulted him in the course of their debate), that al-Shāfi'ī complained to the governor of being insulted, that Fityān was chastised, shaven, and paraded about Old Cairo, that his partisans then beat al-Shāfi'ī so severely that he died not long after.[95] The upshot of *mudhākarah* was not chiefly, after all, that one side was reduced to silence, but that those assembled heard more hadith reports than they had known, before.

Mudhākarah also answered to the traditionalists' concern for certainty. In case of disagreement, an authoritative decision was possible.

---

[90] *Munāẓarah* has been described by George Makdisi, *The Rise of Colleges* (Edinburgh: Univ. Press, 1981), 109-111, 133-140.

[91] Ibn Faḍl Allāh al-'Umarī, *Masālik al-abṣār fī mamālik al-amṣār*, Aya Sofya 3418, 140b.

[92] Al-Khaṭīb al-Baghdādī, *Tārīkh* 6:275, 276.

[93] Al-Dhahabī, *Siyar* 13 (ed. 'Alī Abū Zayd, 1983):80.

[94] Ibn Ḥajar, *Lisān* 3:86f. 'Alī ibn al-Madīnī and 'Abd al-Raḥmān ibn Mahdī feared violence between the respective followers of al-Shādhakūnī and Ibn Abī Shaybah when they met for *mudhākarah*: al-Khaṭīb al-Baghdādī, *Tārīkh* 10:69.

[95] Abū al-'Arab, *K. al-Miḥan*, ed. Yaḥyá Wuhayb al-Jubūrī (Beirut: Dār al-Gharb al-Islāmī, 1983), 433f; al-Qāḍī 'Iyāḍ, *Tartīb al-madārik*, ed. Aḥmad Bakīr Maḥmūd, 5 vols. (Beirut: Maktabat al-Ḥayāh, 1967-1968), 2:458. For a slightly later version of the story, which does not blame the denunciation of Fityān on al-Shāfi'ī himself, *v.* Makdisi, *Rise of Colleges*, 136.

'Alī ibn al-Madīnī relates, "Whenever I went to Baghdad, over a period of forty years, it was Aḥmad who engaged me in *mudhākarah*. We often disagreed over something, whereupon we asked Yaḥyá ibn Ma'īn."[96] Similarly, when the prominent traditionists Ibn Wārah (d. 270/884) and Faḍlak (d. 270/883) of Rayy disagreed over a hadith report that had come up in *mudhākarah*, they appealed to Abū Zur'ah al-Rāzī. He was able to tell them precisely where in the library (*bayt al-kutub*) they would find the correct version.[97]

The upshot of *munāẓarah*, by contrast, must often have been continuing disagreement. For example, Dāwūd al-Ẓāhirī explained a generation later what al-Shāfi'ī had meant by his argument against selling the houses of Mecca, which his opponent Isḥāq had allegedly misunderstood.[98] Presumably most of the audience had likewise misunderstood. What can the audience have thought when al-Shāfi'ī reduced his opponent to silence, told him "Now you take up my position and let me take up yours," then reduced him to silence again?[99] The exercise must indeed have convinced them that al-Shāfi'ī was a skillful debater; however, a strict traditionalist would surely notice that the point of determining God's will for his elect community had been entirely lost. (Indeed, there is a contrary Iraqi tradition by which al-Shāfi'ī never debated save for the sake of giving advice [*naṣīḥah*], and never with the object of leading his opponent into a mistake.[100])

It might seem that some traditionists engaged in both *mudhākarah* and *munāẓarah*. Isḥāq ibn Rāhawayh has already come up in connection with both. As we have seen, Isḥāq first came from Khurasan a rationalistic jurisprudent, not understanding that he needed to choose between Ḥanafism and hadith. It is possible that the debate with al-Shāfi'ī took place before his thorough conversion to traditionalism.

---

[96] Al-Khaṭīb al-Baghdādī, *Tārīkh* 14:182. Elsewhere, 'Alī himself is said to have acted as arbiter between Aḥmad and others: *ibid.*, 11:462f.

[97] Ibn Abī Ḥātim, *Jarḥ* 1:327. Many other stories are extant, as well. By one account, the great Nishapuran traditionist Muslim actually died from eating too many dates while he sat up, one night, looking for the hadith report that had escaped him in a session for *dhākirah*. He did find the report: al-Ḥākim al-Naysābūrī, *apud* al-Khaṭīb al-Baghdādī, *Tārīkh* 13:103.

[98] Al-Bayhaqī, *Manāqib al-Shāfi'ī*, ed. al-Sayyid Aḥmad Ṣaqr, 2 vols. (Cairo: Dār al-Turāth, 1970, 1971), 1:215f.

[99] By the testimony of Yūnus ibn 'Abd al-A'lá, *apud* al-Bayhaqī, *Manāqib* 1:179.

[100] Ibn Abī Ḥātim, *Ādāb al-Shāfi'ī wa-manāqibuh*, ed. 'Abd al-Ghanī 'Abd al-Khāliq (Cairo, 1954; repr. Aleppo: Maktabat al-Turāth al-Islāmī, n.d.), 92f.

More likely, though, Isḥāq's engagement in *munāẓarah* was typical of the Khurasani traditionalist party, of which Isḥāq was a founding member. It was Ibn Khuzaymah (d. 311 or 312/*circa* 924), leader of Khurasani traditionalism in his time but no enemy to al-Shāfi'ī, who related the story from Yūnus ibn 'Abd al-A'lá of al-Shāfi'ī's playfully changing sides. It was the Baghdadi traditionalists in particular who rejected *munāẓarah*.

By some accounts, admittedly, even the Baghdadis engaged in *munāẓarah*. A Ḥanbali source quotes Abū Zur'ah al-Rāzī as saying he engaged in *munāẓarah* with Aḥmad concerning hadith and juridical questions.[101] Yet shortly thereafter 'Abd Allāh ibn Aḥmad is quoted as saying that they engaged in much *mudhākarah*.[102] Very likely, the quotation from Abū Zur'ah was garbled, or at least their *munāẓarah* more resembled the normal *mudhākarah* than the rationalists' *munāẓarah*. The Shāfi'i biographer al-Subkī tells us the Egyptian Aḥmad ibn Ṣāliḥ came to Baghdad and there debated with (*nāẓara*) Aḥmad ibn Ḥanbal.[103] Al-Subkī even provides the transcription of a debate (*munāẓarah*) between Aḥmad and al-Shāfi'ī.[104] I am inclined to think that al-Subkī's lonely and late references are mistaken: he was in a poor position to notice the difference, or inclined to press it if he did. In a similar class would be the older report from someone at the court of al-Mutawakkil, quoted as recalling,

> Aḥmad ibn Ḥanbal was brought in before the caliph . . . . Two men had been decapitated. Aḥmad looked at Abū 'Abd al-Raḥmān al-Shāfi'ī and asked, "What have you by memory from al-Shāfi'ī concerning brushing off (the feet; *al-masḥ*)?" Ibn Abī Duwād said, "Behold a man who comes to be decapitated yet he debates about jurisprudence (*yunāẓiru fī al-fiqh*)."[105]

The reporter no doubt intended a compliment, but did not comprehend Aḥmad's actual disinclination to ask about the opinions of late

---

[101] Ibn Abī Ya'lá, *Ṭabaqāt* 1:199.

[102] Ibn Abī Ya'lá, *Ṭabaqāt* 1:199. Cf. Al-Khaṭīb al-Baghdādī, *Tārīkh* 10:327, referring only to *mudhākarah*.

[103] Al-Subkī, *Ṭabaqāt al-shāfi'īyah al-kubrá*, ed. Maḥmūd Muḥammad al-Ṭanāḥī & 'Abd al-Fattāḥ al-Ḥulw, 10 vols. (Cairo: 'Īsá al-Bābī al-Ḥalabī, 1964-76), 2:7.

[104] Al-Subkī, *Ṭabaqāt* 2:61.

[105] Abū Nu'aym, *Ḥilyat al-awliyā'*, 10 vols. (Cairo: Maktabat al-Khānjī & Maṭba'at al-Sa'ādah, 1932-38), 9:186.

jurisprudents.[106] At least, we have many more references to *mudhākarah* among the Baghdadi traditionalists than to *munāẓarah*. By contrast, moreover, *mudhākarah* is almost never associated with rationalistic jurisprudents.

DISADVANTAGES OF TRADITIONALIST JURISPRUDENCE

Pure traditionalism proved untenable in the long run. In its purest form, it was never maintained for long outside Iraq. We have seen already how aversion to *munāẓarah* was weaker among the traditionalists of Khurasan than of Baghdad. Too, as the reader may have noticed, the sharpest depreciations of Abū Ḥanīfah are nearly all from Iraqis. In Khurasan, attacks on the Ḥanafīyah were never so sharp; for example, al-Bukhārī would include Abū Ḥanīfah in his directory of weak transmitters of hadith but would not explicitly associate him with the doctrine of a created Qur'an.[107] More Khurasanis are known to have gone to Egypt to hear the jurisprudence of al-Shāfi'ī than Baghdadis, including leaders of the Khurasani traditionalist movement such as Ibn Khuzaymah. The party of *ḥadīth* in the developing Māliki school was never strong in Medina, and largely died away in Basra and Egypt. In the West, the Māliki school was traditionalized, in ways, as the Ḥanafi school was in Iraq, but not in all ways; for example, Saḥnūn (d. 240/854), qadi for Qayrawan, may have stood up against the Inquisition, but his highly influential juridical program put *fiqh* before *ḥadīth*, the fixed code and *taqlīd* in place of continual re-examination of the sources.[108] Perhaps the

[106] Abū 'Abd al-Raḥmān had studied under al-Shāfi'ī' in Baghdad and made himself known by his defense of al-Shāfi'ī's juridical system. He later became attached to the qadi Ibn Abī Duwād: *v.* Ibn Ḥajar, *Lisān* 7:76. Aḥmad's question refers to a well-known point of contention with the Shī'ah, and may have implied, tauntingly, that Abū 'Abd al-Raḥmān had strayed towards Shī'ism away from al-Shāfi'ī's orthodoxy. Yet in this aspect, too, the quotation agrees better with the polemical position of al-Mutawakkil's court than with the position of Aḥmad, who strongly opposed Shī'ism but did not, by any other account, attribute the Inquisition to Shī'i influence.

[107] Ibn 'Abd al-Barr, *Intiqā'*, 149f. Wilferd Madelung finds reluctance to attack Abū Ḥanīfah in Aḥmad and the Ḥanābilah generally ("Origins," 509f), but the many stories against Abū Ḥanīfah in 'Abd Allāh ibn Aḥmad's *K. al-Sunnah*, to mention no other collection, indicate that the Baghdadis felt scant reluctance.

[108] *V.* M. Talbi, "Kairouan et le mālikisme espagnol," *Etudes d'orientalisme dédi-*

Muslims outside Iraq felt more beleaguered, amidst non-Muslim majorities, and therefore inclined more strongly to compromise.

I know of no Muslim observer who commented on the decline of purely traditionalist jurisprudence, but I will propose some technical reasons. It must have maintained itself with difficulty in part because of its resisting any regular system of succession from teacher to student. The traditionalists related how the Successor al-Sha'bī (d. 109/727-728?) was asked, "Whom are you leaving to succeed you?" Al-Sha'bī answered, "I am not a jurisprudent, and I am not leaving as my successor (*mā ukhallifu*) any jurisprudent." Sufyān al-Thawrī is the common link in two chains of authorities for the story, and may have invented it.[109] Certainly, it illustrates the traditionalists' reluctance to identify authoritative teachers of jurisprudence, as opposed to faithful transmitters of hadith.

The story of Asad ibn al-Furāt's study in Egypt illustrates how refusal to identify authoritative teachers of jurisprudence might impede the spread of traditionalism. Asad studied first in Iraq under Muḥammad ibn al-Ḥasan, then entered Egypt a second time with Muḥammad's questions for the leading scholars there to answer. He first approached Ibn Wahb, a student under Mālik and the Egyptian al-Layth ibn Sa'd (d. 175/791); however, in good traditionalist fashion, Ibn Wahb refused to give any answers but hadith reports he had heard. Next, Asad went to Ashhab (d. 204/819), a student under Mālik and enemy to al-Shāfi'ī; however, Ashhab was too independent, too willing to give his own opinion, not that of Mālik or Abū Ḥanīfah, and so Asad left him, as well. He finally went to Ibn al-Qāsim (d. 191/806-807), who was willing to give answers exactly as Mālik might have.[110] Later, Saḥnūn brought Asad's *Mudawwanah* back to Ibn al-Qāsim, who changed many answers to bring them yet closer in line with the teaching of Mālik.[111] The resultant book, his own *Mudawwanah*, was practically the basis of African Māliki jurispru-

---

ées à la mémoire de Lévi-Provençal (Paris: G.-P. Maisonneuve et Larose, 1957) 1:337. His name is also pointed "Suḥnūn." Both options are approved by Ibn Ḥajar, *Tabṣīr al-mushtabih*, ed. 'Alī Muḥammad al-Bijāwī, 4 vols. (Cairo: al-Dār al-Miṣrīyah lil-Ta'līf wa-al-Tarjamah, 1967), 2:677.

[109] Aḥmad ibn Ḥanbal, *K. al-'Ilal*, ed. Waṣī Allāh, 1:281, 283.

[110] Abū Bakr al-Mālikī, *K. Riyāḍ al-nufūs*, ed. Bashīr al-Bakkūsh, 2 vols. (Beirut: Dār al-Gharb al-Islāmī, 1983), 1:261. Talbi, "Kairouan," 1:322.

[111] Abū Bakr al-Mālikī, *Riyāḍ* 1:263.

dence thenceforward.[112] Whether it was really more faithful to the teaching of Mālik, I cannot say; however, it is plain what sold well in Africa: faithful transmission of the master's doctrine, neither greatly extended by independent reasoning nor requiring much independence in the one who learnt it. Orthodoxy, guaranteed by association with Mālik, mattered more than maintaining the traditional flexibility.

Traditionalist jurisprudence suffered, too, from certain theoretical weaknesses. If Schacht is misleading about the stress that traditionalists placed on hadith reports going all the way back to the Prophet, he is probably correct to state that al-Shāfi'ī's logic was irresistible, or at least to suggest that Muslims found it so. (Had his logic alone been irresistible, then presumably medieval Jews should also have discarded the opinions of jurisprudents in favor of teaching from Moses himself.) Schacht observes the difficulty with which al-Shāfi'ī found any logical authority for relying on hadith reports from the Companions.[113] The traditionalists themselves told the story of Aḥmad's impressing Wakī' ibn al-Jarrāḥ with his hadith reports from the Prophet. Aḥmad argued before him with some followers of Abū Ḥanīfah. As noted before, Wakī' adhered to the juridical position of Abū Ḥanīfah. Yet when a Ḥanafi complained to him of Aḥmad's aspersing Kufans, Wakī' answered, "A man who says, 'The Messenger of God said . . . '—what shall I say to him?"[114]

Among Aḥmad's closest followers there were clearly some who felt the lack of a juridical theory like that of the Shāfi'īyah and others. Abū Bakr al-Athram (d. 273/886-887?) of Iskāf had studied jurisprudence and disagreements among jurisprudents before coming to study under Aḥmad, whereupon he left it in favor of hadith from the Prophet and his Companions.[115] He evidently treated Aḥmad's juridical opinions in the same fashion, though, ordering them by topic.[116] This work Aḥmad repudiated: "I have forbidden anyone to write from him. I did not say not to write down hadith from him: what I dislike

---

[112] Sezgin, *Geschichte* 1:465, 469-471.

[113] Schacht, *Origins*, 19.

[114] Al-Dhahabī, *Siyar* 11:186f, probably quoting from al-Khallāl, *K. Akhlāq Aḥmad*.

[115] Ibn Abī Ya'lá, *Ṭabaqāt* 1:72.

[116] Ibn Abī Ya'lá, *Ṭabaqāt* 1:66.

is these juridical problems that he has brought out . . . ."[117] Significantly, it is he who described Aḥmad as following the standard (Shāfi'i) distinction between hadith reports from the Prophet and hadith reports from Companions, preferring one from the Prophet to any number of contrary positions from the Companions, and so forth.[118] No such formal procedure is related of Aḥmad directly. It is a definite step toward the formation of a Ḥanbali school just like the others.

Another disadvantage of pure traditionalist jurisprudence must have been the demands it placed on jurisprudents—demands probably too high to be universally accepted. The number of hadith reports it required the jurisprudent to know was prodigious. Abū Zur'ah al-Rāzī was impeccably traditionalist, and measured expertise in the law by expertise in hadith.[119] "I am amazed by one who gives juridical opinions concerning questions of divorce," he said, "and knows by heart fewer than a hundred thousand hadith reports."[120] Abū Sa'īd al-Dārimī (d. 280/894?), of Herat, stated, "Whoever has not combined the hadith of Shu'bah, Sufyān (al-Thawrī), Mālik, Ḥammād ibn Zayd, and Sufyān ibn 'Uyaynah is bankrupt in hadith."[121] Al-Dhahabī estimates that the hadith of Sufyān al-Thawrī alone would come to ten volumes.[122]

Aḥmad ibn Ḥanbal may have required the most of all. He was once asked,

> "How many hadith reports will suffice a man to give juridical opinions? Will 100,000 suffice?" He said, "No." He was asked, "200,000?" He said, "No." He was asked, "300,000?" He said, "No." He was asked, "400,000?" He said, "No." He was asked, "500,000?" He said, "I hope so."[123]

---

[117] Ibn Ḥajar, *Tahdhīb* 1:78.

[118] Ibn al-Jawzī, *Manāqib*, 230.

[119] For example, his reported evaluations of Sufyān al-Thawrī and Mālik ibn Anas have nothing to do with their powers of reasoning but only their skill at sifting traditions by weak and strong transmitters: al-Dhahabī, *Siyar* 13:79.

[120] Al-Dhahabī, *Siyar* 13:69.

[121] Al-Dhahabī, *Siyar* 13:323. Al-Dārimī was claimed by later jurisprudents of the Ḥanbali, Shāfi'i, and Ḥanafi schools: *v.* al-'Abbādī, *K. Ṭabaqāt al-fuqahā' al-shāfi'īyah*, ed. Gösta Vitestam, Veröffentlichungen der "De Goeje Stiftung," 21 (Leiden: E. J. Brill, 1964), 45f; Ibn Abī Ya'lá, *Ṭabaqāt* 1:221. In his call for knowing hadith, as in his polemics against the Jahmīyah, he seems thoroughly traditionalist.

[122] Al-Dhahabī, *Siyar* 13:323.

[123] Ibn Abī Ya'lá, *Ṭabaqāt* 1:131.

A modern edition of the *Ṣaḥīḥ* of al-Bukhārī, which comprises some 7,000 hadith reports, occupies four volumes. Aḥmad's 500,000 would occupy hundreds.

There were traditionists with prodigious memories. A man reported to Isḥāq ibn Rāhawayh that Aḥmad ibn Ḥanbal had said there were 700,000 sound hadith reports, while Abū Zur'ah knew 600,000.[124] A man who dreamt of Abū Zur'ah after his death asked him how he had attained to flying amongst the angels. Abū Zur'ah told him, "By writing with my hand a million hadith reports in which I said 'From the Messenger of God . . . .'"[125] Reports directly from Abū Zur'ah reduce the numbers but leave them awesomely large; e.g., he assured someone that he had not actually written 100,000 hadith reports from the Rāzi traditionist Ibrāhīm ibn Mūsá (d. after 222/837), as reported, but only 60,000 or 70,000.[126] Other traditionists knew far fewer hadith reports. Isḥāq ibn Rāhawayh asserted that he had 100,000 in his notebooks.[127] If this was the case with so prominent a jurisprudent as he, how could the ordinary student aspire to meet Aḥmad's standard?

Knowledge of hadith on this order must have been far beyond the power of most men. Aḥmad and other traditionalist authorities did alleviate the potential burden by warning their followers away from books of jurisprudence (including records of their own opinions) in favor of hadith.[128] Yet the temptation must have been overwhelming to learn rather the books of jurisprudence and such hadith reports as they relied on; or, alternatively, to learn a small body of reliable hadith.

Several traditionists of the generation after Aḥmad did indeed assemble small bodies of reliable hadith, namely al-Bukhārī (d. near Samarqand, 256/870), Muslim (d. near Nishapur, 261/875), Ibn Mājah (d. Qazvin, 273/887), Abū Dāwūd (d. Basra, 275/889), and al-Tirmidhī (d. Tirmidh, 279/892). Al-Bukhārī's collection included only some 7,000 sound hadith reports, selected from over 600,000

---

[124] Al-Khaṭīb al-Baghdādī, *Tārīkh* 10:332; al-Ḥākim al-Naysabūrī, *apud Siyar* 13:69. Al-Dhahabī comments that one transmitter in al-Ḥākim's chain (in al-Khaṭīb's, too) is not trustworthy.

[125] Al-Khaṭīb al-Baghdādī, *Tārīkh* 10:336.

[126] Ibn Abī Ḥātim, *Jarḥ* 1:334f.

[127] Ibn Ḥajar, *Tahdhīb* 1:217.

[128] Warnings collected in Ibn al-Jawzī, *Manāqib*, 249f.

that he had heard[129]; Abū Dāwūd his 4,800 sound hadith reports from 500,000[130]; Muslim his 12,000 sound hadith reports from 300,000 that he had heard.[131] (Even Aḥmad's *Musnad* included only, by most estimates, some 30,000 hadith reports, selected from 750,000, and Aḥmad recommended it as sufficient for juridical purposes.[132]) It would plainly be easier to memorize ten or twenty thousand hadith reports than a hundred thousand, not to speak of six hundred thousand. Moreover, the sound hadith reports in these new books were already arranged by the categories of jurisprudence.

(In addition to the sheer number of hadith reports that the traditionalist approach required one to memorize, it would seem that the attached chains of transmitters must have become increasingly more difficult. That is, with each generation, the chain of transmitters attached to each hadith report must lengthen, so that with every new generation any given number of hadith reports must occupy a greater number of pages and more of a traditionist's memory. Moreover, a chain of names must be more or less meaningless; for example, "Aḥmad ibn Ṣāliḥ" is just as good a name as "Ṣāliḥ ibn Aḥmad," and must require special effort to keep straight, whereas it requires minimal effort to recall that a text reads, say, *innamā al-a'māl bi-al-nīyāt* and not *bi-al-nīyāt al-a'māl innamā*, which is nonsense. There are many stories of someone's testing a famous traditionist by deliberately altering the chains of transmitters attached to known hadith reports to see whether he would detect the change. I have never seen a story about altering actual texts. As a given number of reports came to occupy more and more space, it was precisely the more difficult part that was increasing. If the chain could stop at, say, al-Bukhārī, or if the traditionist need memorize only one chain from al-Bukhārī to himself, hadith must become more manageable. However, the only discussion I have seen of the relative difficulty of memorizing chains and texts suggests that texts were trickier, and more liable to be confused if the traditionist did not know jurisprudence.[133])

---

[129] Al-Khaṭīb al-Baghdādī, *Tārīkh* 2:8, 14.

[130] Al-Khaṭīb al-Baghdādī, *Tārīkh* 9:57.

[131] Al-Khaṭīb al-Baghdādī, *Tārīkh* 13:101.

[132] Ibn Abī Ya'lá, *Ṭabaqāt* 1:143.

[133] Ibn Ḥibbān, *K. al-Majrūḥīn*, *apud* Ibn Rajab, *Sharḥ "'Ilal" al-Tirmidhī*, ed. Hammām 'Abd al-Raḥīm Sa'īd, 2 vols. (al-Zarqā', Jordan: Maktabat al-Manār, 1987), 1:430. Ibn Rajab comments that no one before Ibn Ḥibbān (d. 354/965) had

Some traditionalists were unhappy with the new enterprise. Abū Zur'ah assailed Muslim on the ground that he included hadith reports from certain weak transmitters, also on the ground that he had made it easier for heretics to resist hadith reports cited against them: they had only to say, "This is not in the *Ṣaḥīḥ*."[134] Muslim explained that it was intended to help those for whom learning was a burden; that is, Muslim laymen, *'awāmm al-nās*.[135] He expected experts such as Abū Zur'ah to continue in the old style, and even put together, himself, an old-style collection by transmitter, *al-Musnad al-kabīr*.[136] Evidently, Abū Zur'ah could not be persuaded; however, approval among the general is easy to understand, as likewise among ordinary students of jurisprudence. The author of one of the new, abridged collections, Abū Dāwūd, was actually a follower of Aḥmad ibn Ḥanbal, who attended Aḥmad's session and asked him subtle questions concerning both the roots and branches of jurisprudence.[137]

It must have been difficult not only to collect but also, afterwards, to keep such large numbers of hadith reports. Abū Zur'ah himself needed constant practice.

> When I become ill for a month or two, it becomes apparent to me in the memorization of the Qur'an. As for hadith, if you leave it for (a few) days, it will become apparent to you.
>
> We see a number of our comrades who have written hadith but left off sitting (for dictation) twenty years or less. If they sit today with the young men, it is as if they knew nothing, or were not good in hadith.
>
> Hadith is like the sun: if one did not observe the sun rise for five days, he would not know when its setting was. This is something you must take on in perpetuity (*tata'āhaduhu abadan*).[138]

Yaḥyá ibn Ma'īn would write down every hadith report fifty

---

taken this position.

[134] Al-Khaṭīb al-Baghdādī, *Tārīkh* 4:274.

[135] Al-Nawawī, introduction, *Ṣaḥīḥ Muslim bi-sharḥ al-Nawawī*, 18 vols. (Cairo: al-Maṭba'ah al-Miṣrīyah, 1929), 1:47.

[136] Significantly, though, al-Ḥākim states that no one related it from Muslim, and no manuscript has survived: al-Dhahabī, *Siyar* 12 (ed. Ṣāliḥ al-Samr, 1983):579; Sezgin, *Geschichte* 1:136-143.

[137] Al-Dhahabī, *Siyar* 13:215. Cf. Ibn Abī Ya'lá, *Ṭabaqāt* 1:159-162.

[138] Al-Dhahabī, *Siyar* 13:79.

times.[139] The traditionalist Abū Mas'ūd (d. 258/871-872) would repeat every one five hundred times in order to memorize it.[140] The Qazvini traditionist Abū al-Ḥasan al-Qaṭṭān (d. 345/956-957) furnishes an illustration of what must happen to one who did not continually practice: he complained that he had known 100,000 hadith reports by heart when he was travelling, in his youth, but now knew scarcely a hundred.[141]

Work like this must have made hadith science a full-time activity, scarcely to be practiced alongside most trades; yet the traditionalists forbade the dictation of hadith or the giving of juridical opinions for a fee. Sufyān al-Thawrī was supposed to have said, "The scholar (*'ālim*) is the physician of religion, the dirham the plague of religion, so what if the physician draws the plague to himself as he treats another?"[142] Aḥmad forbade his followers to write down the hadith of anyone who demanded money for it, "even to honor him."[143] His follower Ibrāhīm al-Ḥarbī (d. 285/899) once accepted beans to the value of one *fals* in exchange for an opinion, otherwise never in his life.[144] The Kufan traditionist al-Faḍl ibn Dukayn (d. 219/834?) lamented that he was blamed for taking payment (*ajr*), yet had thirteen dependents and not a loaf of bread in the house.[145]

It is almost entirely among *aṣḥāb al-ra'y* or those close to them that we read of direct payment for religious knowledge. Al-Shāfi'ī paid 50 or 60 dinars for the books of al-Shaybānī.[146] He allegedly warned his followers not to pay Abū 'Abd al-Raḥmān al-Shāfi'ī to tutor them, but on the grounds of unreliability, not that payment was wrong.[147] Yaḥyá ibn Yaḥyá al-Laythī (d. 234/849) boasted of bribing ("*arshaytu*") Ḥabīb Ibn Abī Ḥabīb (d. 218/833-834) a thousand dirhams to relate to him a thousand hadith reports from Mālik.[148]

---

[139] Ibn Ḥajar, *Tahdhīb* 11:282.

[140] Ibn Ḥajar, *Tahdhīb* 1:67, ll. 9f from bottom.

[141] Al-Dhahabī, *Siyar* 15 (ed. Ibrāhīm al-Zaybiq, 1983):463.

[142] Ibn Faḍl Allāh, *Masālik*, 138b.

[143] Al-Khaṭīb al-Baghdādī, *K. al-Kifāyah fī 'ilm al-riwāyah* (Hyderabad: Dā'irat al-Ma'ārif al-'Uthmānīyah, 1938), 154.

[144] Al-Khaṭīb al-Baghdādī, *Tārīkh* 6:33f.

[145] Ibn Ḥajar, *Tahdhīb* 8:275.

[146] Stories in al-Dhahabī, *Siyar* 10 (ed. Muḥammad Nu'aym al-'Araqasūsī, 1982):14f.

[147] Al-Khaṭīb al-Baghdādī, *Tārīkh* 5:200.

[148] Al-Qāḍī 'Iyāḍ, *Tartīb* 1:379.

Yaḥyá's reputation in hadith was poor, but he returned to Andalusia to became a leading counsellor to the ruler, and the giving of juridical opinions, there, devolved on him: it was evidently a worthwhile investment.

Indirect payment for hadith must have been common, to be sure. We often read of men who expended large legacies on gathering hadith; for example, Yaḥyá ibn Ma'īn spent a million dirhams.[149] But men of religion commonly lived on charity—we continually read of rulers' handing over large sums to be distributed (e.g., al-Ma'mūn to Muḥammad ibn 'Abd Allāh al-Anṣārī)—and traditionalists preferred to maintain the forms of free giving. Hence, for example, 'Īsá ibn Yūnus al-Sabī'ī (d. 191/806-807?) once refused 100 dinars with the words "No, by God: the scholars *(ahl al-'ilm)* shall not relate that I took money for the Sunnah unless this was before they (the donors) have asked me. As for hadith, no, not even to drink water."[150] Yet Aḥmad was famous for refusing gifts that fellow traditionists accepted.[151] His example must have been hard on his followers; conversely, made his program unattractive to others.

Perhaps in consequence of how difficult it was to be a thorough traditionalist, the early Baghdadi followers of Aḥmad ibn Ḥanbal gained little renown as traditionists. Aḥmad's most important student in jurisprudence, al-Marrūdhī, does not appear in either of Ibn Ḥajar's compendia, *Tahdhīb "al-Tahdhīb"* or *Lisān "al-Mīzān,"* indicating that he was practically ignored by subsequent *rijāl* critics. Ibrāhīm al-Ḥarbī did merit an evaluation from al-Dāraquṭnī *(thiqah)*,[152] but he, too, appears in neither work of Ibn Ḥajar's.

A list of leading scholars in the ninth century shows clearly the ebb and flow of traditionalist influence. 'Alī ibn al-Madīnī is quoted as describing how the religious knowledge (*'ilm*) of past generations had all ended up with Yaḥyá ibn Ma'īn. Al-Dhahabī adds that it was also with Aḥmad, Abū Bakr Ibn Abī Shaybah, 'Alī ibn al-Madīnī, and others; then passed to al-Bukhārī, Abū Zur'ah al-Rāzī, Abū Ḥātim al-Rāzī (d. 277/890-891), and Abū Dāwūd; after them to al-Nisā'ī (d. 303/915?), Muḥammad ibn Naṣr al-Marwazī (d. 294/907?), Ibn

---

[149] Al-Khaṭīb al-Baghdādī, *Tārīkh* 14:180.
[150] Ibn Ḥajar, *Tahdhīb* 8:239.
[151] Abū Nu'aym, *Ḥilyah* 9:174-179, 181, 186.
[152] *Apud* al-Khaṭīb al-Baghdādī, *Tārīkh* 6:40.

Khuzaymah, and al-Ṭabarī before beginning to dwindle away.[153] The earliest generation, of Aḥmad, is fairly solidly traditionalist. The next generation has been profoundly influenced by him: all four were students under Aḥmad, and although al-Bukhārī died in exile for suggesting that his pronunciation of the Qur'an was created, he explicitly identified his creed with Aḥmad's. The next generation, to the contrary, is only weakly traditionalist: al-Nisā'ī is difficult to characterize, but he was fatally wounded for too warmly commending 'Alī; al-Marwazī trained students in jurisprudence like a Ḥanafi; Ibn Khuzaymah adhered to a more traditionalist form of Shāfi'ism, but still told the story of al-Shāfi'ī's playfully changing sides; and al-Ṭabarī is said to have ended his life under siege by the Ḥanābilah of Baghdad. The future of jurisprudence belonged not to pure traditionalism but to compromise forms: the Ḥanbali school, submitted to the forms of jurisprudence, and the Shāfi'i, Ḥanafi, and Māliki schools, submitted to the forms of hadith.

[153] Al-Dhahabī, *Siyar* 11:78.

CHAPTER TWO

FROM REGIONAL SCHOOLS TO PERSONAL

The great schools of Islamic law in the eighth century were regional: the school of Iraq, the school of the Hijaz, a secondary Syrian school, and so on. In the middle of the eighth century, there arose the traditionalist movement, based not on a region (although it was strongest in Iraq) but rather a principle: exclusive reliance on Scriptuary authority, mostly hadith reports of what the Prophet, the Companions, and the Successors had said. In the ninth century, the old regional schools were largely redefined as personal schools; that is, collections of jurisprudents who upheld the teaching of one man. Some jurisprudents evidently felt more secure when they identified their jurisprudence with an individual teacher, not a region, perhaps in reaction to the traditionalist challenge. Over time, more and more jurisprudents were persuaded to follow their example, until no one identified any longer with a region. An example of the efficiency of personal authority at securing the loyalties of jurisprudents is the demise of the old Basran school, which the new Ḥanafi and Māliki schools absorbed by the mid-ninth century.

FROM THE KUFAN SCHOOL TO THE ḤANAFI

We owe our perception of the shift from regional to personal schools to Joseph Schacht, once again. He describes the ancient regional schools of Iraq and the Hijaz as transforming themselves into personal schools.

> There existed within the 'Iraqi [school] of Kūfa the "followers of Abū Ḥanīfa," a group which included Abū Yūsuf and Shaybānī; in addition, Abū Yūsuf had followers of his own . . . . The followers of Abū Ḥanīfa were only part of the Kūfians. But the extensive literary activity of the followers of Abū Ḥanīfa, particularly of Shaybānī, in 'Iraq . . . , together with other factors, some of them accidental, brought it about that the ancient school of Kūfa survived

only in the followers of Abū Ḥanīfa (or Ḥanafīs) . . . .

In much the same way, the literary activity of certain North Africans caused the old Hijazi school to survive only as the school of Mālik.[1]

The formation of a Ḥanafi school shows up first in the evidence to which Schacht points, mainly the extant writings of Abū Ḥanīfah's followers Abū Yūsuf (d. Baghdad, 182/798) and Muḥammad al-Shaybānī (d. near Rayy, 189/804). For example, al-Shaybānī's *Kitāb al-Āthār* comprises a series of juridical problems, to each of which are attached relevant hadith reports (mostly from Companions and Successors), then, at the end, the opinion of Abū Ḥanīfah. Norman Calder suggests that the extant writings attributed to Abū Yūsuf and al-Shaybānī were actually put together at the middle of the ninth century or later.[2] But even he pronounces authentic the attribution of *Kitāb Aḥkām al-awqāf* to Hilāl al-Ra'y (d. Basra, 245/859-860), student under Abū Yūsuf and Zufar, and it appears to present in the first place what seems reasonable, in the second what Abū Ḥanīfah and his closest disciples held.[3] The same might be said of the extant works of al-Khaṣṣāf (d. Baghdad, 261/874), *Adab al-qāḍī* and *Kitāb al-Ḥiyal wa-al-makhārij*.[4] Such works as these imply a specifically Ḥanafi school, both inasmuch as they collect the doctrine (*madhhab*) of one jurisprudent (and a few close to him) and inasmuch as they suggest that his doctrine (and theirs) is all one need know.

The biographical literature furnishes more evidence of the forma-

---

[1] Joseph Schacht, "The Schools of Law and Later Developments of Jurisprudence," *Law in the Middle East* 1: *Origin and Development of Islamic Law*, ed. Majid Khadduri & Herbert J. Liebesny (Washington: Middle East Institute, 1955), 63.

[2] Norman Calder, *Studies in Early Muslim Jurisprudence* (Oxford: Clarendon Press, 1993), chaps. 3, 6.

[3] Calder, *Studies*, 50f. In the first fifty pages of Hilāl al-Ra'y, *Kitāb Aḥkām al-waqf* (Hyderabad: Majlis Dā'irat al-Ma'ārif al-'Uthmānīyah, 1355), I count 28 references to Abū Ḥanīfah, six to the caliph 'Umar, three or four to Abū Yūsuf, &c.

[4] Al-Khaṣṣāf, *Adab al-qāḍī*, is not extant by itself, and the text is difficult to disengage from the extant commentaries on it. The most helpful edition is that of Farḥat Ziyādah (Cairo: American Univ. in Cairo Press, 1978). Ziyādah states that the Turkish manuscripts enumerated by Fuat Sezgin, *Geschichte des arabischen Shrifttums*, 9 vols. (Leiden: E. J. Brill, 1967-), 1:437, #2, are all abridgements of a later commentary: "Introduction," 7. I have examined Feyzullah Efendi 660 and Köprülü 546. Joseph Schacht edited *K. al-Ḥiyal wa-al-makhārij* as his doctoral dissertation: *Das Kitāb al-ḥiial ual-maḫāriǧ*, Beiträge zur semitischen Philologie und Linguistik, ed. G. Bergsträsser, 4 (Hanover: Heinz Lafaire, 1923).

tion of a personal school. At his death, it is said, Abū Ḥanīfah was succeeded in his circle by Zufar ibn al-Hudhayl (d. Basra, 158/774-775), then Abū Yūsuf, then al-Shaybānī.[5] A continuously existing group of students with a regular succession of teachers is a mark of a functioning school.

In Kufa, some jurisprudents initially resisted becoming known as adherents of Abū Ḥanīfah in particular. The Kufan littérateur and qadi al-Qāsim ibn Ma'n (d. 175/791-792) was asked, "Are you willing to be among the devotees (*ghilmān*) of Abū Ḥanīfah?" "The Muslims," he answered, "have not sat with anyone more beneficial than . . . Abū Ḥanīfah."[6] Plainly, in this story, the nascent Kufan school of jurisprudence was already being identified with Abū Ḥanīfah, and some Kufan jurisprudents resented it, as al-Qāsim ibn Ma'n was expected to but would not.

Unfortunately, the extant stories of Kufan jurisprudents in the eighth century may better reflect conditions in the ninth. If Abū Ḥanīfah's circle passed in turn to Zufar, then Abū Yūsuf, then al-Shaybānī, what happened to it after that? Very likely, there was no regular circle, and the succession story simply accounts for the importance of these teachers in later Ḥanafi doctrine. Al-Qāsim ibn Ma'n is supposed to have expressed willingness to identify himself with Abū Ḥanīfah, but no source states that he learnt jurisprudence from any particular teacher, including Abū Ḥanīfah. The story of his willing to be called a (slavish) follower of Abū Ḥanīfah was very likely put forward by Ḥanafizers of the ninth century.

The biographical sources also identify as followers of Abū Ḥanīfah men whose contemporaries seem to have considered them independent. Nūḥ ibn Darrāj (d. 182/798-799) was qadi at times in Kufa and Baghdad, known for relating hadith but repudiated by the great *rijāl* experts.[7] He is almost certainly to be counted, then, amongst *aṣḥāb al-ra'y*. The fourteenth-century Ḥanafi biographer Ibn Abī al-Wafā' states that he learnt jurisprudence from Abū Ḥanīfah and Zufar[8]; yet

---

[5] Ibn 'Abd al-Barr, *al-Intiqā' fī faḍā'il al-thalāthah al-a'immah al-fuqahā'* (Cairo: Maktabat al-Qudsī, 1350), 174.

[6] Wakī', *Akhbār al-quḍāh*, ed. 'Abd al-'Azīz Muṣṭafá al-Marāghī, 3 vols. (Cairo: Maṭba'at al-Istiqāmah, 1947-50), 3:176.

[7] His name appears in none of the Six Books. *V.* Ibn Ḥajar, *K. Tahdhīb "al-Tahdhīb,"* 12 vols. (Hyderabad: Majlis Dā'irat al-Ma'ārif al-Niẓāmīyah, 1325-27), 10: 482-484.

[8] Ibn Abī al-Wafā', *al-Jawāhir al-muḍīyah*, 2 vols. (Hyderabad: Majlis Dā'irat

Wakīʻ, writing in the late ninth century, speaks of his inclining toward the position of the qadi Ibn Abī Laylá (d. Kufa, 148/765-766).[9]

Similarly, Ibn Abī al-Wafā' says that Ḥafṣ ibn Ghiyāth (d. 195/811?), qadi for Kufa and a district of Baghdad, was a *ṣāḥib* of Abū Ḥanīfah's.[10] Writing in Ottoman times, al-Kaffawī includes him among Abū Ḥanīfah's pupils (*talāmidhah*), then says expressly that he learnt jurisprudence from him.[11] To the contrary, though, Abū Ḥanīfah does not appear in Ibn Ḥajar's long list of shaykhs from whom Ḥafṣ related hadith reports.[12] Neither does Abū Ḥanīfah appear in the earliest biographies of Ḥafṣ.[13] Moreover, a story of Abū Yūsuf's attempting to discredit him presents Ḥafṣ as ruling (most acceptably) according to the position of Ibn Abī Laylá.[14] Presumably, there was once some chance that the ancient Kufan doctrine should survive not as Ḥanafism but Laylism.

The biographical dictionaries do negatively confirm Schacht's assertion that the old Kufan school, narrowly speaking, was fully made over into a Ḥanafi school by about the middle of the ninth century. After this point, one finds adherents of the opinion of the Kufans (not specifically of Abū Ḥanīfah) only outside Iraq. This said, I must acknowledge that there are severe limits to how precisely we can know when the school of Kufa became completely, by self-definition, Ḥanafi. The juridical literature of the time should be our most reliable guide to the progress of personalization, but in fact little survives from the ninth century, none from adherents of Kufan jurisprudence who did not consider themselves followers of Abū Ḥanīfah. Much of the biographical literature shows clear signs that later conditions have been projected backward.

Schacht speaks also of jurisprudents who considered themselves

---

al-Maʻārif al-Niẓāmīyah, 1332), 2:202.

[9] Wakīʻ, *Akhbār* 3:182.

[10] Ibn Abī al-Wafā', *al-Jawāhir al-muḍīyah*, ed. ʻAbd al-Fattāḥ Muḥammad al-Ḥulw, 2 vols. (Cairo: ʻĪsá al-Ḥalabī, 1978), 2:138; likewise Ibn Duqmāq, *Naẓm al-jumān fī ṭabaqāt aṣḥāb imāminā al-Nuʻmān*, Serez (Istanbul) 1827, 10a.

[11] Al-Kaffawī, *Katā'ib aʻlām al-akhyār min fuqahā' madhhab al-Nuʻmān al-mukhtār*, Esat Efendi (Istanbul) 548, 46b.

[12] Ibn Ḥajar, *Tahdhīb* 2:415.

[13] E.g., Ibn Saʻd, *al-Ṭabaqāt al-kubrá*, 8 vols. + index (Beirut: Dār Ṣādir, 1957-1968), 6:390.

[14] Ibn Abī al-Wafā', ed. Ḥulw, 2:140. Future references to this edition unless otherwise specified.

followers first of Abū Yūsuf or al-Shaybānī, not Abū Ḥanīfah, but these are harder to find. Some followers of Abū Yūsuf did disparage al-Shaybānī. Asad ibn 'Amr (d. 190/805-806), a fellow student with Abū Yūsuf, is said to have called al-Shaybānī a great liar (*kadhdhāb*).[15] Bishr ibn al-Walīd al-Kindī (d. Baghdad, 238/852-853), who studied under Abū Yūsuf, scorned him.[16] One wonders, however, whether such disparagements had not mainly to do with the doctrine of the created Qur'an: in traditionalist accounts, both Abū Ḥanīfah and al-Shaybānī preached it, as Abū Yūsuf did not, but Bishr ibn al-Walīd denied it of Abū Ḥanīfah as well.[17]

It remains to explain why the adherents of Kufan jurisprudence personalized their school at all. The traditionalist challenge seems to have been the main reason. Schacht has pointed out the overwhelming logical advantage of al-Shāfi'ī's case for hadith reports from the Prophet over hadith reports from the Companions and Successors: this was only an extension of the logical advantage of the traditionalist case for Scriptuary authority over local custom. Many of *aṣḥāb al-ra'y* must have been made uncomfortable. I have already cited the story of Wakī' ibn al-Jarrāḥ unable to deny what Aḥmad ibn Ḥanbal had asserted on the authority of the Prophet.[18]

Defending themselves against the traditionalists, the adherents of *ra'y* might have relied to some extent on the sophistication of their legal thinking, compared with the traditionalists'. When al-Ma'mūn announced the Inquisition in 218/833, evidently a move to establish some style of Ḥanafism, he began with a scornful depreciation of "the people of ignorance" with their weak opinions, defective minds, and inability to think and reflect.[19] His letter goes on to argue by reason

[15] Al-'Uqaylī, *K. al-Ḍu'afā' al-kabīr*, ed. 'Abd al-Muṭī' Amīn al-Qal'ajī, 4 vols. (Beirut: Dār al-Kutub al-'Ilmīyah, 1984), 4:54.

[16] Ibn Abī al-Wafā', 1 (Hyd.):166.

[17] Ibn 'Abd al-Barr, *Intiqā'*, 166; al-Khaṭīb al-Baghdādī, *Tārīkh Baghdād*, 14 vols. (Cairo: Maktabat al-Khānjī, 1931), 13:377.

[18] Two who have recently pointed out a tendency among Muslims to locate authority in righteous individuals, as opposed to self-evidently true texts, are William A. Graham, "Traditionalism in Islam," *Journal of Interdisciplinary History* 23 (1992-93):495-522, and Sherman A. Jackson, *Islamic Law and the State*, Studies in Islamic Law and Society 1 (Leiden: E. J. Brill, 1996), xxxif.

[19] Al-Ṭabarī, *Annales*, ed. M. J. de Goeje, 3 vols. in 15 (Leiden: E. J. Brill, 1879-1901), 3:1113 = *Tārīkh al-Ṭabarī*, ed. Muḥammad Abū al-Faḍl Ibrāhīm, Dhakhā'ir al-'Arab 30, 10 vols. (Cairo: Dār al-Ma'ārif, 1960-1969), 8:632. On the connection

and the Qur'an, not hadith. Over the following century, there lived a number of Iraqi rationalists whom Mu'tazili biographers describe as experts in jurisprudence but who are not found in Ḥanafi biographical dictionaries. For example, a Mu'tazili describes Muways ibn 'Imrān (*fl.* mid-ninth cent.) as knowing much about *kalām* theology and the giving of juridical opinions, also as upholding *irjā'*, Murji'ism: he must have been close to the nascent Ḥanafi school.[20] Nevertheless, I have found his name in no Ḥanafi biographical dictionary. Similarly, he describes al-Jubbā'ī (d. 303/915-916) as giving juridical opinions, while another Mu'tazili biographer states that he was seldom seen consulting any book but once *al-Jāmi' al-kabīr* of al-Shaybānī.[21] A Ḥanafi source suggests that he taught Ḥanafi jurisprudence to Abū al-Ḥasan al-Ash'arī.[22] Nevertheless, I have found al-Jubbā'ī himself in no Ḥanafi biographical dictionary. The Ḥanafi biographical dictionaries do include other reputed Mu'tazilah, such as Ibn Abī Duwād (d. 240/854), mastermind of the Inquisition under al-Mu'taṣim and al-Wāthiq[23]; therefore, it can hardly be argued that the Ḥanafīyah systematically excluded the Mu'tazilah and other rationalists from their self-description. It seems possible that many rationalists disdained to put themselves under the protection of a previous jurisprudent, implying some lack of faith in themselves (and in independent reason).

To the traditionalists, reliance on oneself, as opposed to reliance on the Book, the Prophet, and the Companions and Successors, bespoke

---

of the Inquisition with Ḥanafism, *v. The Encyclopaedia of Islam*, new edn., s.v. "Miḥna," by Martin Hinds.

[20] 'Abd al-Jabbār, *Faḍl al-i'tizāl*, *apud* Fu'ād Sayyid, ed., *Faḍl al-i'tizāl wa-ṭabaqāt al-mu'tazilah* (Tunis: al-Dār al-Tūnisīyah lil-Nashr, 1974), 74. For the pointing of his name, *v.* Ibn Ḥajar, *Tabṣīr al-muntabih*, ed. Muḥammad 'Alī al-Najjār, 4 vols. (Cairo: al-Dār al-Miṣrīyah lil-Ta'līf wa-al-Tarjamah, 1964?-67), 4:1330.

[21] 'Abd al-Jabbār, *Faḍl*, 318; Ibn al-Murtaḍá, *Die Klassen der Mu'taziliten*, ed. Susanna Diwald-Wilzer, Bibliotheca Islamica 21 (Wiesbaden: Franz Steiner, 1961), 80, 83.

[22] Mas'ūd ibn Shaybah, *K. al-Ta'līm*, *apud* Ibn Abī al-Wafā', *Jawāhir* 2:544f; cf. Ibn Abī al-Wafā', *Jawāhir* 2 (Hyd.):247f.

[23] Owned as a Ḥanafi by Ibn Abī al-Wafā', *Jawāhir* 1:134f; 2 (Hyd.):390; Ibn Duqmāq, *Naẓm*, 45b. Identified as a Mu'tazili by Ibn al-Nadīm, *apud* J. W. Fück, "Some Hitherto Unpublished Texts on the Mu'tazilite Movement From Ibn al-Nadīm's *Kitāb al-Fihrist*," *Professor Muhammad Shafī' Presentation Volume*, ed. S. M. Abdullah (Lahore: Majlis-e-Armughān-e-'Ilmī, 1955), 64f; Abū al-Qāsim al-Balkhī, "Bāb Dhikr al-mu'tazilah," *apud* Sayyid, ed., *Faḍl*, 105; Ibn al-Murtaḍá, *Klassen*, 62.

appalling arrogance. Reliance on a late authority such as Abū Ḥanīfah seemed little better. Later Ḥanafi tradition would stress Abū Ḥanīfah's own reliance on the Book, the Prophet, and the Companions and Successors.[24] To the earliest of his followers, however, reliance on Abū Ḥanīfah flowed from proper humility, not arrogance. This deathbed prayer is reported of Abū Yūsuf:

> O God, you know that I never deliberately did wrong in a decision I made concerning your servants. I exerted myself in judging according to what agreed with your book and the Sunnah of your prophet. For everything that was obscure to me, I put Abū Ḥanīfah between myself and you. I thought him, by God, one who knows your command and would not depart from the truth when he knew it.

The chain of transmitters is solidly Ḥanafi.[25] This is indeed to treat Abū Ḥanīfah like the patron saint that customarily headed a guild in the Latin world.[26]

It might even be said that the adherents of *ra'y*, in personalizing their jurisprudence, were taking over a traditionalist technique. The traditionalists did not trust the late figures on whom the adherents of *ra'y* relied; however, they were accustomed, already, to measuring the soundness of their texts by the trustworthiness of the persons whose names were attached to them ("so-and-so related to me, so-and-so related to me, so-and-so related to me, the Messenger of God said . . ."). To learn and relate the opinions of Abū Ḥanīfah was not the same as learning and relating by much longer chains the opinions of Successors, Companions, and the Prophet himself; however, it was closer to the practice of the traditionalists than reliance on a vague regional school.

---

[24] *V.* a selection of stories in Ibn 'Abd al-Barr, *Intiqā'*, 143-145.

[25] Al-Khaṭīb al-Baghdādī, *Tārīkh* 14:254, ll. 19-22.

[26] George Makdisi, "La Corporation à l'époque classique de l'Islam," *Présence de Louis Massignon: Hommages et témoignages* (Paris: Maisonneuve & Larose, 1987), 46; *The Rise of Humanism in Classical Islam and the Christian West* (Edinburgh: Univ. Press, 1990), 19.

FROM THE HIJAZI TO THE MĀLIKI

The Africans and Egyptians evidently turned the Medinese school into the Māliki in a similar search for security. We have already considered how Asad ibn al-Furāt insisted on hearing the position of Mālik himself, as opposed to either an array of hadith reports from Companions and Successors, such as Ibn Wahb was willing to give him; as opposed also to the position of a later jurisprudent such as Ashhab. For Asad, the name of a great teacher guaranteed orthodoxy, or rather orthopraxy, as nothing else could.

Admittedly, the traditionalist offensive probably does not explain why Asad, Saḥnūn, and other Maghribis so stressed the Māliki character of Hijazi jurisprudence. For one, it is difficult to make out any traditionalist presence in the West to which Asad or Saḥnūn might have reacted. Roger Idris has pointed out the Aghlabid dynasty's tendency to favor the Kufans and interprets the African Māliki jurisprudents as representatives of the African middle class.[27] On this account, African jurisprudents such as Saḥnūn and his students may have stressed the Māliki character of their jurisprudence chiefly in opposition to a Kufan aristocracy, borrowing the weapon of personal authority from their rationalist adversaries long before the traditionalists of Iraq. In other words, to reliance on a vague Kufan school, they opposed reliance on one heroic jurisprudent of Medina. Idris' scheme seems unable, though, to explain Asad's zeal to find out the opinion of Mālik himself, since Asad was close enough to the dynasty to become its governor of Sicily. Moreover, Saḥnūn was not the only Māliki qadi of the century: the Aghlabids went back and forth between the Māliki and Kufan schools. An optimistic view makes their policy look like an attempt at balance, a pessimistic view like simple confusion. They can hardly be said to have systematically promoted just one school.

It seems more likely to me that the Maghribis felt insecure chiefly because of their position as a tiny minority ruling over a great mass of pagans and Christians, on the one hand, and heretical (Khāriji) Muslims on the other. On this account, the appeal of following the teaching of one man would have been its apparent certainty, as op-

---

[27] Roger Idris, "Réflexions sur le Mālikisme sous les umayyades d'Espagne," *Atti del terzo congresso di studi arabi e islamici* (Naples: Istituto Universitario Orientale, 1967), 399.

posed to the uncertainty of having to chose among many opinions (pure traditionalism) or relying on the judgement of individual jurisprudents (pure *ra'y*). The more certain the jurisprudence, the stronger a front would be presented to the hostile masses outside the chief cities. Mālikism in Andalusia was established by royal authority, probably for similar defensive reasons.

Asad's questions were avidly taken up by the jurisprudents of Egypt. One reason is doubtless a similar sense of insecurity before the non-Muslim majority. Another is the traditionalist challenge. Unlike in Africa, the traditionalist offensive can easily be made out there; for example, several men related of the Egyptian Ibn Wahb (d. 197/813) the hadith report from the Prophet, "My community will divide into seventy-odd sects, the worst of them being those who apply analogy according to their opinion."[28] Al-Shāfi'ī and his Egyptian disciples made their own contribution: they combined the Scriptuary basis of the traditionalists with the legal sophistication of the rationalists, but failed to convert all parties, then tended by their polemical approach to reinforce personal allegiances.

The traditionalists of Iraq held out against personalization for another century longer than the rationalistic jurisprudents of Egypt and Iraq, but they eventually went over to a personal school of law, as well. They went over partly for technical reasons, mainly the difficulty of learning and remembering so many thousands of hadith reports from so many different teachers. They went, however, with many of the same feelings as the Kufans a hundred years before: humility before the eminence of an earlier, more heroic jurisprudent, security under his guarantee.[29]

---

[28] Al-Khaṭīb al-Baghdādī, *Tārīkh* 13:308.

[29] The Nishapuran traditionist Muḥammad ibn Yaḥyá al-Dhuhlī (d. 258/872) would say, "I have made Aḥmad ibn Ḥanbal an *imām* in what is between me and my Lord (be he exalted and glorified)": al-Dhahabī, *Siyar a'lām al-nubalā'*, 25 vols. (Beirut: Mu'assasat al-Risālah), 12 (ed. Ṣāliḥ al-Samr, 1983):282. The caliph al-Rāḍī, in the course of forbidding the followers of al-Barbahārī to assemble, would reproach them for calumniating those who visited the tombs of the (Shī'i) imams when they themselves visited the tomb of their own imam (Aḥmad ibn Ḥanbal) and called for prayers to be made by it: Ibn Miskawayh, *The Concluding Portion of the Experiences of the Nations* 1: *Reigns of Muqtadir, Qahir and Radi*, ed. H. F. Amedroz, The Eclipse of the 'Abbasid Caliphate, Original Chronicles of the Fourth Islamic Century 1 (London: Basil Blackwell, 1920), 322; trans. D. S. Margoliouth, 4:364f. The irresistible personalization of Iraqi traditionalism will be treated more fully in chapter 7 on al-

THE BASRAN SCHOOL OF *RA'Y*

In the late eighth and early ninth centuries, one can dimly make out a Basran school of *ra'y*. Like the Kufan school of *ra'y*, it resisted assimilation with Ḥanafism until about the middle of the ninth century; unlike the Kufan school, however, it appears to have furnished adherents to both the Ḥanafi and Māliki schools. One often sees references to the opinion of the Kufans in the literature of *khilāf*, almost never to the opinion of the Basrans; yet, for example, Hilāl al-Ra'y refers to the opinion of "the people of Basra," particularly its qadis, as distinct from the opinion of Abū Ḥanīfah and Abū Yūsuf.[30]

Ḥanafi sources state that Zufar ibn al-Hudhayl introduced the jurisprudence of Abū Ḥanīfah to Basra. According to one story, he went to Basra as qadi and won its people over to Ḥanafism by the reasonableness of his arguments.[31] His name does not appear in *Akhbār al-quḍāh* ("the stories of the judges") of Wakī', though, so the alternative story seems more plausible: that Zufar went to Basra, joined the circle of 'Uthmān al-Battī (d. 143/760-761), and gradually persuaded his students to take up Ḥanafi jurisprudence.[32] Traditionalists would later accuse 'Uthmān of introducing jurisprudence by *ra'y* to Basra, but it was evidently not quite Ḥanafi jurisprudence.[33] The qadi Sawwār ibn 'Abd Allāh (d. Basra, 156/773) is also said to have resisted Zufar's introduction of Ḥanafi legal methods, initially forbidding Zufar to teach.[34] According to al-Maqrīzī, 'Uthmān al-Battī and Sawwār were the leading jurisprudents of Basra in their time.[35] Ibn Ḥazm states that Ḥanafi jurisprudence, or rather the *ra'y* of Abū Ḥanīfah, was introduced to Basra by Yūsuf ibn Khālid al-Samtī (d.

Khallāl and the Ḥanbali school.

[30] Hilāl al-Ra'y, *Aḥkām al-waqf*, 5. Joseph Schacht supposes that these Basrans were a group within the Ḥanafi school: "Early Doctrines on Waqf," *60. doğum yılı münasebetiyle Fuad Köprülü armağanı* (Istanbul: Osman Yalçın Matbaası, 1953), 449.

[31] Ibn 'Abd al-Barr, *Intiqā'*, 173f.

[32] Ibn Abī al-'Awwām, *Manāqib Abī Ḥanīfah*, *apud* Ibn Ḥajar, *Lisān "al-Mīzān,"* 7 vols. (Hyderabad: Majlis Dā'irat al-Ma'ārif, 1329-31), 2:477f.

[33] Al-Khaṭīb al-Baghdādī, *Tārīkh* 13:394f.

[34] Ibn Ḥajar, *Lisān* 2:477.

[35] Al-Maqrīzī, *K. al-Mawā'iẓ wa-al-i'tibār bi-dhikr al-khiṭaṭ wa-al-āthār*, ed. Muḥammad ibn 'Abd al-Raḥmān Quṭṭah al-'Adawī, 2 vols. (Bulaq: Dār al-Ṭibā'ah al-Miṣrīyah, 1853), 2:332, ll. 15f from bottom.

189/805).[36]

Some leading Basran jurisprudents can be identified after 'Uthmān al-Battī and Sawwār. 'Umar ibn Ḥabīb (d. Baghdad, 207/822-823?) was qadi for Basra, later for a district of Baghdad. He was identified with *ra'y* and his hadith was generally rejected.[37] He is included in Ḥanafi biographical dictionaries[38]; however, the sources name no Ḥanafi teacher, whereas the historian of Basra al-Sājī (d. 307/919-920) counts him among the *aṣḥāb* of the Basran qadi 'Ubayd Allāh ibn al-Ḥasan (d. 168/785).[39]

Muḥammad ibn 'Abd Allāh al-Anṣārī (d. 215/830?) was likewise qadi in Basra and Baghdad. By some accounts, his teachers in jurisprudence were the Basrans Sawwār, 'Uthmān al-Battī, and 'Ubayd Allāh ibn al-Ḥasan.[40] The story has been told in the previous chapter of his quarrel with Hilāl al-Ra'y. It makes Muḥammad al-Anṣārī attentive to hadith, in opposition to the Ḥanafi Hilāl al-Ra'y.

Yet Muḥammad al-Anṣārī also showed signs of being a Ḥanafi. Another Basran source states that he was a follower (*ṣāḥib*) of Zufar's and Abū Yūsuf's.[41] Muḥammad al-Anṣārī is the source for one report from Zufar of Abū Ḥanīfah's juridical position, another from Abū Yūsuf.[42] Al-Sājī quotes him as saying he had changed his mind and ruled the same way as Mu'ādh ibn Mu'ādh (d. 196/811-812) because no other opinion was supported by the books of Abū Ḥanīfah.[43] Indeed, when a group of prominent Basrans met in 166/782-783 to nominate a new qadi, one put forward Muḥammad al-Anṣārī as chaste, honorable, and discerning (*faqīh*) but another objected,

> "He has spoken truly; however, his counsel is mistaken. This man follows after (*ya'tammu bi-*) Abū Ḥanīfah and inclines toward his opinion. We in our city have rulings that Abū Ḥanīfah would nullify,

---

[36] Ibn Ḥazm, *al-Iḥkām fī uṣūl al-aḥkām*, 8 vols. in 2 (Cairo: al-Khānjī, 1345), 5:98 = ed. Muḥammad Aḥmad 'Abd al-'Azīz, 2 vols. (Cairo: Maktabat 'Āṭif, 1978), 2:875 = 8 vols. in 2 (Beirut: Dār al-Kutub al-'Ilmīyah, n.d.), 2:94.

[37] Ibn Ḥajar, *Tahdhīb* 7:432, with derogatory comments from Aḥmad, Ibn Ma'īn, Abū Ḥātim, Abū Zur'ah, &al.

[38] Ibn Abī al-Wafā', *Jawāhir* 2:643; Ibn Duqmāq, *Naẓm*, 68b; al-Fīrūzābādhī, *al-Mirqāh al-wafīyah fī ṭabaqāt al-ḥanafīyah*, Reisülküttâb (Istanbul) 671/1, 50b.

[39] Ibn Ḥajar, *Tahdhīb* 7:432, presumably quoting from *Tārīkh al-Baṣrah*.

[40] Wakī', *Akhbār* 2:65; al-Khaṭīb al-Baghdādī, *Tārīkh* 5:408.

[41] Ibn Kāmil < Ismā'īl ibn Isḥāq, *apud* al-Khaṭīb al-Baghdādī, *Tārīkh* 15:412.

[42] Wakī', *Akhbār* 2:161; 3:259.

[43] *Apud* al-Khaṭīb al-Baghdādī, *Tārīkh* 5:411; Ibn Ḥajar, *Tahdhīb* 9:276.

> whereas nothing else suits us. Were we judged by other than our rulings, they would become null and our monies would vanish."

They turned from al-Anṣārī and the caliph appointed someone else.[44] Here is clear evidence both that the Basrans had their own juridical tradition distinct from the Kufans' and that they felt threatened even at this early date by the spread of Ḥanafi doctrine (particularly concerning *waqf* foundations, pointed out later by Hilāl al-Ra'y[45]).

The Basran school of *ra'y* did not disappear for lack of caliphal patronage. Ibn Ḥazm states that the Ḥanafi and Māliki schools prevailed because Abū Yūsuf, as chief qadi for Hārūn al-Rashīd, saw to it that only Ḥanafīyah were appointed to judgeships anywhere in the empire, while Yaḥyá ibn Yaḥyá similarly influenced the Umayyad 'Abd al-Raḥmān ibn al-Ḥakam (*r.* 206-238/822-852).[46] Yet we know of a number of Basran jurisprudents who were appointed to judgeships right in Baghdad. 'Umar ibn Ḥabīb and Muḥammad al-Anṣārī have been mentioned already, the latter appointed by Hārūn over Abū Yūsuf's head.

Another Basran even became chief qadi after Abū Yūsuf: Yaḥyá ibn Aktham (d. al-Rabadhah, 242/857?). Like Muḥammad al-Anṣārī, he has been claimed for the Ḥanafīyah. Ibn Abī al-Wafā' so claims him, although without naming any teacher in jurisprudence.[47] The later biographer al-Kaffawī not only claims him for the Ḥanafīyah but goes on to state that he learnt from the Kufan Wakī' ibn al-Jarrāḥ and related hadith reports of Muḥammad al-Shaybānī.[48] Wakī' ibn al-Jarrāḥ (d. 197/812) was a Kufan sometimes said to give juridical

---

[44] Wakī', *Akhbār* 2:131.

[45] Involving material property, foundations were a touchy issue everywhere. Ismā'īl ibn al-Yasa' (*fl.* 164/780-781) is said to have introduced the Ḥanafi *madhhab* to the people of Egypt, who had not heard of it before. As qadi, he took to nullifying foundations (*aḥbās*), and on this account al-Layth ibn Sa'd (d. 175/791, usually identified with the nascent Māliki school but arguably rather the chief of a nascent Egyptian school) wrote to the caliph and procured Ismā'īl's dismissal: Raif Georges Khoury, *'Abd Allāh ibn Lahī'a (97-174/715-790)*, Codices arabici antiqui 4 (Wiesbaden: Harrasowitz, 1986), 41, 176f; Robert Brunschvig, "Polémiques médiévales autour du rite de Mālik," *al-Andalus* 15 (1950):379; al-Kindī, *The Governors and Judges of Egypt*, ed. Rhuvon Guest, E. J. W. Gibb Memorial Ser. 19 (Leiden: E. J. Brill, 1912), 371, 372f.

[46] Ibn Ḥazm, *al-Iḥkām fī uṣūl al-aḥkām* (al-Khānjī) 4:230 = (Beirut) 1:625.

[47] Ibn Abī al-Wafā', *Jawāhir* 2 (Hyd.):210f.

[48] Al-Kaffawī, *Katā'ib*, 59a.

opinions according to the position of Abū Ḥanīfah.[49] He was also, though, a chief transmitter from Sufyān al-Thawrī, known for his hostility towards Abū Ḥanīfah.[50] Neither studying under Wakī' nor relating hadith reports from al-Shaybānī necessarily implies Ḥanafi jurisprudence. Moreover, one story makes Yaḥyá ibn Aktham only 20 or 21 when he was appointed qadi for Basra in 202/817-818, which means he must have been only 16 at the death of Wakī', eight at the death of al-Shaybānī: it seems doubtful whether he could have learnt Ḥanafi jurisprudence from either.[51] Al-Dāraquṭnī counted Yaḥyā ibn Aktham a Shāfi'i, but those who report his identification go on to express their doubt of it.[52] Ibn Ḥazm simply names him one of the jurisprudents of Basra,[53] and this seems the most likely identification: that he worked in the tradition of Basran *ra'y* before it was absorbed by Ḥanafism.

Yaḥyá ibn Aktham became a close associate of the caliph al-Ma'mūn's. He was removed from the judgeship of Basra in 210/825, but became chief qadi then or shortly thereafter.[54] Al-Ma'mūn came to depend on him to the degree that the viziers, it was said, would do nothing without consulting him.[55] The courtier al-Ṣūlī related that

---

[49] Ibn Ḥajar, *Tahdhīb* 11:127; cf. Ibn 'Abd al-Barr, *Intiqā'*, 151, where Wakī' is made to complain that Abū Ḥanīfah differed with 200 hadith reports of the Prophet.

[50] His Kufan contemporary Yaḥyá ibn Yamān (d. 188 or 189/*ca.* 804) said that when Sufyān died, Wakī' sat in his place (Ibn Ḥajar, *Tahdhīb* 11:128). The Basran al-Qa'nabī related that people said he was the great relator (*rāwiyah*) from Sufyān (*ibid.* 11:125). Al-Marrūdhī quoted Aḥmad ibn Ḥanbal as saying that the three (greatest) followers of Sufyān had been Wakī', Yaḥyá ibn Sa'īd al-Qaṭṭān, and 'Abd al-Raḥmān ibn Mahdī (*loc. cit.*).

[51] Al-Khaṭīb al-Baghdādī, *Tārīkh* 14:199. Reports of how old he was at his death push back his date of birth: about 166/782-783, according to his nephew, *apud* Wakī', *Akhbār* 2:166; about 159/775-776, according to Ibn al-Jawzī, *al-Muntaẓam fī tārīkh al-mulūk wa-al-umam*, ed. Muḥammad 'Abd al-Wahhāb Faḍl, 2 vols. (Cairo: Maṭba'at al-Amānah, 1985), 1:372 = ed. Muḥammad 'Abd al-Qādir 'Aṭā' & Muṣṭafá 'Abd al-Qādir 'Aṭā', w/ Nu'aym Zurzūr, 18 vols. (Beirut: Dār al-Kutub al-'Ilmīyah, 1992), 11:320.

[52] Al-'Aynī, *'Iqd al-jumān*, s.a. 243; Veli (Istanbul) 2385, 180; similarly, al-Fīrūzābādhī, *Mirqāh*, 85b.

[53] Ibn Ḥazm, *Iḥkām* (al-Khānjī) 5:99 = ed. 'Abd al-'Azīz, 2:875 = (Beirut) 2:94.

[54] Wakī', *Akhbār* 2:167, 3:273; *contra* Louis Massignon, "Cadis et naqibs baghdadiens," *Opera minora*, Recherches et documents, 3 vols. (Beirut: Dar al-Maaref, 1963), 1:259, where 'Abd al-Raḥmān ibn Isḥāq is named chief qadi A.H. 205-218. Massignon's list was prepared without the benefit of Wakī'.

[55] Al-Khaṭīb al-Baghdādī, *Tārīkh* 14:197.

when he was in Syria, al-Ma'mūn actually had it proclaimed that marriage for a term (*mut'ah*) was licit, a position usually identified with the Shī'ah; then Yaḥyá ibn Aktham dissuaded him, and he had it proclaimed that it was forbidden, after all.[56]

Yaḥyá ibn Aktham came to Egypt with al-Ma'mūn in 217/832,[57] but evidently fell from grace over some fiscal malfeasance shortly thereafter.[58] This was not the end of Basran influence, though, for al-Mu'taṣim appointed in his place the Basran Mu'tazili Ibn Abī Duwād, whom Yaḥyá ibn Aktham had himself recommended to be his chief adviser.[59] Some Ḥanafi biographers say that Ibn Abī Duwād was of their school, but name no teacher.[60] He was more likely a follower of Basran jurisprudence, like his patron Yaḥyá ibn Aktham. In the year when al-Mutawakkil rescinded the last measures of the Inquisition, 237/851, he sacked Ibn Abī Duwād and his son but re-appointed Yaḥyá ibn Aktham to the chief judgeship.[61] He sacked him again two or three years later for pederasty, but appointed in his place another Basran: Ja'far ibn 'Abd al-Wāḥid (d. 258/871-872?).[62]

When in office, Yaḥyá ibn Aktham promoted many fellow Basrans, but not only them. When he left the judgeship of the East Side to follow al-Ma'mūn to the Byzantine frontier, he appointed as his substitute the Basran Ja'far ibn 'Īsá (d. 219/834), a descendant of al-Ḥasan al-Baṣrī. Al-Ma'mūn briefly replaced him with the Medinese Hārūn ibn 'Abd Allāh (d. 232/847), a Māliki, but then reinstated Ja'far ibn 'Īsá.[63] Ja'far ibn 'Īsá dutifully professed the Qur'an created at the

---

[56] Al-Khaṭīb al-Baghdādī, *Tārīkh* 14:199f.

[57] Al-Kindī, *Governors*, 442.

[58] So he was denounced by al-Ma'mūn in his final instructions to his heir Abū Isḥāq al-Mu'taṣim, *apud* al-Ṭabarī, *Annales* 3:1139 = *Tārīkh* 8:649. Al-Khaṭīb al-Baghdādī quotes a story of apparent defalcation, *Tārīkh* 14:194f.

[59] Wakī', *Akhbār* 3:294. According to al-Ṣūlī, Ibn Abī Duwād was actually advanced to spy on al-Mu'taṣim for al-Ma'mūn. He ignored requests for information, though, and when al-Ma'mūn ordered him sent back to Iraq in chains, he confirmed his favor with al-Mu'taṣim by showing him the requests he had ignored: *apud* al-Maqrīzī, *al-Tārīkh al-kabīr al-muqaffá*, Pertev Paşa (Istanbul) 496, 122a, b. The story is difficult to reconcile with al-Ma'mūn's recommending Ibn Abī Duwād in his last testament, as reported by al-Ṭabarī (previous note).

[60] *V. supra*, n. 23.

[61] Al-Ṭabarī, *Annales* 3:1410 = *Tārīkh* 9:188.

[62] In 239/853, according to Ibn al-Jawzī, *Muntaẓam*, ed. Faḍl, 1:245 = 'Aṭā' & 'Aṭā', 11:266; in 240/860, according to al-Ṭabarī, *Annales* 3:1421 = *Tārīkh* 9:197.

[63] Al-Khaṭīb al-Baghdādī, *Tārīkh* 7:161. On Hārūn ibn 'Abd Allāh's Mālikism,

Inquisition, for which traditionalists repudiated him.[64] When Yaḥyá became chief qadi under al-Mutawakkil, the Basran Sawwār ibn 'Abd Allāh (d. 245/860), grandson of the Basran qadi, was appointed to the judgeship of the East Side[65]; however, the judgeship of al-Sharqīyah was given at the same time to Ḥayyān ibn Bishr (d. 237 or 238/*c.* 852), onetime student under Abū Yūsuf, who had prosecuted the Inquisition in Isfahan.[66] Yaḥyá ibn Aktham had other priorities besides promoting the Basran school of *ra'y*.

Ja'far ibn 'Abd al-Wāḥid is probably also to be assigned to the Basran school. No source states from whom he learnt jurisprudence, which suggests something other than strict Ḥanafism or Mālikism. The list of his shaykhs in hadith is dominated by Basrans, and the famous Basran Māliki al-Qa'nabī is quoted as cursing him for falsifying hadith reports.[67] He immediately appointed as his deputy another Basran, al-Ḥasan Ibn Abī al-Shawārib. As we have seen, his juridical affiliation is just as obscure as Ja'far ibn 'Abd al-Wāḥid's; however, his brother was said to follow the *madhhab* of the people of Iraq, which here probably means the wing of Basran *ra'y* that inclined towards Ḥanafism.[68] Al-Mutawakkil may have chosen Ja'far chiefly for his lineage—he was an 'Abbāsid—and not from opposition to the Ḥanafīyah.

Another of al-Mutawakkil's Basran appointees would dominate the Baghdadi judiciary for most of the later ninth century: Ismā'īl ibn Isḥāq (d. Baghdad, 282/896). I shall treat his formation in Basra and later advocacy of Mālikism in chapter 9: suffice it to say here that his father Isḥāq had been confidant (*amīn*) to Yaḥyá ibn Aktham, and was sent with Ibn Abī Duwād to accompany al-Mu'taṣim to Egypt, where Isḥāq oversaw the *maẓālim*.[69] Al-Mutawakkil appointed Ismā'īl qadi for the East Side of Baghdad on the death of Sawwār ibn 'Abd Allāh.

---

v. Wakī', *Akhbār* 3:274, and Abū Isḥāq al-Shīrāzī, *Ṭabaqāt al-fuqahā'*, ed. Iḥsān 'Abbās (Beirut: Dār al-Rā'id al-'Arabī, 1970), 153.

[64] Ibn Abī Ḥātim, *K. al-Jarḥ wa-al-ta'dīl*, 9 vols. (Hyderabad: Jam'īyat Dā'irat al-Ma'ārif al-'Uthmānīyah, 1360), 2:486.

[65] Al-Khaṭīb al-Baghdādī, *Tārīkh* 9:210.

[66] Abū al-Shaykh, *Ṭabaqāt al-muḥaddithīn bi-Iṣbahān*, ed. 'Abd al-Ghafūr 'Abd al-Ḥaqq Ḥusayn al-Balūshī, 4 vols. (Beirut: Mu'assasat al-Risālah, 1987-), 2:131f; al-Khaṭīb al-Baghdādī, *Tārīkh* 8:285; Ibn Abī al-Wafā', *Jawāhir* 2:158.

[67] Al-Khaṭīb al-Baghdādī, *Tārīkh* 7:173f.

[68] Al-Khaṭīb al-Baghdādī, *Tārīkh* 12:60.

[69] Ibn Ḥajar, *Lisān* 1:352; Wakī', *Akhbār* 3:280.

Through the influence of al-Muwaffaq, brother to the later caliph al-Mu'tamid and the true power behind him, he transferred to the West Side in 258/871-872 despite opposition from the chief qadi al-Ḥasan Ibn Abī al-Shawārib. A few years later, he became qadi for both the East and West Sides of Baghdad, and henceforward ruled independently of the chief qadi.[70] This was the beginning of a long preponderance of Mālikīyah among the qadis of Baghdad. It had begun, itself, as a preponderance of Basrans, but by this point the Basran school seems to have survived mainly as Ḥanafism and Mālikism.

The Ḥanafi side of surviving Basran jurisprudence is seen in Bakkār ibn Qutaybah, whom al-Mutawakkil appointed qadi for Egypt in 246/860. He was certainly identified with Basra, for the Egyptians acclaimed him as reviving the religious knowledge of the Basrans.[71] He was also Ḥanafi, though. He had learnt the craft of composing official documents from Hilāl al-Ra'y, and was said to adopt the position of Abū Ḥanīfah.[72] His immediate charge as qadi for Egypt was to reverse a ruling of his Māliki predecessor's. Al-Ḥārith ibn Miskīn had been qadi for Egypt since 237/851. In 245/859, some would-be heirs against whom he had ruled appealed to Baghdad, where the caliph al-Mutawakkil summoned some Kufan jurisprudents to review the ruling. They decided the opposite way, whereupon al-Ḥārith ibn Miskīn requested to be excused and Bakkār ibn Qutaybah, his designated successor, was instructed to overturn his ruling.[73] The story indicates that al-Mutawakkil did not systematically favor any juridical tendency, contrary to al-Suyūṭī's declaration that he adhered to the school of al-Shāfi'ī.[74] Bakkār ibn Qutaybah remained qadi until his death. It seems possible that, through him, Basran *ra'y* constituted another source of al-Ṭaḥāwī's relative traditionalism, as the classical Ḥanafi school took shape.

---

[70] Al-Khaṭīb al-Baghdādī, *Tārīkh* 6:288.
[71] Ibn Abī al-Wafā', *Jawāhir* 1:458.
[72] Aḥmad ibn 'Abd al-Raḥmān, *Dhayl*, *apud* al-Kindī, *Governors*, 477.
[73] Al-Kindī, *Governors*, 474f.
[74] Al-Suyūṭī, *Tārīkh al-khulafā'* (Beirut: Dār al-Thaqāfah, 1970's), 379f.

CHAPTER THREE

THE ḤANAFI SCHOOL OF THE LATER NINTH CENTURY

The previous chapter has treated the development of a personal Ḥanafi school; that is, the identification of jurisprudents with the teaching of Abū Ḥanīfah rather than vaguely with the teaching of all the jurisprudents of Kufa or Basra. Reliance on personal authority was evidently a response, in part, to the traditionalist challenge. The Ḥanafīyah of the ninth century met the traditionalist challenge in another fashion, as well, mainly traditionalizing their own jurisprudence. On the one hand, this meant fitting out their tenets with a basis in hadith reports from the Prophet; on the other hand, it meant dissociating Abū Ḥanīfah from dubious, anti-traditionalist theological positions. By the end of the century, moreover, jurisprudents loyal to Abū Ḥanīfah finally began to produce commentaries on works by earlier Ḥanafi loyalists, particularly by Muḥammad al-Shaybānī, the first great collector of the opinions of Abū Ḥanīfah and Abū Yūsuf. All the pieces of the classical school were now in place, save possibly the classical method of teaching.

THE TRADITIONALIZATION OF ḤANAFI JURISPRUDENCE

The traditionalization of the Ḥanafi school, by which certain Ḥanafīyah endeavored to render it more or less acceptable to traditionalist sentiment, is visible over the course of the ninth century. It had three main aspects: the fitting out of Ḥanafi doctrines originally based on common sense with a new basis in hadith reports from the Prophet; actual alteration of Ḥanafi doctrines to agree with traditionalist jurisprudence; and the rewriting of history to disguise hostility between Abū Ḥanīfah and contemporary traditionalists. Traditionalist triumph at the Inquisition probably strengthened the impulse to traditionalize, but in fact it is visible before then, as well.

Indeed, the fitting out of Ḥanafi juridical preferences with hadith reports to justify them was largely a mere extension of what is evident already in the late eighth century, when Abū Yūsuf and Muḥammad al-Shaybānī each had to accommodate more hadith reports than his predecessors.[1] Little Ḥanafi writing from the ninth century has survived to our time, and still less has been published. It is clear what went on, though, from a comparison of the works of al-Shaybānī and others in the late eighth century with the works of al-Ṭaḥāwī and later Ḥanafīyah in the tenth. (The comparison remains valid even if, following Norman Calder, we reassign the supposed works of al-Shaybānī to the ninth century.[2])

Schacht points out the usefulness of the various collections of hadith reports related by Abū Ḥanīfah: those from the late eighth and early ninth centuries, by Muḥammad al-Shaybānī and al-Ḥasan ibn Ziyād al-Lu'lu'ī, show Abū Ḥanīfah as working on the basis mainly of the opinions of Companions and Successors, whereas later versions, from the tenth century and after, show him as working on the basis of hadith from the Prophet.[3] The qadi al-Khʷārizmī (d. Baghdad, 655/1257-58) synthesized all earlier collections of hadith that Abū Ḥanīfah was supposed to have used. In a hundred pages of the printed edition of his synthesis, the early books are the source of 19 hadith reports from the Prophet, 110 (over five times as many) from Companions and Successors. By contrast, the later books are the source for 51 hadith reports from the Prophet, 77 (scarcely one and a half times as many) from Companions and Successors.[4] These additional hadith reports from the Prophet, although all supposedly transmitted by Abū Ḥanīfah, must have been worked up between the time of al-Shaybānī and al-Lu'lu'ī, on the one hand, and al-Ushnānī (d. 339/951?), al-Ustādh (d. 340/951), &al., on the other.

The actual alteration of Ḥanafi doctrine is more difficult to demonstrate, at this point in our knowledge; however, some outlines can be made out. A convenient test is Ḥanafi doctrine concerning *nabīdh*, a drink of fermented dates that the Ḥanafīyah were notorious for allowing in the face of traditionalist opposition to all potentially intoxicating liquors. On no other juridical position do the biographers comment so often. Abū Ḥanīfah was said to have approved of *nabīdh*.[5]

---

[1] Joseph Schacht, *The Origins of Muhammadan Jurisprudence* (Oxford: Clarendon Press, 1950), 33f, 277, 301, 306.

[2] Norman Calder, *Studies in Early Muslim Jurisprudence* (Oxford: Clarendon Press, 1993), chap. 3.

[3] Schacht, *Origins*, 149.

[4] Muḥammad ibn Maḥmūd al-Khʷārizmī, *Jāmi' masānīd al-imām al-a'ẓam*, 2 vols. (Hyderabad: Dā'irat al-Ma'ārif, 1332), 2:155-255.

[5] Ibn 'Abd al-Barr, *al-Intiqā' fī faḍā'il al-thalāthah al-a'immah al-fuqahā'* (Cairo:

The Kufan Mūsá ibn Ṭarīf (8th century?), said to follow the opinion of the people of Syria, was rejected for it.[6] Isḥāq ibn Rāhawayh blamed Abū Yūsuf for approving of it.[7] Various Iraqi jurisprudents in the first part of the next century were still associated with it; e.g., Khalaf ibn Hishām (d. Baghdad, 229/844), who drank according to the opinion of the Kufans,[8] and Ibn Abī al-Layth (d. Baghdad, 250/864-865), sometime qadi for Old Cairo.[9]

There are signs of change in the earlier ninth century. Khalaf ibn Hishām drank, but then was convinced of his error and repeated forty years of ritual prayers. Certain Khurasani adherents of *ra'y* are quoted in outright opposition to it. When Abū Ḥafṣ al-Kabīr (d. Bukhara, 217/832) forbade the drinking of *al-muthallath* (perhaps a liquor allowed to ferment for three days), he was asked whether this was not to differ with the two shaykhs (Muḥammad al-Shaybānī, his teacher, and Abū Yūsuf). He said, "No, for they permitted it when taken for pleasure in its taste (*istimrā'an*), whereas the people in our time drink for purposes of abandon and dissipation."[10] Abū Yūsuf's and al-Shaybānī's approval was evidently too well known to be denied, and so Abū Ḥafṣ brought in the familiar argument of *fasād al-zamān* ("the decadence of the age") to excuse accommodation with popular opinion. The important Ḥanafi teacher Muḥammad ibn Salamah (d. 278/891-892), likewise of Balkh, related a hadith report from the Prophet against *nabīdh*.[11]

The growing circulation of such hadith reports against *nabīdh* among the Ḥanafīyah is evident in the collections of hadith reports al-

---

Maktabat al-Qudsī, 1350), 148.

[6] Al-'Uqaylī, *K. al-Ḍu'afā' al-kabīr*, ed. by 'Abd al-Mu'ṭī Amīn Qal'ajī, 4 vols. (Beirut: Dār al-Kutub al-'Ilmīyah, 1984), 4:158; Ibn Ḥajar, *Lisān "al-Mīzān,"* 7 vols. (Hyderabad: Majlis Dā'irat al-Ma'ārif, 1329-31), 6:121.

[7] Ibn Ḥajar, *Lisān* 6:300.

[8] Al-Khaṭīb al-Baghdādī, *Tārīkh Baghdād*, 14 vols. (Cairo: Maktabat al-Khānjī, 1931), 8:327.

[9] For stories of his drinking, including in the mosque, *v.* al-Kindī, *The Governors and Judges of Egypt*, ed. Rhuvon Guest, E. J. W. Gibb Memorial Series 19 (Leiden: E. J. Brill, 1912), 466f.

[10] Al-Kaffawī, *Katā'ib a'lām al-akhyār*, Esat Efendi (Istanbul) 548, 51b; cf. Ibn Abī al-Wafā', *al-Jawāhir al-muḍīyah*, 2 vols. (Hyderabad: Dā'irat al-Ma'ārif al-Niẓāmīyah, 1914), 2:471, where it is said that the people of the present day drink alcohol for strength (*taqawwī*).

[11] Ibn 'Adī al-Qaṭṭān, *al-Kāmil fī al-ḍu'afā'*, 6 vols. (Beirut: Dār al-Fikr, 1984), 3:1296.

legedly related by Abū Ḥanīfah. Al-Khʷārizmī reports fourteen hadith reports that Abū Ḥanīfah related, all from Companions or Successors, by which *nabīdh* was licit. Ten of these are in the early books (by al-Shaybānī and al-Lu'lu'ī), seven in the late. Three hadith reports from the Prophet forbid all intoxicating liquors, however weak: they are all in the late books. Other sections show the same evolution toward traditionalist positions; for example, concerning the raising of the hands during ritual prayer.

A leader in the transformation of Ḥanafi jurisprudence was evidently the Baghdadi Muḥammad ibn Shujā' al-Thaljī (d. 266/880). He was among the *aṣḥāb* of al-Ḥasan ibn Ziyād al-Lu'lu'ī.[12] As a personalizer, he stressed adherence to the exact doctrine of Abū Ḥanīfah; for example, it was he who related from four witnesses Abū Yūsuf's saying, "I have never taken up a position in which I differed with Abū Ḥanīfah, save when it was a position that he himself had taken up."[13] Al-Sājī would accuse him of inventing reasons to prefer the opinion of Abū Ḥanīfah to hadith reports from the Prophet.[14] He was not uninterested in hadith, though, for among his known works is a *Kitāb Taṣḥīḥ al-āthār* (Book of Judging Sound Hadith Reports).[15] It presumably found sound hadith reports to back up Ḥanafi doctrine. Indeed, Ibn al-Nadīm states outright that Ibn al-Thaljī reinforced the jurisprudence of Abū Ḥanīfah with hadith.[16]

He defended Abū Ḥanīfah against traditionalist attack; for example, he is the source of the story defending him against the charge that his *ra'y* changed from year to year and was therefore unreliable:

> I told 'Abbād ibn Ṣuhayb, "Bring out for me what you have from Abū Ḥanīfah."
>
> He said, "I have a box (*qimṭar*, full of notes), but I will not relate to you his opinion, only however much you like of his hadith."
>
> I said, "Why?"
>
> He said, "I went to Kufa and heard him give juridical opinions, so I wrote down his answers. Then I was away from Kufa for ten

[12] Al-Khaṭīb al-Baghdādī, *Tārīkh* 5:350.

[13] Ibn Abī al-Wafā', *Jawāhir* 2 (Hyd.):221.

[14] Al-Khaṭīb al-Baghdādī, *Tārīkh* 5:351.

[15] Fuat Sezgin, *Geschichte des arabischen Schrifttums*, 9 vols. (E. J. Brill, 1967-), 1:436.

[16] Ibn al-Nadīm, *Kitâb al-Fihrist*, ed. Gustav Flügel, w/ Johannes Roediger & August Mueller (Leipzig: F. C. W. Vogel, 1872), 206 = *fann* 2, *maqālah* 6.

> years. When I returned, I heard him give juridical opinions concerning those questions but not those same answers."
>
> That bothered me as it had bothered 'Abbād. I went to 'Abd Allāh ibn Dāwūd [al-Khuraybī, d. 213/828] and mentioned that to him. He told me, "This indicates the breadth of his learning: if his learning had been narrow, his answer would have been one; however, his affair was broad, so he would treat it however he liked."[17]

Plainly, traditionalist attacks had generated insecurity among the adherents of *ra'y*, and Ibn al-Thaljī was trying to assuage them.

He went on the offensive, as well. In *Kitāb al-Radd 'alá al-mushabbihah* (Refutation of the Anthropomorphists), he attacked traditionalist theologians.[18] The *Kitāb al-Naqḍ 'alá Bishr al-Marīsī* (Refutation of Bishr al-Marīsī) of al-Dārimī (d. 282/890) is largely, it seems, a refutation of Ibn al-Thaljī's book.[19] Ibn 'Adī al-Qaṭṭān would accuse him of making up absurd hadith reports and attributing them to *aṣḥāb al-ḥadīth*.[20]

Some traditionalists accused Ibn al-Thaljī of maintaining that the Qur'an was created.[21] Alternatively, he was said to maintain a position of *waqf*; that is, refusing to declare the Qur'an either created or uncreated.[22] It seems more likely that he upheld a middle position like that of Dāwūd al-Ẓāhirī, al-Karābīsī, and others, confessing that the Qur'an itself was uncreated but that its pronunciation, earthly copies, and so on, were not. Certain Ḥanbali traditions explicitly associate him with al-Karābīsī and the doctrine that one's pronunciation of the Qur'an is created.[23] The Ḥanafism he envisaged was evi-

---

[17] Ibn Abī al-Wafā', *al-Jawāhir al-muḍīyah*, ed. 'Abd al-Fattāḥ Muḥammad al-Ḥulw, 2 vols. (Cairo: 'Īsá al-Ḥalabī, 1978), 2:285. Future references to this edition unless otherwise specified. Another version at 2:309, attributed also to Ibn al-Thaljī by al-Dhahabī, *Tārīkh al-islām*, ed. 'Umar 'Abd al-Salām Tadmurī, 40+ vols. (Beirut: Dār al-Kitāb al-'Arabī, 1987-), 15 (A.H. 211-220):208f.

[18] Sezgin, *Geschichte* 1:436, #4.

[19] Al-Dārimī, *Radd al-imām al-Dārimī 'Uthmān ibn Sa'īd 'alá Bishr al-Marīsī al-'anīd*, ed. Muḥammad Ḥāmid al-Fiqī (Cairo: Maṭba'at Anṣār al-Sunnah, 1358), 76 et seq.

[20] Ibn 'Adī, *Kāmil* 6:2293; *apud* Ibn Ḥajar, *Tahdhīb "al-Tahdhīb,"* 12 vols. (Hyderabad: Majlis Dā'irat al-Ma'ārif al-Niẓāmīyah, 1325-27), 9:221.

[21] Ibn Ḥajar, *Tahdhīb* 9:221.

[22] Al-Khaṭīb al-Baghdādī, *Tārīkh* 5:351.

[23] Ibn Abī Ya'lá, *Ṭabaqāt al-ḥanābilah*, ed. Muḥammad Ḥāmid al-Fiqī, 2 vols. (Cairo: Maṭba'at al-Sunnah al-Muḥammadīyah, 1952), 1:94, 120.

dently close to the compromise systems of Abū Thawr, Dāwūd al-Ẓāhirī, the qadi Ismāʿīl, &al.

Somewhat later, the Baghdadi Aḥmad ibn al-Ṣalt (d. 308/921?) would work to further obscure differences between Abū Ḥanīfah and early traditionalists. Al-Khaṭīb al-Baghdādī states that he invented statements from Bishr ibn al-Ḥārith, the barefoot ascetic, and the famous traditionists Yaḥyá ibn Maʿīn and ʿAlī ibn al-Madīnī in praise of Abū Ḥanīfah. For example, he related with the chain ʿAbd Allāh ibn Muḥammad al-Ḥulwānī < Mukram ibn Aḥmad < Aḥmad ibn Muḥammad (i.e., al-Ḥimmānī) < Muḥammad ibn al-Ḥasan ibn al-Muthanná, *ṣāḥib* to Bishr ibn al-Ḥārith < Ibn ʿUyaynah: "The scholars are Ibn ʿAbbās in his time, al-Shaʿbī in his time, Abū Ḥanīfah in his time, and al-Thawrī in his time." Al-Khaṭīb considers "Abū Ḥanīfah in his time" an interpolation of Aḥmad ibn al-Ṣalt's for two reasons: Ibn ʿUlayyah was elsewhere quoted as naming only three, and he was known for his condemning Abū Ḥanīfah.[24] Since, moreover, Abū Ḥanīfah and Sufyān al-Thawrī were near-contemporaries, al-Khaṭīb's charge of inauthenticity seems highly credible.

Aḥmad ibn al-Ṣalt was concerned to vindicate leading followers of Abū Ḥanīfah in the same fashion; for example, he is the source for the statement from Abū ʿUbayd, "I have seen no one who knows more of the Book of God than Muḥammad ibn al-Ḥasan (al-Shaybānī)."[25] In the short run, it seems, Aḥmad ibn al-Ṣalt's enterprise was unsuccessful: *rijāl* critics of the next century such as al-ʿUqaylī and Ibn ʿAdī include many harsh criticisms of Abū Ḥanīfah in their books on weak transmitters, and none of Aḥmad ibn al-Ṣalt's praises.[26] In the long run, though, even so thorough a traditionalist as Ibn Taymīyah would refuse to believe ill of a man whose jurisprudence was followed by so many Muslims.

---

[24] Al-Khaṭīb al-Baghdādī, *Tārīkh* 4:207f. Further praise for the *aṣḥāb* of Abū Ḥanīfah related by Aḥmad ibn al-Ṣalt < Bishr ibn al-Walīd (d. 238/853) *apud* al-Khaṭīb al-Baghdādī, 7:82.

[25] Al-Khaṭīb al-Baghdādī, *Tārīkh* 2:175.

[26] *V.* Eerik Dickinson, "Aḥmad b. al-Ṣalt and His Biography of Abū Ḥanīfa," *Journal of the American Oriental Society* 116 (1996):406-417.

THE TRADITIONALIZATION OF ḤANAFI THEOLOGY

The traditionalization of the Ḥanafi school over the ninth century involved also its dissociation from dubious theological tenets and dubious patrons. The most important of these dubious theological tenets were the created Qur'an and *irjā'*, after them a particular loyalty to 'Alī. The dubious patrons from whom they had to distance themselves were, of course, the 'Abbāsids.

Ḥanafi association with the created Qur'an is fairly well-established. Abū Ḥanīfah was widely accused by traditionalists of teaching that the Qur'an was created. Al-Sājī preserved multiple accusations; e.g., Abū Ḥātim al-Rāzī < al-'Abbās ibn 'Abd al-'Aẓīm < Muḥammad ibn Yūnus: "Abū Ḥanīfah was asked to repent only for saying that the Qur'an was created. 'Īsá ibn Mūsá asked him to repent."[27] Abū Ḥanīfah's grandson Ismā'īl ibn Ḥammād (d. 212/827-828) professed that the Qur'an was created and testified that his father and grandfather had believed the same.[28] An unfriendly source adds that traditionalists heard this testimony and dismissed Abū Ḥanīfah as a *zindīq*, or secret unbeliever.[29]

Adherents of the nascent Ḥanafi school were divided by the controversy over the Qur'an. Abū Sulaymān al-Jūzajānī (d. shortly after 200/815?) studied under both Abū Yūsuf and al-Shaybānī (Ibn al-Nadīm states that he related the books of al-Shaybānī in particular[30]) but held them to be unbelievers who said the Qur'an was created.[31] His younger friend al-Mu'allá ibn Manṣūr (d. Baghdad, 211/826-827) likewise studied under both Abū Yūsuf and al-Shaybānī, and likewise held them to be unbelievers who said the Qur'an was created.[32] Bishr ibn al-Walīd al-Kindī (d. Baghdad, 238/853) is said to have denied the report of Ismā'īl ibn Ḥammād that his father and grandfather (Abū Ḥanīfah) had confessed the Qur'an created: "As for your

---

[27] Al-Sājī, *apud* Ibn 'Abd al-Barr, *Intiqā'*, 151. Further reports 149f, mostly through the Basran qadi Mu'ādh ibn Mu'ādh (d. 196/812). 'Īsá ibn Mūsá (d. 167/783-784) was governor of Kufa for the first two 'Abbāsid caliphs.

[28] Al-Khaṭīb al-Baghdādī, *Tārīkh* 6:245.

[29] Al-Khaṭīb al-Baghdādī, *Tārīkh* 12:349.

[30] Ibn al-Nadīm, *Fihrist*, 206 = *f.* 2, *q.* 6.

[31] Ibn Abī Ḥātim, *K. al-Jarḥ wa-al-ta'dīl*, 9 vols. (Hyderabad: Jam'īyat Dā'irat al-Ma'ārif al-'Uthmānīyah, 1360), 8:145.

[32] Ibn Ḥajar, *Tahdhīb* 10:240.

opinion, yes, but as for the opinion of your fathers, no."[33] Bishr himself lost his judgeship and was briefly imprisoned for refusing to confess that the Qur'an was created, and other Ḥanafīyah suffered in the Inquisition as well.

Later traditionalizers circulated reports denying altogether that Abū Ḥanīfah had professed the creation of the Qur'an. Al-Jūzajānī and al-Mu'allá were together quoted as saying that Abū Ḥanīfah, Abū Yūsuf, Zufar, and Muḥammad (al-Shaybānī) did not talk of the Qur'an, but only Bishr al-Marīsī and Ibn Abī Duwād, who disgraced the followers of Abū Ḥanīfah.[34] Considering that both died well before Ibn Abī Duwād became prominent, their denial seems incredible, surely an invention of later Ḥanafi traditionalizers.[35] Ibn al-Thaljī related of the Baghdadi qadi Ibn Samā'ah (d. 233/848) of Abū Yūsuf, "I debated with Abū Ḥanīfah for six months, until he said, 'Whoever says the Qur'an is created is an unbeliever.'"[36] Aḥmad ibn al-Ṣalt related of Bishr ibn al-Walīd < Abū Yūsuf < Abū Ḥanīfah, "Whoever says the Qur'an is created is an unbeliever: no one may go by his (juridical) position, nor may anyone pray behind him."[37] Of course, Aḥmad ibn al-Ṣalt could hardly have heard Bishr, so al-Khaṭīb's chain of transmitters belies his report.[38]

As for Abū Ḥanīfah's having been beaten for professing the Qur'an created, later defenders (a Maghribi tradition?) insisted, "Abū Ḥanīfah was beaten on account of the judgeship (for refusing to become qadi): his enemies were delighted by that, and said that he had been asked to repent."[39] Others asserted that Abū Ḥanīfah had twice said "I repent of every (act of) unbelief" in the course of debating with

---

[33] E.g., Ibn 'Abd al-Barr, *Intiqā'*, 166.

[34] Al-Khaṭīb al-Baghdādī, *Tārīkh* 13:378.

[35] Al-Khaṭīb al-Baghdādī, *Tārīkh* 13:378. Perhaps the inventor in al-Khaṭīb's chain of transmitters can be identified: the Nakha'ī (*fl.* mid-200's/800's) who also related of Abū Bakr al-Marrūdhī that Aḥmad ibn Ḥanbal himself disbelieved reports that Abū Ḥanīfah said the Qur'an was created (*loc. cit.*).

[36] Al-Khaṭīb al-Baghdādī, *Tārīkh* 13:377.

[37] Al-Khaṭīb al-Baghdādī, *Tārīkh* 13:377.

[38] Cf. the report by a chain of unknowns < Abū Yūsuf: "The first to say the Qur'an was uncreated was Abū Ḥanīfah" (Wakī', *Akhbār al-quḍāh*, ed. 'Abd al-'Azīz Muṣṭafá al-Marāghī, 3 vols. [Cairo: Maṭba'at al-Istiqāmah, 1947-50], 3: 257f). Here, one suspects textual corruption, namely that "created" has become "uncreated."

[39] Ibn 'Abd al-Barr, *Intiqā'*, 150.

some Khārijites, and that this was what his opponents had twisted to mean something else.[40] No school could appear orthodox whose founder had preached such a heresy as the created Qur'an, and so the formation of a viable Ḥanafi school required the dissociation of Abū Ḥanīfah from it.

The association of Abū Ḥanīfah and his followers with the theology of *irjā'*, Murji'ism, seems yet better established.[41] This theological school held that faith did not increase or decrease, and did not include works such as the ritual prayer.[42] Traditionalists certainly made the association, sometimes with a sinister turn:

> When Ibrāhīm died, five of the people of Kufa met, among them 'Umar ibn Qays al-Māṣir and Abū Ḥanīfah. They gathered 40,000 dirhams and went to al-Ḥakam ibn 'Utaybah and told him, "We have gathered 40,000 dirhams and come to you with them. If you will be our leader (*ra'īs*) in *irjā'* (we shall give them to you)." Al-Ḥakam refused, so they went to Ḥammād Ibn Abī Sulaymān and asked him. He said yes, and took the 40,000 dirhams.[43]

Here, Abū Ḥanīfah is a ringleader of the Murji'ah. Ḥammād Ibn Abī Sulaymān was an early Kūfan jurisprudent (d. *ca.* 120/737-738) sometimes accused of introducing *irjā'*.[44] When al-Ḥārith ibn Surayj (d. 128/746), leader of a Murji' revolt in Gūzgān, Fāryāb, Ṭaliqān, and Balkh, sought a caliphal pardon in 126/744, his emissaries procured a letter of introduction from Abū Ḥanīfah in Kufa before going

---

[40] Al-Qāri' al-Harawī, *Manāqib al-imām al-a'ẓam, apud* Ibn Abī al-Wafā', *Jawāhir* 2 (Hyd.):486f.

[41] Hence, for example, Joseph Schacht acknowledges that Abū Ḥanīfah was a Murji' but ignores charges that he professed a created Qur'an: *Encyclopaedia of Islam*, new edn., s.v. "Abū Ḥanīfa." Modern Muslim scholars usually deny that Abū Ḥanīfah believed the Qur'an to be created but admit a harmless sort of *irjā'*; e.g., 'Alī 'Abd al-Fattāḥ al-Maghribī, *al-Firaq al-kalāmīyah al-islāmīyah* (Cairo: Maktabat Wahbah, 1986), 363f (denying that he believed the Qur'an to be created on the basis of a commentary on *al-Fiqh al-akbar*), 368f (admitting that Abū Ḥanīfah did not think works part of *īmān*), 374 (holding that his *irjā'* was praiseworthy, for it amounted only to hoping for *ṣāḥib al-kabīrah*, perpetrator of a cardinal sin).

[42] On the Murji'ah, *v.* W. Montgomery Watt, *The Formative Period of Islamic Thought* (Edinburgh: Univ. Press, 1973), 119-148; J. Merie Pessagno, "The Murji'a, Īmān, and Abū 'Ubayd," *Journal of the American Oriental Society* 95 (1975):382-394.

[43] Al-'Uqaylī, *Ḍu'afā'* 1:303f.

[44] *Qāla fīhī bi-ra'yih*; *apud* Ibn Ḥajar, *Tahdhīb* 3:18.

to the caliph himself.[45]

Leading followers of Abū Ḥanīfah's are equally identified with the Murji'ah. Nūḥ ibn Abī Maryam (d. 173/789-790), qadi for Marv and a student under Abū Ḥanīfah in Kufa, was said to be a Murji'.[46] Al-Sājī accused al-Shaybānī outright of being a Murji'.[47] The Kufan qadi Sharīk ibn 'Abd Allāh (d. 187/803?) is said to have rejected the testimony of al-Shaybānī, explaining "I do not permit (to testify) one who says the ritual prayer is not a part of faith," a tenet of the Murji-'ah.[48] Abū Muṭī' al-Balkhī (d. 199/814), qadi for Balkh, possibly a sometime student under Abū Ḥanīfah, and the source of *al-Fiqh al-akbar* (alternatively, *al-Fiqh al-absaṭ*), was condemned by later *rijāl* critics as a Murji'.[49] Ismā'īl ibn Ḥammād, grandson of Abū Ḥanīfah, is credited with a comprehensive treatment of Ḥanafi law, a refutation of Qadari arguments, and a *Kitāb al-Irjā'*, presumably setting out the Murji' system.[50] Abū Ḥafṣ al-Kabīr was recalled to have said that faith was (mere) profession and was condemned as a Murji'.[51] And Ibrāhīm ibn Yūsuf (d. Baghdad, 239/853?) was expelled from the circle of Mālik in Medina for being a Murji'.[52] He may have studied law under Abū Yūsuf and was sometime *ra'īs* of Balkh. Easing the entrance requirements to Islam, *irjā'* probably reinforced Ḥanafi predominance in the eastern provinces.[53]

---

[45] Al-Ṭabarī, *Annales*, ed. M. J. de Goeje, 3 vols. in 15 (Leiden: E. J. Brill, 1879-1901), 2:1867, cited by Wilferd Madelung, "The Early Murji'a in Khurāsān and Transoxania and the Spread of Hanafism," *Der Islam* 59 (1982):34.

[46] Abū al-Rajā' Muḥammad ibn Ḥamdawayh, *Tārīkh*, *apud* Ibn Ḥajar, *Tahdhīb* 10:488, ll. 5f from bottom.

[47] Ibn Ḥajar, *Lisān* 5:122, ll. 8f.

[48] Ibn Ḥajar, *Lisān* 5:122, ll. 1-3.

[49] *V.* Ibn Ḥajar, *Lisān* 2:334-336; Sezgin, *Geschichte* 1:414, II.

[50] Ibn Abī al-Wafā', *Jawāhir* 1:401.

[51] Al-Dhahabī, *Siyar a'lām al-nubalā'*, 25 vols. (Beirut: Mu'assasat al-Risālah, 1983), 13 (ed. 'Alī Abū Zayd):36.

[52] Al-Dhahabī, *Siyar* 11 (ed. Ṣāliḥ al-Samr, 1982):63.

[53] For more on *irjā'* in Khurasan, *v.* Madelung, "The Early Murji'a," 32-39. The spread of Ḥanafism in Khurasan and Transoxania is a major topic I do not treat. Madelung's survey is only the beginning of what might be done. *V.* also Muḥammad Maḥrūs 'Abd al-Laṭīf Mudarris, *Mashāyikh Balkh min al-Ḥanafīyah wa-mā infaradū bihi min al-masā'il al-fiqhīyah*, Iḥyā' al-turāth al-islāmī, 2 vols. (Baghdad: Wizārat al-Awqāf, 1978, 1979). Mudarris always minimizes the differences between Muslims then and Muslims today, but he cites virtually all the extant biographical information. The second volume is given over to a review of peculiar juridical positions ascribed

It is difficult to find any Murji'ah at all in the biographical dictionaries after this time; i.e., from the mid-ninth century. Perhaps they were absorbed by the Mu'tazilah. Several ninth-century figures in our standard biographical dictionary of the Mu'tazili school were said to incline towards *irjā'*.[54] Certainly, later traditionalists would associate the Murji'ah with the Mu'tazilah. For example, Abū Muḥammad Ibn Abī Ḥamzah would warn against reading the qur'anic commentary of al-Zamakhsharī lest one unwittingly become a Mu'tazili and a Murji'.[55] The association of the Ḥanafīyah with the Murji'ah would linger. Hence, for example, the Ḥanafīyah would appear in al-Khwārizmī's *Mafātīḥ al-'ulūm*, a vade mecum for secretaries of the later tenth century, not with other jurisprudents (the Mālikīyah, Shāfi'īyah, Ḥanbalīyah, and Dāwūdīyah) but among the Murji'ah.[56]

Shī'i accounts emphasize Abū Ḥanīfah's special views on the 'Alids. The Twelver al-Nawbakhtī (d. 310/922?) names Abū Ḥanīfah, Abū Yūsuf, and Bishr al-Marīsī as the Murji'ah who held that 'Alī was right to fight Ṭalḥah and al-Zubayr (by contrast with the rest of the Murji'ah and certain of the Mu'tazilah, who held that although one side was right, the Muslims were in effect unable to judge which).[57] Less credibly, al-Nawbakhtī also identifies the people of *irjā'* and *ahl al-ḥadīth* together as the Muḥaddithah, who once recognized Mūsá al-Kāẓim (seventh imam of the Twelvers, d. 183/799) and 'Alī al-Riḍā (eighth imam, d. 203/819) but after that left the 'Alids for worldly ends.[58] On the other hand, Ibn al-Nadīm identifies with the Zaydīyah the early traditionists (his examples are Sufyān al-Thawrī, Sufyān ibn 'Uyaynah, and Ṣāliḥ ibn Ḥayy) but not Abū Ḥanīfah and *aṣḥāb al-ra'y*.[59] W. Montgomery Watt suggests that the Murji'ah were originally defined as those who refused to decide be-

---

to the Ḥanafīyah of Balkh.

[54] Ibn al-Murtaḍá, *Die Klassen der mu'taziliten*, ed. Susanna Diwald-Wilzer, Bibliotheca Islamica 21 (Wiesbaden: Franz Steiner, 1961), 57.

[55] Ibn Ḥajar, *Lisān* 6:4, l. 10 from bottom.

[56] Al-Khwārizmī, *Liber Mafâtîh al-olûm*, ed. G. Van Vloten (Leiden: E. J. Brill, 1895), 28.

[57] Al-Nawbakhtī, *Die Sekten der Schi'a*, ed. Helmut Ritter, Bibliotheca Islamica 4 (Istanbul: Staatsdruckerei, 1931), 13. The work may belong rather to Sa'd ibn 'Abd Allāh al-Qummī (d. 301/913-914?).

[58] Al-Nawbakhtī, *Sekten*, 72f.

[59] Ibn al-Nadīm, *Fihrist*, 178 = *f.* 2, *q.* 5.

tween 'Uthmān and 'Alī.[60]

Whatever their variety of loyalty to 'Alī, it must have been compatible with loyalty to the 'Abbāsids. Claude Cahen has observed that the relatively rationalistic and flexible Ḥanafi jurisprudence was favorable to the practical demands of administration and justice, and that the Ḥanafīyah were thus natural auxiliaries to the 'Abbāsids. Their influence in the provinces was strongest precisely where 'Abbāsi authority was strongest.[61] On the other hand, we have the report, which Schacht accepts, that Abū Ḥanīfah was imprisoned at the end of his life neither for refusing the judgeship nor for professing the Qur'an created but for too freely criticizing the caliph al-Manṣūr at the time of an 'Alid revolt.[62]

As the Ḥanafi school was traditionalized, its adherents jettisoned their old associations with *irjā'* and the 'Abbāsids. They did not exactly repudiate such doctrines as the created Qur'an and *irjā'*, but rather pushed them to the side, divorcing their theological interests and their jurisprudential. Hence, for example, Abū Yūsuf was said to have been asked whether Abū Ḥanīfah had been a Murji'. "Yes," he answered. Next he was asked whether he had been a Jahmi (a believer in the created Qur'an). "Yes," Abū Yūsuf replied again. Then asked where he stood in relation to him, Abū Yūsuf explained, "Abū Ḥanīfah was only a teacher (*mudarris*). What was good of his position, we accepted; what was bad, we left."[63] Many important Ḥanafīyah were associated with dubious theological schools, particularly the Mu'tazili; for example, the most important teachers of the tenth century, al-Barda'ī, al-Karkhī, and al-Jaṣṣāṣ.[64] However, they pre-

---

[60] Watt, *Formative*, 124f.

[61] Claude Cahen, "La changeante portée sociale de quelques doctrines religieuses," *L'Elaboration de l'Islam* (Paris: Presses Universitaires de France, 1961), 18 = *Les Peuples musulmanes dans l'histoire médiévale* (Damascus: Institut Français de Damas, 1977), 205.

[62] Al-Khaṭīb al-Baghdādī, *Tārīkh* 13:329f; *Encyclopaedia of Islam*, new edn., s.v. "Abū Ḥanīfa," by J. Schacht.

[63] Al-Khaṭīb al-Baghdādī, *Tārīkh* 13:375.

[64] The association of all three with the Mu'tazilah has been energetically denied by A. Kevin Reinhart, *Before Revelation* (Albany: State Univ. of New York Press, 1995), 46f. His argument is marred by little mistakes and depends on a narrow definition of Mu'tazilism. For example, he states, "It is an accusation that *none* of the non-Mu'tazilī biographical dictionaries makes"—Reinhart's emphasis. Cf. al-Dhahabī, *Tārīkh* 26 (A.H. 351-380):432. To show that al-Jaṣṣāṣ was a Mu'tazili, al-Dhaha-

tended to authority only as teachers of law (precisely, *mudarrisūn*), not theology, and theological traditionalists as well as Mu'tazilah were happy to study law under them. Similarly, al-Karkhī would not only refuse to become a qadi himself, he refused even to associate with any student of his who accepted an appointment. The old connections had helped the Ḥanafīyah in their time, but the enduring, classical school was stronger without those connections.

THE GROWTH OF A COMMENTARY LITERATURE

One essential feature of the classical school of law is a body of authoritative doctrine ascribed to the eponym of the school. Abū Ḥanīfah himself left no considerable body of juridical writings, whereas his disciples Abū Yūsuf and especially Muḥammad al-Shaybānī did; hence some scholars' characterizing them as the true founders of the Ḥanafi school. It was not yet the classical Ḥanafi school, though, until, among other things, a body of jurisprudents began to treat the work of Abū Ḥanīfah and his two disciples as the basis of a school. In the first place, this meant transmitting it to students. It also meant writing commentaries on it. To write a commentary was to acknowledge that some writings had incomparably more weight than anything coming after. The chronology of commentaries on earlier writings should reveal when and where the classical school took shape. Nearly all the known commentaries written in the twelfth century or before dealt with the two summations of Ḥanafi doctrine by Muḥammad al-Shaybānī, *Kitāb al-Jāmi' al-ṣaghīr* and *al-Jāmi' al-kabīr*. Here is a list of those who wrote commentaries on one or both of these works during the four centuries after al-Shaybānī's death.

Commentaries on al-Jāmi' al-ṣaghīr.

Abū Ja'far *al-Ṭaḥāwī* (d. Baghdad, 321/933).[65]

---

bī cites his position concerning the sight of God in the afterlife. This is admittedly not one of the five principles by which the Mu'tazilah were classically defined. Reinhart is right to remind us that we have no hard evidence concerning the theological views of most jurisprudents of the period, that one might agree with a party on some questions without agreeing on every question, and that we must use labels with care.

[65] Kātib Çelebī, *Kashf al-ẓunūn 'an asāmī al-kutub wa-al-funūn*, ed. Şerefettin

Muḥammad ibn 'Īsá *Ibn Abī Mūsá* (d. Baghdad, 334/945).[66]

Abū Ṭāhir Muḥammad ibn Muḥammad ibn Sufyān *al-Dabbās* (*fl.* Baghdad, early tenth cent.; d. Mecca).[67]

Abū 'Amr Aḥmad ibn Muḥammad *al-Ṭabarī* (d. Baghdad? 340/951-952).[68]

Abū al-Ḥasan *al-Karkhī* (d. Baghdad, 340/952).[69]

Muḥammad *ibn* Aḥmad *'Abdak* al-Jurjānī (d. Basra? 347/958-959).[70]

Abū Ja'far Muḥammad ibn 'Abd Allāh *al-Hinduwānī* (d. Bukhara, 362/973).[71]

Abū Bakr *al-Jaṣṣāṣ* al-Rāzī (d. Baghdad, 370/981?).[72]

Abū al-Layth al-Samarqandī (d. 373/983?).[73]

Abū Sa'd (Sa'īd) 'Abd al-Raḥmān ibn Muḥammad *al-Ḥākim al-Fuzzī* (d. 374/984-985), qadi for Tirmidh.[74]

Abū al-Ḥasan Muḥammad ibn Aḥmad ibn Muḥammad *al-Za'farānī* (d. 393 or 394/*ca.* 1003).[75]

Shams al-A'immah al-Ḥalwānī (d. Kashsh, 448/1056-57?).[76]

Yaltkaya & Rifat Bilge, 2 vols. (Istanbul: Maarif Matbaası, 1941, 1943), 1:562.

[66] A *murattab*; i.e., presumably, a re-ordering of al-Shaybānī's material according to current juridical categories: Kātib Çelebī, *Kashf* 1:564.

[67] *Tartīb al-Jāmi' al-ṣaghīr*, copied by his *tilmīdh* at his house in Baghdad, 322/933-934, according to Kātib Çelebī, *Kashf* 1:563. This is evidently the version of *al-Jāmi' al-ṣaghīr* extant today: Fuat Sezgin, *Geschichte* 1:428, V.

[68] Kātib Çelebī, *Kashf* 1:562.

[69] A *murattab*: Kātib Çelebī, *Kashf* 1:563f.

[70] Kātib Çelebī, *Kashf* 1:562; cf. Ibn Abī al-Wafā', *Jawāhir* 2 (Hyd.):265.

[71] Kātib Çelebī, *Kashf* 1:563.

[72] Anon. list of commentaries on the two *Jāmi*'s of al-Shaybānī, *apud* Ibn Abī al-Wafā', *Jawāhir* 2 (Hyd.):449.

[73] Kātib Çelebī, *Kashf* 1:563.

[74] Ibn Abī al-Wafā', *Jawāhir* 2:390f; a *murattab*, according to Kātib Çelebī, *Kashf* 1:563f.

[75] No direct reference, but several references to his reordering of the *Jāmi'*. Al-Za'farānī studied under al-Jaṣṣāṣ': Ibn Abī al-Wafā', *Jawāhir* 2 (Hyd.):6.

[76] Kātib Çelebī, *Kashf* 1:563.

Abū al-Qāsim ʻAlī ibn Bundār al-Rāzī (d. 474/1081-82).[77]

Fakhr al-Dīn (al-Islām) ʻAlī al-Pazdawī (d. Samarqand, 482/1089).[78]

Shams al-A'immah *al-Sarakhsī* (d. *ca.* 483/1090).[79]

Abū al-Yusr Muḥammad ibn Muḥammad al-Pazdawī (d. Bukhara, 493/1100).[80]

Muḥammad ibn Aḥmad *al-Isbījābī al-Khujandī* (d. *ca.* 500/1106-7).[81]

Abū al-Maʻīn Maymūn ibn Muḥammad *al-Nasafī al-Makḥūlī* (d. 508/1114-15).[82]

al-Ṣadr al-Shahīd Ibn Māzah (d. Samarqand, 536/1141).[83]

Aḥmad al-Nasafī (*fl.* 515/1121).[84]

Abū Ḥafṣ al-Nasafī (d. 537/1142-43).[85]

Abū al-Faḍl ʻAbd al-Raḥmān ibn Muḥammad *al-Kirmānī* (d. 543/1149).[86]

Abū Bakr Aḥmad ibn ʻAlī al-Ẓahīr al-Balkhī (d. 553/1158-59).[87]

Tāj al-Dīn ʻAbd al-Ghaffār ibn Luqmān *al-Kardarī* (d. Aleppo, 562/1166-67).[88]

Burhān al-Dīn Muḥammad ibn Aḥmad *Ibn Māzah* (d. *ca.* 570/1174?).[89]

---

[77] According to the order of al-Zaʻfarānī: Kātib Çelebī, *Kashf* 1:562.
[78] Sezgin, *Geschichte* 1:428, a.
[79] Sezgin, *Geschichte* 1:428, b.
[80] Kātib Çelebī, *Kashf* 1:563.
[81] According to the order of al-Zaʻfarānī: Kātib Çelebī, *Kashf* 1:562. *V.* also Sezgin, *Geschichte* 1:428, c.
[82] Kātib Çelebī, *Kashf* 1:563.
[83] According to the edition of Abū Ṭāhir al-Dabbās: Sezgin, *Geschichte* 1:429, f.
[84] Sezgin, *Geschichte* 1:428, d.
[85] Versification: Sezgin, *Geschichte* 1:430, a.
[86] Kātib Çelebī, *Kashf* 1:563.
[87] Kātib Çelebī, *Kashf* 1:562.
[88] Sezgin, *Geschichte* 1:429, f.
[89] Sezgin, *Geschichte* 1:429, j.

Mas'ūd ibn al-Ḥusayn al-Yazīdī (d. Baghdad? 571/1175-76).[90]

'Alā' al-Dīn Muḥammad ibn 'Abd al-Ḥamīd *al-Samarqandī* (d. 563/1167-68).[91]

Abū Sa'īd (Sa'd) Muṭahhar ibn Ḥasan (al-Ḥusayn) al-Yazdī (*fl.* 559/1163-64).[92]

Ḥusayn ibn Muḥammad al-Najm (d. Aleppo? 580/1184-85).[93]

Aḥmad ibn Muḥammad *al-'Attābī* (d. Bukhara, 586/1190-91).[94]

Fakhr al-Dīn *Qāḍī Khān* (d. 592/1196).[95]

'Alī ibn Abī Bakr *al-Marghīnānī* (d. Marghinan, 593/1197).[96]

Burhān al-Dīn Imām al-Ḥaramayn (*fl.* 6th/12th cent.?).[97]

Ḥusām al-Dīn 'Alī ibn Aḥmad *Ibn al-Makkī* al-Rāzī (d. Aleppo, 598/1201-2).[98]

Commentaries on al-Jāmi' al-kabīr.

Abū Khāzim 'Abd al-Ḥamīd ibn 'Abd al-'Azīz (d. Baghdad, 292/905).[99]

'Alī *al-Qummī* (d. Nishapur? 305/917-918).[100]

Abū Ja'far *al-Ṭaḥāwī* (d. Baghdad, 321/933).[101]

Abū Bakr Muḥammad ibn Aḥmad *al-Iskāf al-Balkhī* (d. 333/944-

---

[90] Kātib Çelebī, *Kashf* 1:562.
[91] Sezgin, *Geschichte* 1:429, g.
[92] Grandson to 'Alī ibn Bundār al-Rāzī (d. 474/1081-82), a commentary on his commentary, called *al-Tahdhīb*: Kātib Çelebī, *Kashf* 1:562f.
[93] Kātib Çelebī, *Kashf* 1:562.
[94] Sezgin, *Geschichte* 1:429, h.
[95] Sezgin, *Geschichte* 1:429, i.
[96] Anon., *apud* Ibn Abī al-Wafā', *Jawāhir* 2 (Hyd.):449.
[97] Sezgin, *Geschichte* 1:429, j.
[98] Sezgin, *Geschichte* 1:429, k.
[99] Kātib Çelebī, *Kashf* 1:569.
[100] Kātib Çelebī, *Kashf* 1:570.
[101] Kātib Çelebī, *Kashf* 1:568.

945?).[102]

Muḥammad ibn ʿĪsá *Ibn Abī Mūsá* (d. Baghdad, 334/945).[103]

Abū ʿAmr Aḥmad ibn Muḥammad *al-Ṭabarī* (d. Baghdad? 340/951-952).[104]

Muḥammad *ibn* Aḥmad *ʿAbdak* al-Jurjānī (d. Basra? 347/958-959).[105]

Abū ʿAbd Allāh Yūsuf ibn ʿAlī ibn Muḥammad al-Jurjānī (*fl.* Baghdad, before 340/951-952).[106]

Abū Bakr *al-Jaṣṣāṣ* al-Rāzī (d. Baghdad, 370/981?).[107]

Abū al-Layth al-Samarqandī (d. 373/983?).[108]

Abū ʿAbd Allāh Muḥammad ibn Yaḥyá *al-Jurjānī* (d. Baghdad, 398/1008).[109]

Abū Zayd al-Dabūsī (d. Bukhara, 430/1038-39).[110]

Shams al-A'immah *al-Ḥalwānī* (d. Kashsh, 448/1056-57?).[111]

Aḥmad ibn Manṣūr *al-Isbījābī* (d. Samarqand? 480/1087-88).[112]

Fakhr al-Dīn (al-Islām) ʿAlī al-Pazdawī (d. Samarqand, 482/1089).[113]

Muḥammad ibn al-Ḥusayn *Khʷāharzādah* (d. Bukhara, 483/

---

[102] Kātib Çelebī, *Kashf* 1:570.
[103] A *murattab*: Kātib Çelebī, *Kashf* 1:564.
[104] Kātib Çelebī, *Kashf* 1:569.
[105] Kātib Çelebī, *Kashf* 1:568; cf. Ibn Abī al-Wafā', *Jawāhir* 2 (Hyd.):265.
[106] Al-Kaffawī, *Katā'ib aʿlām al-akhyār*, Esad Efendi 548, 70a. The identity of this man is somewhat doubtful: only al-Kaffawī ascribes to him a commentary on *al-Jāmiʿ al-kabīr*, possibly confusing him with the Jurjānī who died 398/1008. Al-Kaffawī and Ibn Abī al-Wafā' (*Jawāhir* 2 [Hyd.]:228f) both ascribe to him a work called *Khizānat al-akmal* in six volumes; however, Kātib Çelebī (*Kashf* 1:702) ascribes that to Abū Yaʿqūb Yūsuf ibn ʿAlī ibn Muḥammad al-Jurjānī (*fl.* 522/1128).
[107] Sezgin, *Geschichte* 1:424, #1.
[108] Kātib Çelebī, *Kashf* 1:568; doubted by Sezgin, *Geschichte* 1:424, #7.
[109] Kātib Çelebī, *Kashf* 1:569.
[110] Kātib Çelebī, *Kashf* 1:568.
[111] Kātib Çelebī, *Kashf* 1:568.
[112] Sezgin, *Geschichte* 1:424, #2.
[113] Ibn Abī al-Wafā', *Jawāhir* 2:595.

1090).[114]

Shams al-A'immah *al-Sarakhsī* (d. *ca.* 483/1090-91).[115]

Abū al-Ma'īn Maymūn ibn Muḥammad *al-Nasafī al-Makḥūlī* (d. 508/1114-15).[116]

Abū Bakr Muḥammad ibn al-Ḥusayn ibn Muḥammad al-Arsābandī (d. 515/1121-22?).[117]

Aḥmad Ibn Abī al-Mu'ayyad al-Maḥmūdī al-Nasafī (*fl.* 515/1121).[118]

al-Ṣadr al-Shahīd Ibn Māzah (d. Samarqand, 536/1141).[119]

Ṣadr al-Islām al-Pazdawī (d. Sarakhs, 542/1147).[120]

Abū al-Faḍl 'Abd al-Raḥmān ibn Muḥammad *al-Kirmānī* (d. Marv, 543/1149).[121]

'Alā' al-Dīn Muḥammad ibn 'Abd al-Ḥamīd al-Samarqandī *al-'Ālimī* (d. 552/1157-58).[122]

Maḥmūd ibn Aḥmad *ibn Māzah* (d. *ca.* 570/1174-75).[123]

Aḥmad ibn Muḥammad *al-'Attābī* (d. Bukhara, 586/1190-91).[124]

Fakhr al-Dīn *Qāḍī Khān* (d. 592/1196).[125]

'Alī ibn Abī Bakr *al-Marghīnānī* (d. Marghinan, 593/1197).[126]

Plainly, the great explosion of activity took place about a hundred years after the death of al-Shaybānī. That should be about the time

[114] Sezgin, *Geschichte* 1:424, #5.
[115] Sezgin, *Geschichte* 1:424, #3.
[116] Kātib Çelebī, *Kashf* 1:570.
[117] Kātib Çelebī, *Kashf* 1:569.
[118] Versification: Kātib Çelebī, *Kashf* 1:570.
[119] Sezgin, *Geschichte* 1:424, #4.
[120] Anon., *apud* Ibn Abī al-Wafā', *Jawāhir* 2 (Hyd.):449.
[121] Sezgin, *Geschichte* 1:424, #6.
[122] Sezgin, *Geschichte* 1:424, #7.
[123] Sezgin, *Geschichte* 1:424, #8.
[124] Sezgin, *Geschichte* 1:424f, #9. Also an abridgement: Sezgin, 1:426, #1.
[125] Ibn Abī al-Wafā', *Jawāhir* 2:94.
[126] Kātib Çelebī, *Kashf* 1:569.

when the classical school came together, or at least began to. (Following Norman Calder's lead, we may also detect at this point a *terminus ad quem* for the edition of the works of al-Shaybānī.[127]) As for where the school came together, there were thirteen commentators who died in the late 200's or the 300's (900's-early 1000's C.E.), of whom seven were active mainly in Iraq, three in Khurasan, two in Transoxania, and one in Egypt. Not only a majority were thus Iraqi, themselves, but the one Egyptian, al-Ṭaḥāwī, was trained by Iraqis and ended his life in Baghdad, while the Khurasani and Transoxanian commentators all either trained, themselves, in Iraq (al-Qummī, Abū Bakr al-Iskāf, al-Ḥākim al-Fuzzī) or were taught by an earlier commentator who had (al-Hinduwānī, Abū al-Layth al-Samarqandī). In sum, activity during the tenth century was mainly Iraqi, in the eleventh and twelfth mainly Transoxanian. No one teacher can be identified with certainty as the common link among all these commentaries, but Abū Khāzim and Abū Sa'īd al-Barda'ī (d. 317/929) come close; that is, nearly all the commentators whose teachers can be identified at all either studied directly under one of these two or had teachers who had. Therefore, inasmuch as the commentary is a hallmark of the classical school, these two come close to being the founders of the Ḥanafi school.

From time to time, collections appeared of hadith reports that Abū Ḥanīfah was supposed to have used: their chronology, too, points to a major change at the beginning of the tenth century, while their geographical distribution suggests that the chief center of new-style Ḥanafi activity was Iraq, with additional activity in Transoxania. Al-Khʷārizmī's synthesis of previous collections has been mentioned already. In his introduction, al-Khʷārizmī lists the fifteen collections of which he knew.[128] The chronological pattern of these collections is similar to that of the commentaries on *al-Jāmi' al-kabīr* and *al-Ṣaghīr*: *five* from the late eighth century (most only rarely quoted—they must have been insubstantial), *none* from the ninth century, then *six* from the

---

[127] Calder, *Studies*, chap. 3. Unfortunately, the book that Calder analyzes in detail is *al-Aṣl*, much used by modern students of Ḥanafi law but less important to medieval Ḥanafi jurisprudents than the two *Jāmi'*s. Still, his finding is entirely consistent with the evidence of the commentary literature: "A plausible dating for the final redaction of these early Ḥanafī polemical texts would be . . . *c*. 250 AH" (*Studies*, 66).

[128] Al-Khʷārizmī, *Jāmi'* 1:4f. Sezgin names one additional tenth-century *musnad*, that of Abū Bakr Ibn al-Muqri' (d. 381/991-992): *Geschichte* 1:205, 415.

tenth century, *four* from the eleventh. Few of the tenth-century collectors were known as Ḥanafi jurisprudents, and the collection of hadith reports related by Abū Ḥanīfah was clearly not central to the formation of the school, as the writing of commentaries on the works of al-Shaybānī was. (Similarly, the first *musnad* for Mālik was prepared by the traditionist al-Nisā'ī [d. Palestine? 303/915?], not known to have studied jurisprudence under any Māliki teacher, while the most important for al-Shāfi'ī was worked up from the teaching of Abū al-'Abbās al-Aṣamm [d. Nishapur, 346/957], not known to have studied jurisprudence under any Shāfi'i.[129]) However, the collection of hadith reports does indicate where and when Ḥanafi doctrine was finally provided with a basis in hadith.

[129] Kātib Çelebī, *Kashf* 1:1685, 1683.

CHAPTER FOUR

THE NINTH-CENTURY SHĀFI'Ī SCHOOL OF LAW AND THEOLOGY

Al-Shāfi'ī is the point at which Norman Calder's redatings most radically affect the history of Islamic law. This is because the theory of the guild schools—the classical schools of law as we are familiar with them from the eleventh century onwards—was so largely the theory of al-Shāfi'ī, particularly *al-Risālah*. If *al-Risālah* in its familiar form was first published around 300/912-913, almost a century after al-Shāfi'ī's death, the juridical theory of the guild school must be reassigned to the ninth-century Shāfi'i school, not al-Shāfi'ī himself.[1] My own observations tend to confirm Calder's redating. Among other things, Aḥmad and other traditionalists continued to heed the opinions of Companions and Successors, contrary to al-Shāfi'ī's arguments for Prophetic hadith; commentaries on *al-Risālah* (and rebuttals) appeared only after 300/912-913; and traditionalists came to regard al-Shāfi'ī more positively about then.[2] It is still important to show the relation between the putative writings of al-Shāfi'ī and the practice of the later guild schools, likewise to locate these writings as between the rival schools of *ra'y* and *ḥadīth*; however, historians have already made a good start at treating these.[3] What I shall stress here is the peculiar juridical and theological tendency of the ninth-century Shāfi'i school—a looser formation than the guild school of the tenth century and after, yet in important ways prefiguring the guild school more clearly than any other grouping of its time.

---

[1] For the redating of *al-Risālah*, *v*. Norman Calder, *Studies in Early Muslim Jurisprudence* (Oxford: Clarendon Press, 1993), chap. 9, esp. 242.

[2] For growing Ḥanbali friendliness, *v. infra*, chap. 7.

[3] Outstandingly, of course, Joseph Schacht, *The Origins of Muhammadan Jurisprudence* (Oxford: Clarendon Press, 1950) for the theory of the classical schools; *v. infra*, note 8, for al-Shāfi'ī between the schools of *ra'y* and *ḥadīth*.

THE SEMI-RATIONALIST PARTY

In Chapter One, I discussed the emergence of the *traditionalist* party in the late eighth century. In Chapters Two and Three, I discussed the evolution of jurisprudence among what I conventionally call, by default, the *rationalist* party. In discussing the Shāfi'i personal school of the ninth century, I will propose a new category, the *semi-rationalist*, a third party in the middle. Josef van Ess noticed Ibn Kullāb (d. *ca*. 240/854-855) and some associates who took up the tools of *kalām* in defence of traditionalist doctrines, and has suggested the name *ahl al-ithbāt*.[4] My own attention was drawn to them by a survey of Aḥmad ibn Ḥanbal's polemics against various opponents. He is seldom quoted against contemporary Mu'tazilah, often against semi-rationalists: al-Ḥusayn al-Karābīsī (d. 248/862-863?), Abū Thawr (d. 240/854), and al-Ḥārith al-Muḥāsibī (d. 243/857-858); also against Dāwūd al-Ẓāhirī (d. 270/884). These are all variously associated with Ibn Kullāb, although there is no record of Aḥmad's saying anything about Ibn Kullāb himself, and only one report, from outside the Ḥanbali tradition, by which Aḥmad severely condemned the Kullābīyah.[5]

It is striking that most of these semi-rationalists whom Aḥmad and his followers opposed were loosely associated with the Shāfi'i school of law. George Makdisi has identified the Ḥanbali school of law as the only one to comprise both one system of jurisprudence, fairly traditionalist, and one theological tendency, staunchly traditionalist. Each of the other three schools of law comprised one system of juris-

---

[4] Josef van Ess, "Ibn Kullāb und die Miḥna," *Oriens* 18-19 (1965-1966):92-141, trans. with additional notes by Claude Gilliot, "Ibn Kullāb et la *Miḥna*," *Arabica* 37 (1990):173-233.

[5] Ibn Khuzaymah (d. 311 or 312/ca. 924) asserted that Aḥmad had severely condemned the Kullābīyah: al-Ḥākim al-Naysābūrī, *Tārīkh Naysābūr*, *apud* al-Dhahabī, *Siyar a'lām al-nubalā'*, 25 vols. (Beirut: Mu'assasat al-Risālah, 1981-1988), 14 (ed. Akram al-Būshayyī, 1983):379f; likewise Ibn Ḥajar, *Lisān "al-Mīzān,"* 7 vols. (Hyderabad: Majlis Dā'irat al-Ma'ārif, 1329-31), 3:291. For Ibn Kullāb and Abū Thawr, *v*. Ibn 'Abd al-Barr, *al-Intiqā' fī faḍā'il al-thalāthah al-a'immah al-fuqahā'* (Cairo: Maktabat al-Qudsī, 1350), 156. For Ibn Kullāb and Dāwūd al-Ẓāhirī, *v*. al-Dhahabī, *Siyar* 11 (ed. Ṣāliḥ al-Samr, 1982):174; Ibn Ḥajar, *Tahdhīb "al-Tahdhīb,"* 12 vols. (Hyderabad: Majlis Dā'irat al-Ma'ārif al-Niẓāmīyah, 1325-27), 2:361f. For Ibn Kullāb and al-Muḥāsibī, *v*. Ibn Khuzaymah, *apud* al-Dhahabī, *Siyar* 11:174, 14:380.

prudence but no one theological tendency: rather, the other three comprised both traditionalists and rationalists.[6] However, in the ninth and early tenth centuries, it appears that there was also a vague Shāfi'i school, wider than the later, guild school, that comprised both a particular system of jurisprudence and a particular theological tendency. On both sides, it was a compromise, semi-rationalist school: its jurisprudence was formally based on textual sources but with heavier reliance on reason to combine texts than the extreme traditionalists allowed; in theology, it upheld the essential traditionalist tenets but elaborated rationalist apologies for them and made concessions that appalled the extreme traditionalists.

AL-SHĀFI'Ī BETWEEN RATIONALISM AND TRADITIONALISM

Joseph Schacht is ambiguous, sometimes characterizing al-Shāfi'ī as a traditionalist, sometimes pointing out his differences with contemporary traditionalists[7]; however, Wael B. Hallaq has now firmly established that al-Shāfi'ī himself was at least somewhere between the rationalists and pure traditionalists.[8] Al-Shāfi'ī's insistence on deriving law from hadith going back to the Prophet contravened continuing traditionalist willingness to consider the opinions of Companions. Even more, his resort to reason, in particular his willingness to apply analogy to the hadith reports of the Prophet rather than to rely on the opinions of Companions, together with his willingness to examine and lay down rules for the practice of jurisprudence, separated his practice from the traditionalists'.[9] It was doubtless for such resort to reason

---

[6] George Makdisi, "Hanbalite Islam," in *Studies on Islam*, trans. & ed. Merlin Swartz (New York: Oxford Univ. Press, 1981), 239. Makdisi's sketch of a monolithic, traditionalist Ḥanbali school must now be qualified by A. Kevin Reinhart, *Before Revelation*, SUNY Ser. in Middle Eastern Studies (Albany: State Univ. of New York Press, 1995), esp. 21-25.

[7] Joseph Schacht, *Origins*, 47, 55, 57, 253f, &c.

[8] Wael B. Hallaq, "Was al-Shafi'i the Master Architect of Islamic Jurisprudence?" *International Journal of Middle East Studies* 25 (1993):593f. Cf. Christopher Melchert, "The Formation of the Sunni Schools of Law, Ninth-Tenth Centuries C.E.," Ph.D. diss., Univ. of Pennsylvania, 1992, chap. 3.

[9] For a succinct characterization of Aḥmad's juridical practice, *v.* Susan A. Spectorsky, "Aḥmad Ibn Ḥanbal's *Fiqh*," *Journal of the American Oriental Society* 102 (1982):461-465.

that Aḥmad, for example, recommended that one avoid the books of al-Shāfi'ī.[10]

THE DISCIPLES OF AL-SHĀFI'Ī IN BAGHDAD

According to al-Nawawī, al-Shāfi'ī's Baghdadi teaching ("*al-qadīm*") was transmitted by four: al-Karābīsī, al-Za'farānī (d. 260/874), Abū Thawr, and Aḥmad ibn Ḥanbal (d. 241/855).[11] Al-Karābīsī was allegedly the most important. Two eleventh-century biographers report that he wrote on both the theory of jurisprudence (*uṣūl al-fiqh*) and the ramifications (*al-furū'*).[12] Hallaq has expressed doubt over al-Karābīsī's contribution in both fields on the ground that we have no particular information about it.[13] However, we know of so many lost works from this century, it seems more likely that we lack information because his works were lost than because he simply wrote little. Moreover, we do have a report of al-Karābīsī's position concerning one classic question of *uṣūl al-fiqh*, namely whether a report necessarily brings about certain knowledge.[14]

In *kalām*, al-Karābīsī seems to have been the first and most prominent to assert that his pronunciation of the Qur'an was created.[15] Aḥ-

[10] Ibn Abī Ya'lá, *Ṭabaqāt al-ḥanābilah*, ed. Muḥammad Ḥāmid al-Fiqī, 2 vols. (Cairo: Maṭba'at al-Sunnah al-Muḥammadīyah, 1952), 1:38, 318; Ibn al-Jawzī, *Manāqib al-imām Aḥmad ibn Ḥanbal*, ed. 'Abd Allāh ibn 'Abd al-Muḥsin al-Turkī & 'Alī Muḥammad 'Umar (Cairo: Maktabat al-Khānjī, 1979), 249; al-Dhahabī, *Siyar* 13 (ed. 'Alī Abū Zayd, 1983):350; Ibn Ḥajar, *Lisān* 2:291. Contrary accounts of Aḥmad's praise for al-Shāfi'ī are mostly to be found in non-Ḥanbali sources such as Ibn Abī Ḥātim, *Ādāb al-Shāfi'ī*, and al-Bayhaqī, *Manāqib al-Shāfi'ī*.

[11] Al-Nawawī, *Tahdhīb al-asmā' wa-al-lughāt*, 3 vols. in 2 (Cairo: Idārat al-Ṭibā'ah al-Munīrīyah, 1927), 2:284.

[12] Al-'Abbādī, *Kitāb Ṭabaqāt al-fuqahā' al-shāfi'īyah*, ed. Gösta Vitestam, Veröffentlichungen der "De Goeje Stiftung" 21 (Leiden: E. J. Brill, 1964), 24f; Abū Isḥāq al-Shīrāzī, *Ṭabaqāt al-fuqahā'*, ed. Iḥsān 'Abbās (Beirut: Dār al-Rā'id al-'Arabī, 1970), 102.

[13] Hallaq, "Was al-Shafi'i?" 602, n. 23.

[14] Al-'Abbādī, *Ṭabaqāt*, 24. Cf. Bernard Weiss, *The Search for God's Law* (Salt Lake City: Univ. of Utah Press, 1992), 294f.

[15] Abū al-Ḥasan al-Ash'arī, *Die dogmatischen Lehren der Anhänger des Islam*, ed. Helmut Ritter, Bibliotheca Islamica 1, 2nd edn. (Wiesbaden: Franz Steiner, 1963), 602; Ibn al-Nadīm, *Kitâb al-Fihrist*, ed. Gustav Flügel, w/ Johannes Roediger & August Mueller (Leipzig: F. C. W. Vogel, 1872), 181 = *fann* 3, *maqālah* 5.

mad identified al-Karābīsī himself as a successor to Bishr al-Marīsī (d. 218/833-834), whose doctrine of the created Qur'an was taken up by al-Ma'mūn.[16] Al-Karābīsī expressed exasperation: "What shall we do with this boy? If we say 'created,' he says 'innovation'; if we say 'uncreated,' he says 'innovation.'"[17] Al-Karābīsī's doctrine of the pronunciation was taken up after him by Abū Thawr, Ibn Kullāb, al-Ḥārith al-Muḥāsibī, Dāwūd al-Ẓāhirī, and possibly al-Bukhārī (d. near Samarqand, 256/870).[18]

Al-Za'farānī is presented as having merely transmitted what al-Shāfi'ī said, without additions or extensions of his own. He must have stayed out of theological discussions. Asked by an envoy of al-Mutawakkil's vizier, Aḥmad professed to have heard of him nothing but good.[19]

According to Ḥanbali tradition, Aḥmad was most bothered, after al-Karābīsī, by Abū Thawr. In jurisprudence, Abū Thawr aligned himself with the traditionalists, renouncing *ra'y* as a form of innovation (*bid'ah*).[20] He is included among the Shāfi'īyah by Ibn al-Nadīm (who states, like some others after him, that Abū Thawr went on to develop his own doctrine on the basis of al-Shāfi'ī's), al-'Abbādī, Ibn al-Ṣalāḥ, and al-Subkī.[21] He was not on good terms with al-Ka-

---

[16] Al-Khaṭīb al-Baghdādī, *Tārīkh Baghdād*, 14 vols. (Cairo: al-Khānjī, 1931), 8:65f; Ibn Abī Ya'lá, *Ṭabaqāt* 1:41, 62, 111, 288. On Bishr al-Marīsī and the Inquisition, *v.* Josef van Ess, "Ḍirār b. 'Amr und die 'Cahmiya': Biographie einer vergessenen Schule," *Der Islam* 44 (1968):34, where he points out particular differences between Mu'tazili thought concerning the created Qur'an and Bishr al-Marīsī's; also *idem*, *Theologie und Gesellschaft im 2. und 3. Jahrhundert Hidschra*, 6 vols. (Berlin: de Gruyter, 1991-95), 3:175-188.

[17] Al-Khaṭīb al-Baghdādī, *Tārīkh* 7:65.

[18] For Ibn Kullāb, Dāwūd al-Ẓāhirī, and al-Bukhārī, *v.* Ibn Ḥajar, *Tahdhīb* 2:361f.

[19] Al-Khaṭīb al-Baghdādī, *Tārīkh* 7:409.

[20] Al-Khaṭīb al-Baghdādī, *Tārīkh* 6:67f.

[21] Ibn al-Nadīm, *Fihrist*, 211 = *f.* 3, *q.* 6; al-'Abbādī, *Ṭabaqāt*, 22; Ibn 'Abd al-Barr, *al-Intiqā' fī faḍā'il al-thalāthah al-a'immah al-fuqahā'* (Cairo: Maktabat al-Qudsī, 1350), 107; Ibn al-Ṣalāḥ al-Shahrazūrī, *Ṭabaqāt al-fuqahā' al-shāfi'īyah*, ed. al-Nawawī, al-Mizzī, & Muḥyī al-Dīn 'Alī Najīb, 2 vols. (Beirut: Dār al-Bashā'ir al-Islāmīyah, 1992), 1:299-301; al-Subkī, *Ṭabaqāt al-shāfi'īyah al-kubrá*, ed. Maḥmūd Muḥammad al-Ṭanāḥī & 'Abd al-Fattāḥ al-Ḥulw, 10 vols. (Cairo: 'Īsá al-Bābī al-Ḥalabī, 1964-76), 2:74-80. *V.* also al-Nisā'ī, "Tasmiyat fuqahā' al-amṣār," *Majmū'at rasā'il fī 'ulūm al-ḥadīth*, ed. Ṣubḥī al-Badrī al-Sāmarrā'ī (Medina: Muḥammad 'Abd al-Muḥsin, 1969), 8.

rābīsī, reportedly joining Aḥmad in questioning whether al-Karābīsī had really studied under al-Shāfi'ī.[22] Yet Aḥmad is several times quoted against Abū Thawr, whom he sometimes condemns by himself, sometimes alongside al-Karābīsī.[23] When a particular error is named, it actually concerns not the pronunciation of the Qur'an but the hadith report, "God created Adam in his image": Abū Thawr interpreted it, *contra* Aḥmad, to mean "in Adam's image," not "in God's image."[24]

Al-Khaṭīb al-Baghdādī does quote contrary reports of Aḥmad's praising Abū Thawr; for example, comparing his stature to that of Sufyān al-Thawrī.[25] The Ḥanbali jurisprudent Abū Bakr al-Khallāl (d. Baghdad, 311/923) would explain that Aḥmad had praised Abū Thawr until he heard of his heretical doctrines, then condemned him; however, this explanation is impossible to reconcile with the particular report that Aḥmad praised Abū Thawr when his son 'Abd Allāh had just returned from his funeral.[26] Al-Khallāl also reported that Abū Thawr called Aḥmad his shaykh and imam.[27] Al-Khaṭīb al-Baghdādī was a Shāfi'ī in jurisprudence, an Ash'ari in theology, while al-Khallāl, as we shall see, led the development of a Ḥanbali school of law along Shāfi'i lines. Probably, then, both were eager to relate a later tradition by which Aḥmad approved of al-Shāfi'ī and Abū Thawr.

Aḥmad ibn Ḥanbal's hostility seems to have inspired violence against one of his semi-rationalist contemporaries, al-Ḥārith al-Muḥāsibī. Al-Muḥāsibī first fled to Kufa, where he announced his repentance of all that Aḥmad held against him. When Aḥmad refused to accept his repentance, perhaps on the ground of its vagueness, al-Muḥāsibī returned to Baghdad but hid. When he died and was buried there, two years after Aḥmad's death, only four persons prayed over him.[28]

---

[22] Ibn Ḥajar, *Tahdhīb* 2:361.

[23] Ibn Abī Ya'lá, *Ṭabaqāt* 1:211, 212, 255, 414.

[24] Ibn Abī Ya'lá, *Ṭabaqāt* 1:93, 212, 309.

[25] Al-Khaṭīb al-Baghdādī, *Tārīkh* 6:66-69.

[26] Al-Khallāl, *apud* Ibn Abī Ya'lá, *Ṭabaqāt* 1:328; al-Khaṭīb al-Baghdādī, *Tārīkh* 6:68f.

[27] Al-Khaṭīb al-Baghdādī, *Tārīkh* 4:417, ll. 19f.

[28] Al-Dhahabī, *Tārīkh al-islām*, ed. 'Umar 'Abd al-Salām Tadmurī, 40 vols. to date (Beirut: Dār al-Kitāb al-'Arabī, 1987-), 18 (A.H. 241-250):209 (Kufa, repentance); al-Khaṭīb al-Baghdādī, *Tārīkh* 8:216 (hiding, death). On the contrary, al-

No early Ḥanbali source explicitly states Aḥmad's complaint with al-Muḥāsibī; however, it seems most likely to have been, again, his position concerning the pronunciation of the Qur'an. The early Sufi biographer Ibn al-A'rābī (d. Mecca, 341/952?) states that al-Muḥāsibī talked (theologized) about the pronunciation of the Qur'an (*lafẓ*) and about faith (*īmān*).[29] Aḥmad himself associated al-Muḥāsibī with Jahmism, probably for saying that a man's pronunciation of the Qur'an was created, possibly also for arguing that faith must be created.[30] (On the nature of faith, Aḥmad is quoted inconsistently: that one should say of faith neither "created" nor "uncreated," a position of *waqf*; alternatively, that the faith that is heard is uncreated, the faith that comprises human actions created.[31]) Aḥmad also heard of al-Muḥāsibī's casting doubt on the audibility of God's voice.[32]

There is one report that Aḥmad shunned al-Muḥāsibī simply for engaging in *kalām*, dialectical theological reasoning.[33] Although vague, this agrees with Aḥmad's distrust of all *kalām*, even apologetic: with his excluding the practitioner of *kalām* from Ahl al-Sunnah, and forbidding a follower to sit with practitioners, even though they defend the Sunnah.[34] It also agrees with al-Muḥāsibī's own denial that he upheld any special doctrine of the pronunciation.[35] Abū al-Ḥasan al-Ash'arī may have preserved one of al-Muḥāsibī's positions in *kalām* in his report that one Ḥārith held that God is not other than his characters (*ṣifāt*), although they are different from one another.[36] By contrast, Bishr al-Marīsī evidently proposed that God's hearing is not different from his sight, his face from his hand, and so on—an exam-

'Abbādī states that al-Muḥāsibī died in Basra, *Ṭabaqāt*, 27.

[29] Ibn al-A'rābī (*Ṭabaqāt al-nussāk*), *apud* al-Dhahabī, *Tārīkh* 18 (A.H. 241-250):209.

[30] Ibn Abī Ya'lá, *Ṭabaqāt* 1:62f, 233f.

[31] Ibn Abī Ya'lá, *Ṭabaqāt* 1:93f, 2:176; cf. Aḥmad ibn Ḥanbal (i.e., al-Khallāl), *al-'Aqīdah lil-imām Aḥmad ibn Ḥanbal*, ed. 'Abd al-'Azīz 'Izz al-Dīn al-Sayrawān (Damascus: Dār Qutaybah, 1988), 117f.

[32] Al-Dhahabī, *Tārīkh* 18 (A.H. 241-250):209f.

[33] *Apud* al-Sulamī, probably *Miḥan al-ṣūfīyah*, *apud* al-Khaṭīb al-Baghdādī, *Tārīkh* 8:215f.

[34] Ibn Abī Ya'lá, *Ṭabaqāt* 1:242, 334.

[35] Josef van Ess, *Die Gedankenwelt des Ḥāriṯ al-Muḥāsibī*, Bonner orientalische Studien, n.s., 12 (Bonn: Selbstverlag des orientalischen Seminars der Universität Bonn, 1961), 205f.

[36] Abū al-Ḥasan al-Ash'arī, *Dogmatischen*, 546.

ple of what al-Muḥāsibī opposed, if indeed this Ḥārith was al-Muḥāsibī.[37] Al-Muḥāsibī's connection with the Shāfi'i school of law is difficult to make out, but he is included amongst the Shāfi'īyah by the eleventh-century biographers Ibn Ṭāhir al-Baghdādī and al-'Abbādī.[38] Al-'Abbādī preserves a position of his concerning *uṣūl al-fiqh*, mainly that the consensus of the scholars in one age was not a source of law if the scholars of a previous age had disagreed over the same question.[39]

Some medieval sources count Dāwūd al-Ẓāhirī a Shāfi'i. Today, he is usually counted the founder of his own school of traditionalist jurisprudence.[40] He is more accurately classified with the semi-rationalists. The same goes for his sometime student, the well-known jurisprudent, historian, and Qur'an commentator Muḥammad ibn Jarīr al-Ṭabarī (d. Baghdad, 310/923). I shall treat them and their difficulties with Aḥmad and the Ḥanābilah at length in Chapter Nine.

Another early student of al-Shāfi'ī's was 'Abd al-Azīz ibn Yaḥyá al-Kinānī (d. *ca.* 240/854-855?). Dāwūd al-Ẓāhirī identifies him as having learnt from al-Shāfi'ī and accompanied him to Yemen.[41] Al-'Abbādī states that he learnt from al-Shāfi'ī until he died, suggesting an Egyptian acquaintance.[42] Ibn al-Nadīm connects him not at all with al-Shāfi'ī, rather places him in the section on Sufis as a contemporary of al-Muḥāsibī. He does state that he wrote books on *kalām* as well as *zuhd* (asceticism).[43] It is difficult to identify his precise tendency in *kalām*, for the only extant work attributed to him, the record of a debate over the Qur'an with Bishr al-Marīsī, is inauthentic.[44] He did evidently comment on questions of *uṣūl al-fiqh*.[45]

---

[37] Abū Sa'īd al-Dārimī, *Radd al-imām al-Dārimī 'alá Bishr al-Marīsī al-'anīd*, ed. Muḥammad Ḥāmid al-Fiqī (Cairo: Maṭba'at Anṣār al-Sunnah al-Muḥammadīyah, 1358), 22 = (Cairo: Dār al-Furqān, 1985?), 24f.

[38] Ibn al-Ṭāhir al-Baghdādī, *apud* Ibn al-Ṣalāḥ, *Ṭabaqāt*, 1:439; al-'Abbādī, *Ṭabaqāt* 27.

[39] Al-'Abbādī, *Ṭabaqāt*, 27. For later Shāfi'i discussions, *v.* Weiss, *Search*, 247f.

[40] E.g., *v.* Fuat Sezgin, *Geschichte des arabischen Schrifttums*, 9 vols. to date (Leiden: E. J. Brill, 1967-), 1:521.

[41] Dāwūd al-Ẓāhirī, *Faḍā'il al-Shāfi'ī*, *apud* al-Khaṭīb al-Baghdādī, *Tārīkh* 10:449.

[42] Al-'Abbādī, *Ṭabaqāt*, 38.

[43] Ibn al-Nadīm, *Fihrist*, 184 = *f.* 5, *q.* 5.

[44] *K. al-Ḥaydah*, for which *v.* Sezgin, *Geschichte* 1:617, #2.

[45] Notably *khuṣūṣ*, *'umūm*, and *bayān*, for which *v.* al-Khaṭīb al-Baghdādī, *Tārīkh*

The only members of the supposed ninth-century Kullābi school *not* associated with al-Shāfi'ī were Ibn Kullāb himself and, in the next generation, al-Qalānisī.[46] At that, Ibn Kullāb appears in some biographical dictionaries of the Shāfi'i school, although without information and probably from association with other semi-rationalist Shāfi'īyah.[47] So very little is known of Ibn Kullāb, it seems possible that later generations made him a scapegoat, exaggerating his importance and blaming him for the worst of semi-rationalist doctrine in order to exonerate the Shāfi'īyah. It is easy to see how Ibn Khuzaymah, for example, would have felt uncomfortable condemning the Shāfi'īyah. A possible parallel would be Jahm ibn Ṣafwān (d. 128/746), blamed for the doctrine of the created Qur'an to exonerate the Ḥanafīyah.[48]

OTHER BAGHDADI SHĀFI'ĪYAH

It is probably for tending toward semi-rationalist theology that the Baghdadi philologist Abū 'Ubayd al-Qāsim ibn Sallām (d. Mecca, 224/839?) is often reckoned a Shāfi'i in law.[49] Other reports conflict. Al-Khalīlī reports that he usually inclined toward the Kufans (i.e., the Ḥanafīyah).[50] Alternatively, his jurisprudence is said to have come from the books of the Hijazi jurisprudent and historian al-

---

10:449.

[46] The material on Abū al-'Abbās al-Qalānisī has been gathered by Daniel Gimaret, "Cet autre théologien sunnite: Abū l-'Abbās al-Qalānisī," *Journal asiatique* 277 (1989):227-261. Gimaret cites no evidence of his affiliation in jurisprudence, and cites Ibn Ṭāhir al-Baghdādī to the effect that all his works concerned *kalām* (234). He doubts whether we should consider al-Qalānisī a follower of Ibn Kullāb (234f), which agrees with my contention that we should refer to a loose semi-rationalist grouping rather than, with misleading precision, a Kullābi school.

[47] *V.* al-'Abbādī, *Ṭabaqāt*, 70; al-Subkī, *Ṭabaqāt* 2:299.

[48] On the supposed party of the Jahmīyah, *v.* esp. W. Montgomery Watt, *The Formative Period of Islamic Thought* (Edinburgh: Univ. Press, 1973), 143-147. On the Ḥanafīyah and the Inquisition, *v. The Encyclopaedia of Islam*, new edn., s.v. "Miḥna," by Martin Hinds.

[49] Al-'Abbādī, *Ṭabaqāt*, 37; Ibn 'Abd al-Barr, *Intiqā'*, 107f; al-Nawawī, *Tahdhīb* 2:257.

[50] Al-Khalīlī, *Irshād fī ma'rifat 'ulamā' al-ḥadīth*, abr. al-Silafī, Aya Sofya (Istanbul) 2951, 101a. Abū 'Ubayd highly praised Muḥammad al-Shaybānī, according to al-Khaṭīb al-Baghdādī, *Tārīkh* 2:175. Al-Dhahabī lists him among al-Shaybānī's students, *Siyar* 9 (ed. Kāmil al-Kharrāṭ, 1982):135.

Wāqidī (d. Baghdad, 207/823).[51] A tenth-century grammarian states that he merely took his jurisprudence from Mālik and al-Shāfi'ī, repeating what they had said rather than coming up with his own doctrine but then fitting it out with literary citations.[52] Abū 'Ubayd must certainly have known something of jurisprudence, for at least two men are remembered as having learnt jurisprudence from him, mainly the Nishapuran Aḥmad ibn Naṣr al-Muqri' (d. 245/860)[53] and the Baghdadi Aḥmad ibn Yūsuf (d. 273/886-887).[54] Additionally, I have come across another Baghdadi, Muḥammad ibn al-Ḥasan ibn Ḥaydarah (d. 287/900), who was said to have practiced jurisprudence after his books.[55]

Specific identifications of Abū 'Ubayd's contribution almost always point to *Gharīb al-ḥadīth*; for example,

> God obliged this community with four in their time: with al-Shāfi'ī, from whom is learnt *fiqh* according to hadith; with Aḥmad, who stood firm during the Inquisition; with Yaḥyá ibn Ma'īn, who deflected lying from hadith; and with Abū 'Ubayd, who explained rare locutions.[56]

Abū 'Ubayd must have known many hadith reports, as the basis of his philological work, but not enough that he appears in a single chain in the Six Books, for example. Probably, his high repute in philology became a juridical reputation because traditionalists considered expertise in hadith more or less equivalent to expertise in the law—a position not widely shared after the later ninth century, when Abū 'Ubayd's reputation as a jurisprudent seems to have declined.[57]

Another Baghdadi usually reckoned among the disciples of al-Shā-

---

[51] Al-Khaṭīb al-Baghdādī, *Tārīkh* 3:11f; Ibn Ḥajar, *Tahdhīb* 9:366.

[52] Ibn Darastawayh (d. 347/958), *apud* al-Khaṭīb al-Baghdādī, *Tārīkh Baghdād* 12:405.

[53] Al-Dhahabī, *Siyar* 12 (ed. Ṣāliḥ al-Samr):239.

[54] Al-Dhahabī, *Tārīkh* 20 (A.H. 261-280):291.

[55] Al-Khaṭīb al-Baghdādī, *Tārīkh* 2:185.

[56] Opinion of Hilāl ibn al-'Alā' al-Raqqī, *apud* al-Khaṭīb al-Baghdādī, *Tārīkh Baghdād* 12:410, ll. 11-17. Cf. Abū Qudāmah: "Al-Shāfi'ī understood the most, but knew little hadith; Aḥmad was the most prudent; Isḥāq (ibn Rāhawayh) had memorized the most; and Abū 'Ubayd was the most knowledgeable of them of the words of the Arabs," *loc. cit.*, ll. 17-22.

[57] *V.* the disparaging remarks of Ibn Surayj and al-Ṭabarī, *apud* al-Dhahabī, *Siyar* 13 (ed. 'Alī Abū Zayd, 1983):102, 301.

fi'ī was Abū 'Abd al-Raḥmān al-Shāfi'ī (d. after 221/836). According to Ibn 'Abd al-Barr, Abū 'Abd al-Raḥmān was the first to follow al-Shāfi'ī in Iraq, and later defended his principles and fought for his position.[58] Ibn Kathīr relates that he was always faithful to al-Shāfi'ī in jurisprudence, and that his opinions were heeded to his own day (the fourteenth century).[59] The famous Iraqi traditionist Abū Dāwūd al-Sijistānī, close to the Ḥanābilah of Baghdad, described him as "a man not praiseworthy: Abū 'Abd al-Raḥmān . . . called 'the Shāfi'i,' for he would invert things and upheld Mu'tazilism."[60] He has been placed in Baghdad at the trial of Aḥmad ibn Ḥanbal before al-Mu'taṣim, when he and a Ghassān (possibly the Kufan qadi Ghassān ibn Muḥammad) argued privately with Aḥmad in a futile attempt to persuade him to confess the Qur'an created.[61] Al-Subkī provides one example (concerning divorce) of his juridical position, one that relies on what the Shāfi'īyah would call a falsified hadith report but that does agree, interestingly, with the Ẓāhiri position.[62] No students of his can be identified save, according to al-Dhahabī, Dāwūd al-Ẓāhirī.[63] His identification with Mu'tazilism at least confirms Ḥanbali fears that any interest in *kalām* might lead to heresy. The association with Ẓāhirism might indicate that this was al-Shāfi'ī's own early position (or close to it), taken up from him by both Abū 'Abd al-Raḥmān and Dāwūd al-Ẓāhirī.

---

[58] *Apud* Ibn Ḥajar, *Lisān* 7:76.

[59] Ibn Kathīr, *Ṭabaqāt al-fuqahā' al-shāfi'īyīn*, ed. Aḥmad 'Umar Hāshim & Muḥammad Zaynuhum Muḥammad 'Azib, 3 vols. (al-Ẓāhir, Egypt: Maktabat al-Thaqāfah al-Dīnīyah, 1993), 1:116.

[60] Al-Subkī, *Ṭabaqāt* 2:65.

[61] Ṣāliḥ ibn Aḥmad and Abū Nu'aym say "*ṣāḥib al-Shāfi'ī wa-Ghassān*": Ṣāliḥ ibn Aḥmad, *Sīrat al-imām Aḥmad ibn Ḥanbal*, ed. Fu'ād 'Abd al-Mun'im Aḥmad (Alexandria: Mu'assasat Shabāb al-Jāmi'ah, 1981), 59; Abū Nu'aym, *Ḥilyat al-awliyā'*, 10 vols. (Cairo: Maṭba'at al-Sa'ādah, 1932-38), 9:200. Ḥanbal ibn Isḥāq says "*Ghassān wa-al-shāfi'ī al-a'má*": *Dhikr miḥnat al-imām Aḥmad ibn Ḥanbal*, ed. Muḥammad Naghash (Cairo: Dār Nashr al-Thaqāfah, 1977), 54. Al-Khaṭīb al-Baghdādī states that Abū 'Abd al-Raḥmān was weak-sighted, *Tārīkh* 5:200. *V.* also Abū Nu'aym, *Ḥilyah* 9:186, relating the story that when Aḥmad was brought before the caliph (al-Mu'taṣim), he looked at Abū 'Abd al-Raḥmān al-Shāfi'ī and asked him, "What do you remember from al-Shāfi'ī regarding the wiping off of one's shoes?" The question may have implied that Abū 'Abd al-Raḥmān had strayed towards Shiism, as Aḥmad also accused al-Shāfi'ī of having done.

[62] Al-Subkī, *Ṭabaqāt* 2:65.

[63] Al-Dhahabī, *Siyar* 10 (ed. Muḥammad Nu'aym al-'Araqasūsī, 1982):555.

THE SHĀFI'I SCHOOL OF IRAQ IN THE LATER NINTH CENTURY

The uncertainty of the connection between al-Shāfi'ī and his alleged followers in Baghdad makes it dubious to identify men as Shāfi'īyah because at some time they endorsed a position also endorsed by some allegèd Shāfi'i. Joshua Finkel identifies the littérateur al-Jāḥiẓ as a Shāfi'i in law because of his complaining that a majority of judges would execute a Muslim for the murder of a Christian.[64] It seems hard to believe that a ninth-century Muslim need even have heard of al-Shāfi'ī to make such a complaint. Louis Massignon supposes that willingness to depose a caliph betrayed Shāfi'ism, citing Abū Zur'ah al-Dimashqī's willingness to depose the regent al-Muwaffaq.[65] Actually, the deposition was also signed by leading adherents of the nascent Ḥanafi school.[66]

According to al-Subkī, Abū Ja'far al-Tirmidhī (d. 295/907) was leader (*shaykh*) of the Shāfi'īyah in Iraq before Ibn Surayj.[67] Abū Isḥāq says that no one in Iraq was superior to him (in debate).[68] Abū 'Abd Allāh al-Zubayrī (d. 320/932?) was known as a reciter of the Qur'an and a jurisprudent according to the *madhhab* of al-Shāfi'ī.[69] Al-Māwardī would refer to him in *al-Ḥāwī* as "the shaykh of our *aṣḥāb* in his time," to which al-Subkī comments that al-Māwardī must have meant the shaykh of the Basrans, being a Basran himself.[70] We can

---

[64] Joshua Finkel, "A Risāla of al-Jāḥiẓ," *Journal of the American Oriental Society* 47 (1927):329.

[65] Louis Massignon, *The Passion of al-Hallāj*, trans. Herbert Mason, Bollingen Ser. 98, 4 vols. (Princeton: Univ. Press, 1982), 2:146.

[66] Text in al-Maqrīzī, *K. al-Muqaffá al-kabīr*, ed. Muḥammad al-Ya'lawī, 8 vols. (Beirut: Dār al-Gharb al-Islāmī, 1991), 2:449f, with subscriptions of 'Ubayd Allāh ibn Muḥammad al-'Umarī, then qadi for the border and militia (d. 294/906-907), Abū Khāzim 'Abd al-Ḥamīd ibn 'Abd al-'Azīz, then qadi for Damascus, Jordan, and Palestine (d. 292/905), and Bakkār ibn Qutaybah, qadi for Old Cairo and Alexandria (d. 270/884). Massignon probably never saw *K. al-Muqaffá*. However, Ibn Abī al-Wafā' includes Ibn Zūlāq's quotation of al-Ṭaḥāwī to the effect that Bakkār did sign the deposition, which source Massignon should have seen: *al-Jawāhir al-muḍīyah*, ed. 'Abd al-Fattāḥ Muḥammad al-Ḥulw, 2 vols. (Cairo: 'Īsá al-Ḥalabī, 1978), 1:461.

[67] Al-Subkī, *Ṭabaqāt* 2:167.

[68] Abū Isḥāq, *Ṭabaqāt al-fuqahā'*, 105.

[69] Al-Khaṭīb al-Baghdādī, *Tārīkh* 8:471.

[70] Al-Subkī, *Ṭabaqāt* 3:295.

say from whom he learnt the readings of the Qur'an,[71] but no source mentions his teachers in jurisprudence. The convention of one man's leading the local adherents of a particular sort of jurisprudence was evidently established in Iraq by the early tenth century, as it may have been in Egypt a century before. The convention of each man's having an identifiable teacher and identifiable students was evidently not established until after al-Tirmidhī. If there existed in Baghdad a Shāfi'i school in the sense of a body of doctrine, which is uncertain, it plainly lacked a regular means of transmitting that doctrine from one generation to the next. That is, the classical, guild school of law did not yet exist.

THE DISCIPLES OF AL-SHĀFI'Ī IN EGYPT

The leading transmitters of al-Shāfi'ī's Egyptian teaching were traditionally six: al-Muzanī (d. 264/878?), al-Rabī' ibn Sulaymān al-Murādī (d. 270/884), al-Rabī' ibn Sulaymān al-Jīzī (d. 256/870), al-Buwayṭī (d. 231/846?), Ḥarmalah (d. 243/857), and Yūnus ibn 'Abd al-A'lá (d. 264/879).[72] From the juridical point of view, al-Muzanī was by far the most important. His *Mukhtaṣar* was the literary basis of the guild Shāfi'i school more or less founded in the next century by Ibn Surayj.[73] In theology, al-Muzanī was highly interested in *kalām*. Indeed, one famous traditionalist, Abū Zur'ah al-Rāzī (d. 264/878), avoided studying under him, for he was interested only in hadith, whereas al-Muzanī was teaching only *kalām* and disputation (*naẓar*).[74] One of his positions in *kalām* is known, and it clearly identifies him with the semi-rationalists of Baghdad: that the name is other than the named.[75] The same position was attributed to Ibn Kullāb.[76]

---

[71] Al-Dhahabī, *Siyar* 15 (ed. Ibrāhīm al-Zaybiq, 1983):57.

[72] Al-Nawawī, *Tahdhīb* 2:284.

[73] *V. infra*, chap. 5. Cf. Halm, who observes that it effectively eclipsed the works of al-Shāfi'ī himself: Heinz Halm, *Die Ausbreitung der šāfi'itischen Rechtsschule*, Beihefte zum tübinger Atlas des vorderen Orients, B (Geisteswissenschaften), 4 (Wiesbaden: Ludwig Reichert, 1974), 21.

[74] Ibn Abī Ḥātim, *K. al-Jarḥ wa-al-ta'dīl*, 9 vols. (Hyderabad: Jam'īyat Dā'irat al-Ma'ārif al-'Uthmānīyah, 1360), 2:204.

[75] Al-Khushanī, *Ṭabaqāt 'ulamā' Ifrīqīyah*, *apud* Abū al-'Arab, *Classes des savants de l'Ifriqiya*, ed. Mohammed ben Cheneb, Publications de la Facultée des lettres d'Alger, Bulletin de Correspondance africaine 51 (Paris: Leroux, 1915), 213 =

Al-Rabī' ibn Sulaymān al-Murādī is the only other Egyptian student important for the transmission of al-Shāfi'ī's juridical positions. (Traditionally, he has been credited with compiling the basic collection of al-Shāfi'ī's writings, *Kitāb al-Umm*.[77] Norman Calder guesses that the oldest strata of the extant *Kitāb al-Umm* are from the time of al-Rabī' ibn Sulaymān himself.[78] Unfortunately, although medieval Shāfi'i writers assigned a central role to al-Rabī' ibn Sulaymān's transmission of al-Shāfi'ī's doctrine, it is never *Kitāb al-Umm* they cite, so that Calder's findings do more to qualify Schacht's findings than to characterize the actual development of Shāfi'i doctrine.) However, al-Rabī' was said to know virtually nothing of jurisprudence, only hadith. In the transmission of al-Shāfi'ī's opinions, this must mean that he could relate by rote but knew nothing of combining texts to come up with answers to new problems, or even, perhaps, that he could not recall hadith reports relevant to a particular problem. There is no evidence for his tendency in *kalām*, probably indicating that he had nothing to do with it.

As for the rest, al-Rabī' ibn Sulaymān al-Jīzī seems to have been fairly insignificant in all respects. Al-Buwayṭī wrote his own *Mukhtaṣar*, but it did not survive to rival al-Muzanī's. He himself was sufficiently traditionalist to be imprisoned at the Inquisition, denounced by none other than al-Muzanī, Ḥarmalah, and al-Shāfi'ī's son.[79] Aḥmad found his learning unimpressive.[80] Ḥarmalah and Yūnus ibn 'Abd al-A'lá are said to have identified themselves with the Māliki school.[81]

---

apud Abū al-'Arab, *Quḍāt Qurṭubah wa-'Ulamā' Ifrīqiyah*, ed. 'Izzat al-'Aṭṭār al-Ḥusaynī, Min turāth al-Andalus 2 (Cairo: Maktabat al-Khānjī, 1953), 179.

[76] Al-'Abbādī, *Ṭabaqāt*, 27.

[77] V. Sezgin, *Geschichte* 1:486f.

[78] Calder, *Studies*, chap. 4, esp. 82f.

[79] Al-Dhahabī, *Tārīkh al-islām* 17 (A.H. 231-240):423f; al-Subkī, *Ṭabaqāt* 2:164

[80] Abū Bakr al-Ṣayrafī, *Sharḥ "K. Ikhtilāf al-Shāfi'ī wa-Mālik,'"* *apud* Ibn al-Ṣalāḥ, *Ṭabaqāt*, 2:684.

[81] Al-Qāḍī 'Iyāḍ, *Tartīb al-madārik*, ed. Aḥmad Bakīr Maḥmūd, 5 vols. in 3 (Beirut: Maktabat al-Ḥayāh, 1967, 1968?), 3:77, 80; cf. Ibn al-Nadīm, *Fihrist*, 234 = *f*. 6, *q*. 6, where Yūnus ibn 'Abd al-A'lá is identified as the teacher of al-Ṭabarī in Māliki jurisprudence.

THE SHĀFI'I SCHOOL IN EGYPT AFTER THE DISCIPLES OF AL-SHĀFI'Ī

It hardly appears from the biographies of those who studied under al-Shāfi'ī that the master left behind any coherent school in the later sense. The school of Ibn Surayj and his successors was based on the work of al-Shāfi'ī's Egyptian students, especially of al-Muzanī, but those Egyptian students constituted no school themselves. The unlikeness of the later ninth-century Egyptian school to the classical school of, say, eleventh-century Baghdad is nowhere plainer than in the nature of the students it formed. The only very prominent jurisprudents of the Egyptian school were the blind poet Manṣūr ibn Ismā'īl (d. 306/918-919), who enjoyed a sort of paramountcy in his time, and Ibn al-Ḥaddād (d. 345/956?). Al-Subkī states that Manṣūr learnt jurisprudence from al-Muzanī and al-Rabī', but Ibn al-Nadīm classifies him as a follower of Abū Thawr.[82] One Transoxanian is known to have learnt jurisprudence from him, Abū Aḥmad al-Mulqī (d. Istirābādh, 362/973).[83] Ibn al-Ḥaddād's *Kitāb al-Furū'* was long studied by other Shāfi'i jurisprudents, and inspired a number of commentaries.[84] He was not, however, beyond the influence of Ibn Surayj and the Shāfi'i school of Baghdad, for he spent some time in that city in 310/922-923 and sat with the leading Shāfi'i jurisprudents there.

Altogether, al-Subkī mentions nineteen Shāfi'i jurisprudents who died some time in the fourth/tenth century and seem to have lived in Egypt. A majority died in the first quarter of the century, over three-quarters in the first half. There are several qadis among them, but none except Ibn al-Ḥaddād whose teachers are named. The Egyptian Shāfi'i school never managed, then, a regular system of transmitting its doctrines, with identifiable teachers and students, and it seems to have died away like the Ḥanafi school with the advent of the Fāṭimids. The regular system of transmitting doctrine from teacher to student is a feature of the school that developed from the teaching of Ibn Surayj in Baghdad, the classical Shāfi'i school of law.

---

[82] Al-Subkī, *Ṭabaqāt* 3:478; Ibn al-Nadīm, *Fihrist*, 211 = *f.* 3, *q.* 6.

[83] Al-Idrīsī, *Tārīkh Istirābādh,*, *apud* al-Sahmī, *Tārīkh Jurjān* (Hyderabad: Maṭba'at Majlis Dā'irat al-Ma'ārif al-'Uthmānīyah, 1950), 489. Al-Idrīsī does not expressly identify Abū Aḥmad as a Shāfi'i.

[84] Kātib Çelebī, *Kitāb Kashf al-ẓunūn 'an asāmī al-kutub wa-al-funūn*, ed. Şerefettin Yaltkaya and Rifat Bilge, 2 vols. (Istanbul: Maarif Matbaası, 1941, 1943), 2:1257.

IMĀMĪYAH, MU'TAZILAH, AND OTHERS IN THE TENTH CENTURY

In the tenth century, the vague, semi-rationalist Shāfi'i school of Baghdad widened to the point of dispersion. Geographically, it travelled from Baghdad to Khurasan, Persia, and other regions of which we are less well informed. The semi-rationalists of the ninth century were not necessarily on good terms with one another; however, they did have teachers in common, starting with al-Shāfi'ī himself. Whether because the Shāfi'i school looked like a convenient cover for their rationalist theological interests or because it was sufficiently sophisticated to interest them itself, Shī'ah, Mu'tazilah, and others of increasingly disparate backgrounds pressed in. Meanwhile, the leading Iraqi semi-rationalist of the age, Abū al-Ḥasan al-Ash'arī (d. 324/935-936?), is only shakily identified with the Shāfi'i school at all.[85]

To begin with, certain semi-rationalist Imāmi Shī'ah were associated with the Shāfi'i school: the Nishapuran al-Faḍl ibn Shādhān (d. 260/873-874)[86]; one Mūsá ibn al-Ashyab (d. 339/950?)[87]; Abū al-Ḥasan Muḥammad ibn Aḥmad ibn Ibrāhīm (b. 281/894-895)[88]; al-Mas-

---

[85] Abū al-Ḥasan al-Ash'arī is claimed for the Shāfi'i school by Ibn al-Ṣalāḥ, *Ṭabaqāt*, 1:605, Ibn Kathīr, *Ṭabaqāt* 1:209, and al-Subkī, *Ṭabaqāt* 3:366. They assert that he learnt Shāfi'i jurisprudence from Abū Isḥāq al-Marwazī. He is claimed for the Ḥanafīyah by Ibn Abī al-Wafā', *Jawāhir*, ed. al-Ḥulw, 2:545; *idem*, *al-Jawāhir al-muḍīyah*, 2 vols. (Hyderabad: Dā'irat al-Ma'ārif al-Niẓāmīyah, 1914), 2:247f.

[86] *V.* Ibn al-Nadīm, *Fihrist*, 231 = *f.* 6, *q.* 6; al-Najāshī, *Rijāl*, ed. Muḥammad Jawād al-Nā'īnī, 2 vols. (Beirut: Dār al-Aḍwā', 1988), 2:168f; al-Ṭūsī, *Ikhtiyār ma'rifat al-rijāl al-ma'rūf bi-"Rijāl al-Kashshī,"* ed. Ḥasan al-Muṣṭafawī, Dānishgadah-yi ilāhīyāt va ma'ārif-i islāmī (Mashhad: Dānishgāh-i Mashhad, 1348), 540; *idem*, *al-Fihrist*, ed. Muḥammad Ṣādiq Āl Baḥr al-'Ulūm, Nashrīyāt al-maktabah al-murtaḍawīyah 95 (Najaf: n.p., 1937), 150f.

[87] Al-Mas'ūdī, *Murūj al-dhahab*, ed. C. A. C. Barbier de Meynard & B. M. M. Pavet de Courteille, 9 vols. (Paris: Imprimerie Impériale, 1861-77), 8:284 = Charles Pellat, ed., Manshūrāt al-Jāmi'ah al-lubnānīyah, Qism al-dirāsāt al-tārīkhīyah, 11, 7 vols. (Beirut: al-Jāmi'ah al-Lubnānīyah, 1973-74), 5:208; Ibn al-Nadīm, *Fihrist*, 214 = *f.* 3, *q.* 6.

[88] Ibn al-Nadīm, *Fihrist*, 197 = *f.* 5, *q.* 5. The later Imāmi al-Ṭūsī cites Ibn al-Nadīm as his authority for a different name, Abū al-Ḥusayn Muḥammad ibn Ibrāhīm ibn Yūsuf al-Kātib: al-Ṭūsī, *Fihrist*, 159f. So his name appears also in al-Najāshī, *Rijāl* 2:280. Ibn Shahrāshūb gives the name Abū al-Ḥasan Muḥammad ibn Ibrāhīm ibn Yūsuf: *Ma'ālim al-'ulamā'*, ed. Muḥammad Ṣādiq Āl Baḥr al-'Ulūm (Najaf: al-Maṭba'ah al-Ḥaydarīyah, 1961), 97.

'ūdī the littérateur (d. Giza, 345 or 346/*ca.* 957)[89]; and the Kufan Abū al-Qāsim 'Alī ibn Aḥmad (d. 352/962).[90] Adherence to the Shāfi'i school fit well with a widespread disposition among the proto-Imāmīyah toward semi-rationalism. Additionally, these Shī'ah may have been repelled by the association of Ḥanafism with *irjā'*, a largely anti-Shī'i movement. In time, however, the Shī'ah developed their own systems of jurisprudence: Abū al-'Abbās al-Ḥasanī (*fl.* mid-4th/10th cent.) taught a Zaydi system,[91] while al-Sharīf al-Murtaḍá (d. 436/1044) laid out an independent Imāmi system.[92]

As for Mu'tazilah in the Shāfi'i school, Abū 'Abd al-Raḥmān al-Shāfi'ī lived before the formation of the classical Mu'tazili school, and the identification is not to be pressed.[93] One late biographer of the Mu'tazilah would claim Abū 'Abd al-Raḥmān's student Dāwūd al-Ẓāhirī for that party, as well, but the claim seems doubtful.[94] Most of the proto-Mu'tazilah of whose juridical preferences we are informed adhered to the personal Ḥanafi school.

Less doubtful is that a number of later Mu'tazilah adhered to the personal Shāfi'i school. The Mu'tazilah of the tenth century were divided between the so-called Basran and Baghdadi schools. It would be convenient if the adherents of one school were associated with the Ḥanafi school of jurisprudence, adherents of the other with the Shāfi'i; however, such was not the case. Leading figures of both schools were Ḥanafīyah; among the Basrans, al-Jubbā'ī (d. 303/915-916),[95]

---

[89] Al-Subkī, *Ṭabaqāt* 3:456f.

[90] On the works of Abū al-Qāsim, *v.* al-Najāshī, *Rijāl* 2:96; al-Ṭūsī, *Fihrist*, 117. For more on these men, *v.* Christopher Melchert, "The Proto-Imāmīyah Between Rationalism and Traditionalism," forthcoming in *Shī'ī Islam: Faith, Experience, and Worldview*, ed. Lynda S. Clarke w/ Mahmoud Ayoub.

[91] Ibn al-Murtaḍá, *Die Klassen der Mu'taziliten*, ed. Susanna Diwald-Wilzer, Bibliotheca Islamica 21 (Wiesbaden: Franz Steiner, 1961), 114. Al-Dā'ī learnt Zaydi law from him, then transferred to al-Karkhī and the Ḥanafi school (*loc. cit.*).

[92] "The first to expatiate on the talk of the Imāmīyah concerning jurisprudence": Ibn Ḥajar, *Lisān* 4:224.

[93] *V. The Encyclopaedia of Islam*, new edn., s.v. "Mu'tazila," by D. Gimaret, for a summary of recent research (mainly by Josef van Ess).

[94] Ibn al-Murtaḍá, *Klassen*, 138.

[95] The Qadi 'Abd al-Jabbār tells a story of al-Jubbā'ī's giving opinions in a mosque, *Faḍl al-i'tizāl, apud* Sayyid, ed. & comp., *Faḍl al-i'tizāl*, 318. Al-Jubbā'ī is not acknowledged by the Ḥanafi biographer Ibn Abī al-Wafā', who admits Abū al-Qāsim al-Balkhī and other Mu'tazilah; however, a Ḥanafi affiliation is suggested by the report that Abū al-Ḥasan al-Ash'arī must have been Ḥanafi, having been

Abū 'Abd Allāh al-Baṣrī (d. 369/979-980?),[96] and Abū al-Ḥusayn al-Baṣrī (d. 426/1044)[97]; among the Baghdadis, Abū al-Qāsim al-Balkhī (d. 319/931?).[98] Other leading figures of both schools were Shāfi'īyah: of the Basrans, the vizier and littérateur al-Ṣāḥib ibn 'Abbād (d. 385/995)[99] and his protégé the Qadi 'Abd al-Jabbār (d. 415/1025?)[100]; of the Baghdadis, Ibn al-Ikhshīdh (d. 326/938?).[101] Another leader of the Baghdadis, Ibn al-Munajjim (d. 327/938-939), studied jurisprudence under al-Ṭabarī and wrote polemics in favor of his school of law.[102]

As for why Mu'tazilah should have taken up Shāfi'i jurisprudence at this time, it seems likely that rationalists began to press in under pressure of persecution. Membership in the school had been useful as a badge of orthodoxy, to fend off persecution, already by 264/877, when al-Junayd saved himself from the Sufi Inquisition of Ghulām Khalīl by asserting that he was no Sufi but a student of jurisprudence according to the school of Abū Thawr.[103] Abū Hāshim (d.

---

brought up by al-Jubbā'ī: Mas'ūd ibn Shaybah, *K. al-Ta'līm*, *apud* Ibn Abī al-Wafā', *Jawāhir*, ed. Ḥulw, 2:545; 2 (Hyd.):260.

[96] Ibn al-Nadīm, *Fihrist*, 174 = *f.* 1, *q.* 5; 'Abd al-Jabbār, *Faḍl*, 325; Ibn Abī al-Wafā', *Jawāhir* 2 (Hyd.):260.

[97] Ibn Abī al-Wafā', *Jawāhir* 2 (Hyd.):93f.

[98] Ibn Abī al-Wafā', *Jawāhir*, ed. Ḥulw, 2:296f = 1 (Hyd.):271.

[99] Ibn al-Najjār, *apud* Ibn Ḥajar, *Lisān* 1:413. As for al-Ṣāḥib ibn 'Abbād's adherence to Mu'tazilism, Abū Ḥayyān al-Tawḥīdī (a hostile source) is quoted to the effect that he sent out propagandists to commend it particularly to the grocers, druggists, bakers, and the like (*apud Lisān* 1:415). Wilferd Madelung characterizes al-Ṣāḥib ibn 'Abbād as essentially a Mu'tazili, who restricted the traditionalist wing of the Imāmīyah in Rayy ("Imāmism and Mu'tazilite Theology," *Le Shî'isme imâmite*, ed. T. Fahd [Paris: Presses universitaires de France, 1979], 20). He is also claimed by the Mu'tazili biographer al-Bayhaqī, *Sharḥ "'Uyūn al-masā'il," apud* Sayyid, ed., *Faḍl al-i'tizāl*, 381. On the other hand, any such Mu'tazili adherence is questioned by some Shī'ah; mainly, the theologian al-Shaykh al-Mufīd and the biographer Ibn Abī Ṭayy (*apud Lisān* 1:416). Ibn Ḥajar also reports a contradictory identification from Abū Ḥayyān al-Tawḥīdī, that al-Ṣāḥib ibn 'Abbād was rather a Ḥanafi. However, Ibn Ḥajar's direct quotation from Abū Ḥayyān concerns not jurisprudence but loyalty to 'Alī: "He was a Shī'i according to the doctrine of Abū Ḥanīfah and the position of the Zaydīyah" (*K. al-Atbā'*, *apud Lisān* 1:414).

[100] Al-Khaṭīb al-Baghdādī, *Tārīkh* 11:113; al-Rāfi'ī, *Tārīkh Qazvīn*, *apud* Ibn Ḥajar, *Lisān* 3:387; al-Subkī, *Ṭabaqāt* 5:97; Ibn al-Murtaḍá, *Klassen*, 112.

[101] Ibn Ḥazm, *apud* Ibn Ḥajar, *Lisān* 1:231.

[102] Ibn Ḥajar, *Lisān* 1:324, perhaps quoting al-Marzubānī, *Mu'jam*; Ibn al-Nadīm, *Fihrist*, 144 = *f.* 3, *q.* 3.

[103] Ibn 'Aṭā', *apud* Ibn al-Jawzī, *Talbīs Iblīs* (Cairo: Idārat al-Ṭibā'ah al-Munīrī-

321/933), leader in his time of the Basran Mu'tazili school, identified himself as a grammarian when he came to Baghdad in order to avoid persecution by the Ḥanābilah.[104] It may be, too, that shifts in Mu'tazili thought made adherence to a semi-rationalist school of law more attractive than hitherto.

Meanwhile, the Shāfi'i guild school grew from the work of Ibn Surayj (d. 306/918): a school with a fairly regular method of forming jurisprudents, a strong interest in *uṣūl al-fiqh* along Shāfi'i lines, but less strongly identified with any tendency in theology than the wider Shāfi'i school of the ninth century. Between the numbers of Shī'ah and Mu'tazilah pressing into the school and the growing rivalry of Ibn Surayj's purely juridical school, the semi-rationalist Shāfi'i school of law and theology effectively broke up over the tenth and eleventh centuries.

---

yah, 1368), 167 = ed. Khayr al-Dīn 'Alī (Beirut: Dār al-Wa'y al-'Arabī, 1970?), 193. For the Inquisition of Ghulām Khalīl, *v.* Carl Ernst, *Words of Ecstasy* (Albany: State Univ. of New York Press, 1985), 101; Christopher Melchert, "The Transition From Asceticism to Mysticism at the Middle of the Ninth Century C.E.," *Studia Islamica* 83 (1996):65f.

[104] Abū al-Ḥasan Ibn al-Azraq, *apud* 'Abd al-Jabbār, *Faḍl*, 307.

CHAPTER FIVE

IBN SURAYJ
AND THE CLASSICAL SHĀFI'I SCHOOL

It is clear that in neither Iraq nor Egypt did there flourish, in the ninth century, a continuous Shāfi'i school in the later sense. The classical Shāfi'i guild school dates back, in most of its essentials, not all the way to al-Shāfi'ī but to Abū al-'Abbās Ibn Surayj (d. Baghdad, 306/918). From his time forward, Shāfi'i jurisprudents have normally had an identifiable teacher and identifiable students. Before his time, the learning of Shāfi'i jurisprudence was less like the learning of Ḥanafi jurisprudence, organized as a regular course of study under one teacher, than like the gathering of hadith reports from a number of teachers, the more the better. From his time forward, there was a normal course of advanced study leading to the production of a *ta'līqah*, virtually a doctoral dissertation, describing the juridical opinions chosen by the Shāfi'i school. No such literary production regularly characterized the study of law before Ibn Surayj. It was a mark of the classical school of law that it had a local chief, and Ibn Surayj seems to be the first jurisprudent described as having the chieftaincy of the Shāfi'īyah. From his time forward, someone was usually identified as having inherited that title, but no one before him is said to have had it. Finally, from his time forward, Shāfi'i jurisprudents were usually but not necessarily familiar with Sunni *kalām* theology. Before him, al-Karābīsī, Abū Thawr, and Dāwūd al-Ẓāhirī in Baghdad and al-Muzanī in Old Cairo had pursued *kalām*, but with less success in persuading traditionalists of their orthodoxy. After Ibn Surayj, indeed, the Shāfi'īyah continued to find difficulty in persuading Ḥanbali traditionalists in Baghdad; yet for only a short time was there trouble in Egypt and Khurasan. The only marks of the classical school of law that did not appear first in the lifetime of Ibn Surayj were explicit distinction between graduate students (*aṣḥāb*) and undergraduates (*talāmīdh*) and the biographical dictionary of adherents of the school. The first appeared with a student of his, the second about a century after his death.

IBN SURAYJ AS JURISPRUDENT

Abū al-'Abbās Ibn Surayj was born in Baghdad in 249/863-864. Nothing can be said of his parents. His formation seems to have been entirely in Baghdad. Al-Khaṭīb al-Baghdādī reports that he began early to hear hadith, but nothing indicates that he travelled widely in search of it. Al-Khaṭīb names four traditionists from whom he related a little, but reports no opinions of his reliability from *rijāl* critics.[1] His name does not appear in Ibn Ḥajar, *Lisān "al-Mīzān,"* the comprehensive digest of *rijāl* criticism for men not found in the Six Books.

Ibn Surayj is continually said to have learnt jurisprudence from (*tafaqqaha 'alá*) Abū al-Qāsim al-Anmāṭī (d. Baghdad, 281/893-894?), who in turn is always identified as the *ustādh* (teacher) of Ibn Surayj. Al-Anmāṭī is usually said to have learnt the jurisprudence of al-Shāfi'ī from al-Rabī' and al-Muzanī in Egypt. Additionally, Muḥammad ibn Jarīr al-Ṭabarī (d. Baghdad, 310/923) asserted that he himself had taught al-Anmāṭī what he knew of Shāfi'i jurisprudence.[2] Such is just what we should expect if Ibn Surayj indeed established a new style of teaching jurisprudence: he must have named his own teacher, as his students would name him, but his teacher's own training was unsystematic and vaguely known. Additionally, an early source names one Abū al-Ḥasan al-Mundhirī as the *ustādh* of Ibn Surayj.[3] He is otherwise completely unknown. Al-Mundhirī wrote some sort of handbook of Shāfi'i doctrine like the *Mukhtaṣar* of al-Muzanī. Ibn Surayj would also write a *Mukhtaṣar*, and perhaps this was the origin of his practice.

A Māliki source tells us that Ibn Surayj worked for a time as secretary for the qadi Ismā'īl ibn Isḥāq (d. Baghdad, 282/896).[4] Ismā'īl ibn Isḥāq was first elevated to the judgeship under al-Mutawakkil, in 246/860-861. From 258/871-872 until his death, he was qadi for

---

[1] Al-Khaṭīb al-Baghdādī, *Tārīkh Baghdād*, 14 vols. (Cairo: Maktabat al-Khānjī, 1931), 4:287.

[2] Al-Dhahabī, *Siyar a'lām al-nubalā'*, 25 vols. (Beirut: Mu'assasat al-Risālah), 14 (ed. Akram al-Būshayyī, 1983):275.

[3] Al-'Abbādī, *K. Ṭabaqāt al-fuqahā' al-shāfi'īyah*, ed. Gösta Vitestam, Veröffentlichungen der "De Goeje Stiftung," 21 (Leiden: E. J. Brill, 1964), 51.

[4] Al-Qāḍī 'Iyāḍ, *Tartīb al-madārik*, ed. Aḥmad Bakīr Maḥmūd, 5 vols. (Beirut: Maktabat al-Ḥayāh, 1967-1968?), 3:178.

the West Side and more powerful than the nominal chief qadi, Ibn Abī al-Shawārib. I shall say more of Ismā'īl ibn Isḥāq in Chapter Eight; however, it needs stating here that he was formed by the Māliki school of Basra, particularly its wing that inclined toward *ra'y* more than *ḥadīth*; that is, he was of the Māliki party more interested in the ramifications of the law, on the one hand, than the Prophetic and other hadith reports, of the party that laid more stress on knowing and following the doctrine of previous jurists (especially Mālik), on the other hand, than on knowing the diverse ancient sources and choosing one's own solutions to problems as they arose. His position concerning hadith science must then have been close to that of Ibn Surayj.

Ibn Surayj was himself appointed qadi for Shiraz.[5] There is little evidence concerning his judgeship. Al-Subkī guesses that it was early in his career, although mainly to make way for a dubious story of his refusing another judicial appointment.[6] One would guess the appointment came through the influence of the qadi Ismā'īl ibn Isḥāq. However, Massignon guesses it was A.H. 296-301, near the end of Ibn Surayj's life.[7] Indeed, the Persian mystic Ibn Khafīf (d. 371/982) is said to have studied under him there, which would have to have been very late in Ibn Surayj's life.[8] Ibn Khayrān (d. 320/932), a contemporary among the Shāfi'i jurisprudents of Baghdad, is remembered as bitterly deprecating Ibn Surayj's acceptance of a judgeship: "This matter did not use to be found among our comrades, but only the followers of Abū Ḥanīfah."[9] As Heinz Halm has suggested, he does not refer to any formal Shāfi'i doctrine but rather the sentiment of a grouping within the traditionalist camp of Baghdad.[10] His complaint

---

[5] Abū Isḥāq al-Shīrāzī, *Ṭabaqāt al-fuqahā'*, ed. Iḥsān 'Abbās (Beirut: Dār al-Rā'id al-'Arabī, 1970), 109.

[6] Al-Subkī, *Ṭabaqāt al-shāfi'īyah al-kubrá*, ed. Maḥmūd Muḥammad al-Ṭanāḥī & 'Abd al-Fattāḥ al-Ḥulw, 10 vols. (Cairo: 'Īsá al-Bābī al-Ḥalabī, 1964-1976), 3:22.

[7] Louis Massignon, *The Passion of al-Hallāj*, trans. Herbert Mason, Bollingen ser. 98, 4 vols. (Princeton: Univ. Press, 1982), 2:183.

[8] Al-Dhahabī, *Tārīkh al-islām*, ed. 'Umar 'Abd al-Salām Tadmurī, 40 vols. to date (Beirut: Dār al-Kitāb al-'Arabī, 1987-), 26 (A.H. 351-380):503, 509f.

[9] Abū Isḥāq, *Ṭabaqāt*, 110.

[10] Heinz Halm, *Die Ausbreitung der šāfi'itischen Rechtsschule*, Beihefte zum tübinger Atlas des vorderen Orients, B, 4 (Wiesbaden: Ludwig Reichert, 1974), 27. But cf. Ibn Khuzaymah, who, charged by the first Samanid governor of Khurasan to

does indicate how Ibn Surayj's program meant a marked reduction of tension with the world and a shift toward the traditional Ḥanafi position.

The juridical works of Ibn Surayj survive mainly in quotation, and the quotations are difficult to assess.[11] In the first place, we know too little of Islamic jurisprudence to tell the importance of any particular opinion; for example, that, failing unambiguous indications, one should determine the direction of Mecca for oneself if there is much time, accept another's determination of the direction of Mecca if time is short, *contra* Abū Isḥāq al-Marwazī, who says one should determine the direction for oneself, and al-Muzanī, who says one should accept another's determination.[12] Sometimes, different authorities will quote him differently.[13] In the second, what survives in quotation may not indicate his actual importance. Abū Ḥāmid al-Isfarāyinī, most highly regarded Iraqi Shāfi'i of his time (d. Baghdad, 406/1016), would say, "We go along with Abū al-'Abbās (Ibn Surayj) on the broad outlines of jurisprudence, not the details (*najrī ma'a Abī al-'Abbās fī ẓawāhir al-fiqh dūna al-daqā'iq*)"[14] In scattered quotations concerning particular problems, it is precisely the broad outlines that are least likely to survive.

The biographical literature does suggest some of the broad outlines. One concerns the relations between Ibn Surayj's Shāfi'ism and other schools. On the one hand, Ibn Surayj defined his jurisprudence by opposition to the Ḥanafi and Ẓāhiri schools. Of the five books

choose a qadi for Nishapur, nominated Ḥanafīyah: Ibn Abī al-Wafā', *al-Jawāhir al-muḍīyah*, ed. 'Abd al-Fattāḥ Muḥammad al-Ḥulw, 2 vols. (Cairo: 'Īsá al-Bābī al-Ḥalabī, 1978), 2:310f; (Hyderabad: Majlis Dā'irat al-Ma'ārif al-Niẓāmīyah, 1332) 2:55.

[11] The only work extant in manuscript seems to be *K. al-Aqsām wa-al-khiṣāl*, 43 ff., Chester Beatty 5115, not published. I have been able to examine the fascicle mentioned by Sezgin, *Geschichte des arabischen Schrifttums*, 9 vols. (Leiden: E. J. Brill, 1967-), 1:495, *Ajwibat Abī al-'Abbās*, &c., Şehit Ali 2763/4: the attribution to Ibn Surayj is extremely dubious.

[12] Abū Isḥāq al-Shīrāzī, *al-Muhadhdhab*, 2 vols. (Cairo: 'Īsá al-Bābī al-Ḥalabī, n.d.), 1:68.

[13] E.g., Abū Ḥāmid al-Isfarāyinī and al-Māwardī would report that he held a certain sort of water not usable for ritual ablutions, al-Bandanījī and the author of *al-Ibānah* that he did hold it usable: al-Nawawī, *al-Majmū'*, ed. Zakarīyā' 'Alī Yūsuf, 9 vols. + continuations (Cairo: Maṭba'at al-'Āṣimah, 1966-, & Maṭba'at al-Imām, n.d.), 1:211.

[14] Abū Isḥāq, *Ṭabaqāt*, 109.

whose titles Ibn al-Nadīm presents, two are refutations of Ḥanafi doctrine.[15] "He composed books," says al-Khaṭīb, "to refute those who disagreed by way of the people of *ra'y* and the adherents of the *ẓāhir*."[16] On the other hand, Ibn Surayj evidently took his juridical categories from Muḥammad ibn al-Ḥasan al-Shaybānī, as al-Muzanī and, indeed, al-Shāfi'ī himself had done.[17] One of his books, a large one, was called *al-Tawassuṭ bayna Muḥammad ibn al-Ḥasan wa-al-qāḍī Ismā'īl*, or "Placing oneself in the middle between Muḥammad ibn al-Ḥasan and Ismā'īl (ibn Isḥāq)."[18] Plainly, Ibn Surayj meant to establish a position intermediate between the Iraqi and Medinese, Ḥanafi and Māliki. Significantly, this was to establish a position intermediate between two adherents of *ra'y* rather than *ḥadīth*, unlike the looser traditionalist Shāfi'ism that stood for *ḥadīth* against *ra'y*.

The biographical literature also suggests that Ibn Surayj placed great emphasis on the jurisprudence of al-Shāfi'ī himself. This was somewhat in the spirit of Asad ibn al-Furāt and Saḥnūn as they sought out the true teaching of Mālik in Egypt. Another of the five books that Ibn al-Nadīm names in his entry on Ibn Surayj is *Kitāb al-Taqrīb bayna al-Muzanī wa-al-Shāfi'ī*, evidently a reconciliation of apparent differences between the two.[19] Al-Khaṭīb al-Baghdādī quotes the conclusion to a debate between Ibn Surayj and his contemporary Abū Sa'īd al-Iṣṭakhrī (d. Baghdad, 328/940): Ibn Surayj uses insulting language and blames him for giving other than the position of al-Shāfi'ī—not, as a pure traditionalist might have complained, for neglecting the evidence of the Book, the Sunnah, or what the Companions said.[20] Al-Subkī quotes Ibn Surayj as boasting,

> On the Day of the Resurrection, al-Shāfi'ī will be brought forth and with him al-Muzanī. He will say, "This one has corrupted my sciences." I shall say, "Be clement toward Abū Ibrāhīm, for I have

---

[15] *K. al-Radd 'alá Muḥammad ibn al-Ḥasan* and *K. al-Radd 'alá 'Īsá ibn Abān*: Ibn al-Nadīm, *Kitâb al-Fihrist*, ed. Gustav Flügel, w/ Johannes Roediger & August Mueller (Leipzig: F. C. W. Vogel, 1872), 213 = *fann* 3, *maqālah* 6.

[16] Al-Khaṭīb al-Baghdādī, *Tārīkh*, 4:287.

[17] *Farra'a 'alá kutub Muḥammad ibn al-Ḥasan*; i.e., ramified the problems raised in his books: Abū Isḥāq, *Ṭabaqāt*, 109.

[18] Al-Qāḍī 'Iyāḍ, *Tartīb* 3:178.

[19] Ibn al-Nadīm, *Fihrist*, 213 = *f.* 3, *q.* 6.

[20] Al-Khaṭīb al-Baghdādī, *Tārīkh* 7:269.

not ceased to repair what he corrupted."[21]

In al-Subkī's estimation, Ibn Surayj differed as often as al-Muzanī with the known positions of al-Shāfi'ī, more often than the great Shāfi'i jurisprudents of the eleventh century; however, he differed much less often than his contemporaries Muḥammad ibn Naṣr al-Marwazī, al-Ṭabarī, Ibn Khuzaymah, and Ibn al-Mundhir.[22] That is, he started a trend toward closer adherence to what al-Shāfi'ī had taught, reversing the tendency of the looser Shāfi'i school of his time.

TEACHERS AND STUDENTS

Al-Subkī names fifteen who studied under Ibn Surayj (*tafaqqaha 'alayh*), and other sources name half as many more.

The Students of Ibn Surayj

Abū Bakr Aḥmad ibn al-Ḥasan ibn Sahl *al-Fārisī* (d. 305/917-918?), the first to teach Shāfi'i law in Balkh, 2:185. (Also reported to have learnt Shāfi'i jurisprudence directly from al-Muzanī.) Mu'tazili.[23]

Abū al-Ṭayyib Muḥammad ibn al-Faḍl (al-Mufaḍḍal) *ibn Salamah* (d. 308/920), no entry in al-Subkī.[24]

Muḥammad ibn Ja'far *Ibn Abī al-Qāḍī* (d. 318/930), of Khʷārizm, 3:129f.

Abū 'Alī Aḥmad ibn Muḥammad ibn al-Qāsim *al-Rūdhabārī* (d. Old Cairo, 322 or 323/*ca.* 934), Baghdadi Sufi, 3:48-54.

Abū Ghānim 'Umar ibn Muḥammad ibn Mas'ūd (n.d.), *mulqī* to Ibn Surayj, which al-Subkī guesses to mean something like *mu'īd* of later date, 3:471.

---

[21] Al-Subkī, *Ṭabaqāt* 3:23.
[22] Al-Subkī, *Ṭabaqāt* 2:104.
[23] 'Abd al-Jabbār, *Faḍl al-i'tizāl, apud Faḍl al-i'tizāl*, ed. & comp. Fu'ād Sayyid (Tunis: al-Dār al-Tūnisīyah lil-Nashr, 1974), 321.
[24] Al-Khaṭīb al-Baghdādī, *Tārīkh* 3:308; Abū Isḥāq, *Ṭabaqāt*, 109. Cf. al-'Abbādī, *Ṭabaqāt*, 72, where no teacher is mentioned.

Abū al-Ṭayyib al-Baghdādī (n.d.), *mulqī* to Ibn Surayj, which according to al-Sam'ānī means that he was charged with repetition; also said to have been his student.[25]

Abū Ja'far Muḥammad ibn Ja'far ibn Muḥammad *Ibn Khāzim* (d. 324/935-936), of Gurgan, 3:130.

Abū al-Ḥasan Muḥammad ibn Shu'ayb ibn Ibrāhīm *al-Bayhaqi* (d. 324/935-936), Nishapuran, 3:173. Studied under both Ibn Khuzaymah and Ibn Surayj.

Abū al-Ḥasan 'Alī ibn al-Ḥasan ibn Muḥammad *al-Sanjānī* al-Marwazī (*fl.* 316/928-929, d. mid-320's?), qadi for Nishapur from 316, 3:444f.[26]

Abū al-Ḥusayn Muḥammad ibn Yaḥyá ibn Zakarīyā' al-Rāzī (d. 328/939-940?), studied under Ibn Surayj until his death, then went on to become qadi for Qazvin, A.H. 323-327, and for Hamadhan.[27]

Abū Bakr Aḥmad ibn Ibrāhīm ibn Nawmard (d. 329/940-941), of Gurgan, 3:9.[28]

Abū Ḥafṣ 'Umar ibn Aḥmad (n.d.), son of Ibn Surayj, 3:469.

Abū Bakr Muḥammad ibn 'Abd Allāh *al-Ṣayrafī* (d. 330/941-942), Baghdadi Ash'ari, 3:186f.

Abū Wā'il *'Awf ibn 'Īsá* al-Farghānī (n.d.), sat with Ibn Surayj, then moved to Egypt.[29]

Abū al-'Abbās Muḥammad ibn Ibrāhīm ibn Ḥushmard al-Bakrābādhī (n.d.), of Gurgan.[30]

Aḥmad Ibn Abī Aḥmad *Ibn al-Qāṣṣ* (d. Tarsus, 335/946-947?),

---

[25] Al-Sam'ānī, *al-Ansāb*, E. J. W. Gibb Memorial Ser. 20 (Leiden: E. J. Brill, 1912), 532a.

[26] But he learnt jurisprudence from Muḥammad ibn Naṣr al-Marwazī, according to al-Asnawī, *Ṭabaqāt al-shāfi'īyah*, ed. 'Abd Allāh al-Jabbūrī, Iḥyā' al-Turāth al-Islāmī, 2 vols. (Baghdad: Dīwān al-Awqāf, 1971), 2:34.

[27] Al-Khalīlī, *al-Irshād fī ma'rifat 'ulamā' al-ḥadīth*, abr. al-Silafī, Aya Sofya 2951, 135b; same in al-Dhahabī, *Siyar* 15 (ed. Ibrāhīm al-Zaybaq, 1983):379.

[28] Cf. al-Sahmī, *Tārīkh Jurjān* (Hyderabad: Maṭba'at Majlis Dā'irat al-Ma'ārif al-'Uthmānīyah, 1950), 49f.

[29] Al-Khaṭīb al-Baghdādī, *Tārīkh* 12:292, based on Ibn Yūnus.

[30] Al-Sahmī, *Tārīkh*, 373.

from Tabaristan, 3:59-63.

Muḥammad ibn Yaḥyá (d. 338/949-950?), qadi for Qazvin.[31]

Abū Isḥāq Ibrāhīm ibn Aḥmad *al-Marwazī* (d. Ḥulwān, Egypt, 340/951), Ash'ari.[32]

Abū 'Alī al-Ḥasan ibn al-Ḥusayn *Ibn Abī Hurayrah* (d. 345/956), Baghdadi, 3:256-263. Studied under both Ibn Surayj and Abū Isḥāq al-Marwazī (256).

Abū Ḥāmid Aḥmad ibn Muḥammad ibn Ismā'īl al-Ismā'īlī (d. 345/956-957), Tabaristāni, 3:40.

'Alī ibn al-Ḥasan (al-Ḥusayn) *al-Mas'ūdī* (d. 345 or 346/*ca.* 957), 3:456f, said to be Mu'tazili. Dictated a letter from Ibn Surayj to the Muslims of Shash.

Abū Bakr Muḥammad ibn Yaḥyá ibn al-Nu'mān al-Hamadhānī (d. 347/959).[33]

Abū al-Walīd Ḥassān ibn Muḥammad ibn Aḥmad *al-Naysābūrī* (d. 349/960), Nishapuran, 3:225-229. *Tilmīdh* to Ibn Surayj. *Imām* of *ahl al-ḥadīth*, according to al-Ḥākim (226).

Abū al-Ḥusayn Aḥmad ibn Muḥammad *Ibn al-Qaṭṭān al-Baghdādī* (d. 359/970), no separate entry, but mentioned 3:346.

Abū Bakr Muḥammad ibn 'Alī ibn Ismā'īl *al-Qaffāl al-Shāshī al-Kabīr* (d. 365/976?), Transoxanian, 3:200-222. At first Mu'tazili, then Ash'ari.

Muḥammad *ibn Khafīf* (d. Shiraz, 371/982), the Sufi, 3:149-163. Al-Subkī names no teacher, but other authorities quote a disciple as saying Ibn Khafīf studied under Ibn Surayj when he was a qadi in Shiraz.[34]

Abū Ja'far al-Istirābādhī (d. later tenth century?), Khurasani.[35]

---

[31] Al-Khalīlī, *Irshād*, 135b; *apud* al-Dhahabī, *Siyar* 15:379.

[32] Al-'Abbādī, *Ṭabaqāt*, 68f; al-Khaṭīb al-Baghdādī, *Tārīkh* 6:11; Abū Isḥāq, *Ṭabaqāt*, 112.

[33] Al-Asnawī, *Ṭabaqāt* 2:525.

[34] Ibn al-Ṣalāḥ, *Ṭabaqāt al-shāfi'īyah*, ed. al-Nawawī, Hamidiye (Istanbul) 537, 20b. *V.* also note 8, *supra*.

[35] Al-Asnawī, *Ṭabaqāt* 1:48.

It seems unlikely that the littérateur al-Mas'ūdī received any license to teach. Al-Qaffāl al-Shāshī is said by some sources to have studied under Ibn Surayj but by others to have studied rather under those who had studied under Ibn Surayj.[36] It seems more likely that he studied under the students. Al-Istirābādhī likewise seems too late to have studied under Ibn Surayj.[37] On the other hand, one might add to the list Abū Muḥammad al-Ḥaddād (d. 320's/932-941?), Basran qadi, author of *Adab al-qaḍā'*, who al-Subkī says related hadith of Ibn Surayj, among others. One might also add Abū 'Alī al-Thaqafī (d. Nishapur, 328/940), Sufi and *mutakallim*, who certainly studied under Ibn Surayj in Iraq, although al-Subkī does not use the term *tafaqqaha 'alayh*. Even without these names, though, Ibn Surayj's recorded activity was very great. Al-Subkī has entries for 74 Shāfi'i jurisprudents who died between A.H. 318 and 359, inclusive: five studied under students of Ibn Surayj, two studied under Muḥammad ibn Naṣr al-Marwazī (d. Samarqand, 294/907?), and one each studied under Abū Thawr (d. Baghdad, 240/854), Manṣūr ibn Ismā'īl (d. Old Cairo, 306/918-919), and Abū 'Abd Allāh al-Zubayrī (d. Basra, 318/930-931). In the formation of Shāfi'i jurisprudents, Ibn Surayj plainly had no rival.

The geographical distribution of those who studied under Ibn Surayj (reinforced by the distribution of the students of his students) indicates where the new conception of the Shāfi'i school was welcome:

Iraq: 10 (+ 12 students of students)
Jibal: 3 (+ 3)
Fars: 1
Qumis: (1)

---

[36] Abū Isḥāq al-Shīrāzī is the source of the tradition that al-Qaffāl studied under Ibn Surayj. He gives his date of death as 336/947-948, by which his meeting Ibn Surayj would be more credible (*Ṭabaqāt*, 112). Al-Ḥākim al-Naysābūrī, on the other hand, reports that he died in Shash, 365/976 (*apud* Ibn Khallikān, *Wafayāt al-a'yān*, ed. Iḥsān 'Abbās, 7 vols. + index [Beirut: Dār al-Thaqāfah, 1968], 3:338). Different biographers follow either Abū Isḥāq (e.g., al-Nawawī, *Tahdhīb al-asmā' wa-al-lughāt*, 2 vols. in 3 [Cairo: Idārat al-Ṭibā'ah al-Munīrīyah, 1927], 2:282) or al-Ḥākim (e.g., al-Sam'ānī, *Ansāb*, 325a). Ibn al-Ṣalāḥ doubts whether he met Ibn Surayj (36b), and he is followed by al-Subkī, who states that he must have been seven at the time of Ibn Surayj's death, although he gives al-Qaffāl's date of death as the end of 336 (*Ṭabaqāt* 3:222).

[37] Al-Asnawī states definitely that Ibn al-Qaṭṭān was the last of the *aṣḥāb* of Ibn Surayj (*Ṭabaqāt* 2:298).

Tabaristan: 2
Gurgan: 3 (+ 3)
Khurasan: 6 (+ 14)
Khʷarizm: 1 (+ 1)
Transoxania: 1 (+ 4)
Andalusia: (1)

Syria and Egypt are missing completely: plainly, the would-be jurisprudents of those regions preferred to take their Shāfi'ism directly from the nearby students of al-Muzanī and al-Rabī', as had Ibn Surayj himself. *Kalām* seems to have been weak, in Egypt, so no *mutakallim* felt in need of any *madhhab* affiliation to protect himself, as many did in Baghdad. Moreover, al-Muzanī had set Egyptian Shāfi'ism in resolute opposition to *taqlīd*, upheld by the Egyptian Mālikīyah and al-Ṭaḥāwī, whereas the Shāfi'i tradition of Baghdad, through Abū Thawr, &al., seems not to have stressed it to the same degree; hence, although the line from Ibn Surayj was in some ways opposed to that from Abū Thawr, yet the Baghdadis were readier than the Egyptians to accept a regular school with its peculiar choices and deliberate adjustment to what al-Shāfi'ī himself had reportedly said.

The strength of Egyptian traditionalism may also have prevented the Surayji Shāfi'īyah from receiving the sort of patronage that the Baghdadis enjoyed from 'Alī ibn 'Īsá and others. Abū Isḥāq al-Marwazī emigrated to Egypt and caused a riot in Old Cairo by reading from a book of his on the *sunan*. According to al-Dhahabī, it mentioned *al-istiwā'* (God's sitting on his throne), and therefore was rejected by the Mu'tazilah.[38] It seems hard to believe, though, that the local Mu'tazilah were so strong; moreover, as an Ash'ari, Abū Isḥāq was even more likely to arouse the local traditionalists. Baghdadi Ḥanābilah had incited blind men to assault the Shāfi'īyah in 323/835, although Abū Isḥāq evidently did not travel to Egypt before early 329/October 940.[39] The effective ruler of Egypt, Kāfūr, had evidently heard of Abū Isḥāq's book and written him before the riot not to publicize it.[40] Had he even invited Abū Isḥāq to come? The Egyp-

---

[38] Al-Dhahabī, *Siyar* 15:429f.
[39] Ibn al-Athīr, *al-Kāmil fī al-tārīkh*, *s.a.* 323; ed. C. J. Tornberg, 13 vols. (Beirut: Dār Ṣādir, 1965-1967), 8:308. For 329/940, *v.* al-Khaṭīb al-Baghdādī, *Tārīkh* 11:137, ll. 5f, *contra* Massignon, who dates Abū Isḥāq's emigration to 317/929: *Passion*, trans. Mason, 1:372.
[40] Al-Dhahabī, *Siyar* 15:430.

tians considered him sufficiently close to al-Shāfi'ī that they buried him near the imam's tomb[41]; however, no line of Egyptian Shāfi'īyah begins with Abū Isḥāq, and his assistant Abū al-Ḥasan al-Māsarjisī (d. Nishapur, 383/993?) returned to Baghdad the next year to work as assistant (*mu'īd*) to Ibn Abī Hurayrah, then to Khurasan in 344/955-956.[42]

Also missing is the city of Isfahan—not only from the list of Ibn Surayj's students, but from al-Subkī's dictionary altogether. (Al-Subkī is mainly interested in the great centers, but Isfahan was at least as important a city as, for example, Hamadhan and Qazvin in the Jibal, which do appear.) Abū Nu'aym al-Iṣbahānī indicates in different books that Shāfi'ism was introduced to Isfahan either by al-Ḥasan ibn Muḥammad ibn Mazyad (d. before 280/894), in the form of reports from al-Muzanī and al-Rabī', or by Sahl ibn 'Abd Allāh (d. 270/889-890), in the form of the *Mukhtaṣar* of Ḥarmalah.[43] Another Isfahani, Muḥammad ibn 'Āṣim (d. 299/911-912), was also counted a Shāfi'i in jurisprudence, having learnt that system from the followers of al-Shāfi'ī himself, probably meaning the Egyptians.[44] The pattern was then set for Isfahanis to take their Shāfi'ism directly from Egypt, not Baghdad; however, the same might be said for the Khurasanis, yet many of them did study under Ibn Surayj or his students.

I would hazard the guess that in Isfahan, Ẓāhirism came to occupy the niche that the new Shāfi'ism did in Baghdad and Khurasan; that is, a regular school of law with a body of doctrine going back to its eponym, for men with a strong side interest in Sunni *kalām*. Unfortunately, our data for the original, Mashriqi Ẓāhiri school are extremely sparse, and no history seems possible. Abū Isḥāq al-Shīrāzī suggests that the school was strongest in Sind and Fars, but he knew the Farsi school at first hand, which may explain the attention he gives it.[45]

The situation in Khurasan is complex. On the one hand, it sent Ibn

---

[41] Al-Khaṭīb al-Baghdādī, *Tārīkh* 3:11.

[42] Al-Ḥākim al-Naysābūrī, *apud* Ibn Khallikān, *Wafayāt* 4:202; al-Asnawī, *Ṭabaqāt* 2:380.

[43] Abū Nu'aym, *Geschichte Isbahāns*, ed. Sven Dedering, 2 vols. (Leiden: E. J. Brill, 1931, 1934), 1:260 (al-Ḥasan ibn Muḥammad); *idem*, *Ḥilyat al-awliyā'*, 10 vols. (Cairo: Maṭba'at al-Sa'ādah, 1932-1938), 10:212 (Sahl ibn 'Abd Allāh).

[44] Ibn Ḥajar, *Tahdhīb "al-Tahdhīb,"* 12 vols. (Hyderabad: Majlis Dā'irat al-Ma'ārif al-Niẓāmīyah, 1325-1327), 9:241.

[45] In three generations (*Ṭabaqāt*, 177-179), thirteen Ẓāhirīyah, of whom two from Sind and six from Fars.

Surayj many students—as many as Baghdad. On the other hand, the non-Surayji Shāfi'i tradition remained strong, there. Al-Subkī has entries for some fifty Khurasani Shāfi'i jurisprudents for whom he names no particular teacher of jurisprudence, as against fourteen Khurasanis who studied under Ibn Surayj or under his students. Nearly all these fifty names are drawn from the *Tārīkh* of al-Ḥākim al-Naysābūrī, and evidently represent Shāfi'īyah of the old school; that is, men who represented themselves simply as *ahl al-ḥadīth* (Ibn al-Ṣalāḥ is tireless in reminding us that "of *ahl al-ḥadīth*," in Khurasan, means "*shāfi'ī*") and collected their jurisprudence in the old style, much as traditionists collected hadith. Al-Subkī is at no loss, thanks to al-Ḥākim, to name the shaykhs from whom they heard hadith; only, following al-Ḥākim, he says of no one shaykh *tafaqqaha 'alayh*; that is, he does not tell us from whom these men learnt jurisprudence.

The non-Surayji Shāfi'īyah of Khurasan carried on the tradition begun by Aḥmad ibn Sayyār (d. 268/881) and 'Abdān (d. 293/905-906) of Marv, 'Abd Allāh ibn Muḥammad ibn Ziyād al-Naysābūrī (*fl.* before 264/877) and Ibn Khuzaymah (d. 311 or 312/*ca.* 924) of Nishapur, who all travelled to Egypt to hear the books of al-Muzanī and al-Rabī'.[46] It was only loosely Shāfi'i in jurisprudence. Ibn Khuzaymah stated that the first to bring the *'ilm* of al-Shāfi'ī to Khurasan was Muḥammad ibn Aḥmad ibn Ḥafṣ al-Naysābūrī (d. 263/877). Al-Dhahabī comments that this meant *al-Risālah*, for Muḥammad never travelled to Egypt.[47] Ibn Khuzaymah's comment illuminates his Shāfi'ism, evidently a matter of theology more than jurisprudence. What he may have learnt from al-Muzanī, or had reinforced by him, was above all to renounce *taqlīd*: "I have not resorted to anyone's authority concerning a legal problem (*mā qalladtu aḥadan*)," he boasted, "since I was sixteen."[48] Al-Rabī' ibn Sulaymān is quoted as saying, "We benefitted from him more than he benefitted from us"; that is, he brought with him to Egypt more legal hadith reports than he brought back from there.[49] Ibn al-Ṣalāḥ and al-Subkī

[46] *Contra* Heinz Halm, who names Ibn Khuzaymah as spreading the learning of Ibn Surayj in Nishapur: *Ausbreitung*, 28. For references on Ibn Khuzaymah, *v.* Sezgin, *Geschichte* 1:601; al-Dhahabī, *Siyar* 14:365.

[47] Al-Dhahabī, *Tārīkh al-islām*, Köprülü (Istanbul) 1017, 105; cf. *Siyar* 12 (ed. Ṣāliḥ al-Samr, 1983):616f.

[48] *Apud* Abū Isḥāq, *Ṭabaqāt*, 106.

[49] Al-Dhahabī, *Siyar* 14:371.

must argue that he, like Muḥammad ibn Naṣr al-Marwazī, al-Ṭabarī, and Ibn al-Mundhir, was a follower of al-Shāfi'ī in spite of often disagreeing with him.[50]

Something closer to Surayji Shāfi'ism may have been the nascent school of Muḥammad ibn Naṣr al-Marwazī. Born in Nishapur but active mainly in Transoxania, al-Marwazī had studied in Egypt under al-Rabī' ibn Sulaymān and Ibn 'Abd al-Ḥakam. He is the only Khurasani of the century (besides certain students of Ibn Surayj's) of whom al-Subkī says expressly that someone learnt jurisprudence from him. That is, he followed the Ḥanafi tradition of teachers and students as Ibn Surayj did, too, but as Ibn Khuzaymah, for example, with his strong opposition to *taqlīd*, did not. Al-Marwazī took an interest in *kalām* as well as jurisprudence. Some of his contemporaries refused to consort with him on account of his maintaining that confession (*iqrār*), testimony (*shahādah*), and the recitation of the Qur'an with its pronunciation were all created.[51]

In the event, the nascent Marwazi school of Shāfi'ism seems to have been absorbed by the Surayji. Although al-Subkī has entries for two who studied under Muḥammad ibn Naṣr al-Marwazī, he has no entries for their students. Abū 'Alī al-Thaqafī and Abū al-Walīd, an important teacher of jurisprudence himself, joined the two traditions. Abū 'Alī apparently studied jurisprudence under al-Marwazī and Ibn Khuzaymah but must have communicated with Ibn Surayj, as well, for he is credited with being the first to bring "the sciences of al-Shāfi'ī and the minutiae of Ibn Surayj" from Iraq to Khurasan.[52] Abū al-Walīd studied first under Abū 'Alī but later under Ibn Surayj himself.[53]

The career of Abū 'Alī shows how the Khuzaymi traditionalists of Nishapur, like the Ḥanbali traditionalists of Baghdad, might establish their position by force, for a time. Abū 'Alī was one of Ibn Khuzaymah's most outstanding students, but Ibn Khuzaymah was persuaded near the end of his life to renounce him for adhering to the

[50] Ibn al-Ṣalāḥ, *Ṭabaqāt*, 48b; al-Subkī, *Ṭabaqāt* 3:102.

[51] Al-Dhahabī, *Siyar* 14:39.

[52] Al-Dhahabī, *Siyar* 14:377; cf. 15:282, where he is credited with introducing from Iraq the science of *jadal*. *V.* also, on his studying under al-Marwazī, al-'Abbādī, *Ṭabaqāt*, 49.

[53] Al-Dhahabī, *Siyar* 15:281f.

doctrine of the Kullābīyah.[54] Seventeen years later, Abū 'Alī died under virtual house arrest because of his position concerning the pronunciation of the Qur'an and other problems.[55] Extreme traditionalism ultimately proved untenable, though, and the Khuzaymi variety of Shāfi'ism faded away.

Khurasani traditionalism needs much further study, but I venture to propose two reasons why it must have faltered. On the theological plane, it must have suffered repeated embarrassments before attacks from the Ḥanafi Mu'tazilah. On the juridical plane, it must have been increasingly difficult to occlude all forms of *taqlīd*, and also to maintain the superiority of picking up one's Shāfi'ism piecemeal from shaykhs in Mecca and Egypt over learning it from one authoritative teacher at home. In other words, it suffered the same liabilities as traditionalism everywhere.

Furthermore, Khurasani traditionalists had always been less hostile to compromise than the Baghdadi. The chieftaincy of *aṣḥāb al-ḥadīth* had long been related to military power; for example, Yaḥyá ibn Muḥammad, put to death in 267/881 for leading the militia against an intruding warlord, and Ibn Khuzaymah's student Abū Bakr Ibn Abī 'Uthmān.[56] Unlike Aḥmad in Baghdad, traditionalist leaders from Isḥāq ibn Rāhawayh to Ibn Khuzaymah had associated with sultans and accepted their patronage. Therefore, it was difficult for the Khurasani traditionalists to resist the new style of legal studies, organized around a recognized chief.[57] Khurasani opposition to Ash'arism remained vigorous throughout the eleventh century, but the old style of jurisprudence was bound to become ever less prominent. (The Khurasani school so prominent in later Shāfi'i writings was not the descendant of Khuzaymi traditionalist Shāfi'ism but the product of one systematizer, al-Qaffāl al-Ṣaghīr [d. Sijistan, 417/1026]. His principal teacher was Abū Zayd al-Marwazī [d. 371/982], who studied under Abū Isḥāq

[54] Al-Ḥākim, *apud* al-Dhahabī, *Siyar* 14:379.

[55] Al-Sulamī, *Miḥan al-ṣūfīyah*, *apud* al-Dhahabī, *Siyar* 15:282.

[56] On Yaḥyá ibn Muḥammad, *v.* al-Dhahabī, *Siyar* 12 (ed. Ṣāliḥ al-Samr, 1983):285-294; on Abū Bakr Ibn Abī 'Uthmān, *v.* al-Dhahabī, *Siyar* 14:377.

[57] The term *ra'īs al-madhhab*, "chief of the school," evidently does not appear in Nishapur until about the end of the tenth century (Halm, *Ausbreitung*, 24). Before then, al-Ḥākim uses the term *imām ahl al-ḥadīth*; e.g., of Abū al-Walīd al-Naysābūrī (*apud* al-Subkī, *Ṭabaqāt* 3:226).

al-Marwazī, hence was in the Surayji tradition.[58])

Al-Qaffāl al-Shāshī was at the head of an important Shāfi'i tradition in Transoxania; however, the Surayji variety of Shāfi'ism apparently enjoyed no complete triumph in the tenth century. Al-Subkī names nine Transoxanian jurisprudents who died during the fourth century of the Hijrah (roughly the tenth century C.E.). Almost half of them studied under Ibn Surayj or under his students, a much better ratio than al-Subkī suggests for Khurasan; however, the half whose teachers he does not name includes Abū Bakr al-Ūdanī (d. Bukhara, 385/996), identified as leader (*imām*) of the Transoxanian Shāfi'īyah in his time.[59]

Finally, a survey of al-Subkī's volume on Shāfi'i jurisprudents who died in the fourth (tenth) century suggests two further locations of important activity, namely Mecca and Basra. Mecca is where a number of the traditionalist, teacherless Shāfi'īyah of Nishapur went to study, among other places, and where one shaykh that al-Subkī names lived and died.[60] Al-Shāfi'ī himself was sometimes identified as a Meccan jurisprudent,[61] and there are vestiges of Hijazi law in the doctrine of the classical school.[62] As schools were personalized, it was presumably easy to present Meccan teaching as Shāfi'i. Leading teachers in Basra were Abū 'Abd Allāh al-Zubayrī (3:295-299) and the qadi Abū al-Qāsim al-Ṣaymarī (d. after 386/996; 3:339-342). Abū Ḥāmid al-Marwarrūdhī (d. 362/972-973) was a prominent Basran who studied under Ibn Surayj (3:12f), and Abū al-Ḥasan al-Māwardī, outstanding Shāfi'i jurisprudent of the next century (d. Baghdad, 450/1058), would join the two Iraqi traditions.

---

[58] *V.* Ibn al-Ṣalāḥ, *Ṭabaqāt*, 98a, b; al-Nawawī, *Tahdhīb* 1:18f.

[59] Al-Subkī, *Ṭabaqāt* 3:182f. Al-Ūdanī was an Ash'ari in *kalām*, though (al-Subkī, *Ṭabaqāt* 3:368), so there must have been some Iraqi connection.

[60] Muḥammad ibn al-Ḥusayn al-Ājurrī (d. 360/970): al-Subkī, *Ṭabaqāt* 3:149.

[61] Al-Nisā'ī, "Tasmiyat fuqahā' al-amṣār," *Majmū'at rasā'il fī 'ulūm al-ḥadīth*, ed. Ṣubḥī al-Badrī al-Sāmarrā'ī (Medina: Muḥammad 'Abd al-Muḥsin, 1969), 8; Robert Brunschvig, "Polémiques médiévales autour du rite de Mālik," *al-Andalus* 15 (1950):379.

[62] For example, the Shāfi'īyah justify their form of the *ādhān* (call to prayer) in part on the practice of the people of the two sacred cities, Mecca and Medina: al-Nawawī, *Majmū'* 3:101.

THE COMMENTARY ON THE *MUKHTAṢAR* OF AL-MUZANĪ

Ibn Surayj himself wrote a *Mukhtaṣar*, a handbook of Shāfi'i jurisprudence like those of al-Buwayṭī, Ḥarmalah, and al-Muzanī before him, of Ibn 'Abd al-Ḥakam and Abū Muṣ'ab before him for the Māliki school. His teacher al-Mundhirī composed a *Mukhtaṣar* of his own, presumably based on the teaching of the students of al-Shāfi-'ī.[63] What is new and original with Ibn Surayj is that he not only composed his own handbook, but wrote a commentary on the *Mukhtaṣar* of al-Muzanī and used it as a basis for his teaching, requiring of his advanced students that they produce a similar commentary. Al-Subkī identifies two of Ibn Surayj's students, Abū Isḥāq al-Marwazī and Ibn Abī Hurayrah, as writing what he calls *ta'līqahs*, the earliest application of the term in his dictionary.[64] This meant, in effect, a doctoral dissertation.[65] Other sources tell us of commentaries on the *Mukhtaṣar* of al-Muzanī from two others of Ibn Surayj's students, Ibn al-Qāṣṣ[66] and Ibn Khāzim.[67] To be sure, Ibn Surayj and his students had no monopoly on the writing of commentaries. Abū al-Ḥasan al-Jūrī (d. *ca.* 330/941-942?), of a minor city in Fars, also wrote a commentary on the *Mukhtaṣar* of al-Muzanī.[68] He had no known connection to Ibn Surayj. The prominent Egyptian Shāfi'i Ibn al-Ḥaddād (d. 345/956) wrote his influential book *al-Furū'* based on a treatment of another book by al-Muzanī as related by al-Anmāṭī, Ibn Surayj's teacher.[69] Still, the commentary as *ta'līqah* seems to be a distinguishing characteristic of the Surayji line of Shāfi'i teaching.

---

[63] Al-Asnawī, *Ṭabaqāt* 2:394. Al-Mundhirī, last author of a *Mukhtaṣar* before the series of commentaries began, gives us a *terminus ad quem* for the redaction of the *Mukhtaṣar* of al-Muzanī. Cf. Calder, *Studies*, chap. 5, esp. 104.

[64] Al-Subkī, *Ṭabaqāt* 3:187, 262.

[65] On the *ta'līqah*, v. George Makdisi, *The Rise of Colleges* (Edinburgh: Univ. Press, 1981), 116-122, stressing its connection with organized debate (*munāẓarah*).

[66] Kātib Çelebī, *Kitāb Kashf al-ẓunūn*, ed. Şerefettin Yaltkaya & Rifat Bilge, 2 vols. (Istanbul: Maarif Matbaası, 1941, 1943), 2:1636.

[67] Ibn Ḥajar, *Tabṣīr al-muntabih bi-taḥrīr al-mushtabih*, ed. Muḥammad al-Bijāwī, 4 vols. (Cairo: al-Dār al-Miṣrīyah lil-Ta'līf wa-al-Tarjamah, 1967), 2:483.

[68] Al-Subkī, *Ṭabaqāt* 3:457f.

[69] Al-Subkī, *Ṭabaqāt* 2:105.

CHIEF OF THE SCHOOL

Ibn Surayj's chieftaincy concerned the teaching of Shāfi'i jurisprudence, not politics, and it was a matter of preponderant prestige rather than formal office, much less coercive power. Its chief measure is the line of authoritative teachers that succeeded him. At Ibn Surayj's death, the chieftaincy of the Baghdadi school passed to his student Abū Isḥāq al-Marwazī. Abū Isḥāq had more identified students than any other teacher in the century after Ibn Surayj: nineteen that I have turned up, compared with eleven for Ibn Abī Hurayrah, five for Abū al-Walīd al-Naysābūrī, and only one or two for all others.

The Students of Abū Isḥāq al-Marwazī

Abū al-Ḥasan al-Ash'arī (d. Baghdad, 324/935-936?), the theologian himself, 3:352, 367.

Zāhir ibn Aḥmad al-Sarakhsī (d. 339/950), Ash'ari.[70]

Aḥmad ibn 'Alī *al-Jawbaqī* (d. 340/952), of Nasaf, 3:21.

Ibn Abī al-Qāḍī (d. after 342/954), qadi for Khʷārizm, later teacher to the prominent Shāfi'i jurisprudents al-Māwardī and al-Fūrānī, 3:164-166.

Ibn al-Ḥaddād (d. 345/956), Egyptian, 3:79.[71]

Abū Ḥafṣ 'Umar ibn Muḥammad ibn Mas'ūd al-Isfarāyinī (d. Isfarayin, 345/956-957).[72]

Ibn Abī Hurayrah (d. 345/956), also under Ibn Surayj, 3:256.

Aḥmad ibn Muḥammad al-Ṭabasī (d. 358/968-969), active in Nishapur, 3:44fn. Wrote a *ta'līqah* of 1,000 quires.[73]

---

[70] Ibn Kathīr, *Ṭabaqāt al-fuqahā' al-shāfi'īyīn*, ed. Aḥmad 'Umar Hāshim & Muḥammad Zaynuhum Muḥammad 'Azib, 3 vols. (al-Ẓāhir, Egypt: Maktabat al-Thaqāfah al-Dīnīyah, 1993), 1:251f.

[71] Actually, al-Subkī gives a long list of teachers: Abū Sa'īd Muḥammad ibn 'Uqayl al-Firyābī, Bishr ibn Naṣr Ghulām 'Irq, and Manṣūr ibn Ismā'īl al-Ḍarīr; also Abū Isḥāq al-Marwazī, Muḥammad ibn Jarīr al-Ṭabarī, al-Ṣayrafī, and al-Iṣṭakhrī (*Ṭabaqāt* 3:79).

[72] Ibn al-Ṣalāḥ, *Ṭabaqāt*, 136b; al-Asnawī, *Ṭabaqāt* 1:76.

[73] Al-Dhahabī, *Tārīkh* 26 (A.H. 351-380):174.

Abū Ḥāmid al-Marwarrūdhī (d. 362/972-973), of Basra, 3:12f.

Abū Muḥammad ʻAbd Allāh ibn ʻAlī al-Qūmisī (d. 367/977), qadi for Gurgān, 3:310.[74]

Abū Sahl al-Ṣuʻlūkī (d. 369/980), of Nishapur, also an Ashʻari, 3: 168.

Abū Zayd al-Marwazī (d. 371/982), Ashʻari of Marv, 3:71-77.[75]

Abū Bakr al-Maḥmūdī (*fl.* 4th cent.), 3:225f (al-Subkī's guess).

Abū Bakr Aḥmad ibn Muḥammad Ibn al-Sībī (d. 372/982), of Qaṣr Ibn Hubayrah, 3:47.[76]

Abū al-Fayyāḍ al-Baṣrī (d. *ca.* 375/985-986?), also under al-Marwarrūdhī.[77]

Abū Isḥāq al-Mihrānī (d. later 10th cent.?).[78]

Abū al-Qāsim *al-Dārakī* (d. 375/986), later active in Nishapur,[79] later still became chief teacher in Baghdad, 3:331.

Abū al-Ḥasan *al-Māsarjisī* (d. Nishapur, 384/994?).

Abū ʻAlī Zāhir ibn Aḥmad al-Sarakhsī (d. 389/999), also a student of *kalām* under al-Ashʻarī and the qur'anic readings under Ibn Mujāhid, 3:293.

Abū ʻAlī Muḥammad ibn ʻAlī al-Balādhurī (d. Nishapur, 395/1004).[80]

Abū Muḥammad ʻAbd Allāh ibn Muḥammad al-Bāfī (d. 398/1007), also a student under Ibn Abī Hurayrah, 3:317.

Al-Subkī did have a special reason for emphasizing Abū Isḥāq's importance, namely his explicit identification with Ashʻarism. We cannot

---

[74] Cf. al-Sahmī, *Tārīkh*, 233; al-Dhahabī, *Tārīkh* 26 (A.H. 351-380):372f.

[75] Al-Subkī names no teacher, but Ibn al-Ṣalāḥ and al-Nawawī say he studied under Abū Isḥāq al-Marwazī: *Ṭabaqāt*, 99b; *Tahdhīb* 1:19.

[76] *V.* also al-Dhahabī, *Tārīkh* 26 (A.H. 351-380):516.

[77] No separate entry in al-Subkī, but mentioned, *Ṭabaqāt* 3:12.

[78] Al-Subkī, *Ṭabaqāt* 3:12.

[79] From 353/964-965: Ibn Faḍl Allāh, *Masālik al-abṣār*, Aya Sofya (Istanbul) 3419, 65a, b.

[80] Al-Dhahabī, *Tārīkh* 27 (A.H. 381-400):325.

suppose, however, that he invented names.

Abū Isḥāq's teaching closely followed that of his own master, Ibn Surayj. At least three of his students produced in their turn commentaries on the *Mukhtaṣar* of al-Muzanī: al-Jawbaqī, Abū Ḥāmid al-Marwarrūdhī, and Abū Zayd al-Marwazī. On one point his development of the new style of teaching may have gone further: al-Subkī quotes a source of the early eleventh century as numbering Abū Ḥāmid al-Marwarrūdhī among the *aṣḥāb* of Abū Isḥāq al-Marwazī, Abū Isḥāq al-Mihrānī and Abū al-Fayyāḍ al-Baṣrī among his *talāmīdh*.[81] This is the earliest express distinction I have come across between *aṣḥāb* and *talāmīdh*, graduates and undergraduates.[82] Al-Subkī's contemporary al-Asnawī states that Abū al-Fayyāḍ learnt jurisprudence from (*tafaqqaha 'alá*) Abū Ḥāmid al-Marwarrūdhī,[83] Abū Isḥāq al-Shīrāzī that he was *ṣāḥib* to Abū Ḥāmid.[84] This connection with Abū Ḥāmid would represent the post-graduate portion of Abū al-Fayyāḍ's training. However, since Ibn Surayj employed a repetitor (Abū Ghānim, Abū al-Ṭayyib), he as well probably had two classes of students, besides informal auditors such as al-Mas'ūdī.

Ibn Abī Hurayrah studied under both Ibn Surayj and Abū Isḥāq al-Marwazī. He wrote a commentary on the *Mukhtaṣar* of al-Muzanī that Kātib Çelebi describes as a great *ta'līqah*.[85] When Abū Isḥāq went to Egypt, Ibn Abī Hurayrah succeeded him as chief Shāfi'i teacher of Baghdad. His student Abū 'Alī al-Ṭabarī (d. 350/960-961) wrote a commentary on the *Mukhtaṣar* of al-Muzanī.[86] Abū 'Alī taught jurisprudence in Baghdad after Ibn Abī Hubayrah's death.[87] No source states explicitly who succeeded Abū 'Alī as chief of the school. However, Abū Isḥāq states that the famous jurisprudent Abū Ḥāmid al-Isfarāyinī studied first (*darasa*) under Ibn al-Marzubān (d.

---

[81] 'Umar ibn 'Alī al-Muṭṭawwi'ī, *K. al-Mudhhab fī dhikr shuyūkh al-madhhab*, *apud* al-Subkī, *Ṭabaqāt* 3:12. On *K. al-Mudhhab*, *v.* Kātib Çelebī, *Kashf* 2:1645.

[82] So I take it; however, whereas Makdisi has identified the *aṣḥāb* as advanced, graduate students (*Rise of Colleges*, 128, 175), he has not found the term *talāmīdh/talāmidhah* to refer to rank (175).

[83] Al-Asnawī, *Ṭabaqāt* 1:193.

[84] Abū Isḥāq, *Ṭabaqāt*, 119.

[85] Kātib Çelebī, *Kashf* 2:1636. Cf. Ibn al-Nadīm, *Fihrist*, 215 = *f.* 3, *q.* 6, where the list of his works includes "*K. al-Ta'līq* concerning jurisprudence and (legal) problems."

[86] Kātib Çelebī, *Kashf* 2:1635.

[87] Abū Isḥāq, *Ṭabaqāt*, 115.

366/977), who had studied under Ibn al-Qaṭṭān al-Baghdādī the student of Ibn Surayj, then learnt jurisprudence (*tafaqqaha*) on his death from al-Dārakī (d. Baghdad, 375/986), with whom later ended up, says Abū Isḥāq, the teaching of jurisprudence in Baghdad.[88] Therefore, the sequence of succession to Ibn Surayj was probably this:

Abū Isḥāq al-Marwazī
Ibn Abī Hurayrah
Abū 'Alī al-Ṭabarī
Ibn al-Qaṭṭān al-Baghdādī
Ibn al-Marzubān
al-Dārakī
Abū Ḥāmid al-Isfarāyinī

The comparable Ḥanafi sequence in Baghdad might be said to have begun about the same time, with Abū Sa'īd al-Barda'ī (d. 317/929), but more surely with his student Abū al-Ḥasan al-Karkhī (d. 340/952). As for the Māliki school, various Egyptians are identified from an early date as chiefs of the school in their time; however, their dates leave gaps impossible to fill, a vagueness befitting the earliest system of succession. Abū Bakr al-Khallāl, I shall argue, founded the Ḥanbali school; however, befitting the most stubbornly traditionalist school, no regular succession of chiefs is discernable in the tenth century.

We cannot say certainly that Ibn Surayj was actually called the chief (*ra'īs*) of the Shāfi'īyah in his own time. Ibn al-Jawzī (d. 597/1200) does state that the chieftaincy of the Shāfi'īyah devolved on him (*intahat ilayhi riyāsat aṣḥāb al-Shāfi'ī*).[89] However, Roy Mottahedeh has pointed out that no earlier writer applies the term,[90] and works are extant where we might expect it; for example, the biographical dictionaries of al-Khaṭīb al-Baghdādī and Abū Isḥāq al-

[88] Abū Isḥāq, *Ṭabaqāt*, 117f; however, al-Khaṭīb al-Baghdādī asserts that it was Abū al-Ḥasan Ibn Khayrān (d. 366/976-977) under whom Abū Ḥāmid studied when he first came to Baghdad, *Tārīkh* 11:325.

[89] Ibn al-Jawzī, *al-Muntaẓam*, 6 vols. (Hyderabad: Dā'irat al-Ma'ārif al-'Uthmānīyah, 1357) 6:149 = ed. Muḥammad 'Abd al-Qādir 'Aṭā' & Muṣṭafá 'Abd al-Qādir 'Aṭā', w/ Nu'aym Zurzūr, 18 vols. (Beirut: Dār al-Kutub al-'Ilmīyah, 1992), 13:183.

[90] Roy P. Mottahedeh, *Loyalty and Leadership in an Early Islamic Society*, Princeton Studies on the Near East (Princeton: Univ. Press, 1980), 146.

Shīrāzī. Moreover, the language suits the successors of Ibn Surayj much better than him: *intahat ilayh*, "there ended up with him," suggests that he became the chief when the old one died, but of course there was no Baghdadi of the same pre-eminence before him. It must be concluded that Ibn Surayj's chieftaincy, by that name, became clear mainly in retrospect, as the line of teachers in his style drove out the competition.

More grandly still, Ibn Surayj has regularly appeared on lists of the men sent at the beginning of each century to renew Islam.[91] The story is told that a shaykh in his circle stood up and proposed that he was the predicted renewer (*mujaddid*) of the year 300, as the caliph 'Umar ibn 'Abd al-'Azīz and al-Shāfi'ī had been the respective renewers of A.H. 100 and 200. Ibn Surayj wept, for it meant that soon he should die.[92] Ella Landau-Tasseron has studied the tradition of the centennial renewer, and concludes that it was invented in the early ninth century by students of al-Shāfi'ī's to legitimize his innovations (such as rejecting hadith reports not from the Prophet).[93] She does not examine the identification of Ibn Surayj as renewer for the year 300, but there are signs that it was projected backwards, as well. One is the anonymity of the shaykh who said it. Another is discrepancies in the form of the tradition itself. Abū Nu'aym al-Iṣfahānī (d. 430/1038) quotes Aḥmad ibn Ḥanbal as naming 'Umar ibn 'Abd al-'Azīz (d. A.H. 99) and al-Shāfi'ī (d. 204). However, Abū Nu'aym's version of Aḥmad's identification includes a note that the renewer will be of Qurashi descent, which fits 'Umar II and al-Shāfi'ī but not, of course, Ibn Surayj: Abū Nu'aym could not have thought that Ibn Surayj had been the next renewer.[94] Only in later versions do we find the quotation of Aḥmad without any mention of Qurashi descent.[95]

---

[91] E.g., from al-Khaṭīb al-Baghdādī (*Tārīkh* 4:289), (1) 'Umar ibn 'Abd al-'Azīz, (2) al-Shāfi'ī, (3) Ibn Surayj, (4) Abū Ḥāmid al-Isfarāyinī; from al-Dhahabī (*Siyar* 14:203), (4) Abū Ḥāmid, (5) al-Ghazālī, (6) 'Abd al-Ghanī, (7) Ibn Daqīq al-'Īd.

[92] Al-Bayhaqī, *Ma'rifat al-sunan wa-al-āthār*, ed. Aḥmad Ṣaqr, 2 vols. (Cairo: al-Majlis al-A'lá lil-Shu'ūn al-Islāmīyah, 1969), 1:138f.

[93] Ella Landau-Tasseron, "The 'Cyclical Reform': A Study of the Mudjaddid Tradition," *Studia Islamica*, no. 70 (1989), 99.

[94] Abū Nu'aym, *Ḥilyah* 9:97f.

[95] E.g., from al-Khaṭīb al-Baghdādī (d. 463/1071), *Tārīkh* 2:62; Ibn 'Abd al-Barr (d. 463/1071), *al-Intiqā' fī faḍā'il al-thalāthah al-a'immah al-fuqahā'* (Cairo: Maktabat al-Qudsī, 1350), 75. The hadith report appears in the collection of Abū Dāwūd (d. 275/889) without any mention of Qurashi descent.

On the other hand, Ibn Surayj must have been identified as the renewer of the year 300 no later than about forty years after his death, at least in Nishapur, for a quotation in *Tārīkh Naysābūr* pushes it back to the 340's/950's or earlier.[96] Ibn Surayj was named the renewer of 300 in Baghdad no later than about 400, when Abū Ḥāmid al-Isfarāyinī expressed disgust with a list from al-Maḥāmilī that excluded Ḥanafīyah.[97] We are left, again, to observe that Ibn Surayj's stature grew over the tenth century *pari passu* as prospered the line of teachers that went forth from him.

BESIDES JURISPRUDENCE

Ibn Surayj was involved in Baghdadi high culture well beyond mere

---

[96] Al-Ḥākim al-Naysābūrī, *Tārīkh Naysābūr*, *apud* al-Dhahabī, *Tārīkh* 23 (A.H. 301-320):179.

[97] Al-Nawawī, *Tahdhīb* 2:210. About the same time, the Nishapuran Ash'ari Abū al-Ṭayyib al-Ṣu'lūkī (d. 404/1013-1014) was named renewer of the year 400 (al-Subkī, *Ṭabaqāt* 1:201f, 4:396). The original *mujaddid* hadith report had an anti-Ḥanafi edge: Abū Ḥanīfah was not of Arab stock, and he died right at the middle of his century (150/767), not near the beginning. Moreover, some ninth-century Ḥanafīyah circulated hadith reports making the Prophet predict a renewer named al-Nu'mān ibn Thābit (Abū Ḥanīfah; *v.* Ibn 'Adī, *al-Kāmil fī ḍu'afā' al-rijāl*, 6 vols. [Beirut: Dār al-Fikr, 1984], 1:182), others that Muḥammad had said, "Blessèd are those who have seen me, and those who have seen whoever has seen me, and those who have seen whoever has seen whoever has seen me," which would include Abū Ḥanīfah but not al-Shāfi'ī (Ibn 'Adī, *Kāmil* 1:212; cf. al-Khaṭīb al-Baghdādī, *Tārīkh* 6:200). *V.* also the report of a cynosure arising at the end of each century, with the Ḥanafi Abū Ḥafṣ al-Bukhārī nominated for 200 (al-Dhahabī, *Tārīkh* 15 [A.H. 211-220]:40). If al-Maḥāmilī's suggestion was part of an anti-Ḥanafi polemic, then he may have simply extended an existing tradition that included Ibn Surayj. If, however, the tradition including Ibn Surayj was part of an intra-Shāfi'i polemic between the followers of Ibn Surayj and his students, on the one hand, and the more traditionalist, looser Shāfi'īyah on the other hand, it is possible that Abū Nu'aym actually added the requirement of Qurashi descent, as the Surayji line had not prevailed in Isfahan; or, since Aḥmad ibn Ḥanbal is quoted elsewhere, too, as stressing al-Shāfi'ī's Qurashi descent (e.g., most of the sayings quoted in Ibn Abī Ḥātim [d. 327/ 938], *K. al-Jarḥ wa-al-ta'dīl*, 9 vols. [Hyderabad: Jam'īyat Dā'irat al-Ma'ārif al-'Uthmānīyah, 1360], 7:202-204), Abū Nu'aym did not neglect that addition, as al-Khaṭīb al-Baghdādī would, because the Isfahanis did not recognize Ibn Surayj. Additionally, Ibn 'Asākir reports a tradition by which the renewers of the third and fourth centuries were Abū al-Ḥasan al-Ash'arī and Abū Bakr al-Bāqillānī, respectively (Ibn 'Asākir, *Tabyīn kadhib al-muftarī* [Damascus: al-Qudsī, 1347], 53).

jurisprudence. The sources point to no specific accomplishments in the field of *belles lettres*, but he had his tastes: "Whoever wishes elegance (*ẓarf*)," he said, "must (go to) the jurisprudence (*madhhab*) of al-Shāfi'ī, the (qur'anic) reading of Abū 'Amr, and the poetry of Ibn al-Mu'tazz."[98] It is hard to imagine a Ḥanbali's recommending any particular school of law on the ground of elegance. His own teaching in particular was thought to round out a gentleman's education. The Sufi al-Rūdhabārī is supposed to have boasted, "My professor (*ustādh*) in Sufism was al-Junayd; my professor in jurisprudence, Abū al-'Abbās Ibn Surayj; in grammar and lexicography, Tha'lab; and in the hadith of the Prophet . . . , Ibrāhīm al-Ḥarbī."[99] Several witticisms survive from Ibn Surayj's juridical debates with Abū Bakr al-Ẓāhirī (d. 297/910); for example, Abū Bakr asked Ibn Surayj, "Let me swallow my saliva" (i.e., "Give me a breather"), to which Ibn Surayj retorted, "I will let you swallow the Tigris."[100] No such frivolity is associated with the memory contests (*mudhākarah*) of Baghdadi traditionalists.

Many sources tell us of Ibn Surayj's devotion to *naẓar* and *jadal*; that is, subtle argumentation concerning minutiae of the law. The early Shāfi'i biographer al-Muṭṭawwi'ī (*fl.* Nishạpur, *ca.* 400/1010) actually credits Ibn Surayj with introducing the sciences of *naẓar* and *jadal* (reasoning and argument),[101] and, as we have seen, this is what Abū 'Alī al-Thaqafī learnt from him. Of course, al-Muzanī had been devoted to these sciences long before him; however, they must have been new to traditionalist circles in Baghdad, the circles to which Ibn Khayrān referred in his bitter complaint about Ibn Surayj's accepting a judgeship.

Ibn Surayj was even said to have been as prominent among the fol-

---

[98] Al-Nawawī, *Tahdhīb* 1:64; similarly, al-Bayhaqī, *Manāqib al-Shāfi'ī*, ed. Aḥmad Ṣaqr, 2 vols. (Cairo: Dār al-Turāth, 1970, 1971), 2:281. A like list is attributed to the Qur'an reader Ibn Mujāhid (d. 324/936): "Whoever recites the reading of Abū 'Amr, follows al-Shāfi'ī in law, trades in silk, and relates the poetry of Ibn al-Mu'tazz, his elegance will be complete" (al-Asnawī, *Ṭabaqāt* 2: 394). The reference to trading in silk suggests the social class to which the new Shāfi'ism appealed.

[99] Al-Sarrāj, *The Kitáb al-Luma' fī 'l-taṣawwuf*, ed. Reynold Alleyne Nicholson, E. J. W. Gibb Memorial ser. 22 (London: Luzac, 1914), 104. Slightly different *apud* al-Sulamī, *Ṭabaqāt al-ṣūfiyya*, ed. Johannes Pedersen (Leiden: E. J. Brill, 1960), 369.

[100] Abū Isḥāq, *Ṭabaqāt*, 109.

[101] *Apud* al-Subkī, *Ṭabaqāt* 3:22.

lowers of al-Shāfiʿī in *kalām* as he was in jurisprudence.[102] We have, unfortunately, no identification of the precise tendency in *kalām* to which Ibn Surayj adhered. The half-dozen books of his named by Ibn al-Nadīm, as well as those named by others, seem all to deal with jurisprudence.[103] A. Kevin Reinhart stresses his attention to the methodology of jurisprudence; that is, *uṣūl al-fiqh*, whose classic form he did much to frame.[104] Using the scant available evidence, Reinhart shrewdly reconstructs a stance in *kalām* substantially more open to reason than the stance of earlier traditionalists—indeed, disturbingly more open than the stance of subsequent Shāfiʿīyah, who could not embrace Ibn Surayj's conclusions as they did his methods. This is not precisely the semi-rationalist position sketched in the previous chapter; that is, using the weapons of *kalām* to defend traditionalist tenets. Nor is Ibn Surayj associated with any of peculiar doctrines of the ninth-century semi-rationalists, such as the created pronunciation of the Qur'an. Still, it is clear that Ibn Surayj worked hard at constructing a Sunni *kalām*, without embracing Muʿtazilism.[105]

Ashʿarism was the final form of this (would-be) traditionalist *kalām*, and it became associated with prominent Shāfiʿīyah in the Su-

---

[102] Al-Ḍiyā' al-Khaṭīb, *Ghāyat al-marām fī 'ilm al-kalām*, *apud* al-Subkī, *Ṭabaqāt* 3:22.

[103] Ibn al-Nadīm, *Fihrist*, 213 = *f.* 3, *q.* 6. Cf. Ibn Ṭāhir al-Baghdādī, *al-Farq bayna al-firaq*, ed. Muḥyī al-Dīn ʿAbd al-Ḥamīd (Cairo: Maktabat Muḥammad ʿAlī Ṣabīḥ, n.d.), 363, which names a *Naqḍ kitāb al-Jārūf ʿalá al-qā'ilīn bi-takāfu' al-adillah*, perhaps concerning the sufficiency of juridical evidence (i.e., the Book and Sunnah); al-Qāḍī ʿIyāḍ, *Tartīb* 3:178, which names a *K. al-Tawassuṭ bayna Muḥammad ibn al-Ḥasan wa-al-qāḍī Ismāʿīl*, concerning Māliki and Ḥanafi jurisprudence; Kātib Çelebī, *Kashf* 2:1257f, which names *al-Furūq fī furūʿ al-shāfiʿīyah*, on Shāfiʿi jurisprudence; *ibid.*, 1444, *K. al-ʿAyn wa-al-dīn*, concerning wills; *ibid.*, 2005, *al-Wadā'iʿ li-manṣūṣ al-sharā'iʿ*, giving opinions (presumably on the topic of deposits) without their supporting evidence. Abū Isḥāq states that he wrote over 400 works altogether (*Ṭabaqāt*, 109).

[104] A. Kevin Reinhart, *Before Revelation*, SUNY Series in Middle Eastern Studies (Albany: State Univ. of New York Press, 1995), 15-17. Using mainly bibliographical sources, Wael B. Hallaq proposes much the same characterization: "Was al-Shafiʿi the Master Architect of Islamic Jurisprudence?" *International Journal of Middle East Studies* 25 (1993):595f.

[105] Muʿtazili sources do state that he frequented one of their Baghdadi shaykhs, al-Khayyāṭ (*fl.* later 3rd/9th century): al-Qāḍī ʿAbd al-Jabbār, *Faḍl al-iʿtizāl*, 301; Ibn al-Murtaḍá, *Die Klassen der muʿtaziliten*, ed. Susanna Diwald-Wilzer, Bibliotheca Islamica, ed. Helmut Ritter & Albert Dietrich, 21 (Wiesbaden: Franz Steiner, 1961), 129.

rayji line from the time of his successor at teaching in Baghdad, Abū Isḥāq al-Marwazī. One did not have to be an Ashʻari to study jurisprudence under the successors of Ibn Surayj, or even to teach it as one of his successors. Of the tenth-century successors in Baghdad whom I have identified, the Ashāʻirah themselves have claimed only one, Abū Isḥāq al-Marwazī.[106] Still, it seems excessive to speak of Ashʻari *infiltration* of the Shāfiʻi school[107]: Ibn Surayj himself was notably hospitable to the methods of *kalām*, and followers of his took up Ashʻari *kalām* from the very beginning. Moreover, it is now evident that the followers of al-Ashʻarī considered him merely the first among equals in a line of semi-rationalists going back to the ninth century, hence including most of the ninth-century Shāfiʻi school.[108]

Ibn Surayj is said to have attended lectures by the Sufi leader al-Junayd (d. 298/911?). The Egyptian Ibn al-Ḥaddād was impressed by something Ibn Surayj had said. Ibn Surayj asked him whether he knew from where he had learnt this. Ibn al-Ḥaddād answered, "Let the qadi tell." Ibn Surayj then told him, "This is a blessing from my sitting with Abū al-Qāsim al-Junayd."[109] The Sufi biographer al-Sulamī (d. Nishapur, 412/1021) relates a story of Ibn Surayj's passing by the circle of al-Junayd in the company of his student Ibn al-Qāṣṣ. Ibn al-Qāṣṣ asked him what they were talking about. Ibn Surayj answered, "Allusions (*rumūz*) of a group you do not know," as though he himself did.[110]

Al-Junayd is important as the chief author of classical Sufism. He had studied jurisprudence under Abū Thawr, which connects him to the personal Shāfiʻi school.[111] He also interested the polite circles

---

[106] Al-Subkī, *Ṭabaqāt* 3:368.

[107] *Pace* George Makdisi, "Ashʻarī and the Ashʻarites in Islamic Religious History," *Studia Islamica*, no. 17 (1962), 46f.

[108] Daniel Gimaret, "Un document majeur pour l'histoire du kalām," *Arabica* 32 (1985):191f.

[109] Al-Khaṭīb al-Baghdādī, *Tārīkh* 7:243. Unfortunately, al-Subkī places Ibn al-Ḥaddād's trip to Baghdad in 310/922-923, and denies that he ever met Ibn Surayj (*Ṭabaqāt* 3:79).

[110] Al-Sulamī, *Tārīkh al-ṣūfīyah*, *apud* al-Rāfiʻī, *Tadwīn fī dhikr ahl al-ʻilm bi-Qazvīn*, *s.n.* Aḥmad ibn ʻAlī; Lâleli 2010, 145a.

[111] Al-Khaṭīb al-Baghdādī, *Tārīkh* 7:241, 242. Alternatively, al-Junayd has been reckoned a follower of Sufyān al-Thawrī and (directly) of al-Shāfiʻī (al-Subkī, *Ṭabaqāt* 2:260-275; al-Asnawī, *Ṭabaqāt* 1:334; al-Kaffawī, *Katāʼib aʻlām al-akhyār*, Esat Efendi [Istanbul] 548, 37a.). Later writers may have guessed the school of

of Baghdad in general. The Baghdadi Mu'tazili Abū al-Qāsim al-Balkhī names some of the types who attended his lectures:

> I have seen someone for you in Baghdad. He is called al-Junayd, and I have not seen his like. The writers (*katabah*[112]) go to him for his locutions (*alfāẓ*), philosophers (*falāsifah*) for the subtlety of his concepts, and theologians (*mutakallimūn*) for the mastery of his learning.[113]

Although he would not himself seek out the patronage of the rich and powerful (unlike his disciple Ruwaym, whom he jeered[114]), al-Junayd was plainly sought out by them. The later association of Shāfi'ism with Sufism probably had more to do with religious politics in Khurasan than any inherent attractions of Ibn Surayj's teaching[115]; however, the connection was certainly consistent with Ibn Surayj's interest in al-Junayd and his teaching such Sufis as al-Rūdhabārī and Abū 'Alī al-Thaqafī.

There finally remains to consider the matter of patronage. Socially, it seems clear, Surayji Shāfi'ism appealed to the sophisticates of Baghdad as no rude, Ḥanbali traditionalism could do. There are hints that it was encouraged for its political tendencies, as well. Louis Massignon has pointed out the vizier 'Alī ibn 'Īsá (d. 334/945):

> In dogmatics and canon law, Ibn 'Īsá, who read and consulted, seems to have been a conciliatory Shāfi'ite, although the state was

Sufyān al-Thawrī because several other famous ascetics were counted among its adherents (e.g., Ibrāhīm ibn Ad'ham; Ḥamdūn al-Qaṣṣār, the first Malāmati; Abū Aḥmad al-Julūdī [d. 368/979], a relator of the *Ṣaḥīḥ* of Muslim and a disciple of disciples to Abū Ḥafṣ al-Naysābūrī). Most Sufis of the tenth and later centuries who had any juridical affiliation were affiliated with the Shāfi'i school.

[112] "I.e., the eloquent (*al-bulaghā'*)," glosses al-Dhahabī (*Siyar* 14:67); however, al-Balkhī seems more likely to have meant "state secretaries" or, more broadly, all official recorders (e.g., assistants to qadis).

[113] Al-Khaṭīb al-Baghdādī, *Tārīkh* 7:243. On Abū al-Qāsim al-Balkhī (d. Balkh, 319/931?), *v.* Sezgin, *Geschichte* 1:622f.

[114] Abū Nu'aym, *Ḥilyah* 10:268.

[115] On religious politics in Khurasan, a brilliant beginning has been made by Jacqueline Chabbi, "Remarques sur le développement historique des mouvements ascétiques et mystiques au Khurasan, IIIe/IXe siècle-IVe/Xe siècle," *Studia Islamica*, no. 46 (1977), 5-72. On the affinity of Sufism with Ash'arism in the eleventh century, at least, *v.* Tilman Nagel, *Die Festung des Glaubens* (Munich: C. H. Beck, 1988), and Claude Gilliot, "Quand la théologie s'allie à l'histoire," *Arabica* 39 (1992):241-260.

> Hanafite; he was well-read, exasperated by the narrow rigorism of the Hanbalites, perceiving the need of an orthodox Sunnite metaphysics to pit against that of the Mu'tazilites . . . and against that of the Hellenistic philosophers . . . . He had his new orthodoxy defended by carefully selected associates (in hadīth, by two Jarīrites: Qādī A-b-Kāmil and 'Alī-b-'A 'Azīz Dawlābī; in Shāfi'ite law, by AB M-b-'AA Sayrafī; in Qur'ānic exegesis, by the grammarian AH Khazzāz Wāsitī and, especially, by the head of the Baghdadian *Qurrā'*, Abū Bakr ibn Mujāhid . . .).[116]

As so often, one feels awed by Massignon's perspicuity, then annoyed when one checks his footnotes. Here, his evidence turns out to be a few notices in the *Fihrist* of Ibn al-Nadīm. Al-Dawlābī (d. *ca.* 335/946-947) and Aḥmad ibn Kāmil (d. 350/961) indeed appear there amongst the followers of al-Ṭabarī (235), and the former is credited with a *Risālah* addressed to 'Alī ibn 'Īsá; however, nothing indicates that they were more active in hadith than other fields, nor that Aḥmad ibn Kāmil had any special connection with the vizier. There is no entry for al-Dawlābī in either *Tārīkh Baghdād*, chiefly concerned with traditionists, nor Ibn Ḥajar's *Lisān "al-Mīzān."* Al-Dāraquṭnī characterized Aḥmad ibn Kāmil as lax in his relation of hadith, inclined to chose juridical solutions of his own without any proper basis in the received tradition. He denied that he was a Jarīri.[117] On the other hand, we know that 'Alī ibn 'Īsá paid stipends to the traditionists Ibn Ṣā'id (d. 318/930-931) and Abū Bakr Ibn Abī Dāwūd (d. 316/929).[118] This Abū Bakr led the persecution of al-Ṭabarī.[119] To be sure, Abū Bakr laid his complaint that al-Ṭabarī rejected Abū Bakr and 'Umar before the caliphal door-keeper Naṣr, not the vizier 'Alī ibn 'Īsá; still, it seems difficult to maintain that 'Alī ibn 'Īsá cultivated the new Jarīri school in particular.

The evidence is stronger for a particular interest in the new Shāfi'ism. Ibn al-Nadīm describes Abū Bakr al-Ṣayrafī, Ibn Surayj's student, as a close acquaintance and follower to 'Alī ibn 'Īsá.[120] He

---

[116] Massignon, *Passion*, 1:409f.

[117] Al-Khaṭīb al-Baghdādī, *Tārīkh* 4:358f. He was claimed by the Ḥanafīyah, as well: *v.* Ibn Abī al-Wafā', *Jawāhir* 1 (ed. Ḥulw):238f.

[118] Ibn Ḥajar, *Lisān "al-Mīzān,"* 7 vols. (Hyderabad: Majlis Dā'irat al-Ma'ārif, 1329-31), 3:295.

[119] Ibn al-Jawzī, *Muntaẓam* 6 (Hyd.):172 = ed. 'Aṭā' & 'Aṭā', 13:217.

[120] Ibn al-Nadīm, *Fihrist*, 213 = *f.* 3, *q.* 6.

also mentions, like al-Khaṭīb al-Baghdādī and al-Subkī, that Ibn Surayj himself debated with Abū Bakr al-Ẓāhirī before 'Alī ibn 'Īsá.[121] Al-Muṭṭawwi'ī speaks of 'Alī ibn 'Īsá's friendship for Ibn Surayj. He traces it back to a time when Ibn Surayj was before the vizier in the company of the qadi Abū 'Umar (d. 320/932), who adhered to the Māliki tradition of the qadi Ismā'īl. Ibn Surayj protested that Abū 'Umar had gone against the doctrine of his patron, Mālik (*madhhab ṣāḥibih*), 'Alī ibn 'Īsá called for the book to be brought, and Ibn Surayj turned out to be right.[122] The story is consistent with what other sources tell us of Ibn Surayj's stress on adherence to authoritative teaching, and with 'Alī ibn 'Īsá's interest in establishing orthodoxy.[123] Still, the record shows only that Ibn Surayj's project of developing a Shāfi'i jurisprudence compatible with a broad and sophisticated education was congenial to the famous vizier, not that the vizier gave it any decisive impetus.

Furthermore, 'Alī ibn 'Īsá came in and out of office four times, so his patronage was not constant. Just before his death, indeed, someone identified as a Shāfi'i in jurisprudence, Abū al-Sā'ib (d. Baghdad, 350/961?), was appointed to a judgeship in Baghdad, to the chief judgeship a few years later.[124] He had been born in Hamadhan but had come to Baghdad as a Sufi and may have studied under Ibn Surayj along with al-Rūdhabārī; however, al-Khaṭīb names no teacher in jurisprudence.[125] Abū al-Sā'ib's secretary, then deputy, finally successor as chief qadi, was 'Umar ibn Aktham (d. Baghdad, 357/968), described as the second Shāfi'i qadi in Baghdad but likewise whose teacher in jurisprudence no source names.[126] In any event, Abū al-Sā'ib and 'Umar ibn Aktham must have been appointed on ac-

---

[121] Ibn al-Nadīm, *Fihrist*, 213 = *f.* 3, *q.* 6.

[122] *Apud* al-Subkī, *Ṭabaqāt* 3:30f.

[123] Observe that the jurisprudent pressed for a fixed standard and the vizier approved: this is the opposite of the process suggested by W. Montgomery Watt, whereby scholar-jurists disclaimed any capacity for independent judgement in order to resist political pressures (*Islam and the Integration of Society*, International Library of Sociology & Social Reconstruction [London: Routledge & Kegan Paul, 1961], 207, 243). The school of law was chiefly about orthodoxy, not resistance to rulers.

[124] Al-Khaṭīb al-Baghdādī, *Tārīkh* 11:249; 12:320.

[125] Ibn Abī al-Wafā' even claims him for the Ḥanafīyah, although he, too, names no teacher (*Jawāhir*, ed. Ḥulw, 2:512).

[126] Al-Khaṭīb al-Baghdādī, *Tārīkh* 11:249. The entries of al-Asnawī (*Ṭabaqāt* 1:78f) and al-Subkī (*Ṭabaqāt* 3:470) are merely précis of al-Khaṭīb al-Baghdādī's.

count of connections with the Būyids in Jibāl, not their positions in the Surayji line of Shāfi'i jurisprudents in Baghdad.[127] The new Surayji school would prevail over its competitors not by winning favor in high places but by its efficiency at teaching jurisprudence.

[127] Halm, *Ausbreitung*, 157.

CHAPTER SIX

AL-KARKHĪ AND THE CLASSICAL ḤANAFI SCHOOL

At the end of Chapter Three, I discussed the writing of commentaries on the works of Muḥammad al-Shaybānī. Their chronology suggests the activity of a self-conscious Ḥanafi school from the early tenth century. Can we say more precisely who founded that school? The early commentators are likely candidates. In this chapter, I discuss the careers of four: Abū Jaʿfar al-Ṭaḥāwī in Egypt, then Abū Khāzim, Abū Saʿīd al-Bardaʿī, and Abū al-Ḥasan al-Karkhī in Baghdad. The development of the Ḥanafi school does not seem to change so dramatically with any one teacher as the Shāfiʿi school does with Ibn Surayj; however, if any one man is to be identified as the jurist from whose work descends the classical Ḥanafi guild school, I propose that it is al-Karkhī.

AL-ṬAḤĀWĪ IN EGYPT

If the Ḥanafi school assumed its classical form only in the tenth century, a good candidate for the rôle of founder would seem to be Abū Jaʿfar al-Ṭaḥāwī (d. Baghdad, 321/933). He was the earliest jurisprudent to write a commentary on *al-Jāmiʿ al-ṣaghīr*, and one of the earliest to write one on *al-Jāmiʿ al-kabīr*. He also wrote a *Mukhtaṣar* (epitome), a summation of the doctrine of a school and the first work by that name to treat Ḥanafi jurisprudence.[1] He wrote as well the first work devoted to *Manāqib Abī Ḥanīfah*, the virtues of Abū Ḥanīfah.[2] Finally, the chieftaincy of the Ḥanafi school in Egypt was said to have ended up with him, a statement made of no previous Egyptian.[3] The working up of the doctrine of the school, the exaltation of

[1] Kātib Çelebī, *Kitāb Kashf al-ẓunūn*, ed. Şerefettin Yaltkaya & Rifat Bilge, 2 vols. (Istanbul: Maarif Matbaası, 1941, 1943), 2:1627.

[2] Kātib Çelebī, *Kashf* 2:1836f.

[3] Abū Isḥāq al-Shīrāzī, *Ṭabaqāt al-fuqahāʾ*, ed. Iḥsān ʿAbbās (Beirut: Dār al-Rāʾid al-ʿArabī, 1970), 142.

the eponym, the local chieftaincy—these are all activities characteristic of the classical guild school not to be found in the eighth century or most of the ninth.

If the Ḥanafi school needed to become acceptable to traditionalists, al-Ṭaḥāwī was well-placed to make it so by his close acquaintance with the primitive Shāfi'i school. He was nephew to al-Muzanī and began his legal studies under him. According to one story, often repeated, al-Ṭaḥāwī angrily left his uncle when he scolded him harshly for not understanding some juridical subtlety.[4] According to another story, however, al-Ṭaḥāwī said he had gone over to outright Ḥanafism on account of seeing his uncle spend so much time with the books of Abū Ḥanīfah.[5] Further corroborating the second story, al-Ṭaḥāwī is quoted as highly praising the *Mukhtaṣar* of al-Muzanī.[6] When he composed his own *Mukhtaṣar*, al-Ṭaḥāwī followed al-Muzanī's arrangement of topics.[7] Al-Ṭaḥāwī alone is credited with transmitting al-Muzanī's collection of the hadith of al-Shāfi'ī.[8] This is the collection that circulated in Qazvīn into the eleventh century.[9]

Most often named as the teacher (*ustādh*) of al-Ṭaḥāwī is Ibn Abī 'Imrān (d. 280/893), a blind man of Baghdadi origin who came to Egypt in the company of the tax collector (*ṣāḥib al-kharāj*) Abū Ayyūb in 258/871-872.[10] Al-Khaṭīb al-Baghdādī describes him as one

---

[4] Abū Isḥāq, *Ṭabaqāt*, 142.

[5] Al-Khalīlī, *al-Irshād fī ma'rifat 'ulamā' al-ḥadīth*, abr. al-Silafī, Aya Sofya 2951, 56b. Al-Yāfi'ī, *Mir'āt al-janān wa-'ibrat al-yaqẓān*, 4 vols. (Hyderabad: Dā'irat al-Ma'ārif al-Niẓāmīyah, 1337-1339), 2:281. This was the preferred version of the Ḥanafi jurisprudent al-Qudūrī, according to al-Kaffawī, *Katā'ib a'lām al-akhyār min fuqahā' madhhab al-Nu'mān al-mukhtār*, Esat Efendi (Istanbul) 548, 65b.

[6] "No one will undertake (to duplicate) the book of al-Muzanī. It has become a virgin not to be deflowered": al-Khalīlī, *Irshād*, 56b.

[7] Kātib Çelebī, *Kashf* 2:1627.

[8] *K. al-Sunan*: *v.* al-Khalīlī, *Irshād*, 56a; Ibn Ḥajar, *Lisān "al-Mīzān,"* 7 vols. (Hyderabad: Majlis Dā'irat al-Ma'ārif, 1329-1331), 1:274.

[9] Al-Rāfi'ī, *K. al-Tadwīn fī dhikr ahl al-'ilm bi-Qazvīn*, with examples *s.n.* Muḥammad ibn Yūsuf ibn Bundār, Lâleli (Istanbul) 2010, 109b, 110a; *s.n.* 'Abd al-Salām ibn Muḥammad (d. 488/1095?), Lâleli, 245a, Bağdatlı Vehbi Efendi (Istanbul), 85b.

[10] Al-Khaṭīb al-Baghdādī, *Tārīkh Baghdād*, 14 vols. (Cairo: Maktabat al-Khānjī, 1931), 5:142; al-Maqrīzī, *al-Tārīkh al-kabīr al-muqaffā fī tarājim ahl Miṣr wa-al-wāridīn ilayhā*, *s.n.* Aḥmad ibn Muḥammad ibn Shujā'; Pertev Paşa (Istanbul) 496, 124a, b.

of *aṣḥāb al-ra'y*,[11] while al-Ṣaymarī describes him as the shaykh of his school in Egypt and a former student of Muḥammad ibn Samā'ah, Bishr ibn al-Walīd, and their like.[12] He was the Ḥanafi teacher to whom al-Ṭaḥāwī turned when he first left his uncle al-Muzanī.[13]

Not long afterwards, al-Ṭaḥāwī travelled to Syria, where he met the Baghdadi Abū Khāzim, then qadi for Damascus, and studied jurisprudence under him.[14] Back in Egypt, it is said, he additionally studied jurisprudence under the qadi Bakkār ibn Qutaybah (d. 270/884), who had learnt jurisprudence in Basra under Hilāl al-Ra'y.[15] Al-Ṭaḥāwī was never appointed qadi, himself, but he acted as secretary and deputy to Abū 'Ubayd Allāh al-Baṣrī (d. Baghdad, 313/925-926), qadi for Egypt 277 or 278-284/*ca.* 891-897, then for two months in 292/905.[16]

Al-Ṭaḥāwī had a lively interest in hadith. His teacher the qadi Bakkār ibn Qutaybah had some reputation as a traditionist.[17] The qadi Abū 'Ubayd Allāh al-Baṣrī held sessions in jurisprudence (said to be attended by both the Ḥanafīyah and Shāfi'īyah) and hadith.[18] Al-Ṭaḥāwī likewise attracted praise for his equal mastery of both: "I have seen you in the evening with the jurisprudents (*fuqahā'*) in their place," someone told him, "and I have seen you among the traditionists (*ahl al-ḥadīth*) in theirs: how few are they who combine the

---

[11] Al-Khaṭīb al-Baghdādī, *Tārīkh* 5:141.

[12] Al-Khaṭīb al-Baghdādī, *Tārīkh* 5:142.

[13] Almost immediately on his arrival, according to al-Ṭaḥāwī's own statement *apud* al-Dhahabī, *Siyar a'lām al-nubalā'*, 25 vols. (Beirut: Mu'assasat al-Risālah), 15 (ed. Ibrāhīm al-Zaybaq, 1983):29. Al-Ṭaḥāwī was born in Upper Egypt only in 239/853-854, so he would have been about seventeen when Ibn Abī 'Imrān arrived.

[14] Ibn 'Asākir, *Tahdhīb Tārīkh Ibn 'Asākir*, abr. 'Abd al-Qādir Badrān, 7 vols. (Damascus: Rawḍat al-Shām, 1329?-51), 2:54.

[15] Al-Kaffawī, *Katā'ib*, 65b.

[16] Al-Kindī, *The Governors and Judges of Egypt*, ed. Rhuvon Guest, E. J. W. Gibb Memorial Ser. 19 (Leiden: E. J. Brill, 1912), 479-481; Ibn Ḥajar, *Raf' al-iṣr 'an quḍāt Miṣr*, *apud* al-Kindī, 515.

[17] Al-Dhahabī presents a long list of those who related hadith reports from Bakkār, *Tārīkh al-islām*, 40+ vols. (Beirut: Dār al-Kitāb al-'Arabī, 1987-), 20 (A.H. 261-280):70 = *Siyar* 12 (ed. Shu'ayb al-Arna'ūṭ & Ṣāliḥ al-Samr, 1983):599; however, he mentions no estimate of his reliability, and does not include him in his dictionary of traditionists, *Mīzān al-i'tidāl*.

[18] Ibn Ḥajar, *Raf'*, 516. Alternatively, they were said to be attended by *al-fuqahā'* and *aṣḥāb al-ḥadīth*: Ibn Ḥajar, *Lisān* 1:278.

two."[19]

Al-Ṭaḥāwī would later be attacked for assuming a cavalier attitude toward the science of hadith. According to the Shāfi'i jurisprudent al-Bayhaqī (d. 458/1066), al-Ṭaḥāwī would often claim that a particular transmitter was trustworthy if he appeared in the chain of a hadith report that supported the Ḥanafi position, later claim that the same man was weak if he appeared in the chain of a report contravening the Ḥanafi position.[20] Joseph Schacht has additionally shown that al-Ṭaḥāwī sometimes misrepresents the teaching of earlier Iraqi jurists such as Ibn Abī Laylá and Abū Yūsuf, although without demonstrating any systematic tendency.[21] I am in no position to judge the validity of al-Bayhaqī's charge[22]; however, it does indicate that, with a sure hand or otherwise, al-Ṭaḥāwī engaged in fitting out Ḥanafi doctrine with a basis in hadith.

At this point, it is difficult otherwise to characterize al-Ṭaḥāwī's work in the field of jurisprudence. In the biographical literature are indications both that he was a fanatical partisan of Ḥanafism, seeing no right in differing from it,[23] and that he was thoroughly familiar with other juridical doctrines.[24] Probably, he was a skillful and energetic defender of Ḥanafi positions in debate.

Egypt was a likely place for the establishment of a traditionalized Ḥanafi school. Like Khurasan, Egypt was a frontier of sorts: holding onto an urban island in a sea of peasant Copts, the Muslims of Egypt must have hung together with more fervor than the Muslims of Iraq. In al-Ṭaḥāwī's time, the Copts were in process of conversion to Islam; however, the process could not have gone very far, yet. The traditionist 'Alī ibn Sa'īd (d. Old Cairo, 299/911-912) supported him-

---

[19] Al-Dhahabī, *Siyar* 15:30. Cf. Ibn Ḥajar, *Lisān* 1:279.

[20] Al-Bayhaqī, *Ma'rifat al-sunan wa-al-āthār*, ed. Aḥmad Ṣaqr, 1 vol. published (Cairo: al-Majlis al-A'lá lil-Shu'ūn al-Islāmīyah, 1969), 1:148, with detailed example, 1:344-355.

[21] Joseph Schacht, "Sur la transmission de la doctrine dans les écoles juridiques de l'Islam," *Annales de l'Institut des études orientales* (Algiers) 10 (1952):411.

[22] For one defense of al-Ṭaḥāwī, *v.* Ibn Abī al-Wafā', *K. al-Jāmi'*, *apud al-Jawāhir al-muḍīyah*, 2 vols. (Hyderabad: Dā'irat al-Ma'ārif al-Niẓāmīyah, 1914), 2:431f. For a modern attack (incautiously extended to all of hadith science), *v.* Norman Calder, *Studies in Early Muslim Jurisprudence* (Oxford: Clarendon Press, 1993), 235-240.

[23] Maslamah ibn Qāsim, *al-Ṣilah*, *apud* Ibn Ḥajar, *Lisān* 1:276.

[24] Ibn 'Abd al-Barr, *K. al-'Ilm*, *apud* Ibn Ḥajar, *Lisān* 1:276.

self as a tax collector. It was cited against his reliability that, when the villagers had once refused to pay the *kharāj* tax assessed against them, he had driven all their swine into the mosque.[25] The village mosque appears here as an outpost of alien authority.

The governors of Egypt must have encouraged the men of religion in Egypt to hang together. For one, there was always the temptation to build up a local base of power from which to challenge caliphal control, hence to build up their legitimacy by courting the local men of religion. The Sāmānids and other local dynasties would later be seen at the same endeavor, although we have more abundant evidence for activities in Egypt. Independence-minded governors in Egypt may have felt especially pressed to please the Muslims of the capital because they had so few alternative social bases; for example, local landowners had been reduced to relative insignificance by the civil war of 200-211/815-826, and therefore the impulse to cultivate the most sophisticated tastes, to develop a court culture and leave the Muslim ruck behind, must have been weak. Moreover, ethnically alien régimes and especially personal rulers will always favor the men of religion to tame the subject population.[26] In consequence, a larger proportion of princely patronage may have been directed to the men of religion in Egypt than in Baghdad, where the men of religion had more competitors; for example, poets and musicians, of whom there are many stories from the court in Baghdad but few from the court in Old Cairo.

The soldier Aḥmad ibn Ṭūlūn ruled Egypt from the 250's/870's till his death in 270/884. He certainly strove to make himself independent, and the shadow caliph al-Muwaffaq actually dispatched a military force in 263/877 to remove him. Many stories tell of his bounty to the men of religion. He was said to have assigned 10,000 dinars a month to the jurisprudents, scholars, qur'anic reciters, prayer leaders, and *arbāb al-buyūt* ('Alids?).[27] Still travelling students, al-Ṭabarī,

---

[25] Al-Dhahabī, *Siyar* 14 (ed. Akram al-Būshayyī, 1983):146.

[26] Max Weber, *Economy and Society: An Outline of Interpretive Sociology*, ed. Guenther Roth & Claus Wittich, 2 vols. (Berkeley: Univ. of California Press, 1978), 2:1160, 1176.

[27] Al-'Aynī, *'Iqd al-jumān,*, s.a. 270; Veli (Istanbul) 2385, 455f. Al-Maqrīzī states that he gave 1,000 dinars a month to *ahl al-masājid*: *Kitāb al-Muqaffá al-kabīr*, ed. Muḥammad al-Ya'lawī, 8 vols. (Beirut: Dār al-Gharb al-Islāmī, 1991), 3:425. For comparison's sake, it might be mentioned that the annual *kharāj* tax yield of Egypt was 4,300,000 a year; i.e., almost 360,000 a month (al-Maqrīzī, *Muqaffá*

Ibn Khuzaymah, Muḥammad ibn Naṣr al-Marwazī, and Muḥammad ibn Hārūn al-Rūyānī (d. 307/919-920) each received 50 dinars from him, with the promise of more when that ran out.[28] In 268/881-882, he gave 1,000 dinars to al-Rabī' ibn Sulaymān.[29] When he imprisoned his qadi, Bakkār ibn Qutaybah, there were found in his house eighteen sacks of dinars, 1,000 in each, which Ibn Ṭūlūn had paid him over the years.[30]

In return for his bounty, Ibn Ṭūlūn expected the men of religion to help him realize his political ambitions, most notably when he brought a number of them to his camp outside Damascus in 269/882 and told them to depose the shadow caliph and official heir al-Muwaffaq. There is a story that Bakkār ibn Qutaybah refused and was imprisoned for that reason[31]; however, al-Ṭaḥāwī himself is quoted as saying that Bakkār was imprisoned for not doing something else,[32] and since al-Maqrīzī quotes the document of deposition with Bakkār's subscription *in extenso*, it seems sure that Bakkār did comply.[33] Al-Maqrīzī also quotes the subscription of Abū Khāzim the Ḥanafi, while the Shāfi'i Abū Zur'ah al-Dimashqī is well known for his enthusiastic announcement of the deposition: "I have deposed (stripped off) Abū Aḥmaq ("stupid," rather than Abū Aḥmad) as one strips a ring off a finger."[34] A Māliki source asserts that not only Bakkār ibn Qutaybah but also the chief of the Egyptian Mālikīyah, Ibn al-Mawwāz (d. 269/882-883?), refused to subscribe to the deposition.[35] Whether or not it was so, Ibn Ṭūlūn was able to attract im-

---

1:425; al-Dhahabī, *Tārīkh* 20 [A.H. 261-280]:47). The tribute to Iraq demanded of Ibn Ṭūlūn's son Khumārawayh was 300,000 dinars; i.e., 25,000 a month (al-Maqrīzī, *Muqaffá* 3:821).

[28] Al-Khaṭīb al-Baghdādī, *Tārīkh* 2:165; Ibn Kathīr, *al-Bidāyah wa-al-nihāyah*, 14 vols. (Cairo: Maṭba'at al-Sa'ādah, 1932-1939), 11:146.

[29] Al-Dhahabī, *Tārīkh* 20 (A.H. 261-280):48.

[30] Aḥmad ibn 'Abd al-Raḥmān, *Dhayl*, *apud* al-Kindī, *Governors*, 478.

[31] Al-Kindī, *Governors*, 226.

[32] Ibn Zūlāq, *apud* Ibn Abī al-Wafā', *al-Jawāhir al-muḍīyah*, ed. 'Abd al-Fattāḥ Muḥammad al-Ḥulw. 2 vols. published (Cairo: 'Īsá al-Ḥalabī, 1978), 1:461. Future references to this edition unless otherwise specified.

[33] Al-Maqrīzī, *Muqaffá* 2:449f. In spite of the evidence, al-Maqrīzī himself asserts that Bakkār refused to take part: *Muqaffá* 1:424; *al-Mawā'iẓ wa-al-i'tibār bi-dhikr al-khiṭaṭ wa-al-āthār*, 2 vols. (Bulaq: Dār al-Ṭibā'ah al-Miṣrīyah, 1270), 1:321, ll. 1f.

[34] Ibn Ḥajar, *Raf'*, 520.

[35] Al-Qāḍī 'Iyāḍ, *Tartīb al-madārik wa-taqrīb al-masālik li-ma'rifat a'lām madh-*

portant support from other prominent Mālikīyah; for example, Ibn al-Mawwāz's predecessor, Ibn 'Abd al-Ḥakam (d. 268/882), had been willing to publicly drink and perform his ritual ablutions from a well of the ruler's that the people had stopped using, for which Ibn Ṭūlūn gave him a stipend.[36] In short, the adherents of the different tendencies in law were more or less equally willing to support the ruler, unlike the jurisprudents of Baghdad. With party lines less sharp, it was probably also easier in Egypt to develop juridical compromises.

What keeps me from calling al-Ṭaḥāwī the founder of a mature Ḥanafism is the fewness and insignificance of his students. The Ḥanafī biographer Ibn Abī al-Wafā' names only four.

The Students of al-Ṭaḥāwī

Abū Ṭālib Sa'īd ibn Muḥammad al-Barda'ī (n.d.); among *aṣḥāb* of Abū Ja'far al-Ṭaḥāwī; related hadith of him in Baghdad at the mosque of al-Karkhī, 2:224.

Abū Bakr Muḥammad ibn Badr ibn 'Abd al-'Azīz (d. 330/941-942); qadi; learnt jurisprudence from Abū Ja'far al-Ṭaḥāwī, 2 (Hyd.):37.

Abū Bakr Aḥmad ibn Muḥammad al-Dāmaghānī (n.d.); studied under al-Ṭaḥāwī in Egypt, then al-Karkhī in Baghdad, 1:318.

Abū al-Ḥasan 'Alī ibn Aḥmad ibn Muḥammad al-Ṭaḥāwī (*fl.* Giza, 350/961-962); son of Abū Ja'far, from whom learnt jurisprudence, 2:541f.

Additionally, Ibn Abī al-Wafā' names Abū Sa'īd al-Ḥasan ibn Isḥāq ibn Nabīl al-Naysābūrī (n.d.), who heard hadith from al-Nisā'ī and al-Ṭaḥāwī in Egypt, then became qadi off and on for 40 years over Ma'arrat al-Nu'mān.[37] In a chain of authorities, he also mentions one Abū Ibrāhīm Muḥammad ibn Sa'īd al-Yazīdī (n.d.) who related

---

hab Mālik, ed. Aḥmad Bakīr Maḥmūd, 4 vols. in 2 + index (Beirut: Maktabat al-Ḥayāh, 1967-68?), 3:73.

[36] Al-Quḍā'ī, *K. al-Khiṭaṭ*, *apud* al-Ṣafadī, *Das biographische Lexicon des Ṣalāḥaddīn Ḥalīl ibn Aybak aṣ-Ṣafadī*, Bibliotheca Islamica, 6, *ca.* 20 vols. to date, 3 (ed. Sven Dedering, Damascus: al-Maṭba'ah al-Hāshimīyah, 1953):339.

[37] Ibn Abī al-Wafā', *Jawāhir* 2:37.

Sharḥ ma'ānī al-āthār from al-Ṭaḥāwī.[38] Additionally, we have a list of another dozen men who related hadith of him, none notable save Muḥammad ibn al-Muẓaffar, who would compile the *Musnad* of Abū Ḥanīfah.[39] Certainly, no illustrious line of Egyptian Ḥanafīyah succeeded him. Perhaps, again, the very moderation of religious politics in Egypt hindered the development of formal schools of law: it was less necessary there than in Baghdad to prove one's orthodoxy, hence less necessary to adhere to a clearly identified school of law.

ABŪ KHĀZIM AND AL-BARDA'Ī IN BAGHDAD

There may be a case for naming al-Ṭaḥāwī's teacher Abū Khāzim the founder of the classical Ḥanafi school. The list of his teachers is similar to that of al-Ṭaḥāwī's: Hilāl al-Ra'y, Bakr al-'Ammī, Maḥmūd al-Anṣārī, 'Abd al-Raḥmān ibn Nā'il ibn Najīḥ, and Ibn al-Thaljī.[40] Maḥmūd and 'Abd al-Raḥmān are otherwise virtually unknown, and little more is known of Bakr al-'Ammī than his studying under the Baghdadi qadi Muḥammad ibn Samā'ah (d. 233/848)[41]; however, Hilāl al-Ra'y was a leader of the Basran school of *ra'y*, and Ibn al-Thaljī was an important early traditionalizing Ḥanafi of Baghdad. The list of Abū Khāzim's known works is shorter than al-Ṭaḥāwī's, and no work of his is known to have been the subject of a later commentary.[42] The list of his students is also very short; however, it does include the illustrious al-Ṭaḥāwī and the qadi Abū Ṭāhir al-Dabbās, possibly Abū Bakr al-Iskāf and Ibn Abī Mūsá; i.e., four early commentators of the books of Muḥammad al-Shaybānī. If Abū Khāzim not only wrote the first commentary on a work of al-Shaybānī's but formed students who extended that work of commentary, he significantly advanced the treatment of law as it was practiced in the classical, guild schools. Moreover, he is the first to be identified by Ibn Abī al-Wafā' as chief of the Ḥanafīyah of Baghdad (or

[38] Ibn Abī al-Wafā', *Jawāhir* 2:429.
[39] Ibn Ḥajar, *Lisān* 1:276f.
[40] Al-Khaṭīb al-Baghdādī, *Tārīkh* 11:63.
[41] Al-Kaffawī, *Katā'ib*, 61b.
[42] *V.* Ibn al-Nadīm, *Kitâb al-Fihrist*, ed. Gustav Flügel w/ Johannes Roediger & August Mueller (Leipzig: F. C. W. Vogel, 1872), 208 = *fann* 2, *maqālah* 6.

anywhere).[43]

The next chief of the Baghdadi school, according to Ibn Abī al-Wafā', was Abū Sa'īd al-Barda'ī (d. 317/929). He seems to have trained in Rayy, for Ibn Abī al-Wafā' states that his teachers were Abū 'Alī al-Daqqāq al-Rāzī (n.d.) and 'Alī ibn Mūsá ibn Naṣr (n.d.), who may have been the son of the Mūsá ibn Naṣr al-Rāzī (n.d.) under whom Abū 'Alī al-Daqqāq studied.[44] At the same time, all sources state that al-Barda'ī studied under Mūsá ibn Naṣr himself.[45] Since Mūsá ibn Naṣr was a student of Muḥammad al-Shaybānī's, it seems doubtful that he should have lived to teach al-Barda'ī. Even more doubtful seems the report that al-Barda'ī studied under Ismā'īl ibn Ḥammād, grandson to Abū Ḥanīfah (d. 212/827-828).[46] His training, in short, remains something of a puzzle.

Al-Barda'ī came to Baghdad during the lifetime of Dāwūd al-Ẓāhirī (d. 270/884), whom he met and debated (over a problem of law) in the Friday mosque.[47] He is said to have stayed in Baghdad, instead of continuing on the pilgrimage, in order to confute the Ẓāhirīyah.[48] Only three jurisprudents are named as his students: Abū al-Ḥasan al-Karkhī, Abū Ṭāhir al-Dabbās, and Abū 'Amr al-Ṭabarī. Possibly, the man who succeeded him as teacher of law at his mosque, Sahl ibn Ibrāhīm (d. before 344/956), should also be added.[49] Al-Karkhī, Abū Ṭāhir al-Dabbās, and Abū 'Amr al-Ṭabarī all produced commentaries on *al-Jāmi' al-ṣaghīr*, and Abū 'Amr on *al-Jāmi' al-kabīr* as well. The only extant work of al-Barda'ī's is a *Masā'il al-khilāf*, a survey of disputed juridical questions.[50] Al-Barda'ī's own contribution to Ḥanafi jurisprudence is, again, impossible at this point to identify with precision. His engagement with other schools is consistent, at least, with the development of a Ḥanafi school that would be comparable and acceptable to them.

---

[43] Ibn Abī al-Wafā', *Jawāhir* 2:493.

[44] Ibn Abī al-Wafā', *Jawāhir* 2:618; *Jawāhir* 2 (Hyd.):188, 259.

[45] Al-Khaṭīb al-Baghdādī, *Tārīkh* 4:99; Abū Isḥāq, *Ṭabaqāt*, 141; Ibn Abī al-Wafā', *Jawāhir* 2 (Hyd.):188; al-Kaffawī, *Katā'ib*, 52b.

[46] Al-Kaffawī, *Katā'ib*, 63a.

[47] Al-Khaṭīb al-Baghdādī, *Tārīkh* 4:99.

[48] Al-Khaṭīb al-Baghdādī, *Tārīkh* 4:100.

[49] Ibn Abī al-Wafā', *Jawāhir* 2:238f.

[50] Fuat Sezgin, *Geschichte des arabischen Schrifttums*, 9 vols. to date (Leiden: E. J. Brill, 1967-), 1:439.

AL-KARKHĪ

In spite of possible claims for Abū Khāzim and al-Barda'ī, I am inclined to consider the first teacher of the classical Ḥanafi school al-Barda'ī's student Abū al-Ḥasan al-Karkhī. He is the first Baghdadi with whom Abū Isḥāq al-Shīrāzī says the chieftaincy ended up, and Ibn Abī al-Wafā' identifies Abū Khāzim and al-Barda'ī as chiefs of the Baghdadi school only in retrospect, in his notice for al-Karkhī.[51] Al-Karkhī's was not the earliest commentary on a *Jāmi'* of al-Shaybānī's, nor was his the earliest *Mukhtaṣar* defining Ḥanafi jurisprudence; however, he was the first to leave students who wrote commentaries on his *Mukhtaṣar*, in the style of Ibn Surayj and his students' *ta'līqahs* based on his *Mukhtaṣar*.[52] Befitting one who finally established a system of transmitting authoritative doctrine, his teacher in jurisprudence is always clearly identified, whereas several of the teachers of Abū Khāzim and al-Barda'ī are either unknown or implausibly early.

Most importantly, al-Karkhī had many more known students than any Ḥanafi teacher before him (except, of course, Abū Ḥanīfah and his two disciples).

The Students of al-Karkhī

Abū al-'Alā' ('Abd Allāh) Muḥammad ibn 'Īsá *Ibn Abī Mūsá* al-Ḍarīr (d. Baghdad, 334/945); qadi; also taught law.[53]

Abū al-Qāsim 'Alī ibn Muḥammad ibn Dāwūd *al-Tanūkhī* (d. Basra, 342/953); qadi.[54]

---

[51] Abū Isḥāq, *Ṭabaqāt*, 142; Ibn Abī al-Wafā', *Jawāhir* 2:493.

[52] Ibn Abī Mūsá produced *Mukhtaṣar Kitāb Abī al-Ḥasan al-Karkhī* (Ibn Abī al-Wafā', *Jawāhir* 2 [Hyd.]:260f); al-Jaṣṣāṣ produced a commentary on the *Mukhtaṣar* of al-Karkhī (Ibn Abī al-Wafā', *Jawāhir*, 1:223); Abū 'Abd Allāh al-Baṣrī likewise wrote a commentary on the *Mukhtaṣar* of al-Karkhī (Ibn al-Nadīm, *Fihrist*, 208 = *f.* 2, *q.* 6). Additionally, the verb *'allaqa* appears in connection with al-Qaḥṭānī's learning the book *Adab al-qāḍī* from al-Karkhī (Ibn Abī al-Wafā', ed. Ḥulw, 1:268): perhaps he produced a commentary on it.

[53] No teacher named, but his writing a *Mukhtaṣar Kitāb Abī al-Ḥasan al-Karkhī*, among other books, does suggest it: Ibn Abī al-Wafā', *Jawāhir* 2 (Hyd.):260f.

[54] Al-Khaṭīb al-Baghdādī, *Tārīkh* 12:77-79; Ibn Abī al-Wafā', *Jawāhir* 2:595f, 611f.

Abū 'Alī Aḥmad ibn Muḥammad *al-Shāshī* (d. 344/955-956); taught in succession to al-Karkhī.[55]

Abū al-Ḥusayn Aḥmad ibn Muḥammad al-Naysābūrī *Qāḍī al-Ḥaramayn* (d. Nishapur, 351/962); qadi; also studied under Abū Ṭāhir al-Dabbās; taught law in Nishapur.[56]

Abū Muḥammad Ibn 'Abdak ('Adī) al-Baṣrī (d. Basra? 347/958-959); taught law in Basra.[57]

Abū al-Qāsim ('Abd Allāh) Muḥammad ibn al-Ḥasan Ibn Abī al-Qāsim *(Ibn) al-Dā'ī* (d. 359/969-970?); Mu'tazili.[58]

Abū Bakr Muḥammad ibn Aḥmad ibn 'Alī al-Shāhawayh al-Fārisī *Ibn Shāhawayh* (d. Nishapur, 361/971-972); taught law in Nishapur; qadi.[59]

Abū Bakr Aḥmad ibn Muḥammad al-Anṣārī *al-Dāmaghānī* (d. 360's/970's); also studied under al-Ṭaḥāwī; succeeded al-Karkhī in giving juridical opinions; qadi.[60]

'Alī ibn 'Abd Allāh al-Sadīwarī (d. Bukhara, 365/975); qadi.[61]

Abū 'Abd Allāh al-Ḥusayn ibn 'Alī al-Ju'al al-Kāghadī *al-Baṣrī* (d. 369/980?); chief of the Mu'tazilah.[62]

Abū Bakr Aḥmad ibn 'Alī *al-Jaṣṣāṣ* al-Rāzī (d. Baghdad, 370/981?); also studied under Abū Sahl al-Zujājī; taught law in Nishapur,

---

[55] Al-Khaṭīb al-Baghdādī, *Tārīkh* 4:376; Ibn Abī al-Wafā', *Jawāhir* 1:262.

[56] Al-Dhahabī, *Siyar* 16 (ed. Shu'ayb al-Arna'ūṭ & Akram al-Būshayyī, 1983):25f; Ibn Abī al-Wafā', *Jawāhir* 1:284-288, 2 (Hyd.):249.

[57] Abū Isḥāq, *Ṭabaqāt*, 143; Ibn Abī al-Wafā', *Jawāhir* 2 (Hyd.):265. Associated by al-Ṣaymarī with Abū 'Amr al-Ṭabarī.

[58] Ibn Abī al-Wafā', *Jawāhir* 2 (Hyd.):44f; Ibn al-Murtaḍá, *Die Klassen der Mu'taziliten*, ed. Susanna Diwald-Wilzer, Bibliotheca Islamica, ed. Helmut Ritter & Albert Dietrich, 21 (Wiesbaden: Franz Steiner, 1961), 114.

[59] Ibn Abī al-Wafā', *Jawāhir* 2 (Hyd.):18, names no teacher, but Abū Isḥāq al-Shīrāzī places him amongst the *aṣḥāb* of al-Karkhī (*Ṭabaqāt*, 144).

[60] Al-Khaṭīb al-Baghdādī, *Tārīkh* 5:97f; al-Dhahabī, *Tārīkh* 26 (A.H. 351-380):454f; Ibn Abī al-Wafā', *Jawāhir* 1:318.

[61] Al-Ḥākim al-Naysābūrī, *Tārīkh Naysābūr*, *apud* al-Dhahabī, *Tārīkh* 26 (A.H. 351-380):343; cf. Ibn Abī al-Wafā', *Jawāhir* 2:552.

[62] Ibn al-Nadīm, *Fihrist*, 174f, 208 = *f*. 1, *q*. 5, *f*. 2, *q*. 6; Ibn Abī al-Wafā', *Jawāhir* 2:260; Ibn al-Murtaḍá, *Klassen*, 105.

Baghdad.[63]

al-Ḥusayn ibn Muḥammad ibn 'Abd al-Wahhāb (d. 372/983), qadi for Basra.[64]

Abū al-Ḥasan (al-Ḥusayn) Aḥmad ibn Yūsuf al-Tanūkhī (d. 377/987); Mu'tazili; also taught law?[65]

Abū Ḥāmid Aḥmad ibn al-Ḥusayn al-Marwazī *Ibn al-Ṭabarī* (d. 377/987-988); qadi; also studied in Balkh under Abū al-Qāsim al-Ṣaffār al-Balkhī (d. 336/947-948).[66]

Abū al-Fahm Aḥmad ibn Muḥammad *al-Qaḥṭānī* al-Tanūkhī (*fl.* 327/938-939), brother to Abū al-Qāsim al-Tanūkhī; qadi.[67]

Abū 'Abd Allāh Yūsuf ibn 'Alī ibn Muḥammad al-Jurjānī (n.d.).[68]

Abū Sahl al-Zujājī al-Ghazālī al-Faraḍī (d. Nishapur, n.d.); taught law in Nishapur.[69]

Abū al-Faraj al-'Umānī (n.d.).[70]

Abū Muḥammad (n.d.), not the same as Abū Muḥammad al-Baṣrī (d. 347/958-959).[71]

---

[63] Sezgin, *Geschichte* 1:144f; Ibn Abī al-Wafā', *Jawāhir* 1:220-224.

[64] Al-Dhahabī, *Tārīkh* 26 (A.H. 351-380):517; cf. Ibn Abī al-Wafā', *Jawāhir* 2:89.

[65] Al-Khaṭīb al-Baghdādī, *Tārīkh* 5:221f; Ibn Abī al-Wafā', *Jawāhir* 1:353f; Ibn al-Murtaḍá, *Klassen*, 108.

[66] Al-Khaṭīb al-Baghdādī, *Tārīkh* 4:107f; al-Dhahabī, *Tārīkh* 26 (A.H. 351-380):536; Ibn Abī al-Wafā', *Jawāhir* 1:161-163.

[67] Ibn Abī al-Wafā', *Jawāhir* 1:267f; Ibn Duqmāq, *Naẓm al-jumān fī ṭabaqāt aṣḥāb imāminā al-Nu'mān*, Serez 1827, 93a.

[68] Ibn Abī al-Wafā', *Jawāhir* 2 (Hyd.):228f; al-Kaffawī, *Katā'ib*, 70a. The identity of this man is somewhat doubtful. Only al-Kaffawī identifies him as having learnt jurisprudence from al-Karkhī. Al-Kaffawī also ascribes to him a commentary on *al-Jāmi' al-kabīr*, possibly confusing him with the Abū 'Abd Allāh Muḥammad ibn Yaḥyá al-Jurjānī who died 398/1008, to whom Kātib Çelebī ascribes such a commentary (*Kashf* 1:569)—unless Kātib Çelebī is mistaken, for Muḥammad ibn Yaḥyá does not appear in al-Sahmī, *Tārīkh Jurjān*. Al-Kaffawī and Ibn Abī al-Wafā' both ascribe to him a work called *Khizānat al-akmal* in six volumes; however, Kātib Çelebī (*Kashf* 1:702) ascribes that to Abū Ya'qūb Yūsuf ibn 'Alī ibn Muḥammad al-Jurjānī (*fl.* 522/1128).

[69] Ibn Abī al-Wafā', *Jawāhir* 2 (Hyd.):254. Also studied under al-Barda'ī: al-Kaffawī, *Katā'ib*, 69b.

[70] Ibn Abī al-Wafā', *Jawāhir* 2 (Hyd.):262.

[71] Ibn Abī al-Wafā', *Jawāhir* 2 (Hyd.):265.

Abū Zakarīyā' Yaḥyá ibn Muḥammad al-Ḍarīr al-Farā'iḍī (n.d.).[72]

Abū al-Qāsim Ibn Sahlawayh (n.d.), Mu'tazili.[73]

Abū Bakr al-Bukhārī (n.d.), Mu'tazili.[74]

This makes a total of twenty-two: fourteen whose dates of death are known (at least approximately), eight more whose dates of death are not known. The list is mainly Baghdadi, but students of al-Karkhī's taught in Basra and Nishapur, while others became qadis in cities of Iraq, Khurasan, and Transoxania. It is not so impressive an achievement as Ibn Surayj's, inasmuch as few of al-Karkhī's students had known students, themselves; yet no one other Ḥanafi in his century can be identified with half so many students as he, nor any other than he with so many as can be identified with his student al-Jaṣṣāṣ.

Ibn Abī al-Wafā' gives an example of how the line of students and teachers that starts with al-Karkhī supplanted other lines of succession: the line of teachers that taught at the tomb of Darb 'Abdah.[75] First was Abū Sa'īd al-Barda'ī, then his student Abū 'Amr al-Ṭabarī. Abū 'Amr was succeeded by Sahl ibn Ibrāhīm, of whom I have been able to find out nothing more. Up to this point, prestige among the Ḥanafīyah of Baghdad evidently did not depend on one's having studied under a single prestigious teacher. After Sahl, however, there taught at this mosque Abū 'Alī al-Shāshī (d. 344/955-956), whom al-Karkhī appointed to succeed him in teaching jurisprudence when he was paralysed by a stroke,[76] then al-Karkhī's student al-Jaṣṣāṣ, then al-Jaṣṣāṣ's student Abū Bakr Muḥammad ibn Mūsá al-Khʷārizmī (d. 403/1012). From this point forward, Baghdadi Ḥanafi jurisprudents generally had clearly identified teachers in jurisprudence, usually in a line running from al-Karkhī. George Makdisi names six jurisprudents who were the leading Ḥanafīyah of Baghdad in the fifth/eleventh century.[77] Every one had clearly identified teachers in the

---

[72] Studied under the *aṣḥāb* of al-Karkhī, according to al-Ṣaymarī (*apud* Ibn Abī al-Wafā', *Jawāhir* 2 [Hyd.]:216) but under al-Karkhī himself according to Abū Isḥāq (*Ṭabaqāt*, 144).

[73] 'Abd al-Jabbār, *Faḍl al-i'tizāl*, ed. Fu'ād Sayyid (Tunis: al-Dār al-Tūnisīyah lil-Nashr, 1974), 325.

[74] Ibn al-Murtaḍá, *Klassen*, 109.

[75] Ibn Abī al-Wafā', *Jawāhir* 2:238.

[76] Al-Khaṭīb al-Baghdādī, *Tārīkh* 4:376.

[77] George Makdisi, *Ibn 'Aqīl et la résurgence de l'Islam traditionaliste au XIe siècle*

line running from al-Karkhī through al-Jaṣṣāṣ.

In his personal life, al-Karkhī was notably ascetic, and not only refused to become a qadi himself but dissociated himself from students who became qadis. Nevertheless, a number of them did accept judgeships, and Ibn al-Dā'ī was close to the Būyids. His students arranged for him to receive a stipend just before his death. Like his teacher al-Barda'ī, al-Karkhī was a Mu'tazili in theology. Yet, of course, it was not necessary to be a Mu'tazili to be a prominent jurisprudent of the Ḥanafi school: it was of the essence of the *madhhab* system that law and theology were pursued separately. Abū Bakr al-Khʷārizmī, successor to al-Jaṣṣāṣ and chief of the Ḥanafi school for a time, staunchly opposed *kalām* and prayed behind a Ḥanbali (probably employed him as prayer leader in the mosque where he taught).[78]

When it comes to al-Karkhī's influence on Ḥanafi doctrine, it is necessary again to caution that I do not propose, yet, to write the history of *fiqh*. Some reports suggest that it completed the traditionalization of Ḥanafi doctrine begun in the previous century by partisans such as Ibn al-Thaljī. Ibn Abī al-Wafā' states that whereas 'Īsá ibn Abān had put analogy (*qiyās*) before a hadith report unless the transmitter of that hadith report was also learnèd in jurisprudence, al-Karkhī put the hadith report first regardless of the transmitter's knowledge of jurisprudence.[79] This is less than the total repudiation of *ra'y*, but still a significant step in the direction of traditionalism. On the other hand, al-Kaffawī states that whereas al-Barda'ī had said to follow the opinion of a Companion rather than analogy, al-Shāfi'ī to follow neither, al-Karkhī had said to follow the Companion only if his opinion agreed with analogy, which sounds like a step back from traditionalism.[80]

THE ḤANAFI SCHOOL IN EGYPT AND AFRICA

The Ḥanafi school in Egypt after al-Ṭaḥāwī is almost invisible in Ḥanafi sources. As seen earlier, only four jurisprudents are definitely

---

(Vᵉ siècle de l'Hégire) (Damascus: Institut Français de Damas, 1963), 166-177.

[78] Al-Khaṭīb al-Baghdādī, *Tārīkh* 3:247.

[79] Al-Karkhī, *K. al-Jāmi'*, *apud* Ibn Abī al-Wafā', *Jawāhir* 2 (Hyd.):417.

[80] Al-Kaffawī, 66a. *V.* also Marie Bernand, "Ḥanafī *uṣūl al-fiqh* Through a Manuscript of al-Ǧaṣṣāṣ," *Journal of the American Oriental Society* 105 (1985):623-625.

identified as having learnt jurisprudence from al-Ṭaḥāwī, and two of them moved on (with al-Ṭaḥāwī himself) to Baghdad. Besides them, Ibn Abī al-Wafā' names only one other Ḥanafi active in Egypt in the period after al-Ṭaḥāwī, a Mu'tazili named Aḥmad ibn Z*b*h*rād (d. 344/955-956 or 346/957-958) who moved there from Siraf on the Persian Gulf.[81] Ibn Ḥajar's survey of Egyptian qadis, *Raf' al-iṣr 'an quḍāt Miṣr*, provides the names of three other Ḥanafi jurisprudents from the time of al-Ṭaḥāwī or after who assumed the judgeship. None had identifiable teachers, though, and all left Egypt when their terms in office were up, two for Palestine and one for Iraq. They were part of no flourishing Ḥanafi school in Egypt.

Māliki sources assert that the Fāṭimis, who conquered Africa in 296/909, Egypt in 358/969, favored the Ḥanafīyah. The surviving manual of Fāṭimi law, al-Qāḍī al-Nu'mān's *Da'ā'im al-islām*, is said to be Ḥanafi except for minor details.[82] Al-Qāḍī al-Nu'mān himself speaks of the relative friendliness of the Ḥanafīyah.[83] Perhaps that very favor dealt the *coup de grâce* to Egyptian Ḥanafism, for the Ḥanafīyah seem to have been first eclipsed by Shī'i jurisprudents, then entirely supplanted by the Mālikīyah, always identified with opposition to the Fāṭimis and naturally favored when Fāṭimi rule was overthrown.

The Ḥanafi school of Africa may have put down deeper roots than the school in Egypt, for Māliki sources continually refer to the presence of Kufan jurisprudents; yet we know almost nothing of its constitution. Looking back from Mamluk times, Ibn Faḍl Allāh (d. Damascus, 749/1349) can state that Ibn 'Abdūn (d. 299 or 300/*ca.* 912) was the first and last of the Maghribi Ḥanafīyah, "as if they were on that side (the West) the egg of a rooster."[84] Ibn 'Abdūn was qadi for

---

[81] Ibn Abī al-Wafā', *Jawāhir* 1:169.

[82] H. Monès, "Le Malékisme et l'échec des Fatimides en Ifriqiya," *Etudes d'Orientalisme dédiées à la mémoire de Lévi-Provençal*, 2 vols. (Paris: G.-P. Maisonneuve & Larose, 1962), 1:211. Divergences from Sunni doctrine are pointed out by Rudolf Strothmann, "Recht der Ismailiten," *Der Islam* 31 (1954):131-146, and Robert Brunschvig, "Fiqh Fâtimide et histoire de l'Ifrîqiya," *Mélanges d'histoire et d'archéologie . . . . Hommage à G. Marçais*, 2 vols. (Algiers: Gouvernement général de l'Algérie, 1957), 2:16-19.

[83] Al-Qāḍī al-Nu'mān, *Da'ā'im al-islām*, ed. 'Āṣif ibn 'Alī Aṣghar Fayḍī, 2 vols. (Cairo: Dār al-Ma'ārif, 1952), 1:96.

[84] Ibn Faḍl Allāh, *Masālik al-abṣār fī mamālik al-amṣār*, Aya Sofya (Istanbul) 3419, 43a.

Africa 275/888-889-277/891.[85] He used his office to persecute the students of Saḥnūn and other Medinese jurisprudents.[86] Actually, we have the names of a fair number of Kufan or Iraqi jurisprudents who were active in Africa during the ninth century or early tenth from the African biographer al-Khushanī (d. Cordoba, 371/981).[87] Unfortunately, he says almost nothing on their training or other activity as a school. Of many, al-Khushanī remarks participation in juridical and theological debate. Ibn Khallikān states that the school of Abū Ḥanīfah prevailed in Africa until the advent of al-Mu'izz ibn Bādīs (d. Qayrawan, 454/1062), whose patronage caused all the people of the Maghrib to embrace the school of Mālik.[88] Probably, as in Egypt, it was their identification with the Fāṭimid dynasty that doomed the Ḥanafi school of Africa. Several Kufan jurisprudents actually converted to Shī'ism when the Fāṭimids took over, and of none are told such stories of proud reserve toward the powerful as one so often reads of Māliki jurisprudents.[89] A doctoral dissertation on the spread of the Māliki school in North Africa stresses the connections of that school with several dynasties opposed to the Fāṭimids.[90] It is certainly time for a new study of the Sunni schools under the Fāṭimids, at once more profound, more nuanced, but less given to Māliki triumphalism than previous accounts. I predict that it will confirm, still, the hazard of depending on the wrong patronage.

---

[85] Ibn Faḍl Allāh, *Masālik*, 41b.

[86] Abū al-'Arab, *K. al-Miḥan*, ed. Yaḥyá Wuhayb al-Jubūrī (Beirut: Dār al-Gharb al-Islāmī, 1983), 469-471; al-Qāḍī 'Iyāḍ, *Tartīb* 3:207f, 233, 240.

[87] Al-Khushanī, *Ṭabaqāt 'ulamā' Ifrīqiyah*, *apud* Abū al-'Arab, *Classes des savants de l'Ifriqiya*, ed. Mohammed ben Cheneb (Publications de la Facultée des lettres d'Alger, Bulletin de Correspondance africaine, 51; Paris: Leroux, 1915), 187-241 = *Quḍāt Qurṭubah wa-'Ulamā' Ifrīqīyah*, ed. 'Izzat al-'Aṭṭār al-Ḥusaynī (Min Turāth al-Andalus, 2; Cairo: Maktabat al-Khānjī, 1953), 236-255.

[88] Ibn Khallikān, *Wafayāt al-a'yān wa-anbā' abnā' al-zamān*, ed. Iḥsān 'Abbās, 7 vols. + index (Beirut: Dār al-Thaqāfah, 1968), 5:233f.

[89] *V.* Georges Marçais, *La Berbérie musulmane et l'Orient au Moyen Age* (Les Grandes crises de l'histoire, Paris: Aubier, 1946), 94-99, 138, based on the biographical dictionaries of Abū al-'Arab and al-Khushanī.

[90] Mansour Hasan Mansour, "The Spread and the Domination of the Maliki School of Law in North and West Africa, Eighth-Fourteenth Century," Ph.D. diss., Univ. of Illinois at Chicago Circle, 1981, chaps. 3, 4.

IN KHURASAN AND TRANSOXANIA

By comparison with the Ḥanafi school in Africa and Egypt, a great deal is known of the Ḥanafi school in Khurasan and Transoxania; yet the school remains difficult to characterize. What W. Montgomery Watt says of the Iraqi school through the first half of the third century (to about 865 CE) seems equally true of the Ḥanafi school in Khurasan and Transoxania throughout the fourth century (900's CE):

> Of the earlier scholars to whom notices are given by Ibn-Abī-l-Wafā' in *Al-jawāhir al-muḍī'a fī ṭabaqāt al-Ḥanafiyya* some, though holding views akin to those of Abū-Ḥanīfa, do not appear to have studied under him or his immediate disciples. It seems likely that, until the Shāfi'ite school took shape, most scholars of Iraq who used rational methods, even to a slight degree, were reckoned as Ḥanafites.[91]

Ibn Abī al-Wafā' names almost 200 jurisprudents who died in the 300's, and a few more can be added from other sources. Over half of them seem to have been active in Khurasan or Transoxania. Among these Khurasanis and Transoxanians, those whose teachers in jurisprudence are named are outnumbered four-to-one by those whose teachers are not.

Even leaders of the Khurasani Ḥanafīyah went without well-known teachers in jurisprudence. For example, al-Ḥākim al-Naysābūrī, our principal source for the history of Nishapur, terms Abū Muḥammad Ḥāmid ibn Maḥmūd ibn Ma'qil al-Shāmātī al-Qaṭṭān (d. 319/931-932) "*shaykh* of the *aṣḥāb* of Abū Ḥanīfah in Nishapur."[92] He does not state that al-Qaṭṭān learnt jurisprudence from any particular shaykh, although he does say he related the books of Muḥammad al-Shaybānī from a Ziyād ibn 'Abd al-Raḥmān (otherwise unknown). Similarly, he terms Abū al-'Abbās Aḥmad ibn Hārūn al-Muzanī al-Tabbān (d. 349/960) "shaykh of the *aṣḥāb* of Abū Ḥanīfah in Nishapur."[93] He names a number of shaykhs from whom al-Tabbān heard hadith but names none from whom he learnt jurisprudence in

---

[91] W. Montgomery Watt, *The Formative Period of Islamic Thought* (Edinburgh: Univ. Press, 1973), 285.

[92] Al-Ḥākim al-Naysābūrī, *Tārīkh Naysābūr*, *apud* Ibn Abī al-Wafā', *Jawāhir* 2:29.

[93] Al-Ḥākim al-Naysābūrī, *Tārīkh Naysābūr*, *apud* Ibn Abī al-Wafā', *Jawāhir* 1:343f.

particular.

The same is true outside Nishapur: even leaders seem to lack identifiable students and teachers. Ibn Abī al-Wafā' states that Abū Bakr Aḥmad ibn Ismā'īl (d. 321/933) was chief (*ra'īs*) of Samarqand, but names no teacher.[94] He quotes al-Ḥākim, again, as calling the qadi Abū Sa'īd al-Khalīl ibn Aḥmad al-Sijzī (d. Samarqand, 368/979) "shaykh of *ahl al-ra'y* in his time," but names no teacher.[95] He quotes al-Ḥākim also as saying of Abū Bakr 'Abd Allāh ibn Muḥammad al-Ashqar al-Budaylī (d. 343/954-955), "shaykh of the *aṣḥāb* of Abū Ḥanīfah in his time for Bukhara" without naming a teacher.[96] Apparently drawing on al-Sam'ānī, Ibn Abī al-Wafā' states that Kumayl ibn Ja'far ibn Kumayl al-Bakrābādhī (d. 336/947-948) was "chief of the *aṣḥāb* of Abū Ḥanīfah in his time" (in Gurgan) but names no teacher.[97] These men had teachers, of course, but they could be remembered as leading jurisprudents independently of their training; that is, unlike jurisprudents in the classical, guild system, their authority did not rest on their having been authorized to give juridical opinions or to teach by particular, recognized shaykhs.

The very language that designates leadership in tenth-century Khurasan and Transoxania was not yet fixed. As seen above, al-Ḥākim al-Naysābūrī often identifies one man or another as "the shaykh of the *aṣḥāb* of Abū Ḥanīfah," yet he says of a Muḥammad ibn Ḥāmid (d. 383/993-994) that he was the "imam of the *aṣḥāb* of Abu Ḥanīfah in Bukhara."[98] This is not the regular language of chieftaincy (*riyāsah*) associated with the leadership of Ibn Surayj and his successors, al-Karkhī and his, in Iraq.[99] It will be remembered how al-Ḥākim's distinction between the language of hadith collection (*rawá 'an, sami-'a*, &c.) and the language of jurisprudence (*tafaqqaha 'alá*) reveals the spread among the Khurasani Shāfi'īyah of the more definite Iraqi

---

[94] Ibn Abī al-Wafā', *Jawāhir* 1:148.

[95] Ibn Abī al-Wafā', *Jawāhir* 2:178.

[96] Ibn Abī al-Wafā', *Jawāhir* 2:328.

[97] Ibn Abī al-Wafā', *Jawāhir* 2:717.

[98] Al-Ḥākim al-Naysābūrī, *Tārīkh Naysābūr*, *apud* Ibn Abī al-Wafā', 2 (Hyd.):39f. The accuracy of Ibn Abī al-Wafā's quotation is confirmed by that of Ibn Duqmāq, *Naẓm*, 111b.

[99] Apparently, al-Ḥākim did use the term *ra'īs* as well for the leading adherent of the *madhhab*; e.g., calling the Nishapuran Ḥanafi Abū Naṣr al-Labbād (d. 280/893-894) "shaykh of *ahl al-ra'y* in his time and their *ra'īs*" (Ibn Abī al-Wafā', *Jawāhir* 1:321). The point is that pre-eminence was expressed by no set term.

forms through the students and students of students of Ibn Surayj. The same forms do not seem to have spread in the tenth century, yet, among the Ḥanafīyah of Khurasan, even from the students and students of students of al-Karkhī.

The relatively greater receptivity of the tenth-century Khurasani Shāfi'īyah to new forms from Iraq agrees with the suggestion of Richard W. Bulliet that the Shāfi'īyah were by and large newer converts, eager to prove themselves by taking up the latest forms of orthodoxy:

> Families descended from converts of the seventh and eighth centuries, that is to say the socially respectable converts, were attracted to the orthodoxy of the moment because of the advantages it held out for them. That orthodoxy was Ḥanafī in law and *mu'tazilī* in theology. Subsequent generations of the same families stuck to these doctrines and defended them against later doctrines whose adherents threatened their dominant position. Families which converted during the ninth century, on the other hand, tended to favor what they hoped would be and strived to make the new orthodoxy, that of the Shāfi'ī law school and Ash'arī theology. They hoped to ride this new orthodoxy into positions of dominance in society.[100]

Attractive though Bulliet's social explanation may be, it suffers from lack of evidence: it is only Bulliet's guess that Shāfi'i families had been Muslim for a shorter time than Ḥanafi. Bulliet's explanation is moreover difficult to reconcile with the high degree of power that some traditionalists seem to have enjoyed already in the ninth century (e.g., Isḥāq ibn Rāhawayh and Muḥammad ibn Yaḥyá al-Dhuhlī in Nishapur).

A technical explanation seems more economical: the Shāfi'īyah of Khurasan were more receptive to the new forms of Ibn Surayj than the Ḥanafīyah to the new forms of al-Karkhī because their usual practice was so much more cumbersome. It was much easier to learn the opinions of al-Shāfi'ī himself and the essential hadith reports they were based on, the procedure of Ibn Surayj and his followers, than to learn the opinions of al-Shāfi'ī amongst tens of thousands of other hadith reports from the Prophet, the Companions, and the Successors.

---

[100] Richard W. Bulliet, "Conversion to Islam and the Emergence of a Muslim Society in Iran," *Conversion to Islam*, ed. Nehemia Levtzion (New York: Holmes & Meier, 1979), 39.

Certification by a particular teacher, again the procedure of Ibn Surayj and his followers, was more efficient than picking up learning from many shaykhs, a better guarantee of both the orthodoxy of that learning and the competence of the graduate to give opinions and teach. The Ḥanafīyah of Khurasan were already, in large measure, accustomed to these advantages, and therefore had less need to take over the new system.

It is difficult to prove that Ḥanafi teachers had always made only moderate demands on their students. Negatively, though, we have no such statistics as make contemporary traditionalists look impossibly demanding; that is, no Ḥanafi jurisprudent is said to have known hundreds of thousands of hadith reports, or to have said that knowing that many was a criterion of competence.

As for learning jurisprudence from a particular teacher, it was at least no novelty to the Ḥanafīyah of Khurasan. The phenomenon of identifiable students and teachers begins with the Ḥanafīyah, and several lines were well established in Khurasan before any students of al-Karkhī appeared there. For example, take al-Karkhī's contemporaries Abū al-Qāsim al-Ṣaffār al-Balkhī (d. 336/947-948), teacher to Abū Ja'far al-Hinduwānī and Ibn al-Ṭabarī, and Abū Naṣr al-'Iyāḍī of Samarqand. Al-Ṣaffār is said to have learnt jurisprudence from Nuṣayr ibn Yaḥyá of Balkh (d. 268/881-882), who learnt it from Muḥammad ibn Samā'ah of Baghdad (d. 233/848), a student of Abū Yūsuf's,[101] while Abū Naṣr is said to have learnt jurisprudence from Abū Bakr Aḥmad ibn Isḥāq al-Jūzajānī, who learnt it in turn from Abū Sulaymān al-Jūzajānī of Baghdad (d. 204/819-820?), a student of Muḥammad al-Shaybānī's.[102] These chains of students and teachers are tellingly defective: very little is known of Abū Bakr al-Jūzajānī other than his studying under Abū Sulaymān and teaching Abū Naṣr,[103] Nuṣayr ibn Yaḥyá is alternatively said to have been a student of Abū Sulaymān al-Jūzajānī,[104] and Abū Sulaymān al-Jūzajānī is alternatively said to have been a student of Abū Yūsuf's as well as al-Shaybānī's.[105] We have seen how similar uncertainty characterizes Abū Khāzim's and Abū Sa'īd al-Barda'ī's respective chains

[101] Al-Kaffawī, *Katā'ib*, 66b.
[102] Ibn Abī al-Wafā', *Jawāhir* 1:177-179; al-Kaffawī, *Katā'ib*, 51b, 52a.
[103] *V.* two entries in Ibn Abī al-Wafā', *Jawāhir* 1:144, 145.
[104] Ibn Abī al-Wafā', *Jawāhir* 2 (Hyd.):200.
[105] Ibn Abī al-Wafā', *Jawāhir* 2 (Hyd.):178.

of teachers, and there is no doubt that chains of students and teachers were more systematically registered after al-Karkhī. Still, the fact of having an identifiable teacher in jurisprudence could not give such a competitive advantage to a tenth-century Ḥanafi in Khurasan as it must have given to his Shāfi'i contemporary.

The similarity of Ḥanafi practice in Khurasan to Ḥanafi practice in Iraq apart from the influence of al-Karkhī has already become apparent, moreover, in the chronology of commentaries on the books of al-Shaybānī. Several were produced by Khurasani jurisprudents who had not studied under al-Karkhī or any student of his. By contrast, no Khurasani produced a commentary on the *Mukhtaṣar* of al-Muzanī apart from having studied under Ibn Surayj or a student of his. The Khurasani Ḥanafīyah were slower to take up the new, Iraqi ways because they already had so much more of them.

There are doubtless other reasons as well why al-Karkhī's modern style spread in Khurasan more slowly than Ibn Surayj's. It looks as though the Khurasani Ḥanafīyah were under less pressure than the Iraqi to display some badge of orthodoxy, possibly because Karrāmi preaching had won for them the sort of popular support that the Ḥanābilah enjoyed in Baghdad. Also, patterns of patronage may have shifted in ways undetectable in the extant sources, or at least not detected by me.

In sum, al-Karkhī's way was that of the classical Ḥanafi school, but it would not prevail in all the major centers until the next century. It is because it took relatively long to prevail that the qadi Ibn Qinālīzādah (d. Adrianopolis, 979/1572), looking back from the Ottoman period, would judge that the roots of the Ḥanafi system had been decided in the second century by Abū Ḥanīfah and his immediate disciples but that the period of *ikhtiyār*, free choice, extended for another two centuries after that, until (around) 400/1009-10. Only thenceforth were Ḥanafi jurisprudents limited to *tarjīḥ*, counting one given opinion more weighty than another but no longer daring to propose new solutions.[106]

[106] Ibn Qinālīzādah, *Ṭabaqāt al-masā'il*, Şehit Ali Paşa 2831/6, 57b; Aya Sofya 3407/1, 1b, 2a. Similarly, Ya'akov Meron considers 400/1009-10 the end of the "Ancient Period" in the development of Ḥanafi jurisprudence and the beginning of the "Classical": "The Development of Legal Thought in Hanafi Texts," *Studia Islamica*, no. 30 (1969), 78.

CHAPTER SEVEN

AL-KHALLĀL AND THE CLASSICAL ḤANBALI SCHOOL

The traditionalists of Baghdad held out for exclusive dependence on ancient authority for longer than any group elsewhere; however, as developed in Chapter One, their resistance to any dependence on later teachers was untenable in the long run. By the beginning of the tenth century, there had grown up out of the traditionalist bloc in Baghdad itself a Ḥanbali school of law parallel to the developing Shāfi'i and other schools. The new school developed in two stages: first was the work of Aḥmad ibn Ḥanbal's immediate followers, who gathered his hadith and juridical opinions in spite of his traditionalist opposition to any such enterprise; second, the work of Abū Bakr al-Khallāl. Al-Khallāl might justly be called the founder of the Ḥanbali school, for it was he who made the decisive steps of gathering the jurisprudence of one master, the eponym of the school; of writing a biographical dictionary of those who related that jurisprudence; and of teaching the newly gathered doctrine to disciples of his own. His new forms did not immediately sweep away the old Ḥanbalism, but they had no serious rivals in the long term.

THE COLLECTION OF AḤMAD'S OPINIONS BY HIS IMMEDIATE FOLLOWERS

The first requisite for a school of law was the collection of a body of legal doctrine. Joseph Schacht has located the decisive collection of Aḥmad ibn Ḥanbal's teaching "about the middle of the third century." This work of collection, he says, marks "the beginnings of the Ḥanbalī school."[1] I believe this is too early. What Aḥmad's disciples collected was still only the raw materials from which jurisprudents might work. It included no comprehensive collection of Aḥmad's ju-

[1] Joseph Schacht, "The Schools of Law and Later Developments of Jurisprudence," *Law in the Middle East*, ed. Majid Khadduri & Herbert J. Liebesny (Washington, D.C.: Middle East Institute, 1955), 67.

ridical opinions corresponding to, say, the two *Jāmi'*s and *Āthār* of al-Shaybānī that defined the Ḥanafi school and the *Mukhtaṣar* of al-Muzanī that defined the Shāfi'i.

The only book on jurisprudence with which Aḥmad himself is credited concerned the ritual prayer.[2] It dwells not on disputed questions but rather on humbly following the prayer leader; that is, the moralistic element is far more prominent than any technical, legal reasoning. Otherwise, the books ascribed to him comprise at most theological polemics against secret unbelievers, Murji'ah, and those who affirmed the createdness of the Qur'an, the so-called Jahmīyah.[3]

The greatest extant collection of Aḥmad's learning is his massive *Musnad*. Some stories do suggest that he himself assembled it as a book. He is said to have dictated it to his son 'Abd Allāh (d. 290/903) in 227 or 228/*ca.* 842.[4] According to Aḥmad's cousin Ḥanbal ibn Isḥāq, he, 'Abd Allāh, and Aḥmad's older son, Ṣāliḥ (d. 266/880?), were the only ones to hear it from him in its entirety. In this account, Ḥanbal goes on to say that Aḥmad told them,

> I have collected and selected this book from 750,000 (hadith reports). Whatever the Muslims disagree about by way of the hadith of the Messenger of God . . . consult it. If you find it there (the disputed hadith report, go by it); otherwise, it has no probative value (*laysa bi-ḥujjah*).[5]

In other words, the *Musnad* was to be an adequate basis for the practice of jurisprudence.[6]

Most accounts, though, suggest that what 'Abd Allāh and his

[2] 'Abd al-Qādir Badrān, *al-Madkhal ilá madhhab al-imām Aḥmad* (n.p., n.d.), 46; Fuat Sezgin, *Geschichte des arabischen Schrifttums*, 9 vols. to date (Leiden: E. J. Brill, 1967-), 1:506, no. 4; also *apud* Ibn Abī Ya'lá, *Ṭabaqāt al-ḥanābilah*, ed. Muḥammad Ḥāmid al-Fiqī, 2 vols. (Cairo: Maṭba'at al-Sunnah al-Muḥammadīyah, 1952), 1:348-380.

[3] Sezgin, *Geschichte* 1:507, #7; perhaps also 506, #2, 508, #22.

[4] Al-Dhahabī, *Siyar a'lām al-nubalā'*, 25 vols. (Beirut: Mu'assasat al-Risālah), 11 (ed. Ṣāliḥ al-Samr, 1982):181. 'Abd Allāh was born 213/827-828.

[5] Ibn Abī Ya'lá, *Ṭabaqāt* 1:143.

[6] A similar but still later report from 'Abd Allāh shifts Aḥmad's concern closer to hadith. 'Abd Allāh asked his father, "Why do you disapprove of writing down hadith when you have made the *Musnad*?" Aḥmad answered, "I made this book as a guide. When people differ over the Sunnah of the Messenger of God, it will be turned to (as a reference)": Ibn Abī Ya'lá, *Ṭabaqāt* 1:184.

brother heard was still fairly raw and unorganized. 'Abd Allāh is often quoted as saying, "When I say 'My father related the hadith report to me . . . ,' it usually means I heard it two or three times."[7] This suggests collection piecemeal, not all at once as an orderly book. Al-Dhahabī states,

> The imam Aḥmad did not believe in composition (*taṣnīf*). His book the *Musnad* he did not compose himself, nor order, nor concern himself with pruning. He related it to his son in copies and parts, directing him to put this in the *musnad* of so-and-so (i.e., in the section of hadith transmitted by him), that in the *musnad* of so-and-so.[8]

A cursory examination of the *Musnad* confirms the large part that 'Abd Allāh played in composing it. He added a great many hadith reports of his own. For example, the second volume of the recent edition comprises close to 900 hadith reports, of which almost a third are professedly 'Abd Allāh's, not Aḥmad's.[9] The *Musnad* of Aḥmad dictated by Ṣāliḥ ibn Aḥmad ibn Ḥanbal in Isfahan must have been substantially different.[10] On the whole, the stories by which 'Abd Allāh put together the *Musnad* seem more plausible than those by which Aḥmad did. 'Abd Allāh presumably saw it as the embodiment of Aḥmad's juridical teaching and perhaps the basis for a Ḥanbali school of law (in the sense of a body of doctrine); yet he still more clearly considered it one collection among others of hadith, verified by the chains of transmitters attached to the individual reports (not simply by the final collector), to which he or anyone else might add. Only with the generation after 'Abd Allāh did even the text of the *Musnad* be-

---

[7] Aḥmad Ibn Ḥanbal, *K. al-'Ilal wa-ma'rifat al-rijāl*, ed. Waṣī Allāh ibn Muḥammad 'Abbās, 4 vols. (Beirut: al-Maktab al-Islāmī, 1988), 3:157. Cf. al-Khaṭīb al-Baghdādī, *Tārīkh Baghdād*, 14 vols. (Cairo: Maktabat al-Khānjī, 1931), 9:376; Ibn Ḥajar, *K. Tahdhīb "al-Tahdhīb,"* 12 vols. (Hyderabad: Majlis Dā'irat al-Ma'ārif al-Niẓāmīyah, 1325-1327), 5:142.

[8] Al-Dhahabī, *Siyar* 13 (ed. 'Alī Abū Zayd, 1983):522.

[9] This agrees with the estimate of a traditional scholar, Muḥammad ibn Ja'far al-Kattānī (d. Fez, 1345/1927), that 'Abd Allāh's additions totalled about 10,000 in all. More recently, though, 'Āmir Ḥasan Ṣabrī has asserted that in all the *Musnad*, 'Abd Allāh's additions totalled only 1,300, including duplicates that 'Abd Allāh had by shorter chains than through his father. Unfortunately, Ṣabrī does not explain the precise methodological differences that account for his radically lower estimate. *V.* 'Āmir Ḥasan Ṣabrī, *Zawā'id 'Abd Allāh ibn Aḥmad ibn Ḥanbal fī "al-Musnad"* (Beirut: Dār al-Bashā'ir al-Islāmīyah, 1990), 131.

[10] Al-Dhahabī, *Siyar* 15 (ed. Ibrāhīm al-Zaybaq, 1983):312.

come fixed. (The extant *Musnad* includes a small number of additions attributed to its chief transmitter from 'Abd Allāh, Ibn Mālik al-Qaṭī-'ī [d. 368/979]. They seem to comprise mainly comments from 'Abd Allāh on the chains of authorities.)

Not unlike the *Musnad* is the long *Kitāb al-'Ilal wa-ma'rifat al-rijāl* attributed to Aḥmad but even more plainly than the *Musnad* the work of 'Abd Allāh.[11] Like the *Musnad*, it sometimes includes opinions from other shaykhs than Aḥmad, sometimes includes his juridical opinions (but normally with the hadith report on which he bases them close by), and follows no clear order. In short, the book is thoroughly traditionalist, without juridical reasoning, and not the embodiment of Ḥanbali jurisprudence.

In some respects, 'Abd Allāh and Ṣāliḥ may seem less strongly traditionalist than their father. They were notably freer than he to associate with the mighty of this world. Ṣāliḥ admitted Aḥmad's disgust with their acceptance of gifts from the caliph in his account of the Inquisition.[12] Both would accept judgeships, 'Abd Allāh at the end of his life in Khurasan,[13] Ṣāliḥ for the Byzantine border area,[14] then Isfahan.[15] Additionally, their brother Sa'īd ibn Aḥmad ibn Ḥanbal (d. 303/915-916?) acted as qadi for Kufa.[16]

Nevertheless, 'Abd Allāh and Ṣāliḥ upheld much of Aḥmad's traditionalism. We have seen already how thoroughly traditionalist was the *Musnad* that 'Abd Allāh transmitted: it comprised only the raw materials for traditionalist jurisprudence, without opinions from late jurisprudents (except for some comments on *rijāl*), and was arranged by transmitter, not by juridical category. Ṣāliḥ related the story of Aḥmad's repudiating one who did presume to collect and circulate his opinions, as we shall see. And 'Abd Allāh's *Kitāb al-Sunnah* kept up the bitter attack on Abū Ḥanīfah and his style of jurisprudence by

---

[11] Sezgin, *Geschichte* 1:507, #8.

[12] Ṣāliḥ ibn Aḥmad, *apud* Abū Nu'aym, *Ḥilyat al-awliyā'*, 10 vols. (Cairo: Maṭba-'at al-Sa'ādah, 1932-1938), 9:212-215; Walter M. Patton, *Aḥmed ibn Ḥanbal and the Miḥna* (Leiden: E. J. Brill, 1897), 150f.

[13] Ibn Abī Ya'lá, *Ṭabaqāt* 1:188.

[14] Ibn Abī Ya'lá, *Ṭabaqāt* 1:175.

[15] Al-Khallāl, *Adab al-qaḍā'*, *apud* al-Dhahabī, *Siyar* 12 (ed. Shu'ayb al-Arna'ūṭ & Ṣāliḥ al-Samr, 1983):530.

[16] For Sa'īd's activity in Kufa, as deputy for the prominent Ḥanafi (!) Abū Khāzim (d. Baghdad, 292/905), *v.* Wakī', *Akhbār al-quḍāh*, ed. 'Abd al-'Azīz Muṣṭafá al-Marāghī, 3 vols. (Cairo: Maṭba'at al-Istiqāmah, 1947-1950), 3:199.

ra'y, along with attacks on *kalām*, the Murji'ah, the Qadarīyah, and so on.[17]

Some others did wish to collect not only the hadith reports that Aḥmad thought important to relate but also his personal interpretation of them, more in the style of the rationalistic jurisprudents. The difficulty with collecting the jurisprudence of Aḥmad was in the first place Aḥmad's traditionalist hostility towards it. As we have seen, hadith reports from the Prophet and his Companions were the authority he expected his followers to rely on, not his own fallible opinions. Several stories illustrate both Aḥmad's reluctance to give juridical opinions and the difficulty of restraining others from collecting them. Abū Bakr al-Khallāl related the story of a man who came to Aḥmad and asked him about the efficacy for ritual ablutions of irrigation water, water used to wash beans, and rose water. Aḥmad gave him his opinion (he disapproved of each one), but pulled on his gown to stop him as he left. "What do you say when you enter the mosque?" Aḥmad asked. The man was silent. "What do you say when you leave the mosque?" Again he was silent. "Go and learn this" was Aḥmad's dismissal.[18] A proper reverence for God was more important to cultivate than knowledge of legal minutiae.

When some deliberately collected his juridical opinions, none the less, Aḥmad expressly repudiated them. We have already seen his command not to relate his juridical opinions from Abū Bakr al-Athram. Al-Athram's collection circulated widely nonetheless, and became an important source for later Ḥanbali jurisprudence. However, it cannot be counted the foundation of a Ḥanbali school, for it included juridical problems from Isḥāq ibn Rāhawayh and Yaḥyá ibn Ma'īn as well as Aḥmad.[19]

The Khurasani Isḥāq ibn Manṣūr al-Kawsaj (d. 251/865) was another who collected and transmitted a great number of juridical opinions from Aḥmad. Reports agree that Aḥmad heard of al-Kawsaj's work and repudiated the opinions he was relating: "Witness," he told some people, "that I have gone back on all those."[20] Ṣāliḥ ibn

---

[17] 'Abd Allāh ibn Aḥmad, *Kitāb al-Sunnah*, ed. Muḥammad ibn Sa'īd ibn Sālim al-Qaḥṭānī, 2 vols. (Dammam: Dār Ibn al-Qayyim, 1986).

[18] Ibn Abī Ya'lá, *Ṭabaqāt* 1:41.

[19] Ibn Ḥajar, *Tahdhīb* 1:250. Sezgin, *Geschichte* 1:510, mentions *Masā'il Aḥmad ibn Ḥanbal*, but this is only, of course, a short excerpt.

[20] Al-Khaṭīb al-Baghdādī, *Tārīkh* 6:363.

Aḥmad related a fuller version.

> I told my father that I had heard that Isḥāq ibn Manṣūr had related in Khurasan these questions that he had asked about and was taking dirhams for them. My father became angry at that, then saddened .... He said, "They ask me questions, then they relate them and take (money) for them?" and repudiated him severely.

Aḥmad plainly believed that questions should be asked solely from a pious desire to act as pleased God. Answers to questions of law should no more be sold than the hadith reports themselves. Ṣāliḥ concludes, however, that when Aḥmad saw al-Kawsaj again, he said nothing of the matter.[21]

In Khurasan, where traditionalists were friendlier towards rationalistic jurisprudence, they told another story: that al-Kawsaj heard of Aḥmad's repudiation, was alarmed by it, and walked to Baghdad with his documents on his back to show him them. The great man looked them over, then confirmed that they were indeed his opinions.[22] Certainly, Aḥmad did not succeed in removing the collection of al-Kawsaj from circulation: the Qazvini traditionist al-Khalīlī (d. 446/1055) heard it from Muḥammad ibn Sulaymān al-Fāmī, who had heard it from Abū 'Alī al-Ṭūsī, who had heard the collection from al-Kawsaj. Yet the collection of al-Kawsaj, just like that of al-Athram, cannot be counted the foundation of a Ḥanbali school of jurisprudence, for it, too, included opinions from Isḥāq ibn Rāhawayh alongside opinions from Aḥmad.[23]

Ninth-century students of jurisprudence might well seek to learn Aḥmad's opinions without any desire to adopt them for their own. In his *Ikhtilāf al-fuqahā'*, Muḥammad ibn Naṣr al-Marwazī (d. Samarqand, 294/907?) quotes Aḥmad's opinion on one or another juridical problem less often than he quotes the opinions of al-Shāfi'ī and Sufyān al-Thawrī; however, he quotes the opinions of Aḥmad as often as the opinions of *aṣḥāb al-ra'y*, rather more often than the opinions of Mālik and Isḥāq ibn Rāhawayh.[24] Al-Marwazī is usually iden-

---

[21] Ibn Abī Ya'lá, *Ṭabaqāt* 1:43. Al-Khaṭīb al-Baghdādī, *Tārīkh* 6:363f, reports the same speech but has "You ask me questions," &c.

[22] Al-Ḥākim al-Naysābūrī, *apud* al-Khaṭīb al-Baghdādī, *Tārīkh* 6:364.

[23] Some of it has been translated by Susan A. Spectorsky, *Chapters on Marriage and Divorce* (Austin: Univ. of Texas Press, 1993), ch. 4.

[24] Muḥammad ibn Naṣr al-Marwazī, *K. Ikhtilāf al-fuqahā'*, Yūsuf Ağa (Konya)

tified as a particular follower of al-Shāfi'ī in jurisprudence, having travelled to Egypt to study under al-Muzanī and al-Rabī': he treats Aḥmad's opinions entirely as those of a respected individual jurisprudent, not as the basis of any Ḥanbali school.

THE COLLECTION OF AḤMAD'S OPINIONS BY ABŪ BAKR AL-KHALLĀL

It was Abū Bakr al-Khallāl (d. Baghdad, 311/923) who set out to collect the teachings of Aḥmad ibn Ḥanbal in such a way that they might constitute the basis of a school of law. His crucial importance was recognized well before modern scholars looked into the formation of the schools. It should suffice to quote al-Dhahabī:

> Before him, there was no independent school (*madhhab mustaqill*) of the imam's; not until he followed up Aḥmad's texts, wrote them down, and checked their proofs (*barhamahā*) after 300.[25]

Collecting what Aḥmad had said was then the most important single part of forming a Ḥanbali school, and al-Khallāl accomplished it. The early twentieth-century Ḥanbali jurisprudent Badrān (d. 1346/1927) calls his collection the very root (*aṣl*) of the Ḥanbali school, from which sprang all later books of Ḥanbali jurisprudence.[26]

Al-Khallāl's great work is usually called *al-Jāmi' li-'ulūm Aḥmad ibn Ḥanbal*. It originally comprised some twenty volumes.[27] Quotations indicate that it included much discussion of dogma and piety alongside jurisprudence. Al-Khallāl originally studied in Baghdad under Abū Bakr al-Marrūdhī (d. 275/888), a close associate of Aḥmad's; also under 'Abd Allāh ibn Aḥmad.

Many details of his work remain unclear. Al-Dhahabī says that he travelled to Fars, Syria, and Mesopotamia.[28] Did he travel to Khurasan? Al-Khallāl quoted one Aḥmad ibn al-Ḥasan al-Tirmidhī as saying, "The older men in Khurasan (*al-akābir bi-Khurāsān*) related to us the juridical problems he had from Aḥmad," which suggests that

---

4820/1. *V.* Sezgin, *Geschichte* 1:494, #5.

[25] Al-Dhahabī, *Siyar* 14 (ed. Akram al-Būshayyī, 1983):298.

[26] Badran, *Madkhal*, 47.

[27] Sezgin, *Geschichte* 1:512.

[28] Al-Dhahabī, *Siyar* 14 (ed. Akram al-Būshayyī, 1983):297.

he did travel there; however, he then adds that among these Khurasani informants was Muḥammad ibn al-Mundhir, who outlived al-Khallāl by several years and resided in Mecca.[29] Al-Khallāl could easily have heard him as he passed through Baghdad.

The chronology of al-Khallāl's work is almost as difficult to establish as its geographical extent. Khaṭṭāb ibn Bishr (d. 264/877) sets one *terminus a quo*: of all those of whom Ibn Abī Ya'lá says definitely "al-Khallāl heard him" or "related from him" and whose date of death he gives, his is the earliest.[30] Al-Khallāl must therefore have begun to collect the opinions of Aḥmad by 264/877. However, many names appear without dates, so it is probable that al-Khallāl heard from others before Khaṭṭāb ibn Bishr.

It is difficult to tell even which authorities al-Khallāl definitely met, which escaped him. A rough estimate is that he is mentioned in connection with a third of the men in the first section of Ibn Abī Ya'lá's *Ṭabaqāt al-ḥanābilah*; that is, men known to have met Aḥmad and related hadith or especially juridical opinions from him. Sometimes, though, the connection may be no more than al-Khallāl's mentioning the man in his own biographical dictionary of men who related hadith from Aḥmad. At the same time, one can seldom say with certainty that because al-Khallāl does not appear in any chain of transmitters from a given man, he cannot have met and transmitted anything from him. What is clear is that no other Ḥanbali travelled so widely as al-Khallāl did, or met so many men who had met Aḥmad.[31]

Further limitations of al-Khallāl's work of collection must be acknowledged. Much of the learning of Aḥmad that al-Khallāl did not manage to record was also, evidently, lost to all other jurisprudents of his time and after. For example, al-Khaṭīb al-Baghdādī states that 'Abd al-Raḥmān ibn Yaḥyá ibn Khāqān (d. 262/875-876), brother to al-Mutawakkil's vizier 'Ubayd Allāh, related juridical problems (*masā'il*) from Aḥmad.[32] Al-Khaṭīb does not quote these problems *in extenso*, and I doubt whether any source does.[33] If they included more than Aḥmad's evaluations of various candidates for the judgeship, they are presumably lost forever. A collection that certainly in-

[29] Al-Khallāl *apud* Ibn Abī Ya'lá, *Ṭabaqāt* 1:38.
[30] Ibn Abī Ya'lá, *Ṭabaqāt* 1:152.
[31] Similarly, al-Khaṭīb al-Baghdādī, *Tārīkh* 5:112.
[32] Al-Khaṭīb al-Baghdādī, *Tārīkh* 10:278.
[33] *V.* Ibn Abī Ya'lá, *Ṭabaqāt* 1:207, based on al-Khaṭīb al-Baghdādī, *Tārīkh*.

cluded more than evaluations of candidates for the judgeship but was even more certainly lost to posterity is the *Su'ālāt Aḥmad ibn Ḥanbal* collected by the famous Khurasani traditionist Muslim (d. Nishapur, 261/875).[34]

Other learning of Aḥmad's bypassed al-Khallāl to reach the later Ḥanābilah by means of other reporters. The many juridical problems related from Aḥmad by Ibrāhīm ibn Hāni' al-Naysābūrī (d. 265/878) were surely heard by al-Khallāl: in his biographical notice, Ibn Abī Ya'lá reports a quotation from Aḥmad verified by this chain, al-Khallāl < Abū 'Umar ibn Ḥayyawayh < Abū Dharr al-Bāghandī < Ibrāhīm.[35] Yet the standard chain attached to the collection of his problems is rather through al-Khallāl's contemporary al-Qāf*lānī (d. 325/936-937) < Isḥāq ibn Ibrāhīm ibn Hani' < Ibrāhīm. Among those who heard them from al-Qāf*lānī were Ibn Baṭṭah and 'Umar ibn Badr al-Maghāzilī. Perhaps the shorter chain was more attractive. Ibn Abī Ḥātim mentions Abū Ṭālib Aḥmad ibn Ḥumayd (d. 244/858-859) as having related many juridical problems from Aḥmad.[36] Ibn Abī Ḥātim frequently quotes him as relating an opinion of Aḥmad ibn Ḥanbal's concerning the reliability of some traditionist.[37] Al-Khallāl knew of his activity, and evidently related some opinions concerning oaths and the effect of bat urine on ritual purity; however, he also says that, because he died early, Abū Ṭālib's learning did not reach the young men.[38]

Abū Bakr al-Khallāl's biographical dictionary of transmitters from Aḥmad ibn Ḥanbal was arguably the first devoted to a school.[39] No other school had a biographical dictionary until the early eleventh century, when a Ẓāhiri dictionary appeared from Ibn al-Akhḍar (d. Baghdad, 429/1038)[40]; Shāfi'i dictionaries from al-Muṭṭawwi'ī (*fl.*

---

[34] Al-Ḥākim al-Naysābūrī, *apud* al-Dhahabī, *Siyar* 12:579.

[35] Ibn Abī Ya'lá, *Ṭabaqāt* 1:97.

[36] Ibn Abī Ḥātim, *K. al-Jarḥ wa-al-ta'dīl*, 9 vols. (Hyderabad: Jam'īyat Dā'irat al-Ma'ārif al-'Uthmānīyah, 1360), 2:48.

[37] E.g., Ibn Abī Ḥātim, *Jarḥ* 7:111.

[38] Ibn Abī Ya'lá, *Ṭabaqāt* 1:40.

[39] The *Ṭabaqāt al-fuqahā'* of Ibn Ḥabīb (d. Cordoba, 238/853), for which *v.* al-Dhahabī, *Siyar* 12:103f, probably treated his teachers Ziyād ibn 'Abd al-Raḥmān, Asad ibn Mūsá, &al., and the Medinese and Iraqi jurisprudents under whom they had studied. This is to say, in effect, that it treated the school of *ra'y*, not yet divided between Māliki and Ḥanafi schools; however, Ibn Ḥabīb would have had little reason to think of it as a school, and his title suggests that he did not.

[40] Cited by Abū Isḥāq, *Ṭabaqāt al-fuqahā'*, ed. Iḥsān 'Abbās (Beirut: Dār al-Rā'id

Nishapur, 400/1009-1010),[41] Abū al-Ṭayyib al-Ṭabarī (d. Baghdad, 450/1058),[42] and (the earliest extant) al-'Abbādī (d. Herat, 458/1066)[43]; and a Ḥanafi dictionary from al-Ṣaymarī (d. Baghdad, 436/1045).[44] F. E. Peters has even identified al-Khallāl's composition of a biographical dictionary as the decisive step in forming a Ḥanbali school.[45]

Again, however, one must acknowledge the limitations of al-Khallāl's achievement. His dictionary must have comprised only men who related religious learning directly from Aḥmad. Al-Khallāl himself was of only the second generation. Lacking any account of its transmission to the next generation, his dictionary can be said to define a school only in a limited sense. It will not have been radically different in conception from contemporary works such as the *Manāqib Abī Ḥanīfah* of Aḥmad ibn al-Ṣalt (d. Baghdad, 308/921)[46] and Abū Ja'far al-Ṭaḥāwī (d. Baghdad, 321/933)[47]; the *Manāqib Mālik* of al-Dīnawarī (d. Aswan? 298/310?)[48]; and the *Manāqib al-Shāfi'ī* of Dāwūd al-Ẓāhirī (d. Baghdad, 270/884)[49] and al-Būshanjī (d. Nishapur, 290 or 291/903).[50] None of these others is now extant, but that of al-Ṭaḥāwī, at least, is often quoted concerning the followers of Abū Ḥanīfah, that of Dāwūd al-Ẓāhirī occasionally of the followers of al-Shāfi'ī.

Fittingly, al-Khallāl seems to have been friendlier towards al-Shāfi'ī and the Shāfi'i school than earlier traditionalists. Quotations of Aḥ-

---

al-'Arabī, 1970), 179.

[41] Al-Muṭṭawwi'ī, *K. al-Mudhhab fī shuyūkh al-madhhab*, on which *v.* Kātib Çelebī, *K. Kashf al-ẓunūn 'an asāmī al-kutub wa-al-funūn*, ed. Şerefettin Yaltkaya & Rifat Bilge, 2 vols. (Istanbul: Maarif Matbaası, 1941, 1943), 2:1645.

[42] Kātib Çelebī, *Kashf* 2:1100.

[43] Al-'Abbādī, *K. Ṭabaqāt al-fuqahā' al-shāfi'īyah*, ed. Gösta Vitestam, Veröffentlichungen der "De Goeje Stiftung" 21 (Leiden: E. J. Brill, 1964).

[44] *Manāqib Abī Ḥanīfah*, for which *v.* Sezgin, *Geschichte* 1:411, ll. 3-7. Often quoted concerning followers of Abū Ḥanīfah by al-Khaṭīb al-Baghdādī and Ibn Abī al-Wafā', although never by name. For the biographical dictionary and the school of law, *v.* George Makdisi, "*Ṭabaqāt*-Biography: Law and Orthodoxy in Classical Islam," *Islamic Studies* 32 (1993):371-396.

[45] F. E. Peters, *Allāh's Commonwealth* (New York: Simon & Schuster, 1973), 467.

[46] Kātib Çelebī, *Kashf* 2:1837.

[47] Ibn Abī al-Wafā', *Jawāhir* 1:277; Kātib Çelebī, *Kashf* 2:1836f.

[48] Kātib Çelebī, *Kashf* 2:1841.

[49] Kātib Çelebī, *Kashf* 2:1839.

[50] Kātib Çelebī, *Kashf* 2:1840.

mad by his son 'Abd Allāh ibn Aḥmad stress al-Shāfi'ī's reliance on hadith; for example, that Aḥmad heard from al-Shāfi'ī hadith reports from Mālik and Ḥātim ibn Ismā'īl (d. Medina, 187/803),[51] that al-Shāfi'ī's Iraqi book was superior to his Egyptian because Aḥmad was able to check the Iraqi.[52] Al-Khallāl quotes Aḥmad both for al-Shāfi-'ī and against him; for example, "Al-Shāfi'ī is among the beloved of my heart,"[53] but also, in reply to a question about copying the books of al-Shāfi'ī, "How little the traditionist has need of them."[54] On the other hand, al-Khallāl is the source for no condemnation of the semi-rationalist Shāfi'īyah, al-Karābīsī and others. As we have seen, al-Khallāl maintains that Aḥmad praised Abū Thawr until he heard of his heretical doctrines; that is, so long as he knew him only as a jurisprudent.[55] He also asserts that Abū Thawr weakly opposed the doctrine that one's pronunciation of the Qur'an is created.[56] Against numerous other Ḥanbali witnesses, al-Khallāl credits not al-Karābīsī but the earlier Nu'aym ibn Ḥammād (d. Samarra, 228/843?) with inventing the doctrine of the created pronunciation.[57] Moreover, al-Khallāl associates the doctrine of the created pronunciation mainly with the otherwise unknown Aḥmad al-Sharrāk (*fl. ca.* 240/854-855).[58] It is as if he wished to deflect Ḥanbali ire away from the Shāfi'īyah, whose style of jurisprudence he largely accepted.

AL-KHALLĀL AS CHIEF OF THE SCHOOL

Al-Khallāl sat at the head of a study circle at the Mosque of al-Mahdī

---

[51] Ibn 'Abd al-Barr, *al-Intiqā' fī faḍā'il al-thalāthah al-a'immah al-fuqahā'* (Cairo: Maktabat al-Qudsī, 1350), 76.

[52] Abū Nu'aym, *Ḥilyah* 9:170.

[53] Aḥmad ibn Ḥanbal (i.e., al-Khallāl), *al-'Aqīdah lil-imām Aḥmad ibn Ḥanbal*, ed. 'Abd al-'Azīz Sayrawān (Damascus: Dār Qutaybah, 1988), 127.

[54] Al-Khallāl, *K. al-'Ilm*, *apud* Ibn Abī Ya'lá, *Ṭabaqāt* 1:38.

[55] Al-Khallāl, *apud* Ibn Abī Ya'lá, *Ṭabaqāt* 1:328.

[56] Al-Khallāl, *al-Musnad min masā'il Abī 'Abd Allāh Aḥmad ibn Muḥammad ibn Ḥanbal*, ed. Ẓiyā'uddīn Aḥmad, Asiatic Society of Bangladesh Publication 29 (Dacca: Asiatic Society of Bangladesh, 1975), 544.

[57] Al-Khallāl, *Musnad min masā'il*, 548.

[58] Al-Khallāl, *Musnad min masā'il*, 541-547.

in Baghdad.[59] It was a new departure for the traditionalists of Baghdad, unaccustomed to the specialized study of jurisprudence. His success is to be measured in large part by the impression he made on students. The most prominent jurisprudents of the century after him (to judge by a rough count of citations in the *Mughnī* of Ibn Qudāmah) were Abū al-Qāsim al-Khiraqī (d. Damascus, 334/945-946), Ghulām al-Khallāl (d. Baghdad, 363/974), and Ibn Shāqullā (d. Baghdad, 369/979). Al-Khiraqī, who wrote the first short handbook (*mukhtaṣar*) of Ḥanbali jurisprudence, seems not to have studied under al-Khallāl: rather, he learnt from many of the same teachers as al-Khallāl, above all al-Marrūdhī.[60] Ghulām al-Khallāl, by contrast, not only studied under al-Khallāl but was so closely identified with him that he was named for it.[61] Ibn Shāqullā, at last, evidently came too late to study under al-Khallāl, himself, but Ghulām al-Khallāl is listed among his authorities.[62] Al-Khallāl was influential, we may conclude, inasmuch as no other Ḥanbali teacher of his century had a disciple like Ghulām al-Khallāl; yet, on the other hand, he left no clear line of successors, one after another, like the line of successors to his Shāfi'i contemporary, Ibn Surayj, and no list can be composed of those who learnt jurisprudence from him.

Only, indeed, from about the end of the tenth century can one speak of chiefs of the Ḥanbali school. Ibn al-Jawzī describes Ibn Ḥāmid (d. 403/1013) as "the teacher of the *aṣḥāb* of Aḥmad and their jurisprudent," attributes characteristic of a chief in the style of Ibn Surayj and his successors among the Shāfi'īyah, al-Karkhī and his among the Ḥanafīyah.[63] Ibn Ḥāmid was sufficiently close to the practice of the other schools that he carried on debates with the Shāfi'i leader Abū Ḥāmid al-Isfarāyinī at the caliphal palace.[64] He seems to have held explicitly, against the earlier traditionalists, that one might freely offer one's own juridical opinion even where there was

---

[59] Ibn Abī Ya'lá, *Ṭabaqāt* 2:15.

[60] Al-Khaṭīb al-Baghdādī, *Tārīkh* 11:234f; Ibn Abī Ya'lá, *Ṭabaqāt* 2:75-118.

[61] *V. Encyclopaedia of Islam*, new edn., s.v. "Ghulām al-Khallāl," by H. Laoust.

[62] Ibn Abī Ya'lá, *Ṭabaqāt* 2:128.

[63] Ibn al-Jawzī, *al-Muntaẓam*, 6 vols. (Hyderabad: Dā'irat al-Ma'ārif al-'Uthmānīyah, 1357-1360), 7:264 = ed. Muḥammad 'Abd al-Qādir 'Aṭā' & Muṣṭafá 'Abd al-Qādir 'Aṭā', with Nu'aym Zurzūr, 18 vols. (Beirut: Dār al-Kutub al-'Ilmīyah, 1992), 15:94.

[64] Ibn Abī Ya'lá, *Ṭabaqāt* 2:177.

no precedent.[65] Abū Bakr Ibn al-Khayyāṭ asked Ibn Ḥāmid, whom he calls "imam of the Ḥanbalīyah in his time," under whom he should study while Ibn Ḥāmid was off on the pilgrimage. (He was to die on the way back.) Ibn Ḥāmid indicated the qadi Abū Ya'lá Ibn al-Farrā' (d. Baghdad, 458/1065).[66] This looks very like the chief of the school indicating his successor. Yet Ibn al-Jawzī does not state that Ibn Ḥāmid was chief of the school, nor that Ibn al-Farrā' succeeded him. A century and a half later, al-Dhahabī refers to Abū al-Faḍl al-Tamīmī (d. 410/1020) as chief (in his time) of the Ḥanābilah.[67] He must have succeeded Ibn Ḥāmid, if Ibn Ḥāmid may indeed be called a chief.

Al-Khallāl's enterprise was bound to arouse traditionalist opposition, inasmuch as the systematic collection and teaching of recent juridical opinions was usual among the rationalists but not, before now, the Baghdadi traditionalists. Traditionalist theology, remember, was about accepting dogmatic statements as given by ancient authority. This theology indisposed traditionalists to the study of jurisprudence apart from collecting hadith, to the study of any late teacher's juridical opinions instead of the larger, older body of material with which he had worked; thus al-Khallāl was fighting a strong tide.

The evidence of polemics over jurisprudence, narrowly considered, is difficult to evaluate. Some of his contemporaries are said to have deferred to al-Khallāl on questions of jurisprudence; for example, according to his disciple Ghulām al-Khallāl, the ascetic Abū al-Ḥasan Ibn al-Bashshār (d. 313/925).[68] This suggests respect but also opposition: implicitly, there were other Ḥanābilah who would not defer to al-Khallāl. Ghulām al-Khallāl found sixty questions in the *Mukhtaṣar* of al-Khiraqī over whose solution he disagreed.[69] Ibn Abī Ya'lá found ninety-eight questions over which Ghulām al-Khallāl and al-Khiraqī disagreed.[70] By contrast, he presents only nine over which Ghulām al-Khallāl disagreed with al-Khallāl.[71] Presumably, the

---

[65] Ibn Abī Ya'lá, *Ṭabaqāt* 2:176.
[66] Ibn Abī Ya'lá, *Ṭabaqāt* 2:177.
[67] Al-Dhahabī, *Siyar* 17 (ed. Shu'ayb al-Arna'ūṭ & Muḥammad Nu'aym al-'Araqasūsī, 1983):273.
[68] *Apud* al-Khaṭīb al-Baghdādī, *Tārīkh* 5:113.
[69] Ibn Abī Ya'lá, *Ṭabaqāt* 1:76.
[70] Ibn Abī Ya'lá, *Ṭabaqāt* 2:76-118.
[71] Ibn Abī Ya'lá, *Ṭabaqāt* 2:120f.

numerous disagreements between Ghulām al-Khallāl and al-Khiraqī were largely disagreements between al-Khallāl and al-Khiraqī. At this point in our knowledge of *fiqh*, though, it is difficult to say how significant any of these disagreements actually was.

There is firmer evidence elsewhere of hostility toward al-Khallāl on the part of some traditionalists. Abū Bakr al-Shīrajī (d. 332/943-944), perhaps twenty years younger than al-Khallāl, expressed resentment of his presuming to teach Ḥanbali jurisprudence: "Al-Khallāl has composed his books and wishes us to sit before him and hear from him. This is unlikely (*hādhā ba'īd*)."[72] Ibn Abī Ya'lá once refers to "the shaykhs of the two parties (*ṭā'ifatayn*)" who equally sought the company of Ibn al-Bashshār and exalted him. Ibn Abī Ya'lá somewhat roils the waters when he goes on to name the shaykhs: Abū Muḥammad al-Barbahārī, Abū Bakr al-Khallāl, Abū Bakr 'Abd al-'Azīz (i.e., Ghulām al-Khallāl), "and their like."[73] Who belonged to which party? Ibn Abī Ya'lá's evidence is not unequivocal, but it seems a good guess that al-Barbahārī headed one, al-Khallāl and his student the other. (Ibn Baṭṭah tells a story identifying three parties. A follower of al-Barbahārī's, he relates, once passed a heretic who scoffed at "these Ḥanbalīyah." He told him the Ḥanābilah were of three types [*aṣnāf*]: "the type of the ascetics, who fast and pray; a type who write [hadith] and learn jurisprudence; and a type who slap every scoffer like you," whereupon he slapped him hard.[74])

These two parties represented alternative paths for traditionalism to follow. Under al-Khallāl, traditionalism would be preserved as the elaboration of legal doctrine based on the opinions of Aḥmad ibn Ḥanbal. Under al-Barbahārī (d. 329/941), it would be preserved as a style of public life. Al-Barbahārī has not previously figured in this history of Ḥanbali jurisprudence because his contributions in that field seem to have been negligible: I have never seen a reference to a juridical opinion of his. He was yet another who studied under al-Marrūdhī, and was disciple, as well, to the famous ascetic Sahl al-Tustarī (d. Basra, 283/896?); however, it was not in connection with learning or spirituality that he became prominent, but with rioting. In 317/929, certain Ḥanābilah fought with other Muslims over the interpretation

---

[72] Al-Khaṭīb al-Baghdādī, *Tārīkh* 5:113.
[73] Ibn Abī Ya'lá, *Ṭabaqāt* 2:58.
[74] Ibn Abī Ya'lá, *Ṭabaqāt* 2:43.

of a verse in the Qur'an.[75] Al-Barbahārī was forced into hiding in 321/933 over opposition to a proposal to curse Mu'āwiyah, enemy to 'Alī. In 323/935, the Ḥanābilah looted shops, attacked wine sellers and singing girls, and smashed musical instruments. In 327/939, Ḥanābilah molested people going to festivities at a mosque. Al-Barbahārī hid himself once more, but his lieutenant, Dallā', was put to death. His followers rioted one last time in al-Barbahārī's lifetime in 329/941, when they tried to destroy a Shī'i mosque and also attacked money-changers and bankers. After a month in hiding, again, al-Barbahārī now died of a hemorrhage (*qiyām al-dam*). He was buried in the same house, still in secret.[76]

Al-Barbahārī's program of violent opposition to these disturbers of public decorum went directly against al-Khallāl's teaching. Enforcement of morality by private parties had long been termed "enjoining the good and forbidding the bad," *al-amr bi-al-ma'rūf wa-al-nahy 'an al-munkar*, and al-Khallāl wrote a book by that title which is extant and has been published. Nothing suggests al-Khallāl's approval of wine, singing girls, or festivities in mosques; however, the tendency of his book is again and again to discourage active interference. A man asked al-Awzā'ī, "Who should enjoin the good and forbid the bad?" He answered, relates al-Khallāl, "Whoever sees that it will be accepted from him," presumably without violence.[77] Private reproof is better than public.[78] Confronted with wine, one should indeed pour it out or, if that is impossible, break the container; however, one should not disturb covered containers, search for intoxicating liquors, or interfere with Christian and Jewish wine sellers under the sultan's (caliph's) protection.[79] If one hears singing or drumming, one should not search for the source, and one should break musical instruments only when they are exposed to view.[80] Al-Barbahārī's followers went against practically everything al-Khallāl had told them

---

[75] Ibn al-Athīr, *al-Kāmil fī al-tārīkh*, *s.a.* 317; ed. C. J. Tornberg, 13 vols. (Beirut: Dār Ṣādir, 1965-67), 8:213. *V. infra*, chap. 9.

[76] Henri Laoust, *La Profession de foi d'Ibn Baṭṭa* (Damascus: Institut Français de Damas, 1958), xxxvii-xli; *Encyclopaedia of Islam*, new edn., *s.v.* "al-Barbahārī," by H. Laoust.

[77] Al-Khallāl, *al-Amr bi-al-ma'rūf wa-al-nahy 'an al-munkar*, ed. 'Abd al-Qādir Aḥmad 'Aṭā, Nawādir al-Turāth 2 (Cairo: Dār al-I'tiṣām, 1975), 124.

[78] Al-Khallāl, *Amr*, 101f, 108.

[79] Al-Khallāl, *Amr*, 134f, 138, 141.

[80] Al-Khallāl, *Amr*, 115, 142.

about enjoining the good and forbidding the bad.

Ibn Abī Ya'lá preserves a long creedal statement from al-Barbahārī, evidently an excerpt from his commentary on 'Abd Allāh's *Kitāb al-Sunnah*.[81] It is thoroughly, militantly traditionalist. To avoid using their weapons, al-Barbahārī opposed all discussion with heretics:

> Do not give them power over you. Have you not learnt that Muḥammad ibn Sīrīn (Basran Successor, d. 110/729-730), in spite of his virtue, answered none of the heretics concerning a single problem, nor would hear from any of them a verse from the Book of God . . . ?[82]

He condemned the practice of debate on which rationalistic law and theology depended: "Sitting together (*mujālasah*) for the purpose of counsel (*naṣīḥah*) is to open the gate of benefit (*bāb al-fā'idah*). Sitting together for the purpose of debate (*munāẓarah*) is to close the gate of benefit."[83]

Yet al-Barbahārī's program was not in fact the old traditionalism. By one account, Abū al-Ḥasan al-Ash'arī came to Baghdad and told al-Barbahārī, "I have refuted al-Jubbā'ī [the Mu'tazili leader], the Magians, and the Nazarenes." Al-Barbahārī replied, "I do not know what you say: we know nothing but what the imam Aḥmad said." Al-Ash'arī then went out and wrote *al-Ibānah*, but al-Barbahārī still would not accept it.[84] From a traditionalist point of view, it is disturbing to see al-Barbahārī resort to "what the imam Aḥmad said," not "what the Prophet and the Companions said."

It would seem to have been al-Barbahārī's faction that persecuted the polymath al-Ṭabarī (d. 310/923) during al-Khallāl's lifetime, although traditionalist sources appear to attribute that persecution above all to Abū Bakr Ibn Abī Dāwūd (d. 316/929), son of the famous traditionist associated with Aḥmad. A detailed discussion of al-Ṭabarī's persecution belongs in Chapter Nine, concerning the Ẓāhiri and Jarīri

---

[81] Ibn Abī Ya'lá, *Ṭabaqāt* 2:18-43.

[82] Al-Barbahārī, *Sharḥ K. al-Sunnah*, *apud* Ibn Abī Ya'lá, 2:39.

[83] *Apud* al-Dhahabī, *Siyar* 15:91. Second half also *apud* Ibn Abī Ya'lá, *Ṭabaqāt* 2:43.

[84] Al-Dhahabī, *Siyar* 15:90. The story is rejected by Ibn 'Asākir, but on grounds that Michel Allard considers inadequate: *Tabyīn kadhib al-muftarī* (Damascus: al-Qudsī, 1347), 390f; *Le Problème des attributs divins dans la doctrine d'al-Aš'arī et de ses premiers grands disciples*, Recherches publiées sous la direction de l'Institut de Lettres Orientales de Beyrouth, 28 (Beirut: Imprimerie Catholique, 1965), 46.

schools of law. Suffice it to say here that the reported charges against al-Ṭabarī had to do with espousing Shī'i juridical and theological positions, a semi-rationalist theological position, or with slighting Aḥmad by calling him a mere traditionist, not a jurisprudent. If the last report is valid, then the persecution had to do with the Ḥanābilah's desiring to be recognized alongside the sophisticates of the Shāfi'i school.

Other Ḥanābilah exaggerated Aḥmad's accomplishments in their desire to compete with the Shāfi'īyah. Abū al-Ḥusayn Ibn al-Munādī (d. 336/947) is everywhere associated with a long list of books that 'Abd Allāh ibn Aḥmad heard from his father, including a Qur'an commentary comprising 120,000 hadith reports.[85] Al-Dhahabī points out how unlikely it is that any such commentary existed. Al-Ṭabarī's commentary comprised only fifteen or twenty thousand hadith reports, and all the scholars of Baghdad but Ibn al-Munādī surely would not have neglected to mention another of much greater bulk, nor allowed it to vanish without their copying even parts of it.[86] It seems likely that Ibn al-Munādī attributed a huge *Tafsīr* to Aḥmad lest al-Ṭabarī seem to have outshone him in this important respect.

The party of al-Barbahārī, then, pressed its "me, too" by physical force. It was a costly strategy. The modern Egyptian scholar Abū Zahrah names its violence among just three reasons why the Ḥanbali school spread little outside Baghdad: 1) that the Ḥanbali school developed too late, after Ḥanafism had taken over Iraq, Shāfi'ism Egypt, and so forth; 2) that the Ḥanābilah did not produce qadis (until Abū Ya'lá Ibn al-Farrā', and his activity revitalized the Ḥanbali school as that of Ibn Ḥazm revitalized the Ẓāhiri[87]); and 3) that they alienated the Muslim majority by their severity and fanaticism, especially in forbidding the bad as under al-Barbahārī.[88] The first of these not only presumes that there was a Ḥanafi school from the time of Abū Ḥanīfah, and so on, it also ignores continuing Ḥanafi strength in Egypt, Māliki strength in Iraq, and so forth. Abū Zahrah's second reason seems more credible, but still inadequate. On the one hand, the Ḥanbali school should have benefitted from the judgeships of Ṣāliḥ

---

[85] Al-Khaṭīb al-Baghdādī, *Tārīkh* 9:375f.

[86] Al-Dhahabī, *Siyar* 13 (ed. 'Alī Abū Zayd, 1983):521f.

[87] Abū Zahrah, *Tārīkh al-madhāhib al-islāmīyah* 2: *Fī tārīkh al-madhāhib al-fiqhīyah* (Cairo: Dār al-Fikr al-'Arabī, n.d.), 360.

[88] Abū Zahrah, *Tārīkh* 2:351f.

in Isfahan, 'Abd Allāh in Khurasan, and Sa'īd in Kufa. On the other hand, Shāfi'ism spread without any aid from the occupation of judgeships: the brand of Shāfi'ism that Abū Zur'ah al-Dimashqī encouraged did not survive, while none of Ibn Surayj's Baghdadi successors in the tenth century was a qadi, and few Khurasani qadis of the tenth century were Shāfi'īyah. Abū Zahrah offers no evidence for his third reason except Ibn al-Athīr's report of Ḥanbali rioting and its suppression by caliphal forces. It probably needs at least this refinement: that visiting students who might have spread Ḥanbalism in their own countries must have come mainly from the more prosperous classes, particularly the big landowners and merchants; hence their aristocratic disdain to identify themselves with such rabble as the Ḥanābilah could collect for the breaking of wine jugs in private houses. Second, al-Ṭabarī and Ibn Khuzaymah were scholars of very great stature, their published creeds thoroughly traditionalist: any party that rejected them was quite extreme, and probably seemed too risky in areas far from Baghdad where, as I have said, the Muslims were an insecure minority. Furthermore, it must be acknowledged that Ḥanbalism of some sort did spread to the East in the tenth century, for the geographer al-Maqdisī notes some Ḥanābilah in Egypt, some in Basra, many in Khuzistan, many in Rayy, and some in Qumis and Tabaristan.[89] Their subsequent disappearance belongs to the history of these various regions.

Al-Khallāl's program of collecting and transmitting the teaching of Aḥmad was another way to press "me, too." Small need had the traditionalists to establish their orthodoxy; however, the collection of a basic body of jurisprudence and its treatment by predictable, rational procedures should prove that they were not negligible as elaborators of the holy law. This was about as much as a Baghdadi traditionalist could manage in the tenth century: a system of recognized chiefs, with a regular system of succession, was yet beyond the traditionalists' grasp, at this time.

There was a large element of "me, too" in the formation of the other two successful Baghdadi schools of law. From the Shāfi'īyah and Ḥanafīyah, this meant proving that they were acceptably tradi-

---

[89] Al-Muqaddasī (i.e., al-Maqdisī), *Descriptio imperii moslemici*, ed. M. J. de Goeje, Bibliotheca geographorum Arabicorum 3, 2nd edn. (Leiden: E. J. Brill, 1906), 202 (Egypt), 126 (Basra), 415 (Khuzistan), 395 (Rayy), 365 (Qumis, Tabaristan).

tionalist. The Ḥanafīyah considerably modified the forms of their jurisprudence between al-Shaybānī and al-Karkhī; both the Ḥanafīyah and the Shāfiʿīyah paraded their practice of a discipline that involved no *kalām*, which they practiced for the most part separately from their work as Ḥanafīyah and Shāfiʿīyah. It was a considerable advantage of al-Khallāl's way that it took him to meet other Muslims in the middle. The street-fighting Ḥanbalism of al-Barbahārī lasted for some time, but it was al-Khallāl's semi-rationalist jurisprudence that led to Ibn Taymīyah and the survival of Ḥanbali vitality into modern times.

CHAPTER EIGHT

THE MĀLIKI SCHOOL

There were just four classical schools, the four that survived to the later Middle Ages: the Ḥanafi, Shāfi'i, Māliki, and Ḥanbali, to rank them by their approximate numerical strength and geographic dispersion. In previous chapters, I have discussed the development of the Shāfi'i school as a compromise including elements of both traditionalism and *ra'y*; the development of the Ḥanbali school out of earlier Iraqi traditionalism; and the development of the Ḥanafi school out of earlier Iraqi *ra'y*. I have touched on the early development of the Māliki school in Egypt: its early personalization under the impulse of Asad and Saḥnūn, its rivalry with the nascent Shāfi'i school. Its fortunes in the Maghrib depended heavily on patronage from rulers, and it did not reach its mature form until very late. In its putative homeland, Medina, its creative period came to an end before the mid-ninth century. Its development in Iraq is of interest, though, as an attempt at rationalistic jurisprudence acceptable to the traditionalists, much like the Shāfi'i school of Ibn Surayj that did succeed in the long run. Its dependence on patronage from rulers was probably a leading reason why it failed, in the long run, where the Shāfi'i, Ḥanafi, and Ḥanbali schools succeeded.

THE MĀLIKI SCHOOL IN THE WEST

Ibn Khaldūn distinguishes three lines (*ṭuruq*) within the larger Māliki school: those of Qayrawan, Cordoba, and Iraq.[1] By all accounts, the school of Cordoba was intimately associated with state power from the beginning. Ibn Ḥazm has been quoted already to the effect that the Māliki school was established in Andalusia by the amir 'Abd al-Raḥ-

---

[1] Ibn Khaldūn, *Notices et extraits des manuscrits de la bibliothèque impériale et autres bibliothèques* 16-18: *Prolégomènes d'Ebn Khaldoun*, ed. M. Quatremère (Paris: Didot Frères, &al., 1858), 3:11f.

mān ibn al-Ḥakam (*r.* 206-238/822-852).[2] According to another historian, the Māliki school was established a generation before, not by 'Abd al-Raḥmān but by his grandfather, Hishām ibn 'Abd al-Raḥmān (*r.* 172-180/788-796):

> The shaykh of the jurisconsults at that time was Ṣa'ṣa'ah ibn al-Salām, imam of the Awzā'īyah and their traditionist. A number of the *aṣḥāb* of Mālik had attached themselves to him. Then the people in it (Andalusia) were required (to follow) this *madhhab* (that of Mālik) and altogether forbidden by the sword (to follow) any other.[3]

(Sources agree that the school of al-Awzā'ī [d. Beirut, 157/773-774?] prevailed in Andalusia before the Māliki was introduced.[4] Muhammad Talbi suggests that the Awzā'i school was eventually displaced because it had failed to maintain itself in the East, whose fashions the Andalusians preferred to follow.[5]) The geographer al-Maqdisī (*fl.* 375/985) heard that an un-named ruler had expelled the Ḥanafīyah.[6]

Yaḥyá ibn Muḍar (d. 189/805) was one prominent jurisprudent of the time. He travelled to the East and heard the teachings of Sufyān al-Thawrī and Mālik ibn Anas. He was sufficiently involved in politics to be crucified with other notables for plotting against al-Ḥakam ibn Hishām (*r.* 180-207/796-822) in 189/805.[7] Ziyād ibn 'Abd al-Raḥmān (d. *ca.* 200/814-815) was another prominent jurisprudent of the time, said to have introduced the *Muwaṭṭa'* to Andalusia.[8] Al-Ḥakam ibn Hishām pressed Ziyād to become qadi, but he refused. He did accept private audiences with the monarch, and money.[9]

---

[2] Ibn Ḥazm, *al-Iḥkām fī uṣūl al-aḥkām*, ed. Aḥmad Muḥammad Shākir, 8 vols. in 1 (Cairo: al-Khānjī, 1345), 4:230 = 8 vols. in 2 (Beirut: Dār al-Kutub al-'Ilmīyah, n.d.), 1:625.

[3] Al-Qāḍī 'Iyāḍ, *Tartīb al-madārik*, ed. Aḥmad Bakīr Maḥmūd, 5 vols. (Beirut: Maktabat al-Ḥayāh, 1967, 1968), 1:55.

[4] E.g., al-Qurṭubī, *Tārīkh*, *apud* Ibn Ḥajar, *K. Tahdhīb "al-Tahdhīb,"* 12 vols. (Hyderabad: Majlis Dā'irat al-Ma'ārif al-Niẓāmīyah, 1325-27), 6:242.

[5] Muhammad Talbi, "Kairouan et le mālikisme espagnol," *Études . . . Lévi-Provençal*, 2 vols. (Paris: G.-P. Maisonneuve & Larose, 1957), 1:318.

[6] Al-Maqdisī (Muqaddasī), *Descriptio imperii moslemici*, ed. M. J. de Goeje, Bibliotheca geographorum Arabicorum 3, 2nd edn. (Leiden: E. J. Brill, 1906), 237.

[7] Al-Qāḍī 'Iyāḍ, *Tartīb* 2:355f.

[8] Al-Qāḍī 'Iyāḍ, *Tartīb* 2:350.

[9] Ibn al-Faraḍī, *Historia virorum doctorum Andalusiæ*, ed. Francisco Codera, Bibliotheca arabico-hispana, 7, 8, 2 vols. (Madrid: La Guirnalda, 1890, 1892), 1:132; al-Qāḍī 'Iyāḍ, *Tartīb* 2:351f.

ʿĪsá ibn Dīnār (d. Toledo, 212/827-828) was still better regarded than Yaḥyá ibn Muḍar and Ziyād ibn ʿAbd al-Raḥmān. "It was he who taught jurisprudence to the people of Andalusia," said the later jurisprudent Ibn Waḍḍāḥ (d. 287/900?).[10] "The giving of juridical opinions devolved on him in his time," says the biographer Ibn al-Faraḍī (d. 403/1012). "No one in his time was more prominent."[11] He seems to have travelled to the East too late to hear from Mālik himself, and the learning he spread in Andalusia comprised the teaching of Ibn al-Qāsim of Egypt.[12] Al-Ḥakam made him qadi for Toledo and a councillor in Cordoba.[13] Like Yaḥyá ibn Yaḥyá and Yaḥyá ibn Muḍar, he took part in the plot to overthrow al-Ḥakam.[14] ʿĪsá escaped crucifixion but did have to flee and hide. Later, al-Ḥakam attracted him back by guaranteeing his safety.[15]

On the death of ʿĪsá ibn Dīnār, Yaḥyá ibn Yaḥyá al-Laythī (d. 234/849) became the leading jurisprudent of Andalusia.[16] It is he whom Ibn Ḥazm points out as having established the Māliki school by his influence on the amir.[17] He studied under Yaḥyá ibn Muḍar and ʿĪsá ibn Dīnār before travelling, himself, to the East.[18] Although Ibn Khaldūn places him among the *aṣḥāb* of Mālik, Yaḥyá ibn Yaḥyá was probably formed less by Mālik than by Ibn al-Qāsim, under whom he studied during his second trip to the East.[19]

The next leading figure of the Andalusian school was ʿAbd al-Malik ibn Ḥabīb (d. 238/853?). When he returned to Cordoba from studying in Medina and Cairo (218/833-834?), ʿAbd al-Raḥmān ibn al-Ḥakam summoned him to come forward and enrolled him as an official, paid jurisconsult (*rattabahu fī al-fatwá*) alongside Yaḥyá ibn Yaḥyá. The council (*shūrá*) to which he belonged evidently comprised

[10] Al-Dhahabī, *Siyar aʿlām al-nubalāʾ* 10 (ed. Muḥammad Nuʿaym al-ʿAraqasūsī, Beirut: Muʾassasat al-Risālah, 1982):440.

[11] Ibn al-Faraḍī, *Historia* 1:271.

[12] Ibn Farḥūn, *al-Dībāj al-mudhahhab*, ed. Muḥammad al-Aḥmadī Abū al-Nūr, 2 vols. (Cairo: Dār al-Turāth, 1972, 1976), 2:65.

[13] Al-Qāḍī ʿIyāḍ, *Tartīb* 3:16.

[14] Al-Qāḍī ʿIyāḍ, *Tartīb* 1:356.

[15] Ibn al-Faraḍī, *Tartīb* 1:271.

[16] Ibn ʿAbd al-Barr, *apud* Ibn Ḥajar, *Tahdhīb* 11:301.

[17] *V.* note 2; also al-Qāḍī ʿIyāḍ, *Tartīb* 1:55.

[18] Ibn al-Faraḍī, *Historia* 1:132f, 2:43.

[19] Ibn Farḥūn, *Dībāj* 2:353.

the jurisprudents on whom alone the qadi was supposed to rely.[20] When Yaḥyá ibn Yaḥyá died, 'Abd al-Malik enjoyed the chieftaincy in jurisprudence all by himself.[21] His *magnum opus* was *al-Wāḍiḥah fī al-sunnah wa-al-fiqh*, on which account, evidently, Ibn Khaldūn counts him the founding figure of the Andalusian school.[22] After 'Abd al-Malik ibn Ḥabīb, Andalusian jurisprudence was dominated by a student of his, al-'Utbī (d. 255/869?), whose *magnum opus* was *al-Mustakhrajah*, allegedly containing what the *Mudawwanah* of Saḥnūn had omitted.[23] According to Ibn 'Abd al-Barr, "He had great stature in the view of the general . . . . No one undertook to track those who came before him"[24]; that is, no one bothered any longer to relate hadith from them or from those who had heard from them, but rather contented themselves with learning what they had said by means of the *Mustakhrajah*. According to Ibn Khaldūn, Andalusian jurisprudents became devoted to these two books, especially, in time, to the *'Utbīyah*, sole subject of their commentaries, epitomes, and so on.[25]

The struggle between *ra'y* and *ḥadīth* that raged in the East from the late eighth century was reproduced in Andalusia, but in different terms: the great majority could be said to have favored *ra'y*, yet not as the basis of a flexible, rationalistic jurisprudence, as the Iraqi *aṣḥāb al-ra'y* may have seen it, but more simply as set, known juridical opinions. It is usual to read of the great Andalusian jurisprudents that they knew jurisprudence (*fiqh*) or informed opinion (*ra'y*) but not hadith. Ibn 'Abd al-Barr admits that Yaḥyá ibn Yaḥyá was "not good in hadith."[26] Ibn al-Faraḍī says that 'Abd al-Malik ibn Ḥabīb

---

[20] For a story of its operation, *v.* Ibn al-Faraḍī, *Historia* 1:234f.

[21] Ibn Ḥajar, *Tahdhīb* 6:390.

[22] Ibn Khaldūn, *Prolégomènes* 3:11f.

[23] Fuat Sezgin, *Geschichte des arabischen Schrifttums*, 9 vols. to date (Leiden: E. J. Brill, 1967-), 1:472.

[24] *Apud* al-Qāḍī 'Iyāḍ, *Tartīb* 3:145.

[25] Ibn Khaldūn, *Muqaddimah* (Beirut: al-Maṭba'ah al-Adabīyah, 1900), 450 = *Prolégomènes* 3:11. Admittedly, al-Qāḍī 'Iyāḍ reports, to the contrary, that jurisprudents of the next generation harshly disparaged *al-Mustakhrajah*. Ibn 'Abd al-Ḥakam of Egypt thought it largely false, and gave away his copy rather than risk its being found among his belongings when he died. Ibn Lubābah (d. 314/926), who related the work from al-'Utbī, admitted that it contained many mistakes. Ibn Ḥazm jeered at it: *Tartīb* 3:145f.

[26] Ibn 'Abd al-Barr, *al-Intiqā' fī faḍā'il al-thalāthah al-a'immah al-fuqahā'* (Cairo:

"knew jurisprudence . . . but had no knowledge of hadith, not knowing the sound from the sickly."[27] The Iraqi critic al-Dāraquṭnī identified him as weak.[28]

It was the same at the middle of the century. The giving of juridical opinions in the time of the amir Muḥammad ibn ʿAbd al-Raḥmān (*r*. 238-273/852-886) is said to have devolved on three: Ibn Maṭrūḥ (d. 271/884), Aṣbagh ibn Khalīl (d. 273/886-887?), and ʿAbd al-Aʿlá ibn Wahb (d. 261/874?).[29] Ibn Maṭrūḥ was accused of relating hadith reports from someone he had not met,[30] while Aṣbagh ibn Khalīl and ʿAbd al-Aʿlá ibn Wahb were both said to know *ra'y* but not hadith.[31]

Baqī ibn Makhlad (d. 276/889), who had travelled to Iraq as well as Africa, Egypt, and the Hijaz, is said to have been the first to relate much hadith in Andalusia.[32] The adherents of *ra'y* had him arrested and brought before the amir, but he approved of Baqī's book and ordered that he be allowed to continue teaching.[33] A prominent contemporary, Ibn Waḍḍāḥ, related much hadith but is said to have known nothing of jurisprudence.[34] There is evidence of an active offensive against *ra'y* at mid-century. It was the Andalusian Mālik ibn ʿAlī al-Qaṭanī (d. 268/881-882?) who related of the Basran traditionalist al-Qaʿnabī that Mālik had repented on his deathbed of giving opinions by *ra'y*. Al-Qaʿnabī supposedly came to him, found him weeping, and asked him the reason for it. The sick man replied,

> O Ibn Qaʿnab, how can I not cry? Who has better right to cry? By God, I wish I had been struck for every question on which I gave a juridical opinion according to *ra'y*, a blow of the whip, a blow of the whip . . . . Would that I had never given a juridical opinion according to *ra'y*.[35]

Maktabat al-Qudsī, 1350), 60.

[27] Ibn al-Faraḍī, *Historia* 1:226; Ibn Ḥajar, *Tahdhīb* 6:390.

[28] *Apud* Ibn Ḥajar, *Lisān "al-Mīzān,"* 7 vols. (Hyderabad: Majlis Dā'irat al-Maʿārif, 1329-31), 4:60.

[29] Ibn al-Faraḍī, *Historia* 1:312.

[30] Ibn Ḥajar, *Lisān* 5:435.

[31] Ibn al-Faraḍī, *Historia* 1:71, 235.

[32] Ibn ʿAbd al-Barr, *Akhbār ʿulamā' Qurṭubah*, *apud* al-Dhahabī, *Siyar* 13 (ed. ʿAlī Abū Zayd, 1983):290.

[33] Ibn Ḥazm, *apud* al-Dhahabī, *Siyar* 13:288.

[34] Ibn al-Faraḍī, *Historia* 2:17.

[35] Al-Ḥumaydī, *Jadhwat al-muqtabis fī dhikr wulāt al-Andalus*, ed. Muḥammad ibn

The offensive must have met with some success; hence, for example, it is said that 'Īsá ibn Dīnār set his face against the giving of juridical opinions on the basis of *ra'y* in favor of giving juridical opinions on the basis of *ḥadīth*.[36] In view of other characterizations of 'Īsá's expertise, this report seems improbable; however, it shows what was expected at mid-century to raise a man's reputation.

Yet the old preference for jurisprudence over hadith continued. The two leading jurisprudents of the early tenth century are said to have been Ibn Lubābah (d. 314/926) and Abū Ṣāliḥ al-Ma'āfirī (d. 332/943?).[37] It is said of Ibn Lubābah that he knew the *Muwaṭṭa'* of Mālik but not the proper science of hadith, relating by paraphrase rather than word for word.[38] One biographer calls Abū Ṣāliḥ a traditionist, but no source names anyone who related hadith from him, and he does not appear in the standard compendia of *rijāl* criticism.[39] When Ibn 'Abd al-Barr (d. 463/1071) reports a tradition that Mālik harshly repudiated Abū Ḥanīfah for his presumption (it would have been a lighter thing, he allegedly said, had he come against Islam with a sword), he goes on to say that this is what *ahl al-ḥadīth* relate of Mālik, whereas the followers of Mālik who are *ahl al-ra'y* relate nothing of the kind.[40] As late as the eleventh century, then, the party expressly devoted to *ra'y* continued strong.

In several respects, to conclude, the Māliki school in Andalusia seems in advance of the schools of law in the East. It was personal (Māliki, not merely Medinese) as early as the Māliki school of Egypt, far before the Shāfi'i, Ḥanbali, and Ḥanafi schools of Iraq. Its characteristic literary activity was the commentary on previous works from an earlier date, to judge by the remarks of Ibn Khaldūn, than for any of the eastern schools. And it evidently had recognized chiefs

---

Tāwīt al-Ṭanjī (Cairo, 1953), 347; al-Ḍabbī, *Desiderium quærentis historiam populi Andalusiæ*, ed. Francisco Codera & J. Ribera, Bibliotheca arabico-hispana 3 (Madrid: Rojas, 1882), 449. Joseph Schacht knew the story from Ibn Khallikān and rejected it as an invention of the traditionalists: *Encyclopaedia of Islam*, new edn., s.v. "Mālik"; Ibn Khallikān, *Wafayāt al-a'yān*, ed. Iḥsān 'Abbās, 8 vols. (Beirut: Dār al-Thaqāfah, 1968, 1973), 4:137f.

[36] Al-Dhahabī, *Siyar* 10:440, quoting his son.

[37] Ibn al-Faraḍī, *apud Siyar* 15 (ed. Ibrāhīm al-Zaybaq, 1983):330.

[38] Al-Dhahabī, *Siyar* 14 (ed. Akram al-Būshayyī, 1983):495.

[39] *V.* al-Ḍabbī, *Desiderium*, 223; Ibn al-Faraḍī, *Historia* 1:77; al-Dhahabī, *Siyar* 15:331.

[40] Ibn 'Abd al-Barr, *Intiqā'*, 150f.

from an earlier point than had the Iraqi schools.

On the other hand, certain features sharply distinguish the Māliki school of the ninth century in Andalusia from the classical, guild schools of the tenth century and after. For one, it seems to have been highly derivative, continually catching up with developments in the East. Hence, for example, its leading members without exception travelled east to study, whereas no important jurisprudent of the East went to Andalusia for his training. Hence, too, express devotion to *ra'y* and sloppiness concerning hadith survived much longer in Andalusia than Iraq. If, then, the Andalusian school was personal from the late eighth century, it is more likely evidence that the school of Egypt was already highly personalized, by that time, than evidence of Andalusian advance over the rest. As for the production of commentaries, it may not have begun with the generation immediately after al-'Utbī but only much later, as Shāfi'i commentaries on the *Mukhtaṣar* of al-Muzanī began with Ibn Surayj, two generations away, while Ḥanafi commentaries on the two *Jāmi*'s of al-Shaybānī began with Abū Khāzim and al-Ṭaḥāwī, three generations away.[41] There is no evidence, moreover, that the production of a commentary on the *'Utbīyah* ever became a usual part of a regular course of study, as the production of a commentary on the *Mukhtaṣar* seems to have been among Ibn Surayj's students, a commentary on *al-Jāmi' al-ṣaghīr* among al-Karkhī's, and so forth. Finally, the form of chieftaincy in the Andalusian school was intimately connected with state power, and commonly devolved on several jurisprudents at once. In the classical schools of Iraq, by contrast, chieftaincy was determined by prowess in debate and teaching, never by official appointment.

It has been seen already how the Māliki school was introduced to Africa by Asad ibn al-Furāt (d. 213/828) and Saḥnūn (d. 240/854). African jurisprudence before their time seems to have blended all forms of jurisprudence at the center, much like contemporary Khurasani jurisprudence. For example, there was Ibn Ghānim (d. 190/806),

[41] The earliest reworking of the *'Utbīyah* of which I have found record was not exactly a commentary but an abridgement, the book *al-Muntakhabah* by Yaḥyá ibn 'Umar, born in Cordoba but active mainly in Africa (d. Sūsah, 289/902?): al-Qāḍī 'Iyāḍ, *Tartīb* 3:235. Not mentioned by Abū Bakr al-Mālikī, *K. Riyāḍ al-nufūs*, ed. Bashīr al-Bakkūsh, 2 vols. (Beirut: Dār al-Gharb al-Islāmī, 1983), 1:490-504. The next earliest is a re-arrangement by topic from Muḥammad ibn 'Abd Allāh ibn Rashīd (d. *ca.* 363/973-974): al-Qāḍī 'Iyāḍ, *Tartīb* 4:572.

qadi for Africa from Rajab 171/December 787-January 788: among his authorities were Mālik, Sufyān al-Thawrī, and Abū Yūsuf the qadi.[42] He probably no more realized that these represented contradictory systems of jurisprudence than Isḥāq ibn Rāhawayh as he recited praises of Abū Ḥanīfah to 'Abd al-Raḥmān ibn Mahdī.

Māliki jurisprudence developed in Africa after Saḥnūn much as it did in Andalusia. Indeed, many Andalusians came to Qayrawan to study under Saḥnūn, then returned to Andalusia: Muhammad Talbi has counted fifty-seven mentioned by the biographer al-Qāḍī 'Iyāḍ. According to Talbi, Saḥnūn taught the Andalusians to prefer *fiqh* over *ḥadīth* and to practice *taqlīd*, speaking on someone else's authority.[43] However, figures such as Yaḥyá ibn Yaḥyá must have predisposed the Andalusians to listen to such teaching, and no African Māliki is recorded as explicitly commending speaking on the authority of late teachers. Indeed, Saḥnūn's student Ibn al-Ḥaddād (d. 302/914-915) stated that *taqlīd* came of mental deficiency or mean concerns (*min naqṣ al-'uqūl aw danāyat al-himam*).[44] Ibn al-Ḥaddād had in mind not inflexible Mālikīyah, however, but the local Kufans. The African Māliki school, like the Andalusian, hewed to the procedures of *ra'y* but saw itself as traditionalist. Hence, despite Saḥnūn's reputed zeal to follow the exact doctrine of Mālik, a traditionalist might depreciate *al-Mudawwanah*, Saḥnūn's *magnum opus*, as including the merest speculation.[45]

It is said that near the end of his life, Saḥnūn undertook to purge *al-Mudawwanah* of opinions based on *ra'y* and warned his followers against them.[46] The story that Saḥnūn turned from *ra'y* is probably no more sound than the story that Mālik did, for the term continued to be used long after his death to designate what it had for Mālik; namely, "sound opinion," a virtual synonym for *fiqh* (literally "discernment"), not "irresponsible speculation." For example, Saḥnūn's student Yaḥyá ibn 'Umar (d. 289/902?), who became the only accepted reciter in Qayrawan of *al-Muwaṭṭa'* and *al-Mudawwanah*, is said

---

[42] Abū Bakr al-Mālikī, *Riyāḍ* 1:215, 220-222; Ibn Ḥajar, *Tahdhīb* 5:331.

[43] Talbi, "Kairouan," 1:330-334, 337.

[44] Al-Dhahabī, *Siyar* 14:206.

[45] *Ashyā' lā yanhaḍu dalīluhā bal ra'y maḥḍ*, says al-Dhahabī, *Siyar* 12 (ed. Ṣāliḥ al-Samr, 1983):68.

[46] Al-Dhahabī, *Siyar* 12:68.

to have related great quantities of *ra'y* by memory.[47] It seems unlikely that the term should have been used if Saḥnūn had repudiated the concept. In the eleventh century, Ibn 'Abd al-Barr states that Yaḥyá ibn Yaḥyá was *faqīh ḥasan al-ra'y*, "a jurisprudent good in technical juridical reasoning,"[48] and the Māliki biographer of the twelfth century, al-Qāḍī 'Iyāḍ, regularly refers to *ra'y Mālik* rather than *madhhab Mālik*.

The only notable difference between the African school and the Andalusian is the distance between the Mālikīyah of Africa and the ruling dynasty. Perhaps the Umayyad dynasty in Andalusia inherited a tradition of stricter control over religious affairs than the Aghlabids of Africa, originally governors on behalf of the 'Abbāsid caliphs. The social basis of Aghlabid rule is a topic that calls for further study. Probably, the tradition of tension between the Mālikīyah and the Aghlabids steeled the jurisprudents for their long period of positive disfavor, when the Fāṭimids ruled North Africa. As for the formation of a Māliki school in the later sense, though, the distance between the Mālikīyah of Africa and the dynasty meant only that the leading Mālikīyah there were not usually marked out in the same manner as the leading Mālikīyah of Andalusia, by official appointment. Saḥnūn seems to have been pre-eminent in his time, but it is difficult to name any successor. The Mālikīyah of Africa had no system of chieftaincy such as distinguished the Shāfi'i school of Ibn Surayj and his successors, the Ḥanafi school of al-Karkhī, and so forth. Only with respect to personalization does the African school look even so advanced as the Andalusian: compared with jurisprudents in Iraq, the Mālikīyah of Africa were followers, not leaders, and did not contribute heavily to the development of the classical, guild system of schools.

THE MĀLIKI SCHOOL IN THE EAST

The Māliki school had its origins, of course, in Medina, where Mālik (d. 179/795) was a prominent jurisprudent. Mālik himself cannot be said to have founded a school. It is true that he is credited with a notable collection of juridical doctrines, *al-Muwaṭṭa'*, like no other epo-

---

47 Ibn Ḥajar, *Lisān* 6:271.

48 *Apud* Ibn Ḥajar, *Tahdhīb* 11:301, l. 6; cf. same expression *ibid.* 1:360, l. 3, of Ashhab (d. Old Cairo, 204/819).

nym of a later school. He evidently had personal followers, too, so that Ibn Kinānah is said to have succeeded him in his circle, then Ibn Nāfi'.[49] After that, however, the line of succession is difficult to make out, and it evidently comes of no new method of teaching, as did the line of successors to Ibn Surayj, the line of successors to al-Karkhī, and so on. Moreover, the Māliki line in Medina, even such as it was, ceased to be important after the middle of the ninth century.

For the purposes of this history of the schools, it is enough to locate Mālik and the Medinese after him between *ra'y* and *ḥadīth*. Later tradition had it that the science of *ḥadīth* was born in Medina; so says, for example, Ibn Khaldūn.[50] To counter such claims, Schacht has emphatically pointed out that Mālik practiced jurisprudence by *ra'y* no differently from Abū Ḥanīfah.[51] Certainly, the professed Mālikīyah of the Maghrib supposed that Mālik practiced jurisprudence by *ra'y*. Hence, among other things, they continued to use *ra'y* in its original, positive sense far longer than jurisprudents of the East, more exposed to traditionalist criticism.

Mālik's Medinese contemporaries were equally devoted to *ra'y*. Ibn 'Abd al-Barr reports that five men dominated the giving of juridical opinions in Medina at the end of Mālik's life and afterwards.[52] Four on his list died within a few years of Mālik. Only one of them, Ibn Dīnār (d. 182/798-799), seems to have been uniformly respected by later traditionalists.[53] Aḥmad ibn Ḥanbal said of Ibn Abī Ḥāzim (d. Medina, 184/800-801), "There was no one in Medina after Mālik better than he at legal reasoning (*afqah minh*)," but also that he was not known for seeking hadith.[54] Al-Mughīrah (d. Medina, 186/802) appears in four of the Six Books, but reports of his reliability are mixed; for example, the Baghdadi traditionalist Yaḥyá ibn Ma'īn is quoted as calling him trustworthy, but the later Iraqi traditionalist

---

[49] Al-Qāḍī 'Iyāḍ, *Tartīb* 2:357.

[50] Ibn Khaldūn, *Muqaddimah*, 446 = *Prolégomènes* 3:2f.

[51] Joseph Schacht, *The Origins of Muhammadan Jurisprudence* (Oxford: Clarendon Press, 1950), 114f; *Encyclopaedia of Islām*, new edn., s.v. "*Aṣḥāb al-ra'y*," by J. Schacht.

[52] Ibn 'Abd al-Barr, *Intiqā'*, 54.

[53] *V.* Ibn Ḥajar, *Tahdhīb* 9:7f.

[54] Ibn Abī Ḥātim, *K. al-Jarḥ wa-al-ta'dīl*, 9 vols. (Hyderabad: Jam'īyat Dā'irat al-Ma'ārif al-'Uthmānīyah, 1360), 5:382. Ibn Abī Ḥāzim may not have been a Māliki in any strict sense.

Abū Dāwūd says not only that he was weak but also that Yaḥyá ibn Ma'īn had been misquoted on the matter.[55] The fourth was 'Uthmān ibn Kinānah (d. Mecca, 185/801-802), whom al-Qāḍī 'Iyāḍ, as we have seen, considered the immediate successor to Mālik. Ibn 'Abd al-Barr states that he was given to *ra'y* and showed no concern for hadith.[56] Only the fifth, 'Abd Allāh ibn Nāfi' al-Ṣā'igh (d. Medina, 206/822), might easily be considered a student of Mālik's and successor to him. Aḥmad ibn Ḥanbal belittled him:

> He was master not of hadith (*lam yakun ṣāḥib ḥadīth*), but rather the opinion of Mālik (*kāna ṣāḥib ra'y Mālik*), and gave juridical opinions to the people of Medina according to the opinion of Mālik. He was nothing [i.e., not worth considering] in hadith.[57]

('Abd Allāh ibn Nāfi' nonetheless became a reputed advocate of traditionalist theology. Aḥmad himself related the tradition through 'Abd Allāh ibn Nāfi' that Mālik had said the Qur'an was uncreated, and that whoever said "created" should be beaten and imprisoned.[58] 'Abd Allāh ibn Nāfi' was also the source for Mālik's saying against the Murji'ah that faith was word and deed, increasing and decreasing, whereas Ibn Wahb reported that Mālik had been reluctant to talk of decrease.[59])

A little later, 'Abd al-Malik ibn al-Mājishūn (d. 213/828-829?) is said to have been the leading jurisconsult of Medina in his day. The later Medinese traditionist Muṣ'ab al-Zubayrī (d. Baghdad, 236/851) admitted that he was weak in hadith, while the traditionalist *rijāl* critic al-Sājī identified him as *ṣāḥib ra'y*.[60] Aḥmad was contemptuous: "Who is 'Abd al-Malik?" he asked. "Is 'Abd al-Malik a scholar (*min ahl al-'ilm*)? Who learns (hadith) from 'Abd al-Malik?"[61]

Ibn al-Nadīm lists another Medinese, Ibn Abī Uways (d. 227/841-

---

[55] Ibn Ḥajar, *Tahdhīb* 10:264.
[56] Ibn 'Abd al-Barr, *Intiqā'*, 54f.
[57] Ibn Abī Ḥātim, *Jarḥ* 5:184.
[58] Ibn 'Abd al-Barr, *Intiqā'*, 34f.
[59] Ibn 'Abd al-Barr, *Intiqā'*, 33, 34f.
[60] Ibn Ḥajar, *Tahdhīb* 6:408.
[61] Ibn Ḥajar, *Tahdhīb* 6:408, ll. 5f from bottom. Aḥmad may have been displeased with Ibn al-Mājishūn also because of his theory that the Qur'an was half created, half uncreated: so Abū al-Ḥasan al-Ash'arī, *Die dogmatischen Lehren der Anhänger des Islam*, ed. Hellmut Ritter, 2nd edn., Bibliotheca Islamica 1 (Wiesbaden: Franz Steiner, 1963), 586; cf. Ibn Ḥajar, *Tahdhīb* 6:408, ll. 3f from bottom.

842?), among Mālik's most important *aṣḥāb*.[62] I have seen no source that explicitly identifies Ibn Abī Uways with *ra'y* as opposed to *ḥadīth*; however, he is roundly denounced by the great traditionalist critics, and is said in particular to have been weak and untrustworthy in relating hadith[63]; also to have related the *masā'il* (legal problems) of Ibn Wahb as coming from Mālik.[64] Altogether, the record suggests a concern for jurisprudence such as one expects in *aṣḥāb al-ra'y*.

According to Ibn Ḥazm, Abū Muṣ'ab al-Zuhrī (d. 242/857) was the last important jurisprudent of Medina.[65] His name appears in all of the Six Books, but the traditionalists Abū Ḥātim al-Rāzī and Abū Zur'ah al-Rāzī considered him only *ṣadūq* ("veracious"), a mediocre rating,[66] while some Iraqi traditionalists believed him, too, overly devoted to *ra'y*. Abū Khaythamah told his son to write hadith from whomever he pleased, but not from Abū Muṣ'ab al-Zuhrī. The reproach puzzled al-Dhahabī, but Ibn Ḥajar explains that Abū Khaythamah must have had in mind either Abū Muṣ'ab's assuming the office of qadi or his frequent resort to *ra'y* in giving juridical opinions.[67] Virtually from first to last, then, the Māliki school of Medina was closer to *ra'y* than *ḥadīth*; however, it may have become somewhat more acceptable to Iraqi traditionalists in the fifty years after Mālik's death.

In the generation after Mālik, there did emerge a party of Medinese devoted to *ḥadīth* rather than *ra'y*. Ma'n ibn 'Īsá (d. 198/814) is often associated with traditionalist tendencies. He related that Mālik told him, "I am only human, (sometimes) wrong and (sometimes) right. Look into my opinion (*ra'y*): that which agrees with the Sun-

---

[62] Ibn al-Nadīm, *Kitâb al-Fihrist*, ed. Gustav Flügel, w/ Johannes Roedigger & August Mueller (Leipzig: F. C. W. Vogel, 1872), 199 = *fann* 1, *maqālah* 6.

[63] *V.* Ibn Ḥajar, *Tahdhīb* 1:310f.

[64] Ibn Ḥajar, *Tahdhīb* 1:311, l. 9 from bottom.

[65] Ibn Ḥazm, *al-Iḥkām fī uṣūl al-aḥkām*, ed. Muḥammad Aḥmad 'Abd al-'Azīz (Cairo: Maktabat 'Āṭif, 1978), 2:874 = Shākir, ed., 5:97 = (Beirut) 2:93.

[66] Ibn Abī Ḥātim, *Jarḥ* 2:43. For the meaning of *ṣadūq* and other standard ratings, *v.*, e.g., Ibn Ḥajar, *Taqrīb "al-Tahdhīb,"* ed. 'Abd al-Wahhāb 'Abd al-Laṭīf (Medina: Mūḥammad Sulṭān al-N*m*n*kānī, 1961), 1:4f. *V.* also James Robson, "Standards Applied by Muslim Traditionists," *Bulletin of the John Rylands Library Manchester* 43 (1960-61):459-479; cf. Leonard Librande, "The Supposed Homogeneity of Technical Terms in Ḥadīth Study," *Muslim World* 72 (1982):34-50.

[67] Ibn Ḥajar, *Tahdhīb* 1:20.

nah, go by it."[68] The fierce traditionalist Abū Ḥātim al-Rāzī counted him the most reliable of the *aṣḥāb* of Mālik.[69] Ma'n himself carefully distinguished between what he had heard from Mālik, on the one hand, and what Mālik had simply approved of when recited before him, on the other, the sort of care we associate with the Iraqi traditionalists.[70] Finally, Ma'n asserted that Mālik would not answer the questions of the Iraqis concerning hadith save as Ma'n related the questions.[71] We have seen several examples already of distrust of Iraqi jurisprudence as a hallmark of the traditionalist wing of the Māliki school.

The traditionalist wing of the Māliki school is often associated particularly with Basra. The Basran 'Abd al-Raḥmān ibn Mahdī (d. 198/814), for whom al-Shāfi'ī wrote his famous *Risālah*, is sometimes identified as a Māliki; for example, al-Qāḍī 'Iyāḍ identifies him and al-Qa'nabī (d. 221/835) as the two who spread Mālikism in Basra.[72] Actually, 'Abd al-Raḥmān is doubtfully to be counted a follower of Mālik, whether of the *ra'y* or *ḥadīth* wing of the nascent personal school. The later Basran 'Alī ibn al-Madīnī (d. 234/849) suggested that 'Abd al-Raḥmān succeeded Mālik as chief expert in the *madhhab* of the ancient Medinese jurisprudents, not exactly as a follower of Mālik, himself.[73] Aḥmad ibn Ḥanbal expressed reservations concerning 'Abd al-Raḥmān's knowledge of hadith, and said that he sometimes followed the doctrines (*madhāhib*) of the traditionalists, sometimes the opinion (*ra'y*) of the Medinese.[74]

Al-Qa'nabī (d. 221/835) was late enough for us to consider him a follower of Mālik's own jurisprudence, not merely the jurisprudence of the Medinese. He was also a traditionalist. He is responsible for the story already quoted of Mālik's grieving over what he had said by *ra'y*. Traditionalists praised him most highly: Yaḥyá ibn Ma'īn is said to have put no one's transmission from Mālik ahead of his, Abū Ḥātim said he was trustworthy (rare praise from him), Abū Zur'ah said he had never related from one more glorious in his

[68] Ibn Ḥajar, *Tahdhīb* 10:9, ll. 3f.
[69] Ibn Ḥajar, *Tahdhīb* 10:253, l. 5.
[70] Ibn Abī Ḥātim, *Jarḥ* 8:278.
[71] Ibn Abī Ḥātim, *Jarḥ* 8:278.
[72] Al-Qāḍī 'Iyāḍ, *Tartīb* 1:53.
[73] Ibn Abī Ḥātim, *Jarḥ* 1:252.
[74] Ibn Ḥajar, *Tahdhīb* 6:279.

eyes.[75] Some numbered him among the *abdāl*.[76] He taught in Basra, and reports vary as to whether he died there or on the way to Mecca.[77] He cannot be said to have founded any traditionalist Māliki school of Basra, though, for he is not said to have taught jurisprudence to anyone, and only a few of those who heard hadith from him were thereafter Mālikīyah. Perhaps al-Qa'nabī illustrates the difficulty of founding a traditionalist school: inasmuch as he adhered to hadith against personal opinion, so he rejected servile imitation as against re-examination of the scriptuary sources, and hence could not have followers as might one of *aṣḥāb al-ra'y*.

According to Ibn Ḥazm, the opinion of Mālik was introduced to Iraq by Aḥmad ibn al-Mu'adhdhal (d. *ca.* 240/854-855).[78] He is more plausibly counted a Māliki. On the one hand, Ibn al-Nadīm tells us from whom he learnt jurisprudence: the Egyptians Ibn al-Qāsim and Ibn Wahb and "'Abd al-'Azīz al-Mājishūn," surely a mistake for the Medinese 'Abd al-Malik ibn 'Abd al-'Azīz ibn al-Mājishūn (d. 213/828-829?).[79] The late Māliki biographer Ibn Farḥūn adds the unidentified Muḥammad ibn Maslamah.[80] Al-Qāḍī 'Iyāḍ speaks of him as following 'Abd al-Raḥmān ibn Mahdī and al-Qa'nabī.[81] As a Basran, he may well have heard hadith from them; however, they are less likely than Ibn al-Mājishūn and the others to have turned him into an important Māliki. On the other hand, he was plainly a jurisprudent, not a traditionist. Ibn al-Mājishūn was an adherent of *ra'y*, and Aḥmad ibn al-Mu'adhdhal probably was as well, befitting a teacher of future qadis. According to Abū Dāwūd, he actually discouraged the seeking of hadith out of contempt for the world (*zahādatan*).[82] Biographers identify him as a *mutakallim* (a practitioner of *kalām* theology).[83] He would not say whether the Qur'an

[75] Ibn Abī Ḥātim, *Jarḥ* 5:181.

[76] Al-Dhahabī, *Tārīkh al-islām*, ed. 'Umar 'Abd al-Salām Tadmurī, 40+ vols. to date (Beirut: Dār al-Kitāb al-'Arabī, 1987-), 16 (A.H. 221-230):247.

[77] Ibn Ḥajar, *Tahdhīb* 6:32, ll. 9-12.

[78] Ibn Ḥazm, *Iḥkām*, ed. Shākir, 5:98 = (Beirut) 2:94.

[79] Ibn al-Nadīm, *Fihrist*, 199 = *f.* 1, *q.* 6.

[80] Ibn Farḥūn, *Dībāj* 1:141.

[81] Al-Qāḍī 'Iyāḍ, *Tartīb* 1:53.

[82] Al-Dhahabī, *Siyar* 11 (ed. Ṣāliḥ al-Samr, 1982):520.

[83] Al-Dhahabī, *Tārīkh al-islām* 17 (A.H. 231-240):52-54; al-Ṣafadī, *Das biographische Lexicon*, *ca.* 20 vols to date, Bibliotheca Islamica 6, 8 (ed. Muḥammad Yūsuf Najm; Wiesbaden: Franz Steiner Verlag, 1971):184; Ibn Farḥūn, *Dībāj*

was created or uncreated.[84]

THE MĀLIKI SCHOOL OF BAGHDAD

The Māliki school of Baghdad was historically important as a forerunner of the classical Shāfi'i school. It was students of Aḥmad ibn al-Mu'adhdhal's who initially made it up. Ya'qūb ibn Shaybah (d. 262/875-876) was a Basran who studied under Aḥmad ibn al-Mu'adhdhal and also the Egyptian al-Ḥārith ibn Miskīn[85]—presumably, he moved to Baghdad precisely to hear al-Ḥārith. 'Abd al-Raḥmān ibn Yaḥyá ibn Khāqān, brother to the vizier, asked Aḥmad ibn Ḥanbal about Ya'qūb in the course of reviewing a number of candidates to the judgeship. Aḥmad rejected him as "an innovator, adherent of fancies." His innovation was evidently *waqf*: refusing to say, like his teacher Aḥmad ibn al-Mu'adhdhal and other prominent Mālikīyah, whether the Qur'an was created or not.[86]

A more important student of Aḥmad ibn al-Mu'adhdhal's was Ḥammād ibn Isḥāq (d. 267/880-881), associated with Abū Aḥmad, later the shadow caliph al-Muwaffaq. His correspondence with Abū Aḥmad offended the caliph al-Muhtadī in 255/869 and Ḥammād suffered being chastised and paraded on a donkey, while his brother was removed from his judgeship, for the time.[87] Among his books is a refutation of al-Shāfi'ī.[88]

Aḥmad ibn al-Mu'adhdhal's most important student was this brother of Ḥammād's, Ismā'īl ibn Isḥāq (d. 282/896). His importance is twofold: he began a long line of Māliki qadis in Baghdad, and he seems to have promoted a sort of compromise jurisprudence midway between *ra'y* and *ḥadīth*, a new orthodoxy very like what 'Alī ibn 'Īsá later encouraged. He grew up in Basra and received his license to give juridical opinions from (*udhina lil-futyā 'an*) Aḥmad ibn al-

---

1:141.

[84] Al-Dhahabī, *Siyar* 11:520.

[85] Al-Khaṭīb al-Baghdādī, *Tārīkh Baghdād*, 14 vols. (Cairo: Maktabat al-Khānjī, 1931), 14:283.

[86] Al-Khaṭīb al-Baghdādī, *Tārīkh* 14:282.

[87] Al-Dhahabī, *Siyar* 13:16.

[88] Al-Qāḍī 'Iyāḍ, *Tartīb* 3:182.

Mu'adhdhal.[89] The wording is significant: so far as I know, it is the earliest ascription to any teacher of giving license to his student specifically to give juridical opinions, as opposed to license to relate his hadith or opinions.[90] Ismā'īl enjoyed a long career as qadi for various jurisdictions in Baghdad from 246/860-861 until his death.[91] He is the earliest figure whom Ibn al-Nadīm identifies as spreading Māliki jurisprudence: he publicized Mālikism, argued for it, and wrote books about it.[92]

As for the conflict between *ḥadīth* and *ra'y*, he seems to have taken a position in the middle. In the direction of *ḥadīth*, one of his books has the title *al-Sunan*,[93] normally the mark (certainly for Ibn al-Nadīm) of adherence to *ḥadīth*. He was obviously willing to exercise the office of judge, but the reason he gave for not writing a book on the etiquette of judgeship sounds traditionalist: "Is the etiquette of judging any other than Islam?"[94] He was also known for reluctance to associate with the caliph, preferring to send Muḥammad ibn Yūsuf al-Azdī (his student, later chamberlain, later still deputy) in his place. Finally, the critic Ibn Abī Ḥātim, to whom Ismā'īl sent some of his hadith in writing, had a high opinion of his reliability.[95] In the direction of *ra'y*, his teacher Ibn al-Mu'adhdhal seems to have adhered to that style.

I have said before that Abū al-'Abbās Ibn Surayj marked a turning point in the history of Shāfi'ism because he was the first to have one identifiable teacher in jurisprudence (al-Anmāṭī), on the one hand, a number of identifiable students, on the other. In some respects, Ismā'īl is the comparable figure for Eastern Mālikism: he had one identifiable teacher in jurisprudence (Aḥmad ibn al-Mu'adhdhal), then identi-

---

[89] Ṭalḥah ibn Muḥammad ibn Ja'far, *Tārīkh, apud* al-Qāḍī 'Iyāḍ, *Tartīb* 3:170.

[90] Admittedly, the source (*v.* previous note) is from the later tenth century, so it may be a projection backwards from that time. At that, moreover, it uses not the later technical term, *ajāza*, but a synonym; cf. al-Khaṭīb al-Baghdādī's oral report from 'Alī ibn al-Muḥassin from Ṭalḥah ibn Muḥammad ibn Ja'far: *akhadha al-fiqh 'alá madhhab Mālik 'an* . . . (al-Khaṭīb al-Baghdādī, *Tārīkh* 6:285).

[91] Except for the period of his brother's disgrace, when he went into hiding; however, this could hardly have lasted more than six months. *V.* al-Khaṭīb al-Baghdādī, *Tārīkh* 6:287f.

[92] Ibn al-Nadīm, *Fihrist*, 200 = *f.* 1, *q.* 6.

[93] Al-Qāḍī 'Iyāḍ, *Tartīb* 3:179.

[94] Al-Qāḍī 'Iyāḍ, *Tartīb* 3:179.

[95] Ibn Abī Ḥātim, *Jarḥ* 2:158.

fiable students. Moreover, he may have anticipated Ibn Surayj's new method of teaching, mainly having his leading students compose commentaries on the *Mukhtaṣar* of al-Muzanī. Ismā'īl is not said to have produced any *mukhtaṣar* (epitome), himself, as Ibn Surayj did, nor any commentary on either *Mukhtaṣar* of 'Abd Allāh ibn 'Abd al-Ḥakam (d. 214/829); however, there are hints that some of his students did. 'Abd al-Ḥamīd ibn Sahl (*fl.* later ninth cent.?), said to have been among the *aṣḥāb* of Ismā'īl, is credited with writing two books on jurisprudence called *al-Mukhtaṣar*, one large and one small, which may actually have been commentaries on the large and small epitome of 'Abd Allāh ibn 'Abd al-Ḥakam. Additionally, one Muḥammad ibn al-Jahm (*fl.* later ninth cent.?) produced a commentary on the small *Mukhtaṣar* of 'Abd Allāh ibn 'Abd al-Ḥakam. He is not expressly identified as having studied under Ismā'īl but he did transmit, besides, something called *Kitāb Ismā'īl ibn Isḥāq.*[96]

Ismā'īl was severe towards heretics. It was he who presided over the trial of the Sufis at the Inquisition of Ghulām Khalīl.[97] By the eleventh century, it was said that the Sufi al-Nūrī had so moved Ismā'īl (first by volunteering to be the first to have his head struck off, then by his answers to some juridical questions) that the qadi pardoned them all.[98] A tenth-century report by Ibn al-A'rābī, however, says that most of the seventy-odd persons whose arrest was ordered escaped by hiding, while others were imprisoned for a time.[99] Ibn al-A'rābī's report suggests that al-Nūrī in particular was never brought before the qadi, but rather fled the city.[100] There should have been no need to flee, then stay away for fourteen years, had the qadi pardoned him. In other words, it is more probable that Ismā'īl prosecuted the Inquisition with all the rigor he could muster. Also in defense of orthodoxy (or at least keeping the peace), he exiled Dāwūd al-Ẓāhirī from Baghdad for his denial of *qiyās*.[101] Later Māliki

---

[96] Ibn al-Nadīm, *Fihrist*, 200 = *f.* 1, *q.* 6.

[97] On the Inquisition of Ghulām Khalīl, *v.* Carl W. Ernst, *Words of Ecstasy in Sufism* (Albany: State Univ. of N.Y. Press, 1985), 101; Christopher Melchert, "The Transition From Mysticism to Asceticism," *Studia Islamica* 83 (1996):65f.

[98] Abū Nu'aym, *Ḥilyat al-awliyā'*, 10 vols. (Cairo: Maṭba'at al-Sa'ādah, 1932-38), 10:250f = al-Khaṭīb al-Baghdādī, *Tārīkh* 5:134.

[99] *Apud* al-Dhahabī, *Siyar* 13:284.

[100] *Apud* al-Dhahabī, *Siyar* 14:71.

[101] Al-Qāḍī 'Iyāḍ, *Tartīb* 3:178f.

qadis likewise enforced orthodoxy. It was a grand nephew of Ismā'īl's, Abū 'Umar (d. 320/932), who presided over the execution of al-Ḥallāj. His son, Abū al-Ḥusayn (d. 328/940), presided over the similar execution of al-Shalmaghānī (d. 322/934), an extreme Shī'i.[102]

Socially, Ismā'īl moved comfortably in the highest circles. Besides jurisprudence, he was an expert in Basran grammar, said to know the *Kitāb* of Sībawayh as well as al-Mubarrad. Al-Mubarrad himself said that he might have made off with his own chieftaincy in grammar and *belles lettres* if he had not been distracted by the science of judgeship.[103] One of his books was *Kitāb Shawāhid al-Muwaṭṭa'*, presumably finding lines of old poetry displaying obscure words from the *Muwaṭṭa'* of Mālik.[104]

Ismā'īl employed for some time as his secretary the later Shāfi'i teacher Ibn Surayj.[105] Ismā'īl may have identified al-Shāfi'ī as a follower of Mālik, for Ibn Surayj is reported to have protested to the contrary that al-Shāfi'ī was an independent jurisprudent. "There was less between Mālik and al-Shāfi'ī," he declared, "than between Abū Yūsuf and Abū Ḥanīfah."[106] Nevertheless, among Ismā'īl's works were refutations of al-Shāfi'ī (as well as Abū Ḥanīfah and Muḥammad al-Shaybānī) concerning various legal problems.[107]

Ismā'īl ibn Isḥāq employed as his doorkeeper, later deputy, his nephew Yūsuf ibn Ya'qūb al-Azdī (d. 296/909). The qadi Aḥmad ibn Kāmil, also said to have been a Māliki (but sometimes a Jarīri, sometimes an independent), is quoted as saying of al-Azdī "He was weak in discernment"; i.e., jurisprudence.[108] Be that as it may, al-Azdī became *muḥtasib* for Baghdad in 271/884-885; became qadi for Basra in 276/889-890, which he exercised through substitutes; exercised the judgeship of the East Side of Baghdad in his uncle's place;

---

[102] *V.* al-Qāḍī 'Iyāḍ, *Tartīb* 3:279; Yāqūt, *Irshád al-aríb ilá ma'rifat al-adíb*, ed. D. S. Margoliouth, E. J. W. Gibb Memorial Ser. 6, 7 vols. (Leiden: E. J. Brill, 1907-27), 6/1:296f; Ibn al-Athīr, *al-Kāmil fī al-tārīkh*, *s.a.* 322; (Dār Ṣādir), 8:290f.

[103] Abū Isḥāq al-Shīrāzī, *Ṭabaqāt al-fuqahā'*, ed. Iḥsān 'Abbās (Beirut: Dār al-Rā'id al-'Arabī, 1970), 165.

[104] Ibn al-Nadīm, *Fihrist*, 201 = *f.* 1, *q.* 6.

[105] Al-Qāḍī 'Iyāḍ, *Tartīb* 3:178.

[106] Al-Qāḍī 'Iyāḍ, *Tartīb* 1:386.

[107] Al-Qāḍī 'Iyāḍ, *Tartīb* 3:179; Ibn al-Nadīm, *Fihrist*, 200 = *f.* 1, *q.* 6.

[108] Al-Khaṭīb al-Baghdādī, *Tārīkh* 14:312.

then succeeded him on his death, and remained in office until he fell from favor over the affair of Ibn al-Mu'tazz, to whom his son had sworn allegiance.[109]

Al-Azdī's son Muḥammad, Abū 'Umar the qadi (d. 320/932), presided over the West Side from 284/897-898, served as deputy for the qadi Abū Khāzim over the East Side until his death in 292/905, then succeeded Abū Khāzim over the East Side, where he continued to judge until his disgrace in 296/908.[110] He was restored to favor by the vizier 'Alī ibn 'Īsá, and was chief qadi for the last three years of his life.[111] Abū 'Umar compiled a *musnad*, indicating a certain inclination toward traditionalist methods, and dictated the books of *fiqh* that Ismā'īl ibn Isḥāq had written.[112]

Abū al-Ḥusayn 'Umar ibn Muḥammad (d. 328/940) was grandson to the qadi al-Azdī. He learnt jurisprudence from his father and from disciples of Ismā'īl ibn Isḥāq.[113] He succeeded to the judgeship at Madīnat al-Manṣūr on his father's death in 320/932. In 325/937, he became chief qadi.[114] He debated with Abū Bakr al-Ṣayrafī, successor to Ibn Surayj as chief of the Shāfi'īyah.[115] He also wrote a book defending the consensus of the people of Medina, evidently in refutation of something by al-Ṣayrafī.[116]

One of Abū al-Ḥusayn's witness-notaries and a favorite was Abū al-Ṭāhir al-Dhuhlī (d. 367/978?), son of a qadi for Basra and Wāsiṭ, whom Abū al-Ḥusayn made qadi of Wāsiṭ for a time. Later, Abū al-Ṭāhir became qadi for parts of Baghdad, Medina, then Damascus, and

---

[109] Al-Qāḍī 'Iyāḍ, *Tartīb* 3:183f, 186. On the affair of Ibn al-Mu'tazz, *v.* Harold Bowen, *The Life and Times of 'Alí Ibn 'Ísà* (Cambridge: Univ. Press, 1928), 84-98. From this point, I go over much the same ground as Ahmed Békir, *Histoire de l'école malikite en Orient* (Paris: Université de Paris, n.d.), chap. 6. Békir provides a welcome enlargement of the Shāfi'i-centered history promulgated by Schacht; however, his Māliki-centered history has the weakness of ignoring, more completely even than Schacht's, non-Māliki traditionalism. Hence, for example, in the tradition of Ibn Khaldūn, Békir treats the critique of Ḥanafi jurisprudence as *ra'y* entirely as an outgrowth of the Hijazi tradition.

[110] Al-Khaṭīb al-Baghdādī, *Tārīkh* 3:401f.

[111] Al-Khaṭīb al-Baghdādī, *Tārīkh* 3:402.

[112] Al-Khaṭīb al-Baghdādī, *Tārīkh* 3:402.

[113] Al-Qāḍī 'Iyāḍ, *Tartīb* 3:279.

[114] Al-Qāḍī 'Iyāḍ, *Tartīb* 3:279.

[115] Abū Isḥāq, *Ṭabaqāt*, 166.

[116] Abū Isḥāq, *Ṭabaqāt*, 166; al-Qāḍī 'Iyāḍ, *Tartīb* 3:279.

finally Old Cairo for seventeen years, into the Fāṭimid period.[117] Our sources do not say how Abū al-Ṭāhir learnt jurisprudence, but he is said to have been a Māliki and a moderate, holding debates and choosing a position midway between those of the two opponents.[118] As qadi for Egypt, he was willing to compromise with the Fāṭimid rulers, accepting their position in certain cases.[119] This willingness to compromise contrasts with the reputed steadfastness of the African Mālikīyah, and may have had something to do with the evident demise of the Māliki school in Egypt; for example, with Ibn Khaldūn's not considering it a separate *ṭarīqah*.

Abū al-Ḥasan Ibn Umm Shaybān (d. 369/979) was qadi at times for Medina, Baghdad, and Old Cairo. He was close to Abū 'Umar the qadi and learnt the jurisprudence of Mālik.[120] He was qadi for parts of Baghdad from 334/945, under the Būyids, then for Egypt from 336/947.[121]

To sum up the history so far, the Māliki school of Baghdad under Ismā'īl the qadi seems to have been another early attempt at compromise: a traditionalist style of jurisprudence without the rigid dogmatism or avoidance of the powerful that distinguished the extremists around Aḥmad ibn Ḥanbal and his son 'Abd Allāh. Ismā'īl himself was closely associated through most of his career with al-Muwaffaq, whose policy may have extended that of al-Mutawakkil and his vizier, 'Ubayd Allāh ibn Yaḥyá ibn Khāqān: friendly towards traditionalism (whereas al-Muhtadī, the last caliph before he took power, had been friendly towards rationalism); friendly towards Basran jurisprudence (especially, perhaps, as an alternative to Kufan); unfriendly towards the Shī'ah and perhaps heretics in general (whom he may have identified with the dangerous Zanj rebellion that he suppressed). If the Baghdadi Māliki school was an early attempt at forging a new orthodoxy, blending *ra'y* and *ḥadīth* at the level of jurisprudence, minimizing reason in theology, it seems natural that it should have been associated with the persecution of heretics. It seems natural, too, that

---

[117] Al-Qāḍī 'Iyāḍ, *Tartīb* 3:287.

[118] Muḥammad ibn Ṭalḥah al-Shāhid, *apud* Ibn Ḥajar, *Raf' al-iṣr 'an quḍāt Miṣr*, *apud* al-Kindī, *Governors and Judges of Egypt*, ed. Rhuvon Guest, E. J. W. Gibb Memorial Ser. 19 (Leiden: E. J. Brill, 1912), 583.

[119] Ibn Zūlāq, *apud* Ibn Ḥajar, *Raf'*, *apud* al-Kindī, *Governors*, 582, 586.

[120] Ibn Ḥajar, *Raf'*, *apud* al-Kindī, *Governors*, 573.

[121] Ibn Ḥajar, *Raf'*, *apud* al-Kindī, *Governors*, 574.

Ibn Surayj, another notable compromiser, should have been associated with it. It also seems natural that the Baghdadi Mālikīyah should have been strongly associated with early Ash'arism.[122] Indeed, Abū al-Ḥasan al-Ash'arī himself has been identified as a Māliki in jurisprudence. The ninth-century Baghdadi Māliki school anticipated the successful Shāfi'i guild school of Ibn Surayj in so many respects, it must be counted a very near miss by which the leading schools of the East turned out to be the Ḥanafi and the Shāfi'i, not the Ḥanafi and the Māliki.

It must be asked, then, why the Shāfi'i movement of Ibn Surayj spread and lasted while the Māliki school of Baghdad sputtered and went out. One reason must be its evident dependence on political patronage. The line of prominent Mālikīyah in Baghdad is chiefly a line of qadis, not private jurisconsults. Like the Ḥanafīyah of Baghdad in the early ninth century, the Mālikīyah of Andalusia and Egypt into the ninth and tenth centuries, the Mālikīyah of Baghdad might flourish for a time under favor from the ruling power; however, they necessarily suffered at the eclipse of that ruling power, whether the Umayyads of Andalusia, the Sunni governors of Egypt, or the Sunni caliphs in Baghdad.

There eventually did arise a guild Māliki school of Baghdad on the lines of the Shāfi'ī school of Ibn Surayj, and so on, under Abū Bakr al-Abharī (d. 375/986). He is the earliest teacher to be explicitly identified as chief of the Mālikīyah in Baghdad.[123] He learnt jurisprudence from the qadi Abū al-Ḥusayn and from his father the qadi Abū 'Umar.[124] However, in contrast to all the prominent Baghdadi Mālikīyah before him, he refused the judgeship when it was offered him.[125] Al-Abharī wrote a commentary on both the long *Mukhtaṣar* of 'Abd Allāh ibn 'Abd al-Ḥakam and the short.[126] His student Muḥammad ibn 'Abd Allāh al-Qayrawānī wrote a commentary on one of the *Mukhtaṣars* of Abū 'Abd Allāh ibn 'Abd al-Ḥakam, which Abū

---

[122] For a list of Māliki Ashā'irah of the fourth/tenth century, *v.* al-Subkī, *Ṭabaqāt al-shāfi'īyah al-kubrá*, ed. Maḥmūd Muḥammad al-Ṭanāḥī & 'Abd al-Fattāḥ al-Ḥulw, 10 vols. (Cairo: 'Īsá al-Bābī al-Ḥalabī, 1964-76), 3:370, 372.

[123] Muḥammad Ibn Abī al-Fawāris: *intahat ilayhi al-riyāsah fī madhhab Mālik, apud* al-Khaṭīb al-Baghdādī, *Tārīkh* 5:462.

[124] Al-Qāḍī 'Iyāḍ, *Tartīb* 3:279.

[125] Al-Khaṭīb al-Baghdādī, *Tārīkh* 5:463.

[126] Ibn al-Nadīm, *Fihrist*, 200 = *f.* 1, *q.* 6; Ibn 'Abd al-Barr, *Intiqā'*, 53.

Isḥāq describes as a *ta'līq*, like the commentaries on the *Mukhtaṣar* of al-Muzanī, virtual doctoral dissertations, produced by Ibn Surayj's students.[127] With al-Abharī, then, the Māliki school of Baghdad became associated with exactly the method of teaching that distinguished the classical Shāfi'i and Ḥanafi schools. According to al-Subkī, al-Abharī was an Ash'ari in *kalām*.[128] Despite its transformation under al-Abharī, the Māliki school of Baghdad did not last: according to al-Qāḍī 'Iyāḍ, it died out with another Ash'arī, Abū al-Faḍl Ibn 'Abdūs (d. 452/1060-61).[129] The reasons for its failure belong to the history of the eleventh century.[130]

---

[127] Abū Isḥāq, *Ṭabaqāt*, 167. Jonathan Brockopp has proposed in conversation that this commentary must be rather from Abū Muḥammad 'Abd Allāh Ibn Abī Zayd al-Qayrawānī (d. Qayrawan, 386/996). Al-Qāḍī 'Iyāḍ attributes to him a *K. Mukhtaṣar "al-Mudawwanah,"* which sounds like an abridgement rather than a commentary.

[128] Al-Subkī, *Ṭabaqāt* 3:372.

[129] Al-Qāḍī 'Iyāḍ, *Tartīb* 1:53; cf. Abū Isḥāq, *Ṭabaqāt*, 169, and Ibn 'Asākir, *Tabyīn kadhib al-muftarī* (Damascus: Maṭba'at al-Tawfīq, 1347), 264.

[130] Békir complains of Shāfi'i machinations with the caliph, but examines the problem in no detail: *Histoire*, 141, 144. The disappearance of the tenth-century Māliki school may also be related to the advent of the *madrasah*, a mosque devoted exclusively to the teaching of jurisprudence and increasingly, from the eleventh century, the usual livelihood of teachers of jurisprudence. George Makdisi has observed that Shāfi'i and Ḥanafi law assigns to one who endows a *madrasah* (unlike to one who endows a simple mosque) the right, transmissible to his heirs, of appointing and dismissing the faculty. That this continuing right of appointment accounts for the popularity of the new institution among patrons, Makdisi demonstrates by pointing out the paucity of *madrasahs* in lands where Māliki law prevailed, for Māliki law is peculiar in denying such a right: Makdisi, *Rise of Colleges*, 37f. It is not hard to see why the Māliki school should have quickly lost students if everyone could see that the best Shāfi'i and Ḥanafi jurisprudents might look forward to stipends at *madrasahs* but no one of the Māliki school.

CHAPTER NINE

TWO SCHOOLS THAT DID NOT LAST

THE ORIGINAL ẒĀHIRI SCHOOL

The Māliki school was ultimately successful only in the Maghrib. Another leading unsuccessful school of law was the Ẓāhiri, following the principles of Dāwūd ibn 'Alī (d. Baghdad, 270/884). For a century and a half, it looked like a strong competitor. Covering the later tenth century, Ibn al-Nadīm devotes separate sections of his annotated bibliography to eight schools of law[1]:

Mālik and his followers;
the Iraqi *aṣḥāb al-ra'y*;
al-Shāfi'ī and his followers;
Dāwūd and his followers;
jurisprudents of the Shī'ah;
jurisprudents of the traditionists;
al-Ṭabarī and his followers; and
jurisprudents of the *shurāh* (Kharijites).

(The school of Abū Thawr he treats under the larger head of the Shāfi'īyah, of Aḥmad ibn Ḥanbal under the larger head of traditionist-jurisprudents.) His Khurasani contemporary al-Khʷārizmī, as we have seen, includes the Dāwūdīyah among the four juridical schools of *aṣḥāb al-ḥadīth*.[2] A century later, Abū Isḥāq al-Shīrāzī would divide the later subjects of his biographical dictionary of jurisprudents among five schools: Shāfi'īyah, Ḥanafīyah, Mālikīyah, Ḥanābilah, and Ẓāhirīyah. He notes, however, that the Ẓāhiri school had died out in Baghdad: Abū Isḥāq knew of its survival only in Shiraz.[3] How did

---

[1] Ibn al-Nadīm, *Kitâb al-Fihrist*, ed. Gustav Flügel, w/ Johannes Roediger & August Mueller (Leipzig: F. C. W. Vogel, 1872), 198-237 = *maqālah* 6.
[2] Al-Khʷārizmī, *Liber Mafâtîh al-olûm*, ed. G. Van Vloten (Leiden: E. J. Brill, 1895, repr. 1968), 26.
[3] Abū Isḥāq al-Shīrāzī, *Ṭabaqāt al-fuqahā'*, ed. Iḥsān 'Abbās (Beirut: Dār al-Rā'id al-'Arabī, 1970), 179.

it come to be strong in the tenth century, then, but die away in the eleventh?

Dāwūd was born in Kufa in 200/815-816 or 202/817-818.[4] He is often called "al-Iṣbahānī," but only his mother was from Isfahan. His father was an adherent of the nascent Ḥanafi school.[5] The only man whom I have seen expressly identified as his teacher in jurisprudence is al-Shāfi'ī's Baghdadi student Abū 'Abd al-Raḥmān al-Shāfi'ī (*fl.* 219/834).[6] Dāwūd wrote about al-Shāfi'ī's solutions to various juridical problems and corresponded with students of his in Mecca and Old Cairo, besides writing two versions of *Manāqib al-Shāfi'ī*, the first monographs devoted to the virtues of al-Shāfi'ī or, indeed, any major jurisprudent.[7]

Dāwūd has often been referred to as an extreme traditionalist, like Aḥmad ibn Ḥanbal but carrying his principles yet further. There is admittedly some warrant in the sources for classifying Dāwūd with the traditionalists. "He was the first to employ advocacy of the literal meaning," says Ibn al-Nadīm, "holding to the Book and the Sunnah and nullifying all else by way of *ra'y* and *qiyās*."[8] Aḥmad ibn Ḥanbal could likewise be quoted, as we have seen, in total rejection of *ra'y* (opinion) and *qiyās* (analogy).[9] Dāwūd staunchly rejected *taqlīd*, speaking on someone else's authority, and wrote against it.[10] Likewise, as we have seen, Aḥmad and other traditionalists held that one should study the pronouncements of the Prophet, the Companions, and the Successors, not of late jurisprudents such as Mālik, Ibn al-Mubārak, and al-Shāfi'ī.[11] Dāwūd shared with the traditionalists

[4] Al-Khaṭīb al-Baghdādī, *Tārīkh Baghdād*, 14 vols. (Cairo: al-Khānjī, 1931), 8:375; Abū Isḥāq, *Ṭabaqāt*, 92.

[5] Ibn Ḥazm, *apud* al-Dhahabī, *Siyar a'lām al-nubalā'* 13 (ed. 'Alī Abū Zayd, Beirut: Mu'assasat al-Risālah, 1983):98.

[6] Al-Dhahabī, *Siyar* 10 (ed. Muḥammad Nu'aym al-'Araqasūsī, 1982):555. Abū Isḥāq states that he learnt from Isḥāq ibn Rāhawayh and Abū Thawr (*Ṭabaqāt*, 92), but his expression (*akhadha al-'ilm 'an*) might equally refer to the transmission of hadith.

[7] Ibn al-Nadīm, *Fihrist*, 217, ll. 15, 20f = *fann* 4, *maqālah* 6; Ibn 'Abd al-Barr, *al-Intiqā' fī faḍā'il al-thalāthah al-a'immah al-fuqahā'* (Cairo: Maktabat al-Qudsī, 1350), 105; Kātib Çelebī, *Kashf al-ẓunūn*, ed. Şerefettin Yaltkaya & Rifat Bilge, 2 vols. (Istanbul: Maarif Matbaası, 1941, 1943), 2:1839.

[8] Ibn al-Nadīm, *Fihrist*, 216 = *f.* 4, *q.* 6.

[9] Ibn Abī Ya'lá, *Ṭabaqāt al-ḥanābilah*, ed. Muḥammad Ḥāmid al-Fiqī, 2 vols. (Cairo: Maṭba'at al-Sunnah al-Muḥammadīyah, 1952), 1:31, 241, 2:19.

[10] Ibn al-Nadīm, *Fihrist*, 217, l. 13 = *f.* 4, *q.* 6.

[11] Ibn Abī Ya'lá, *Ṭabaqāt* 1:327, 329, 2:15f; Ibn al-Jawzī, *Manāqib al-imām*

their willingness to rely on *khabar al-wāḥid*, a hadith report transmitted by only one man in his generation. Even his peculiar doctrine of *ijmā'*, that the consensus of the Companions alone might determine the law for later generations, has been ascribed as well to Aḥmad.[12]

To the contrary, however, the neglected literature of *rijāl* criticism shows that Dāwūd had virtually no reputation as a traditionist. Abū al-'Abbās Tha'lab commented, "His *'aql* (reason) was greater than his *'ilm* (religious knowledge, specifically hadith)."[13] Al-Khaṭīb al-Baghdādī states that there are many hadith reports in his books and names six men from whom he heard, four who related hadith of him; however, he admits that his oral transmission was small.[14] Dāwūd appears in neither of the comprehensive *rijāl* encyclopedias of Ibn Ḥajar, *Tahdhīb "al-Tahdhīb"* or *Lisān "al-Mīzān."*

Dāwūd does appear in the early *rijāl* encyclopedia of Ibn Abī Ḥātim (d. Rayy, 327/938), reporting chiefly the opinions of Abū Ḥātim al-Rāzī (d. 277/890-891), his father, and Abū Zur'ah al-Rāzī (d. 264/878). Ibn Abī Ḥātim is usually restrained in his criticism, often omitting the names of men whom his father is elsewhere quoted as condemning. Concerning Dāwūd al-Ẓāhirī, however, he writes with unusual vehemence:

> He was a strayer, a heretic, one who watered down, and a destroyer. I saw him, heard his speech, and related of him to my father and to Abū Zur'ah. They were dissatisfied with his position. As for my father, a book of his (Dāwūd's) was brought to him, called *Kitāb al-Buyū'* ("The Book of Sales"). He went after the people of hadith and castigated and condemned them for their much seeking hadith and travelling for that reason. My father produced a book in refutation that came to about fifty folios.[15]

Dāwūd's position concerning hadith was in some respects, then, very far from Aḥmad's, much closer the position of the rationalistic adher-

---

Aḥmad ibn Ḥanbal, ed. 'Abd Allāh ibn 'Abd al-Muḥsin al-Turkī & 'Alī Muḥammad 'Umar (Cairo: al-Khānjī, 1979), 230, 249f.

[12] *Al-ijmā' ijmā' al-ṣaḥābah*: Abū al-Faḍl al-Tamīmī (d. 410/1020), *K. al-I'tiqād*, *apud* Ibn Abī Ya'lá, *Ṭabaqāt* 2:304.

[13] *Apud* al-Dhahabī, *Tārīkh al-islām*, ed. 'Umar 'Abd al-Salām Tadmurī, 40+ vols. to date (Beirut: Dār al-Kitāb al-'Arabī, 1987-), 20 (A.H. 261-280):91.

[14] Al-Khaṭīb al-Baghdādī, *Tārīkh Baghdād* 8:369f.

[15] Ibn Abī Ḥātim, *Kitāb al-Jarḥ wa-al-ta'dīl*, 9 vols. (Hyderabad: Jam'īyat Dā'irat al-Ma'ārif al-'Uthmānīyah, 1360), 3:410f.

ents of *ra'y*.

In law, Dāwūd evidently considered himself close to al-Shāfi'ī, whom he certainly followed with respect to *taqlīd*, servile imitation of earlier jurisprudents. Possibly, also, Dāwūd's identification of *ijmā'* with the consensus of the Companions was the original Shāfi'i doctrine.[16] As we have seen, he studied under Abū 'Abd al-Raḥmān al-Shāfi'ī (*fl.* 221/836), one of al-Shāfi'ī's students in Baghdad, who is said to have been the first to argue for al-Shāfi'ī's position (although he later argued as well for the createdness of the Qur'an).[17] Dāwūd's publisher (*warrāq*), al-Ḥusayn ibn 'Abd Allāh (d. 283/896?), would relate a report from Abū Bakr al-Athram (d. 273/886-887) that Aḥmad had said of al-Shāfi'ī, "I would often sit with him, here. When he went to Egypt, he changed (*taghayyara wajhan*) and he brought forth *ta'wīl* (implausible interpretation) and *ra'y*." Al-Ḥusayn denied the report, asserting that others suggesting the contrary were more reliable.[18] In other words, the Ẓāhiri defended al-Shāfi'ī against the charge that Aḥmad had disparaged him, and contrary to the Ḥanbali tradition by which Aḥmad had preferred the Iraqi works.[19] Another later Ẓāhiri, the grammarian Nifṭawayh (d. 323/935), would allege that al-Shāfi'ī among the scholars was like the full moon among the stars.[20]

For Dāwūd to identify himself with al-Shāfi'ī was to stand apart from the main body of Iraqi traditionalists. Whereas Dāwūd's teaching on the subject of *taqlīd* agreed with al-Shāfi'ī's, Aḥmad continued to use *taqlīd* in the older sense of accepting the authority of the

---

[16] Abū Nu'aym, *Ḥilyat al-awliyā'*, 10 vols. (Cairo: Maṭba'at al-Sa'ādah, 1932-1938), 9:74. Joseph Schacht finds that al-Shāfi'ī showed progressively less trust in consensus but never sharply defined his position or completely rejected the concept: *Origins of Muhammadan Jurisprudence* (Oxford: Clarendon Press, 1950), 88-94. Al-Shāfi'ī, *K. Jimā' al-'ilm* (Schacht's Treatise IV), sounds very close to the polemics of Ibn Ḥazm against any reckoning of *ijmā'* after the Companions: *apud* al-Shāfi'ī, *K. al-Umm*, 7 vols. (Bulaq: al-Maṭba'ah al-Kubrá al-Amīrīyah, 1325), 7:250-262; Schacht, *Origins*, 91f.

[17] Al-Dhahabī, *Siyar* 10:555; Ibn Ḥajar, *Lisān "al-Mīzān,"* 7 vols. (Hyderabad: Majlis Dā'irat al-Ma'ārif, 1329-1331), 7:76.

[18] Ibn Ḥajar, *Lisān* 2:291.

[19] Cf. Abū Nu'aym, *Ḥilyah* 9:97 (from Ibn Wārah), 170 (from 'Abd Allāh ibn Aḥmad).

[20] Al-Nawawī, *Tahdhīb al-asmā' wa-al-lughāt*, 2 vols. in 3 (Cairo: Idārat al-Ṭibā'ah al-Munīrīyah, 1927), 1:64.

Companions. Dāwūd himself defended al-Shāfi'ī against Isḥāq ibn Rāhawayh, with whom he debated the propriety of selling the houses of Medina. Dāwūd explained what al-Shāfi'ī had said, and accused Isḥāq of misunderstanding him.[21] Aḥmad ibn Ḥanbal witnessed the debate and pronounced Isḥāq the winner.[22] Indeed, the story is told that Aḥmad would not speak to one Muḥammad ibn 'Abdah for his having visited Dāwūd until it was explained to him that he had refuted him concerning a legal question.[23]

This is not to say that Dāwūd was as insignificant a jurisprudent as he was a traditionist, but only that his jurisprudence was not traditionalist. Al-Ṭabarī studied under Dāwūd al-Ẓāhirī for a time, then disagreed with him and convened his own session.[24] He seems to have still admired him. When someone asked Ibn Surayj and al-Ṭabarī about the legal works of Abū 'Ubayd, they disparaged them as lacking a sound basis and recommended instead the works of al-Shāfi'ī, Dāwūd, and their equals.[25] Abū Isḥāq al-Shīrāzī remembered Dāwūd and al-Ṭabarī as the two who denied that a consensus of the jurisprudents might be based on simple analogy.[26] This places the two of them very much in the tradition of al-Shāfi'ī and the developing science of *uṣūl al-fiqh*, which Aḥmad seems to have dismissed as *kalām* ("talk," as well as dialectical theology).

Dāwūd is distant from the traditionalists around Aḥmad in his attitude toward debate as well. On the one hand, befitting one with minimal knowledge of hadith, no extant story associates Dāwūd with *mudhākarah*. On the other hand, befitting one attracted by the tools of the rationalists, many stories associate him with *munāẓarah*. When a session of debate (*majlis al-naẓar*) was convened for him in Nishapur, he made enemies by his poor manners.[27] Abū Sa'īd al-Barda'ī (d. 317/929) was a Mu'tazili and the leading Ḥanafi jurisprudent of Bagh-

---

[21] Al-Bayhaqī, *Manāqib al-Shāfi'ī*, ed. Aḥmad Ṣaqr, 2 vols. (Cairo: Dār al-Turāth, 1970, 1971), 1:215f.

[22] Ibn Abī Ḥātim, *Ādāb al-Shāfi'ī wa-manāqibuh*, ed. 'Abd al-Ghanī 'Abd al-Khāliq (Cairo, 1954; repr. Aleppo: Maktabat al-Turāth al-Islāmī, n.d.), 179.

[23] Al-Dhahabī, *Siyar* 13:103f.

[24] Al-Khaṭīb al-Baghdādī, *Tārīkh* 8:373.

[25] Al-Dhahabī, *Siyar* 13:102, 301.

[26] Abū Isḥāq, *al-Tabṣirah fī uṣūl al-fiqh*, ed. Muḥammad Ḥasan Haytū, Silsilat al-kutub wa-al-dirāsāt al-uṣūlīyah 4 (Damascus: Dār al-Fikr, 1980), 372.

[27] Al-Ḥākim al-Naysābūrī, *Tārīkh Naysābūr*, *apud* al-Dhahabī, *Siyar* 12 (ed. Ṣāliḥ al-Samr, 1983):571f.

dad for a time. The occasion of his staying in Baghdad was seeing Dāwūd confute a fellow Ḥanafi in debate, there.[28] From one Ḥanafi source comes the comment that Dāwūd's followers (*aṣḥāb*) met before al-Barda'ī until Dāwūd's death, further indicating that Dāwūd's position was close to theirs.[29] Another debate with a Ḥanafi, over the validity of *khabar al-wāḥid*, became so heated that the audience gathered stones and threatened Dāwūd's opponent, who fled.[30] Reliance on *khabar al-wāḥid* was certainly part of traditionalist doctrine, but public disputation with Ḥanafīyah was not part of traditionalist practice.

In theology, Dāwūd took up positions quite different from those of Aḥmad and the traditionalists. Concerning the Qur'an, he distinguished between an uncreated heavenly prototype and a created Qur'an in people's hands.[31] Ḥanbali tradition also held that he declared his pronunciation of the Qur'an (*lafẓ*) created.[32] The traditionist Muḥammad ibn Yaḥyá al-Dhuhlī (d. 258/872?), chief (*ra'īs*) of Nishapur, wrote letters to Aḥmad ibn Ḥanbal in Baghdad and to Abū Zur'ah and Abū Ḥātim in Rayy with testimony of Dāwūd's heresy. In consequence, Aḥmad would not open the door to Dāwūd when he called.[33]

Dāwūd is still more closely associated with the theory of a *muḥdath* Qur'an; that is, the proposition that the Qur'an was uncreated yet somehow brought forth in time, so that there had been a time when the Qur'an was not. Al-Khallāl related that Aḥmad repudiated him for this proposition.[34] Abū al-Ḥasan al-Ash'arī associates it with Dāwūd al-Ẓāhirī in his heresiography, the earliest extant.[35] An Abū Ṭāhir al-Dhuhlī identified Dāwūd as a disciple in *kalām* of Ibn

---

[28] Al-Khaṭīb al-Baghdādī, *Tārīkh* 4:99f.

[29] Al-Zayla'ī (d. Cairo, 743/1342), *Sharḥ "Kanz al-daqā'iq," apud* al-Kaffawī, *Katā'ib a'lām al-akhyār*, Esad Efendi (Istanbul) 548, 63b.

[30] Ibn Abī al-Wafā', *al-Jawāhir al-muḍīyah fī ṭabaqāt al-ḥanafīyah*, ed. 'Abd al-Fattāḥ Muḥammad al-Ḥulw, 2 vols. (Cairo: Maṭba'at Īsá al-Ḥalabī, 1978), 1:292f.

[31] Al-Khaṭīb al-Baghdādī, *Tārīkh*, 8:374.

[32] Al-Khallāl, *apud* al-Dhahabī, *Siyar* 13:103.

[33] Al-Khaṭīb al-Baghdādī, *Tārīkh* 8:373f.

[34] Al-Dhahabī, *Tārīkh* 20 (A.H. 261-280):92.

[35] Abū al-Ḥasan al-Ash'arī, *Die dogmatischen Lehren der Anhänger des Islam*, ed. Helmut Ritter, Bibliotheca Islamica 1, 2nd edn. (Wiesbaden: Franz Steiner, 1963), 583.

Kullāb (*fl.* before 240/854-855).[36] Whether or not he was his disciple, his tendency was certainly similar: to establish an orthodox theology in the middle, defending the received sayings of the ancients with dialectical proofs. (Curiously, the later heresiographer al-Shahrastānī groups him not with al-Muḥāsibī and Ibn Kullāb but with Sufyān al-Thawrī, Mālik ibn Anas, and Aḥmad ibn Ḥanbal, men of religion who asserted that the tradition was to be believed without any asking how.[37] Al-Shahrastānī's characterization may have to do with the general movement to exonerate major jurisprudents. At any rate, the Ḥanbali tradition seems more trustworthy.)

In his method of discoursing on the law, Dāwūd was sufficiently close to *aṣḥāb al-ra'y* to have a clear successor in his circle, his son Abū Bakr Muḥammad (d. 297/910). Some doubted whether Abū Bakr was ready, in his mid-teens, but he convinced the doubters with an improvised couplet.[38] This would not be the last time he introduced poetry to the field of law. The story is told of a woman's coming to him with a question about marriage some time later: he answered with a couplet, she repeated her question, he gave her another couplet, and she went away still mystified.[39] The later Shāfi'i Ibn al-Ṣalāḥ al-Shahrazūrī (d. 643/1243) quotes the story as a disgusting example not to be followed.[40]

Abū Bakr's chief literary monument was *Kitāb al-Zahrah*, a collection of poetry and related material. Books of his are also cited in the fields of jurisprudence, theology, and qur'anic readings.[41] There is extant a fairly long transcript of a debate between him and Ibn Surayj, with whom he evidently debated regularly, before the qadi Abū 'Umar. Here again one finds continual resort to poetry.[42] Far from

---

[36] Al-Dhahabī, *Siyar* 11 (ed. Ṣāliḥ al-Samr, 1982):174.

[37] Al-Shahrastānī, *Book of Religious and Philosophical Sects*, ed. William Cureton (London: Society for the Publication of Oriental Texts, 1842, 1846), 1:64 = *al-Milal wa-al-niḥal*, ed. Aḥmad Fahmī Muḥammad (Cairo: Maktabat al-Ḥusayn al-Tijārīyah, 1948), 1:126 = ed. 'Abd al-Laṭīf Muḥammad al-'Abd (Cairo: Maktabat al-Anjilū al-Miṣrīyah [*sic*], 1977), 93 = *Muslim Sects and Divisions*, trans. A. K. Kazi & J. G. Flynn (London: Kegan Paul, 1984), 78.

[38] Al-Khaṭīb al-Baghdādī, *Tārīkh* 5:256.

[39] Al-Khaṭīb al-Baghdādī, *Tārīkh* 5:256f.

[40] Ibn al-Ṣalāḥ, *Adab al-muftī wa-al-mustaftī*, ed. Muwaffaq ibn 'Abd Allāh ibn 'Abd al-Qādir ([Beirut]: Maktabat al-'Ulūm wa-al-Ḥikam, 1986), 132f.

[41] Ibn al-Nadīm, *Fihrist*, 217 = *f.* 4, *q.* 6; Ibn Ḥazm, *apud* al-Dhahabī, *Siyar* 13:110.

[42] Al-Khaṭīb al-Baghdādī, *Tārīkh* 5:260-263. Ibn Khallikān places it before a Jar-

appealing, then, to narrow, uneducated folk, original Ẓāhirism was a movement in court circles appealing to the sophisticates of the age.[43]

When Abū Bakr al-Ẓāhirī died, the chieftaincy of the school passed to his student Ibn al-Mughallis (d. 324/936).[44] He wrote a book on jurisprudence, *al-Mūḍiḥ*, that was evidently a systematic refutation of the *Mukhtaṣar* of al-Muzanī[45]: Ẓāhirism continued to be engaged with the Shāfi'i school. "From him," says al-Khaṭīb al-Baghdādī, "the religious knowledge of Dāwūd spread amongst the countries."[46] Actually, the list of his students is not auspicious. Ibn Ukht al-Walīd (d. Old Cairo, 369/980) studied jurisprudence under Ibn al-Mughallis, became qadi for Old Cairo and Damascus but performed disgracefully, and inclined toward Mu'tazilism in theology.[47] 'Alī ibn Khālid al-Baṣrī (*fl.* early 4th/10th cent.) later converted to Ḥanafism.[48] Abū Isḥāq suggests that Ḥaydarah ibn 'Umar (d. 358/969) was the leading Ẓāhiri teacher in Baghdad after Ibn al-Mughallis, but names none of his students.[49] It appears, indeed, that the Ẓāhiri school of Baghdad narrowly missed extinction already in the tenth century.

What saved the school for a time appears to have been favor from the Būyids, the warlords who protected the caliph from 334/945. Abū Naṣr Yūsuf ibn 'Umar (d. 356/967) was one of the last famous members of that family of Māliki qadis, a grand-nephew of the qadi Ismā'īl. He acted as qadi, himself, 327-329/938-940, under the caliph al-

rāḥid vizier, *Wafayāt al-a'yān*, ed. Iḥsān 'Abbās, 7 vols. (Beirut: Dār al-Thaqāfah, 1968), 4:260.

[43] *Contra* Duncan Black Macdonald, *inter alios*: "How much simpler, it struck the average mind, it would be to follow some clear and unambiguous saying of the Prophet; then one could feel secure. This desire of the plain man to take traditions and interpret them strictly and literally was met by the school of Da'ud az-Zahiri, David the literalist": *Development of Muslim Theology, Jurisprudence and Constitutional Theory* (New York: C. Scribner's Sons, 1903), 108. Characterizations such as Macdonald's are plainly based more on experience with modern literalists than on what the sources say of Dāwūd and his medieval followers.

[44] Ibn al-Nadīm, *Fihrist*, 218 = *f*. 4, *q*. 6.

[45] Ibn al-Nadīm, *Fihrist*, 218 = *f*. 4, *q*. 6; Abū Isḥāq, *Ṭabaqāt*, 177.

[46] Al-Khaṭīb al-Baghdādī, *Tārīkh* 9:385; likewise Abū Isḥāq, *Ṭabaqāt*, 177.

[47] Ibn Zūlāq, *apud* Ibn Ḥajar, *Lisān* 3:251; Ibn Ḥazm, *apud* al-Dhahabī, *Siyar* 16 (ed. Akram al-Būshayyī, 1983):226.

[48] Al-Dhahabī, *Siyar* 15 (ed. Ibrāhīm al-Zaybaq, 1983):77.

[49] Abū Isḥāq, *Ṭabaqāt*, 177.

Rāḍī.[50] By a Ẓāhiri account, Abū Naṣr later transferred to the Ẓāhiri school and became prominent in it, completing a book on jurisprudence begun by Abū Bakr al-Ẓāhirī, *Kitāb al-Ījāz*.[51] A student of Ibn al-Mughallis', 'Alī ibn Muḥammad al-Baghdādī (*fl.* early 10th cent.), left Baghdad for Fars and there had at least one important student: Bishr ibn al-Ḥusayn (d. 380/990), who became the chief qadi for Shiraz, then briefly for Baghdad, as well. He was teacher to 'Abd al-'Azīz ibn Aḥmad al-Kharazī (d. 391/1001), who came to Baghdad, along with the Ash'ari leader and Māliki qadi al-Bāqillānī (d. 403/1013), in the entourage of the Būyid 'Aḍud al-Dawlah.[52] There, he acted as Bishr ibn al-Ḥusayn's deputy over part of the East Side.[53] A Ẓāhiri witness-notary, Ibn al-Akhḍar (d. 429/1038), composed a biographical dictionary of the school, *Akhbār ahl al-ẓāhir*, roughly contemporary with the earliest Shāfi'i biographical dictionaries and the Ḥanafi biographical dictionary of al-Ṣaymarī (d. 436/1045).[54] However, Būyid power would not last in the long term, and neither could the Ẓāhiri school inasmuch as it relied on Būyid patronage. The school continued to flourish for a time in Fars, but evidently disappeared in time. Ibn Ḥazm founded the Andalusian school on books he had read.[55]

---

[50] Al-Khaṭīb al-Baghdādī, *Tārīkh* 14:322f; al-Qāḍī 'Iyāḍ, *Tartīb al-madārik*, ed. Aḥmad Bakīr Maḥmūd, 5 vols. (Beirut: Maktabat al-Ḥayāh, 1967, 1968), 3:282f.

[51] *Apud* Abū Isḥāq, *Ṭabaqāt*, 179. Inasmuch as the Būyids favored the Ẓāhiri school, it seems plausible that an ambitious Māliki should transfer to it. However, the Māliki biographer al-Qāḍī 'Iyāḍ casts doubt on Ibn al-Akhḍar's assertion (*Tartīb* 3:283), and the silence of Ibn al-Nadīm (who names *K. al-Ījāz* among the works of Abū Bakr without comment, *Fihrist*, 217 = *f.* 4, *q.* 6) and al-Khaṭīb al-Baghdādī (*Tārīkh* 14:322) seems to tell against it.

[52] Abū Isḥāq, *Tabaqāt*, 178.

[53] Ibn Miskawayh, *The Concluding Portion of the Experiences of the Nations* 2: *Reigns of Muttaqi, Mustakfi, Muti' and* Ta'i', ed. H. F. Amedroz, Eclipse of the 'Abbasid Caliphate 2 (Oxford: Basil Blackwell, 1921):399f.

[54] On Ibn al-Akhḍar, *v.* al-Khaṭīb al-Baghdādī, *Tārīkh* 3:38, and Abū Isḥāq, *Ṭabaqāt*, 178. On the earliest biographical dictionary of the Shāfi'īyah, *v.* Kātib Çelebī, *Kashf* 2:1645, *s.n. al-Mudhhab fī tārīkh al-madhhab*. On al-Ṣaymarī, *v.* al-Khaṭīb al-Baghdādī, *Tārīkh* 8:78f.

[55] Ibn Khaldūn, *al-Muqaddimah* (Beirut: al-Maṭba'at al-Adabīyah, 1900), 447 = *Notices et extraits des manuscrits de la Bibliothèque impériale* 16-18: *Prolégomènes d'Ebn-Khaldoun*, ed. M. Quatremère, 3 vols. (Paris: Didot Frères, &al., 1858), 3:4. One previous jurisprudent is said to have introduced Ẓāhirism to Andalusia, but no chain of teachers connects him with Ibn Ḥazm: 'Abd Allāh ibn Muḥammad ibn Qā-

We may guess at some of the reasons for the demise of the original Ẓāhiri school. Although close to the center in many ways, Dāwūd may have staked out his position on *qiyās* (analogy) too emphatically, too early: it was simply too far from the position of too many other Muslim jurisprudents. We have seen already how the Ḥanafīyah modified both theory and practice to make their doctrine acceptable to traditionalists, finding support for their opinions in prophetic hadith and disallowing *nabīdh*; how the Ḥanābilah, on the other hand, adopted many of the forms of the more rationalistic jurisprudents, such as teaching jurisprudence apart from hadith reports. We may guess that the rejection of *qiyās* was too important for the Ẓāhiri school to have given it up, too different from the doctrine of the other schools to allow recognition. This is roughly the explanation of Wael B. Hallaq: that the juridical theory of Sunnism recognized *qiyās* and therefore excluded Ẓāhirism.[56] Following George Makdisi, one might add to Hallaq's account that it was formal public debate that made the juridical theory of Sunnism effective.[57]

The Ẓāhiri school of Baghdad may have foundered in part, too, for having staked out a position on *taqlīd* too emphatically, too early. The Egyptian qadi Ibn Ḥarbawayh (d. Baghdad, 319/931) began by learning jurisprudence from Dāwud, then transferred to Abū Thawr.[58] An eleventh-century Shāfi'i source makes him a close follower of Abū Thawr in particular[59]; oddly, Ibn Ḥazm states that he inclined toward the position of al-Shāfi'ī.[60] Similarly, al-Ṭabarī once studied under Dāwūd, then left him to make his own choices.[61]

---

sim (d. 272/885-886), who had studied under al-Muzanī in Egypt and Dāwūd in Iraq, on whom *v.* al-Dhahabī, *Tārīkh* 20 (A.H. 261-280):381.

[56] Wael B. Hallaq, "Was the Gate of Ijtihad Closed?" *International Journal of Middle East Studies* 16 (1984):8.

[57] *V.* George Makdisi, *The Rise of Colleges* (Edinburgh: Univ. Press, 1981), 4.

[58] Ibn Ḥajar, *Raf' al-iṣr 'an quḍāt Miṣr*, *apud* al-Kindī, *Governors and Judges of Egypt*, ed. Rhuvon Guest, E. J. W. Gibb Memorial Ser. 19 (Leiden: E. J. Brill, 1912), 523.

[59] Al-Muṭṭawwi'ī, *Mudhhab*, *apud* al-Subkī, *Ṭabaqāt al-shāfi'īyah al-kubrá*, ed. Maḥmūd Muḥammad al-Ṭanāḥī & 'Abd al-Fattāḥ al-Ḥulw, 10 vols. (Cairo: 'Īsá al-Bābī al-Ḥalabī, 1964-1976), 3:446.

[60] Ibn Ḥazm, *al-Iḥkām fī uṣūl al-aḥkām*, ed. Aḥmad Muḥammad Shākir, 8 vols. in 2 (Cairo: al-Khānjī, 1925), 5:103 = 8 vols. in 2 (Beirut: Dār al-Kutub al-'Ilmīyah, n.d.), 2:98.

[61] Al-Khaṭīb al-Baghdādī, *Tārīkh* 8:373.

If all the most illustrious students of Dāwūd felt free, on the basis of his own teaching, to work out their own doctrines, no coherent body of doctrine could be formed, no school in the most primitive sense. Likewise, it must have been difficult to make any transition to the production of commentaries, the *ta'līqah*, and so on. Certainly, we have no evidence of such activity among the Ẓāhirīyah of Baghdad, as we have among the Shāfi'īyah after Ibn Surayj, the Ḥanafīyah after al-Karkhī, and the Mālikīyah (too late) after al-Abharī.

Yet it will not suffice to say that the Ẓāhiri school died out for rejecting *qiyās* and *taqlīd*: otherwise, the Ḥanbali school should have died out with it. As we have seen, Aḥmad ibn Ḥanbal asserted that there was no *qiyās* in the Sunnah, and important adherents of the school named for him continued to say so into the tenth century. Indeed, Ibn Ḥazm counts as followers of Dāwūd both al-Khallāl and Abū Bakr al-Najjād, virtual founder of the Ḥanbali school and a prominent teacher, respectively.[62]

I would suggest that part of the reason was the dogmatic tendency of each school: the Ḥanbali school of law drew strength from its association with theological orthodoxy, the Ẓāhiri lost by its association with unorthodoxy. Massignon identifies Abū Bakr al-Ẓāhirī as a Mu'tazili.[63] Abū 'Alī Muḥammad ibn Mūsá al-Wāsiṭī (d. 320/932), qadi for Ramlah, was accused of *qadar* (denying divine predestination).[64] Ibn Ukht al-Walīd's Mu'tazilism has been mentioned already. Abū Isḥāq al-Shīrāzī identifies the chief teacher of the Ẓāhiri school in Shiraz in his time as a Mu'tazili.[65] Massignon probably goes too far in suggesting that all Ẓāhirīyah were Mu'tazilah; for example, Abū Ya'lá 'Abd al-Mu'min ibn Khalaf (d. 346/957) of Nasaf was said to be Ẓāhiri for his opposition to *qiyās* and the Mu'tazilah.[66] Still, the continual identification of Ẓāhirīyah with Mu'tazilism surely did obviate the sort of support from below

---

[62] Ibn Ḥazm, *al-Iḥkām*, ed. Shākir, 5:103 = (Beirut) 2:98, reading "al-Najjād" for "al-Najjār," in agreement with al-Dhahabī's quotation, *Tārīkh al-islām*, Köprülü 1017, 60 (although not in al-Tadmurī's edition, 20 [A.H. 261-280]:91). On al-Najjād (d. 348/960), *v.* al-Dhahabī, *Siyar* 15:502-505, with further references.

[63] Louis Massignon, *The Passion of al-Hallāj*, trans. Herbert Mason, Bollingen Ser. 98, 4 vols. (Princeton: Univ. Press, 1982), 1:345.

[64] Al-Dhahabī, *Tārīkh* 23 (A.H. 301-320):612, drawing at least partly on Ibn Yūnus.

[65] Abū Isḥāq, *Ṭabaqāt*, 179, on Abū al-Faraj al-Fāmī.

[66] Al-Dhahabī, *Tārīkh* 25 (A.H. 331-350):354.

that Ḥanbali activists gave Ḥanbali jurisprudents.

Additionally, the Ẓāhiri school seems to have been less fortunate than the others (except the Māliki, which shared its fate) in attracting the right patronage. The qadi Ismā'īl, doubtless executing the policy of his master, the shadow-caliph al-Muwaffaq, actually had Dāwūd removed from Baghdad to Basra, one time, on account of his rejecting *qiyās*.[67] The vizier 'Alī ibn 'Īsá is easier to connect with Ibn Surayj, al-Ṭabarī, and the Qur'an reciter Ibn Mujāhid than with Abū Bakr al-Ẓāhirī and Ibn al-Mughallis. Perhaps the Ẓāhirīyah were indeed too involved with the Mu'tazilah for him to see their usefulness; perhaps, also, too close to the Shī'ah. The support of the Būyids was probably harmful, in the long run, like Fāṭimi friendliness toward the Kufan jurisprudents of Africa.

Finally, the Ẓāhiri school may have been crippled by its reliance on outmoded methods of teaching. Abū Isḥāq al-Shīrāzī, it is true, gives the impression that the leading Ẓāhiri jurisprudents of Baghdad in the century before their extinction had fairly identifiable teachers, like their Baghdadi contemporaries of the Shāfi'i and Ḥanafi schools. Still, neither he nor any other source identifies any characteristic literary production comparable to the commentary on the *Mukhtaṣar* of al-Muzanī among the Shāfi'īyah, on *al-Jāmi' al-ṣaghīr* of al-Shaybānī among the Ḥanafīyah. Neither, to be sure, does any source identify a comparable literary production characteristic of Ḥanbali jurisprudents; however, again, the Ḥanābilah may have gotten away without the *ta'līqah* in part because of their firm popular support.

Not only did Ẓāhiri teachers appear to have developed no regular course of study, they may have fatally dispensed with direct, oral transmission. As we have seen, the Ẓāhirīyah were associated from the beginning with high literary circles. One consequence was a failure to communicate with ordinary Muslims. Might not another have been a tendency to learn jurisprudence from books, rather than directly from a teacher? Reliance on books alone was always more characteristic of literary studies than legal.[68] In the absence of sources such as the biographical dictionary of Ibn al-Akhḍar, it is risky to say much; however, we have at least the case of Ibn Ḥazm, known to

[67] Al-Qāḍī 'Iyāḍ, *Tartīb* 3:178f.

[68] George Makdisi, *The Rise of Humanism in Classical Islam and the West* (Edinburgh: Univ. Press, 1990), 76f.

have learnt his Ẓāhiri jurisprudence from books.[69] 'Ubayd Allāh ibn Aḥmad (d. 361/972) adhered to the Ẓāhiri school in law and related the books of Abū Bakr al-Ẓāhirī. He also carelessly related hadith (and juridical opinions, no doubt) from Dāwūd himself and from Ismā'īl ibn Isḥāq the qadi, although he could hardly have met them: he must rather have learnt of them from books.[70] Ibn Ṭāhir al-Maqdisī (d. 507/1113), can hardly have learnt his Ẓāhirism otherwise than from books,[71] so too the Baghdadi littérateur al-Mulhamī (d. 615/1218-19).[72]

To be sure, the Ẓāhiri school spread far from Baghdad before it faded away. Abū Muḥammad al-'Abasī (d. 292/904-905) introduced the books of Dāwūd (note the telling stress on written transmission) to Andalusia.[73] Abū 'Alī Muḥammad ibn Mūsá al-Wāsiṭī, qadi for Ramlah, Ibn Ukht al-Walīd, qadi for Old Cairo and Damascus, have been noted already. In Transoxania, Abū Ya'lá 'Abd al-Mu'min ibn Khalaf has been noted already. Al-Dārawardī (d. Bukhara, 376/986?), qadi for Bukhara, was reputedly the leading jurisprudent of the Dāwūdīyah in his time in Khurasan.[74] In the third quarter of the tenth century, the geographer al-Maqdisī observed strong Ẓāhiri presences in Fars and Sind.[75] We should better understand the demise of the Ẓāhiri school in these provinces if we had a fuller provincial history. However, the classical forms of the Shāfi'i, Ḥanbali, and Ḥanafi schools of law were developed in Baghdad and spread from there, so that vitality in Baghdad was the foundation of continued vitality in the provinces. In Baghdad and the East, jurisprudents personally authorized by one master to give opinions and teach had a clear advantage over those who had learnt from many teachers or, as here suspected of the Ẓāhirīyah, from books. In time, one might find only personally authorized jurisprudents.

---

[69] Ibn Khaldūn, *Muqaddimah*, 447 = *Prolégomènes* 3:4

[70] Al-Dhahabī, *Tārīkh* 26 (A.H. 351-380):281f, relying on al-Tanūkhī, *Nishwār al-muḥāḍarah*.

[71] Ibn Ḥajar, *Lisān* 5:209.

[72] Yāqūt, *Irshād al-arīb ilá ma'rifat al-adīb*, ed. Iḥsān 'Abbās, 7 vols. (Beirut: Dār al-Gharb al-Islāmī, 1993), 3:1280.

[73] Al-Dhahabī, *Tārīkh* 22 (A.H. 291-300):180.

[74] Al-Ḥākim al-Naysābūrī, *Tārīkh Naysābūr*, *apud* al-Dhahabī, *Tārīkh* 26 (A.H. 351-380):577.

[75] Al-Maqdisī, *Descriptio imperii moslemici*, ed. M. J. de Goeje, Bibliotheca geographorum Arabicorum 3, 2nd edition (Leiden: E. J. Brill, 1906), 439, 481.

THE JARĪRI SCHOOL

Similar to the Ẓāhiri school, but still more evanescent, was the school of jurisprudents who followed Muḥammad ibn Jarīr al-Ṭabarī (d. Baghdad, 310/923). Al-Ṭabarī has already come up in connection with both the Ḥanābilah, accused of besieging him in his house at the end of his life, and Dāwūd al-Ẓāhirī, his sometime teacher in jurisprudence. His was included in the list of schools by Ibn al-Nadīm, it will be remembered, but not of al-Khʷārizmī. The biographer al-Sam'ānī considered the last adherent of his school to be the qadi al-Mu'āfá al-Nahrawānī (d. 390/1000).[76] Al-Khaṭīb al-Baghdādī mentions the witness-notary and deputy qadi Ibrāhīm ibn Makhlad (d. 410/1020).[77]

In jurisprudence, al-Ṭabarī may have been above all a great synthesizer. According to Ibn al-Nadīm, he studied jurisprudence under Dāwūd; Shāfi'i jurisprudence under al-Rabī' ibn Sulaymān in Egypt and al-Za'farānī in Baghdad; Māliki jurisprudence under Yūnus ibn 'Abd al-A'lá, three of the brothers Ibn 'Abd al-Ḥakam, and an Ibn Akhī Wahb; and the jurisprudence of the Iraqis (i.e., Ḥanafism) under Abū Muqātil al-Rāzī.[78] One section of his monumental but unfinished *Tahdhīb al-āthār* is extant in Istanbul.[79] His method is to report a prophetic hadith report on some topic of jurisprudence (the order seems random), discuss its chain of authorities, cite other hadith reports on the same topic, cite the opinions of Companions, cite Arab usage (in the style of Abū 'Ubayd, &al.), and finally explain his own juridical position.[80] The difference between al-Ṭabarī's method and the method of, say, Aḥmad ibn Ḥanbal is in al-Ṭabarī's pushing through to a final decision: rather than arranging a series of hadith reports and expecting them to speak for themselves, al-Ṭabarī proposes

---

[76] Al-Sam'ānī, *The Kitāb al-Ansāb*, E. J. W. Gibb Memorial Ser. 20 (Leiden: E. J. Brill, 1912), 98a.

[77] Al-Khaṭīb al-Baghdādī, *Tārīkh* 6:189-191; Adam Mez, *The Renaissance of Islam*, trans. Salahuddin Khuda Bukhsh & D. S. Margoliouth (London: Luzac, 1937), 213fn.

[78] Ibn al-Nadīm, *Fihrist*, 234 = *f.* 6, *q.* 6.

[79] Köprülü (Istanbul) 269. *V.* Ramazan Şeşen, Cevat İzgi, & Cemil Akpınar, *Catalogue of Manuscripts in the Köprülü Library*, 3 vols. (Istanbul: Research Centre for Islamic History, Art & Culture, 1986), 1:146.

[80] For a detailed résumé, *v.* Claude Gilliot, "Le traitement du *ḥadīṯ* dans le *Tahḏīb al-āṯār* de Tabari," *Arabica* 41 (1994):309-351.

the need for expert interpretation. Indeed, his *Ikhtilāf al-fuqahā'*, "Disagreements of the Jurisprudents," notoriously omits to cite the opinion of Aḥmad ibn Ḥanbal. The difference between al-Ṭabarī's method and the method of, say, al-Ṭaḥāwī in *Bayān mushkil al-ḥadīth* is in al-Ṭabarī's finally presenting his own opinion, not the opinion of some venerated jurisprudent of the past such as Abū Ḥanīfah, Abū Yūsuf, and Muḥammad al-Shaybānī.

In theology, al-Ṭabarī seems to have occupied a compromise position neither traditionalist nor fully rationalist. The Ḥanābilah virtually blockaded his house at the end of his life, preventing anyone from coming to study under him.[81] When he died, he is said to have had to be buried by night, for the Ḥanābilah had met and prevented his burial by day.[82] Others, it will be remembered, had done something similar almost seventy years before to al-Muḥāsibī.

We have four accounts of why the Ḥanābilah were angry with al-Ṭabarī. The best known is that al-Ṭabarī offended the Ḥanābilah by dismissing Aḥmad ibn Ḥanbal as a traditionist, not a jurisprudent.[83] Such is exactly the Shāfi'i tradition, that Aḥmad was basically a traditionist who responded gratefully when al-Shāfi'ī explained the intricacies of juridical reasoning; for example,

> We did not know the abrogating of the ways of the Messenger of God . . . from the abrogated (*nāsikh al-sunan*, *mansūkhuhā*), nor

---

[81] Al-Ḥākim al-Naysābūrī, *Tārīkh Naysābūr*, *apud* al-Dhahabī, *Siyar* 14:272; al-Khaṭīb al-Baghdādī, *Tārīkh* 2:164.

[82] Ibn Miskawayh, *The Concluding Portions of "The Experiences of the Nations"* 1: *Reigns of Muqtadir, Qahir and Radi*, ed. H. F. Amedroz, The Eclipse of the 'Abbasid Caliphate 1 (Oxford: Basil Blackwell, 1920), 84; Thābit ibn Sinān, *Tārīkh*, *apud* Ibn al-Jawzī, *al-Muntaẓam fī tārīkh al-mulūk wa-al-umam*, 6 vols. (Hyderabad: Dā'irat al-Ma'ārif al-'Uthmānīyah, 1357-60), 6:172 = ed. Muḥammad 'Abd al-Qādir 'Aṭā' & Muṣṭafá 'Abd al-Qādir 'Aṭā', w. Nu'aym Zurzūr, 18 vols. (Beirut: Dār al-Kutub al-'Ilmīyah, 1992), 13:217. Both accounts expressly implicate *al-'āmmah* ("the general"), not the Ḥanābilah. However, both go on to explain why the Ḥanābilah were angry with al-Ṭabarī, while Ibn Kathīr changes the term to *'āmmat al-ḥanābilah*: *al-Bidāyah wa-al-nihāyah*, 14 vols. (Cairo: Maṭba'at al-Sa'ādah, 1932-39), 11:146. On *al-'āmmah* as a synonym for "*Ḥanābilah*," *v.* Simha Sabari, *Mouvements populaires à Bagdad à l'époque 'abbaside, IXe-XIe siècles*, Centre "Shiloah" des études du Moyen-Orient et de l'Afrique (Paris: Adrien Maisonneuve, 1981), 148, n. 18.

[83] Ibn al-Athīr, *s.a.* 310; ed. C. J. Tornberg, 13 vols. (repr. Beirut: Dār Ṣādir, 1965-1967), 8:134.

> what has general application from what has only special (*'āmm*, *khāṣṣ*), what was obscure from what was clear (*mujmal*, *mufassar*), until we sat before al-Shāfi'ī.[84]

Ḥanbali tradition, more respectful of *ḥadīth* and less of *fiqh*, tends in the opposite direction. It sometimes makes out that Aḥmad expressly repudiated the work of al-Shāfi'ī. At most, it describes Aḥmad as helping al-Shāfi'ī to assess hadith reports[85]; as saying "He did not benefit from us more than we benefitted from him," as though his followers had assumed that most of the benefit had gone to al-Shāfi'ī.[86] This makes al-Ṭabarī a semi-rationalist in jurisprudence, like the wider Shāfi'i school in general.

There is reason to doubt whether it was really al-Ṭabarī's contempt of Aḥmad's stature as a jurisprudent that provoked the Ḥanābilah, for this account of the conflict comes only in the latest sources. It comes from the Ash'ari Ibn al-Athīr and is repeated by later writers, but it cannot be found from, for example, Ibn Miskawayh or al-Khaṭīb al-Baghdādī. On the other hand, al-Ṭabarī does indeed fail to cite Aḥmad's opinions alongside those of others in the extant portions of his book on disagreements among the jurisprudents.[87]

A second explanation is that al-Ṭabarī ran afoul of the Ḥanābilah by proposing a different interpretation of one or another verse of the Qur'an. In effect, al-Ṭabarī either doubted whether Muḥammad would be seated on God's throne at the Resurrection, thus denying him an honor that the Ḥanābilah insisted was his, or he interpreted away an anthropomorphism ("his two hands are extended").[88] On either ac-

---

[84] Al-Bayhaqī, *Manāqib al-Shāfi'ī*, ed. Aḥmad Ṣaqr, 2 vols. (Cairo: al-Majlis al-A'lá lil-Shu'ūn al-Islāmīyah, 1969), 1:262.

[85] 'Abd Allāh ibn Aḥmad, *apud* Abū Nu'aym, *Ḥilyah* 9:170; Ibn Abī Ya'lá, *Ṭabaqāt* 1:6.

[86] Aḥmad ibn Ḥanbal, *K. al-'Ilal wa-ma'rifat al-rijāl*, ed. Waṣī Allāh ibn Muḥammad 'Abbās, 4 vols. (Beirut: al-Maktab al-Islāmī, 1988), 1:469 = ed. Talât Koçyiğit & Ismail Cerrahoğlu, Ankara Üniversitesi Ilâhiyat Fakültesi Yayınların 49, only first vol. published (Ankara: Doğuş Matbaacılık ve Ticaret Matbaası, 1963), 1:158; Abū Nu'aym, *Ḥilyah* 9:170.

[87] Al-Ṭabarī, *Ikhtilāf al-fuqahā'*, ed. Frederick Kern (Cairo: Maṭba'at al-Mawsū'āt & Maktabat al-Taraqqī, 1320/1902); ed. Josef Schacht (Leiden: E. J. Brill, 1933).

[88] Yāqūt, *The Irshád al-aríb ilá ma'rifat al-adíb*, ed. D. S. Margoliouth, E. J. W. Gibb Mem. ser. 6, 7 vols. (Leiden: E. J. Brill, 1907-1927), 6:436, concerning Q.17.79; Ibn al-Jawzī, *Muntaẓam* 6:172 = 13:217, concerning Q.5.64. On the controversy over Q.17.79, *v.* the helpful summary by Franz Rosenthal, "General Intro-

count, al-Ṭabarī is to be classified a semi-rationalist in theology. To what degree either charge was justified is surprisingly difficult to say.[89] In the year 317/927-928, we hear of bloody fighting between the Ḥanābilah and followers of al-Ṭabarī over the enthronement of Muḥammad, so at least Ḥanbali ire is documented.[90]

The third explanation is that al-Ṭabarī was accused of *rafḍ*, extreme Shī'ism.[91] In particular, he was said to favor a Shī'i juridical position, washing the shod feet at the ritual ablution (not merely wiping). The preponderance of evidence seems clearly against this charge. In response to the accusations of the Ḥanābilah, he produced a creed that seems entirely traditionalist. Claude Gilliot dismisses the creed as an occasional work intended merely to silence his Ḥanbali critics, not to explain his actual position.[92] Howbeit, Dominique Sourdel has examined both the creed and al-Ṭabarī's commentary on the Qur'an to see whether he favors the Shī'i positions at famous points of disagreement. His answer is "never."[93] Al-Ṭabarī is said to have denied that al-Ḥasan al-'Askarī (the eleventh imam of the Twelvers) had any children, and asserted that whoever did not acknowledge Abū Bakr and 'Umar as rightly guided imams should be killed.[94] Finally, Shī'i scholars do not count him one of themselves.[95] Still, being accused of Shī'ism by the Ḥanābilah is not inconsistent with membership in the wider Shāfi'i school of law and

duction," *The History of al-Ṭabarī*, SUNY Ser. in Near Eastern Studies, Bibliotheca Persica, 38 vols. (Albany: State Univ. of New York Press, 1985-), 1:71-77.

[89] *V.* Rosenthal's discussion, "General Introduction," 75-77. *V.* also note 92.

[90] Ibn al-Athīr, *Kāmil*, *s.a.* 317; 8:213. Ibn al-Athīr does not name al-Ṭabarī, but the occasion of the fighting, the interpretation of Q.17.79, was one over which al-Ṭabarī had been at odds with the Ḥanābilah in his lifetime. Ibn al-Athīr describes the Ḥanābilah as followers of Abū Bakr al-Marrūdhī (d. 275/888), disciple to Aḥmad ibn Ḥanbal (*Kāmil* 8:213). Ibn Abī Ya'lá groups hadith reports favoring the Ḥanbali interpretation of Q.17.79 *s.n.* Abū Bakr al-Najjād (d. 348/960), *Ṭabaqāt* 2:9-11.

[91] Ibn Miskawayh, *Concluding Portions* 1:84; Ibn al-Jawzī, *Muntaẓam* 6:172 = 13:217.

[92] Claude Gilliot, *Exégèse, langue et théologie en islam*, Librairie philosophique (Paris: J. Vrin, 1990), 258f.

[93] *V.* Dominique Sourdel, "Une Profession de foi de l'historien al-Ṭabarī," *Revue des études islamiques* 36 (1968):177-199.

[94] Al-Dhahabī, *Siyar* 13:122, 275; Ibn Ḥajar, *Lisān* 5:101.

[95] "He was *'āmmī* of *madhhab*," comments al-Ṭūsī, *al-Fihrist*, ed. Muḥammad Ṣādiq Āl Baḥr al-'Ulūm, Nashrīyāt al-maktabah al-murtaḍawīyah 95 (Najaf: al-Maṭba'ah al-Ḥaydarīyah, 1937), 178.

theology, for Aḥmad had complained that al-Shāfi'ī himself was a Shī'i.[96]

Additionally, a late source states that al-Ṭabarī was attacked for a heresy concerning the pronunciation of the Qur'an (*lafẓ*).[97] The charge looks anachronistic, and is not supported by al-Ṭabarī's creed. However, like the first two explanations of Ḥanbali ire, it clearly places al-Ṭabarī in the same camp as Dāwūd al-Ẓāhirī and the semi-rationalist contemporaries of Aḥmad. Ibn al-Athīr reports that the Ḥanābilah of Baghdad incited blind men to attack Shāfi'īyah at mosques in 323/935. These Shāfi'īyah may have been followers of al-Ṭabarī, with whom there had been bloody street fighting in 317/927-928. They may also have been semi-rationalist Imāmi Shī'is, somewhat as the Ḥanābilah suspected al-Ṭabarī of being, with whom the Ḥanābilah clashed at several other points in the 320's/930's.[98]

Like his contemporary Abū Bakr al-Ẓāhirī, al-Ṭabarī was an accomplished man of letters; indeed, his chief literary monuments are no work of jurisprudence but the history and qur'anic commentaries that he composed. His students and later followers, too, were characterized by literary accomplishment. Among the *talāmīdh* of al-Ṭabarī was Yaḥyá ibn 'Alī (d. 300/912), a Mu'tazili in theology, drinking companion to several caliphs, and a poet.[99] Aḥmad ibn Yaḥyá (d. 327/938-939), also a drinking companion to caliphs, wrote books on *kalām* and poets in addition to expositions of the *madhhab* of al-Ṭabarī and polemics defending it.[100] The recorded works of al-Mu'āfá al-Nahrawānī treated grammar, *kalām* theology, and the Qur'an, as well as jurisprudence.[101]

In the absence of better biographical information, again, explana-

---

[96] Al-Qāḍī 'Iyāḍ, *Tartīb* 1:389, ascribed to "Aḥmad ibn 'Abd Allāh"; 1:390, ascribed to Aḥmad ibn Ḥanbal. Ibn al-Nadīm also states that al-Shāfi'ī was strongly Shī'i, *Fihrist*, 209, l. 18 = *f.* 3, *q.* 6.

[97] Ibn Ḥajar, *Lisān* 3:295.

[98] For résumés of Ḥanbali activism in the 320's, *v.* *The Encyclopaedia of Islam*, new edn., s.n. "al-Barbahārī," by H. Laoust; Henri Laoust, *La profession de foi d'Ibn Baṭṭa* (Damascus: Institut Français de Damas, 1958), xxxvii-xli; Sabari, *Mouvements populaires*, chap. 4.

[99] Al-Dhahabī, *Siyar* 13:405, with further references.

[100] Ibn al-Nadīm, *Fihrist*, 235 = *f.* 6, *q.* 6; Johann Fück, "Neue Materialien zum Fihrist," *Zeitschrift für der deutsche morgenländische Gesellschaft* 90 (1936):307; al-Marzubānī, *apud* Ibn Ḥajar, *Lisān* 1:324.

[101] Ibn al-Nadīm, *Fihrist*, 236 = *f.* 7, *q.* 6.

tions for the failure of the Jarīri school must be tentative. There is no evidence of peculiar tenets like the Ẓāhiri rejection of *qiyās* and *taqlīd* to account for the demise of the Jarīri school. Neither is there evidence of excessive dependence among the Jarīrīyah on official appointments. On the other hand, the Jarīri school may have shared with the Ẓāhiri school an excessively literary character. We have the names of a dozen adherents of the school, but no one after al-Ṭabarī himself is identified as a teacher of jurisprudence. It seems that the Jarīrīyah did think of themselves from the beginning as adhering to a personal school: witness the books defending al-Ṭabarī's *madhhab* ascribed to his immediate follower Aḥmad ibn Yaḥyá (d. 327/938-939).[102] Al-Mu'āfá al-Nahrawānī is credited with a commentary on a work of al-Ṭabarī's, a mark of a functioning school.[103] Still, there is no evidence of any regular form of literary production among the Jarīrīyah, no *ta'līqah*. Moreover, the independence and comprehensiveness of al-Ṭabarī's learning may have been too much for ordinary students of jurisprudence to follow.

Finally, al-Ṭabarī may have come too late to make a convincing "patron saint." His contemporary Ibn Surayj presented himself as restoring the jurisprudence of al-Shāfi'ī, a literary giant of a century before. His contemporary al-Khallāl was the collector of the opinions of Aḥmad ibn Ḥanbal, a man who had died less than a century before but had been, at least, a man of notable austerity in his daily living, outright heroism in his standing firm at the Inquisition. Mālik and Abū Ḥanīfah were older still. Abū Ḥanīfah was dubiously orthodox, but at least he was early. The geographer al-Maqdisī (*fl.* 375/985) gave three reasons for favoring the Ḥanafi school of law: Abū Ḥanīfah's closeness to 'Alī, his opinion concerning a particular juridical problem, and his simply being the oldest of the imams. Al-Maqdisī went on to cite the prophetic hadith report, "The best of you is the generation I am in, then those who follow them, then those who follow them."[104] Abū Ḥanīfah was in the generation after the Successors.[105] Of all the eponyms of schools of law, al-Ṭabarī was the fur-

---

[102] Ibn al-Nadīm, *Fihrist*, 235, ll. 16-18 = *f*. 7, *q*. 6.

[103] Ibn al-Nadīm, *Fihrist*, 236 = *f*. 7, *q*. 6.

[104] Al-Maqdisī, *Descriptio*, 127.

[105] Aḥmad ibn al-Ṣalt even made him out to be a Successor, himself. *V*. Eerik Dickinson, "Aḥmad b. al-Ṣalt and His Biography of Abū Ḥanīfa," *Journal of the American Oriental Society* 116 (1996):409.

thest from the virtuous Companions.

The system of law around which the Sunni community would unite had to have something in it for the most sophisticated tastes. The school as developed by Ibn Surayj met that need. The continuing attraction of Mu'tazilism to leading Ḥanbali jurisprudents shows that they felt it, too. The demise of the Ẓāhiri and Jarīri schools of law may show that the community could not unite around any system that appealed *only* to the most sophisticated tastes.

CONCLUSION

At the beginning of the ninth century, Muslim jurisprudents had not clearly divided themselves amongst the Ḥanafīyah, the Mālikīyah, and the Shāfi'īyah, but mainly, rather, between the adherents of *ra'y* and the adherents of *ḥadīth*. Mutual suspicions ran deep: the adherents of *ra'y* doubted whether the adherents of *ḥadīth* were competent to make out the divine law, the adherents of *ḥadīth* doubted even whether the adherents of *ra'y* were properly Muslims. By the beginning of the eleventh century, most Muslim jurisprudents were adherents of the Ḥanafi, Shāfi'ī, Māliki, or some other school of law. They may have disagreed almost as much as the Muslims of two centuries before over details of the law (say, over how far to raise one's hands at the beginning of the ritual prayer), but their formal procedures were much more uniform and all the schools recognized the legitimacy of the other schools. This study has been the history of how Muslim jurisprudents passed from the earlier state to the later, from bitter discord to substantial harmony. For the period before the late ninth century, it has focused on the development of various components of the classical school. From the late ninth century to the eleventh, it has examined the spread of the classical form.

One leading theme of the history has been the sort of literature associated with different parties. The adherents of *ra'y* were associated with the first systematic collections of juridical opinions: for the nascent Māliki school, the *Muwaṭṭa'* of Mālik, the *Mukhtaṣar*s of 'Abd Allāh ibn 'Abd al-Ḥakam and Abū Muṣ'ab al-Zuhrī, finally the *Mudawwanah* of Saḥnūn; for the nascent Ḥanafi school, the *Jāmi'*s of Muḥammad al-Shaybānī. The adherents of *ḥadīth*, by contrast, collected hadith reports, sayings of both the Prophet and the Companions and Successors after him, and most often organized them not by topic but by transmitter. The adherents of *ra'y* began to operate like schools in the classical sense when they began to produce not new collections but commentaries on the old works, beginning in the late ninth century. For the staunchest traditionalists, conversely, it was the systematic collection and ordering of juridical opinions that marked their beginning to operate, about the same time, as a school in the classical sense.

Another leading theme of the history has been the transmission of knowledge from teacher to student. Befitting their emphasis on expertise, the adherents of *ra'y* had a fairly regular system of transmission from individual teachers to identifiable students from the late eighth century. Befitting their emphasis on knowing a great number of hadith reports, the adherents of *ḥadīth* distrusted reliance on one teacher. Not until the end of the ninth century did the staunchest traditionalists of Iraq, the party loyal to Aḥmad ibn Ḥanbal, accept the principle of instruction in jurisprudence from one authoritative teacher. From the same point dates the classical Ḥanbali school.

What the old adherents of *ra'y* had to learn from the adherents of *ḥadīth* was formal reliance on hadith reports from the Prophet, not merely common sense or logical coherence. Schacht sketched the traditionalization of the Ḥanafi school forty-five years ago: what I have done is largely just to show in more detail how the process worked itself out in the century after al-Shāfiʿī, chiefly in the generation of hadith reports to support Ḥanafi positions. A ramification that Schacht apparently overlooked was the modification of traditionalist practice, for if the Ḥanafīyah progressively minimized personal opinion in favor of hadith reports from the Prophet, likewise the extreme traditionalists came to minimize hadith reports from the Companions and Successors. The Māliki school of Iraq may have dwindled away in part for maintaining its old reliance on the opinions of Successors and later experts, rather than working up a basis for Mālik's opinions solely in hadith reports from the Prophet. It might have dwindled away in the West, as well, if competing schools from the East had been able to penetrate the Fāṭimi domains.

I have repeatedly referred to different regions of the Islamic world, especially Andalusia, Africa, Egypt, the Hijaz, Iraq, Khurasan, and Transoxania. Halfway through my research, indeed, I thought differences among the regions would prove decisively important. The shape of my thesis I saw thus: in Baghdad, in the early ninth century, party lines were drawn too sharply for compromise; however, in outlying regions (particularly Egypt and Khurasan), party lines had been drawn too late for such severity, so that the Muslims there, mindful of their minority status, worked out compromises (like the traditionalist Ḥanafism of al-Ṭaḥāwī, the juridical arrangement of hadith by al-Bukhārī and Muslim) that were finally consummated in Baghdad. In the event, however, I have come to see the Muslim jurisprudents of Baghdad as usually leading the way, almost always at least keeping pace.

Although I suppose that Baghdad will always, indeed, appear to have led the development of Islamic law in the ninth and tenth centuries, I acknowledge that regional developments still call for much further work. For example, I will point to the city of Basra. I know of no earlier treatment than mine of its peculiar school of jurisprudence; however, my treatment here is certainly primitive. Several scholars have associated Basra with a peculiar brand of asceticism, yet without setting forth the history and nature of that asceticism in even such detail as I have set forth the history and nature of the Basran school of *ra'y*. I hope to say more in a future study.

The attitude of the state has been another recurring theme of my history. As Ibn Ḥazm points out, rulers gave decisive early support to the Ḥanafi school in Iraq, the Māliki school in Andalusia. Later, through Saḥnūn, the Aghlabids of Africa gave important support to the Māliki school there. Yet the power of rulers to determine the course of religious evolution ran up against sharp limits in this period, above all when the Inquisition of al-Ma'mūn and his two successors failed to establish the doctrine of a created Qur'an. It was evidently the tremendous popular prestige of the staunch traditionalists that preserved them under al-Ma'mūn, al-Mu'taṣim, and al-Wāthiq; prestige that the caliph al-Mutawakkil designed to attract by ending the Inquisition. From time to time, thereafter, rationalists did enjoy renewed caliphal patronage, most notably under al-Muhtadī; never again, however, did that entail the active suppression of their traditionalist adversaries, and the adherents of *ra'y* in law were forced to traditionalize their jurisprudence, moreover to make no parade of their theology but rather to teach it only in private.

Patronage in the later ninth century and into the tenth was a delicate matter, as liable to hurt the long-term prospects of any religious movement as to help them. On the side of hurt, it seems clear that the prospects for Ḥanafism in Egypt and the West were decisively hurt by the local Ḥanafīyah's tendency to collaborate with the Fāṭimids, while the long-term prospects for Mālikism were aided by Māliki opposition to that dynasty. At the same time, Fāṭimi power probably prevented the new-style Iraqi schools from spreading to the West as they immediately did to the East. Back in Iraq, it seems probable that the Māliki and Ẓāhiri schools were hurt, in the long term, by their reliance on appointment to office by caliphs and warlords. On the side of help, one can make out a tradition of vizierial aid to advocates of rationalistic approaches to traditional materials; for example, 'Ubayd Allāh ibn Yaḥyá ibn Khāqān and al-Ṭabarī, 'Alī ibn 'Īsá and a number of jurisprudents.

Behind vizierial aid to what would be the successful party was probably some calculation that a jurisprudence such as theirs would keep the peace. The successful jurisprudence had to have something in it for both the rationalists and the traditionalists, for both sophisticates around the court and earnest but less refined common people. The theology and law that al-Ma'mūn tried to establish evidently offered too little to the common people of Baghdad and other cities, but the pure traditionalism that Aḥmad ibn Ḥanbal and others opposed to it evidently offered too little to sophisticates at court. The jurisprudence taught by the classical schools of law did offer something to both sides. As for the social movements that religious struggles reflect, our sources support their study less well, and attempts to describe them until now, before the course of the religious struggles has become clear, seem premature. Eventually, though, they must be addressed more searchingly than I or other scholars have done.

If the adherents of *ra'y* were forced to traditionalize their jurisprudence in order to gain the assent, at least, of the middle classes, it must be asked why the traditionalists in their turn took on forms associated with *ra'y*, above all the separate training in jurisprudence by single teachers. I have stressed the technical efficiency of these forms, such as sparing jurisprudents the memorization of many thousands of hadith reports. I have questioned Richard Bulliet's positing of tension between old and new converts as an explanation for the spread of the new forms. At one time, I supposed that another decisive impulse to compromise came from the traditionalists' fear of Shī'ism, to resist which they accepted the necessity of closing ranks, of widening the accepted significance of "Sunni" to include semi-rationalists. Subsequent research has shown me that the Imāmīyah of the early tenth century largely did present themselves as semi-rationalists, so that Ḥanbali opposition to the Shī'ah was continuous with Ḥanbali opposition to al-Ṭabarī and others.[1] Shī'ah do not seem to have developed any of the constituent parts of the classical schools of law, as adherents of both *ra'y* and *ḥadīth* did, which is the reason for my other-

[1] *V.* Christopher Melchert, "The Imāmīyah Between Rationalism and Traditionalism," forthcoming in *Shī'ī Islam*, ed. Lynda S. Clarke with Mahmoud Ayoub.

wise neglecting them in this study. It does appear that Ḥanbali leaders of the later tenth century such as Abū al-Ḥasan al-Tamīmī (d. Baghdad, 371/982) did indeed consort with non-Shī'i semi-rationalists,[2] so that the thesis of anti-Shī'i compromise may be valid, after all, for the Būyid period. It is another subject that calls for further study.

Any study that begins with an institution like the school of law and traces backwards its constituent parts will stress options taken, not options dismissed. I have pointed out some options dismissed; for example, the early traditionalist requirement that one learn a hundred thousand hadith reports before venturing to give juridical opinions, and Ḥanafi reliance on the unsupported personal preference of Abū Ḥanīfah. I have also discussed certain unsuccessful schools, such as the original Ẓāhiri school of Iraq. I would caution, still, that there had to have been many more unsuccessful schools than successful, and that most, being unsuccessful, never attracted the attention of biographers and have therefore escaped my notice.

This said, and without suggesting that any particular development was inevitable, I would urge that a predisposition to compromise, to unify around a middle position, can be made out from the very beginning of the period of this study. The adherents of *ra'y* may have doubted whether the adherents of *ḥadīth* were competent to make out the divine law, the adherents of *ḥadīth* even whether the adherents of *ra'y* were properly Muslims; yet they had already a great deal in common, particularly in the nature of their piety. Austerity of living was doubtless more common among the traditionalists than among courtly adherents of *ra'y*; however, the adherents of *ra'y* included famous ascetics, most prominently Dāwūd al-Ṭā'ī (d. Kufa, 166/782-783) and al-Fuḍayl ibn 'Iyāḍ (d. Mecca, 187/803).[3] *Zuhd* (asceticism) was a popular topic of polite littérateurs such as Ibn Abī al-Dunyā (d. Baghdad, 281/894) as well as traditionalists such as Aḥmad ibn Ḥanbal.[4] And although it was usually traditionalists who made

[2] Ibn 'Asākir, *Tabyīn kadhib al-muftarī* (Damascus: al-Qudsī, 1347), 221. *V.* also A. Kevin Reinhart, *Before Revelation*, SUNY Ser. in Middle Eastern Studies (Albany: State Univ. of New York Press, 1995), 22.

[3] *V.* al-Dhahabī, *Siyar a'lām al-nubalā'*, 25 vols. (Beirut: Mu'assasat al-Risālah), 7 (ed. 'Alī Abū Zayd, 1981):422, 8 (ed. Nadhīr Ḥamdān, 1981):421 with references; also Ibn Abī al-Wafā', *al-Jawāhir al-muḍīyah*, ed. 'Abd al-Fattāḥ Muḥammad al-Ḥulw (Cairo: 'Īsá al-Ḥalabī, 1978), 2:194f, 700.

[4] Jacqueline Chabbi, "Remarques sur le développement historique des mouvements ascétiques et mystiques au Khurasan, IIIe/IXe siècle-IVe/Xe siècle," *Studia Islamica*, no. 46 (1977), 24.

the pilgrimage on foot or were never seen smiling, still the adherents of both *ḥadīth* and *ra'y* included many men noted for their praying much; for example, the traditionalists related that Aḥmad had prayed 300 prostrations a day before his chastisement, 150 a day after, but their opponents related that Abū Yūsuf had prayed 200 prostrations a day.[5] With adherents of *ḥadīth* and *ra'y* holding such values in common, it was likely that bitter divisions in the early ninth century should give way to compromises at the end of it. I hope to offer more on the place of competing pieties in the ninth century elsewhere.

---

[5] Abū Nu'aym, *Ḥilyat al-awliyā'*, 10 vols. (Cairo: Maṭba'at al-Sa'ādah, 1932-38), 9:181; al-Khaṭīb al-Baghdādī, *Tārīkh Baghdād*, 14 vols. (Cairo: Maktabat al-Khānjī, 1931), 14:255, ll. 5f.

WORKS CITED

PRIMARY SOURCES IN MANUSCRIPT

Al-'Aynī (d. Cairo, 855/1451). *'Iqd al-jumān fī tārīkh ahl al-zamān*. Veli (Istanbul) 2385.

Al-Dhahabī (d. Damascus, 748/1348?). *Tārīkh al-islām*. Köprülü (Istanbul) 1017.

Al-Fīrūzābādhī (d. Zabīd, 817/1415). *Al-Mirqāh al-wafīyah fī ṭabaqāt al-ḥanafīyah*, Reisülküttâb (Istanbul) 671/1.

Ibn al-Ṣalāḥ al-Shahrazūrī (d. Jerusalem, 643/1243). *Ṭabaqāt al-shāfi'īyah*. Edited by al-Nawawī. Hamidiye (Istanbul) 537.

Ibn Duqmāq (d. Cairo, 809/1407). *Naẓm al-jumān fī ṭabaqāt aṣḥāb imāminā al-Nu'mān*. Serez (Istanbul) 1827.

Ibn Faḍl Allāh al-'Umarī (d. Damascus, 749/1349). *Masālik al-abṣār fī mamālik al-amṣār*. Aya Sofya (Istanbul) 3418, 3419.

Ibn Qinālīzādah (d. Adrianapolis, 979/1572). *Ṭabaqāt al-masā'il*. Şehit Ali Paşa (Istanbul) 2831/6, 57b; Aya Sofya 3407/1.

Ibn Surayj (attributed; d. Baghdad, 306/918). *Ajwibat Abī al-'Abbās*. Şehit Ali Paşa 2763/4.

Al-Kaffawī (d. Istanbul, 990/1582-83). *Katā'ib a'lām al-akhyār min fuqahā' madhhab al-Nu'mān al-mukhtār*. Esat Efendi (Istanbul) 548.

Al-Khalīlī (d. Qazvin? 446/1055). *Al-Irshād fī ma'rifat 'ulamā' al-ḥadīth*. Abridged by al-Silafī (d. Alexandria, 576/1180). Aya Sofya 2951.

Al-Khaṣṣāf (d. Baghdad, 261/874). *Adab al-qāḍī*. Feyzullah Efendi (Istanbul) 660 and Köprülü 546.

Al-Maqrīzī (d. Cairo, 845/1442). *Al-Tārīkh al-kabīr al-muqaffá fī tarājim ahl Miṣr wa-al-wāridīn ilayhā*. Pertev Paşa (Istanbul) 496.

Muḥammad ibn Naṣr al-Marwazī (d. Samarqand, 294/907). *Kitāb Ikhtilāf al-fuqahā'*. Yūsuf Ağa (Konya) 4820/1.

Al-Rāfi'ī (d. Qazvin, 623/1226). *Kitāb al-Tadwīn fī dhikr ahl al-'ilm bi-Qazvīn*. Lâleli (Istanbul) 2010; Bağdatlı Vehbi Efendi (Istanbul) 1028.

PRIMARY SOURCES IN PRINT

Al-'Abbādī (d. Herat, 458/1066). *Kitāb Ṭabaqāt al-fuqahā' al-shāfi'īyah*. Edited by Gösta Vitestam. Veröffentlichungen der "De Goeje Stiftung" 21. Leiden: E. J. Brill, 1964.

'Abd al-Jabbār (d. Rayy, 415/1025). *Faḍl al-i'tizāl*. Pages 129-350 in *Faḍl al-i'tizāl wa-ṭabaqāt al-mu'tazilah*. Edited by Fu'ād Sayyid. Tunis: al-Dār al-Tūnisīyah lil-Nashr, 1974.

'Abd Allāh ibn Aḥmad (d. Baghdad, 290/903). *Al-Jāmi' fī al-'ilal wa-ma'rifat al-rijāl*. Edited by Muḥammad Ḥusām Bayḍūn. 2 vols. Beirut: Mu'assasat al-Kitāb,

1990.

———. *Kitāb al-Sunnah*. Edited by Muḥammad ibn Saʻīd ibn Sālim al-Qaḥṭānī. 2 vols. Dammam: Dār Ibn al-Qayyim, 1986.

Abū al-ʻArab (d. Qayrawan, 333/945). *Kitāb al-Miḥan*. Edited by Yaḥyá Wuhayb al-Jubūrī. Beirut: Dār al-Gharb al-Islāmī, 1983.

Abū al-Ḥasan al-Ashʻarī (d. Baghdad, 324/935-936?). *Die dogmatischen Lehren der Anhänger des Islam*. Edited by Helmut Ritter. Bibliotheca Islamica 1. 2nd edition. Wiesbaden: Franz Steiner, 1963.

Abū al-Qāsim al-Balkhī (d. Balkh, 319/931?). "Bāb Dhikr al-muʻtazilah." Pages 57-119 in *Faḍl al-iʻtizāl wa-ṭabaqāt al-muʻtazilah*. Edited by Fu'ād Sayyid. Tunis: al-Dār al-Tūnisīyah lil-Nashr, 1974.

Abū al-Shaykh (d. 369/979). *Ṭabaqāt al-muḥaddithīn bi-Iṣbahān wa-al-wāridīn ʻalayhā*. Edited by ʻAbd al-Ghafūr ʻAbd al-Ḥaqq Ḥusayn al-Balūshī. 4 vols. Beirut: Mu'assasat al-Risālah, 1987-.

Abū Bakr al-Mālikī (d. Qayrawan, *ca*. 453/1061-62). *Kitāb Riyāḍ al-nufūs fī ṭabaqāt ʻulamā' Qayrawān wa-Ifrīqīyah wa-zuhhādihim wa-nussākihim*. Edited by Bashīr al-Bakkūsh, under Muḥammad al-ʻArūsī al-Maṭwī. 2 vols. Beirut: Dār al-Gharb al-Islāmī, 1983.

Abū Isḥāq al-Shīrāzī (d. Baghdad, 476/1083). *Al-Muhadhdhab fī fiqh madhhab al-imām al-Shāfiʻī*. 2 vols. Cairo: ʻĪsá al-Bābī al-Ḥalabī, n.d.

———. *Ṭabaqāt al-fuqahā'*. Edited by Iḥsān ʻAbbās. Beirut: Dār al-Rā'id al-ʻArabī, 1970.

———. *Al-Tabṣirah fī uṣūl al-fiqh*. Edited by Muḥammad Ḥasan Haytū. Silsilat al-Kutub wa-al-Dirāsāt al-Uṣūlīyah 4. Damascus: Dār al-Fikr, 1980.

Abū Nuʻaym al-Iṣbahānī (d. Isfahan, 430/1038). *Geschichte Isbahāns nach der leidener Handschrift*. Edited by Sven Dedering. 2 vols. Leiden: E. J. Brill, 1931, 1934. (*Tārīkh Iṣbahān*.)

———. *Ḥilyat al-awliyā' wa-ṭabaqāt al-aṣfiyā'*. 10 vols. Cairo: Maktabat al-Khānjī & Maṭbaʻat al-Saʻādah, 1932-38.

Abū Saʻīd al-Dārimī—*v*. al-Dārimī.

Aḥmad ibn Ḥanbal (attributed; d. Baghdad, 241/855; actually by al-Khallāl). *Al-ʻAqīdah lil-imām Aḥmad ibn Ḥanbal*. Edited by ʻAbd al-ʻAzīz ʻIzz al-Dīn al-Sayrawān. Damascus: Dār Qutaybah, 1988.

———. *Kitāb al-ʻIlal wa-maʻrifat al-rijāl*. Edited by Talât Koçyiğit & İsmail Cerrahoğlu. Ankara Üniversitesi İlâhiyat Fakültesi Yayınlar 49. 1 vol. published. Ankara: Doğuş Matbaacılık ve Ticaret Matbaası, 1963.

———. *Kitāb al-ʻIlal wa-maʻrifat al-rijāl*. Edited by Waṣī Allāh ibn Muḥammad ʻAbbās. 4 vols. Beirut: al-Maktab al-Islāmī, 1988.

———. *Al-Musnad*. Edited by Muḥammad Shākir. 3rd edition. 15 vols. in 8. Cairo: Dār al-Maʻārif, 1949-58.

———. *Kitāb al-Waraʻ*. Edited by Zaynab Ibrāhīm al-Qārūṭ Beirut: Dār al-Kutub al-ʻIlmīyah, 1983.

Anonymous. Untitled (list of commentaries on the two *Jāmi*ʻs of al-Shaybānī). On page 449 of Ibn Abī al-Wafā', *al-Jawāhir al-muḍīyah fī ṭabaqāt al-ḥanafīyah* 2. Hyderabad: Majlis Dā'irat al-Maʻārif al-Niẓāmīyah, 1332.

Al-Asnawī (d. Cairo, 772/1370). *Ṭabaqāt al-shāfiʻīyah*. Edited by ʻAbd Allāh al-Jabbūrī. Iḥyā' al-turāth al-islāmī. 2 vols. Baghdad: Dīwān al-Awqāf, 1971.

Al-Bājūrī (d. 1276/1860). *Ḥāshiyat al-Bayjūrī [sic] 'alá Sharḥ Ibn Qāsim al-Ghazzī.* 2 vols. Cairo: Maṭba'at Wādī al-Nīl al-Miṣrīyah, 1298. Reprinted Beirut: Dār al-Ma'rifah, 1974.

Al-Bayhaqī (d. Nishapur, 458/1066). *Manāqib al-Shāfi'ī.* Edited by al-Sayyid Aḥmad Ṣaqr. 2 vols. Cairo: Dār al-Turāth, 1970, 1971.

———. *Ma'rifat al-sunan wa-al-āthār.* Edited by Aḥmad Ṣaqr. 2 vols. Cairo: al-Majlis al-A'lá lil-Shu'ūn al-Islāmīyah, 1969.

Al-Bayhaqī (al-Ḥākim al-Jushamī, d. Mecca, 494/1101?). "Al-Ṭabaqatān al-ḥādiyah 'ashrah wa-al-thāniyah 'ashrah." Pages 359-393 in *Faḍl al-i'tizāl wa-ṭabaqāt al-mu'tazilah.* Edited by Fu'ād Sayyid. Tunis: al-Dār al-Tūnisīyah lil-Nashr, 1974. (*Sharḥ "'Uyūn al-masā'il fī 'ilm al-uṣūl."*)

Al-Ḍabbī (d. 599/1203). *Desiderium quærentis historiam populi Andalusiæ.* Edited by Francisco Codera & J. Ribera. Bibliotheca arabico-hispana 3. Madrid: Rojas, 1882. (*Bughyat al-multamis fī tārīkh rijāl ahl al-Andalus.*)

Al-Dārimī (d. 280/894?). *Radd al-imām al-Dārimī 'alá Bishr al-Marīsī al-'anīd.* Edited by Muḥammad Ḥāmid al-Fiqī. Cairo: Maṭba'at Anṣār al-Sunnah al-Muḥammadīyah, 1358.

———. *Radd al-imām al-Dārimī 'alá Bishr al-Marīsī al-'anīd.* Cairo: Dār al-Furqān, 1985?

Al-Dhahabī (d. Damascus, 748/1348). *Siyar a'lām al-nubalā'* 8. Edited by Nadhīr Ḥamdān. Beirut: Mu'assasat al-Risālah, 1981.

———. *Siyar a'lām al-nubalā'* 10. Edited by Muḥammad Nu'aym al-'Araqasūsī. Beirut: Mu'assasat al-Risālah, 1982.

———. *Siyar a'lām al-nubalā'* 11. Edited by Ṣāliḥ al-Samr. Beirut: Mu'assasat al-Risālah, 1982.

———. *Siyar a'lām al-nubalā'* 12. Edited by Ṣāliḥ al-Samr. Beirut: Mu'assasat al-Risālah, 1983.

———. *Siyar a'lām al-nubalā'* 13. Edited by 'Alī Abū Zayd. Beirut: Mu'assasat al-Risālah, 1983.

———. *Siyar a'lām al-nubalā'* 14. Edited by Akram al-Būshayyī. Beirut: Mu'assasat al-Risālah, 1983.

———. *Siyar a'lām al-nubalā'* 15. Edited by Ibrāhīm al-Zaybiq. Beirut: Mu'assasat al-Risālah, 1983.

———. *Siyar a'lām al-nubalā'* 16. Edited by Shu'ayb al-Arna'ūṭ & Akram al-Būshayyī. Beirut: Mu'assasat al-Risālah, 1983.

———. *Tārīkh al-islām.* Edited by 'Umar 'Abd al-Salām Tadmurī. 40+ vols. Beirut: Dār al-Kitāb al-'Arabī, 1987-.

Ḥanbal ibn Isḥāq (d. Wasit, 273/886). *Dhikr miḥnat al-imām Aḥmad ibn Ḥanbal.* Edited by Muḥammad Naghash. Cairo: Dār Nashr al-Thaqāfah, 1977.

Hilāl al-Ra'y (d. Basra, 245/859-860). *Kitāb Aḥkām al-waqf.* Hyderabad: Majlis Dā'irat al-Ma'ārif al-'Uthmānīyah, 1355.

Al-Ḥumaydī (d. Baghdad, 488/1095). *Jadhwat al-muqtabis fī dhikr wulāt al-Andalus wa-asmā' ruwāt al-ḥadīth wa-ahl al-fiqh wa-al-adab wa-dhawī al-nabāhah wa-al-shi'r.* Edited by Muḥammad ibn Tāwīt al-Ṭanjī. Cairo, 1953. Reprinted Cairo: al-Dār al-Miṣrīyah, 1966.

Ibn 'Abd al-Barr (d. Jativa, 463/1071). *Al-Intiqā' fī faḍā'il al-thalāthah al-a'immah al-fuqahā' Mālik wa-al-Shā wa-Abī Ḥanīfah wa-dhikr 'uyūn min akhbārihim wa-*

akhbār aṣḥābihim. Cairo: Maktabat al-Qudsī, 1350.
Ibn Abī al-Wafā' al-Qurashī (d. Cairo, 775/1373). *Al-Jawāhir al-muḍīyah fī ṭabaqāt al-ḥanafīyah*. Edited by 'Abd al-Fattāḥ Muḥammad al-Ḥulw. 2 vols. published. Cairo: Maṭba'at 'Īsá al-Ḥalabī, 1978.
———. *Al-Jawāhir al-muḍīyah fī ṭabaqāt al-ḥanafīyah*. 2 vols. Hyderabad: Majlis Dā'irat al-Ma'ārif al-Niẓāmīyah, 1332.
Ibn Abī Ḥātim (d. Rayy, 327/938). *Ādāb al-Shāfi'ī wa-manāqibuh*. Edited by 'Abd al-Ghanī 'Abd al-Khāliq. Cairo, 1954? Also Aleppo: Maktabat al-Turāth al-Islāmī, n.d.
———. *Kitāb al-Jarḥ wa-al-ta'dīl*. 9 vols. Hyderabad: Jam'īyat Dā'irat al-Ma'ārif al-'Uthmānīyah, 1360.
Ibn Abī Shaybah, Abū Bakr (d. Kufa, 235/849). *Kitāb al-Muṣannaf*. Edited by Kamāl Yūsuf al-Ḥūt. 7 vols. Beirut: Dār al-Tāj, 1989.
Ibn Abī Ya'lá (d. Baghdad, 526/1133). *Ṭabaqāt al-ḥanābilah*. Edited by Muḥammad Ḥāmid al-Fiqī. 2 vols. Cairo: Maṭba'at al-Sunnah al-Muḥammadīyah, 1952.
Ibn 'Adī al-Qaṭṭān (d. Gurgan, 360/970-971?). *Al-Kāmil fī ḍu'afā' al-rijāl*. 6 vols. Beirut: Dār al-Fikr, 1984.
Ibn al-Athīr (d. Mosul, 630/1233). *Al-Kāmil fī al-tārīkh*. Edited by C. J. Tornberg. Reprinted in 13 vols. Beirut: Dār Ṣādir, 1965-67.
Ibn al-Faraḍī (d. Cordoba, 403/1013). *Historia virorum doctorum Andalusiæ*. Edited by Francisco Codera. Bibliotheca arabico-hispana 7, 8. 2 vols. Madrid: La Guirnalda, 1890, 1892. (*Tārīkh 'ulamā' al-Andalus*.)
Ibn al-Jawzī (d. Baghdad, 597/1200). *Manāqib al-imām Aḥmad ibn Ḥanbal*. Edited by 'Abd Allāh ibn 'Abd al-Muḥsin al-Turkī & 'Alī Muḥammad 'Umar. Cairo: al-Khānjī, 1979.
———. *Al-Muntaẓam fī tārīkh al-mulūk wa-al-umam*. 6 vols. Hyderabad: Dā'irat al-Ma'ārif al-'Uthmānīyah, 1357.
———. *Al-Muntaẓam fī tārīkh al-mulūk wa-al-umam*. Edited by Muḥammad 'Abd al-Wahhāb Faḍl. 2 vols. Cairo: Maṭba'at al-Amānah, 1985.
———. *Al-Muntaẓam fī tārīkh al-mulūk wa-al-umam*. Edited by Muḥammad 'Abd al-Qādir 'Aṭā & Muṣṭafá 'Abd al-Qādir 'Aṭā, with Nu'aym Zurzūr. 18 vols. Beirut: Dār al-Kutub al-'Ilmīyah, 1992.
———. *Naqd al-'ilm wa-al-'ulamā' aw Talbīs Iblīs*. (Cairo:) Idārat al-Ṭibā'ah al-Munīrīyah, 1368.
———. *Talbīs Iblīs*. Edited by Khayr al-Dīn 'Alī. Beirut: Dār al-Wa'y al-'Arabī, 1970?
Ibn al-Murtaḍá (d. Dhofar, 840/1437). *Die Klassen der Mu'taziliten*. Edited by Susanna Diwald-Wilzer. Bibliotheca Islamica, edited by Helmut Ritter & Albert Dietrich, 21. Wiesbaden: Franz Steiner, 1961. (*K. al-Munyah wa-al-amal fī sharḥ "Kitāb al-Milal wa-al-niḥal."*)
Ibn al-Nadīm (*fl.* 377/987). *Kitāb al-Fihrist*. Edited by Gustav Flügel with Johannes Roediger & August Mueller. Leipzig: F. C. W. Vogel, 1871. (*V.* also s.v. "Fück" among secondary sources, *infra*.)
Ibn al-Ṣalāḥ al-Shahrazūrī (d. Jerusalem, 643/1243). *Adab al-muftī wa-al-mustaftī*. Edited by Muwaffaq ibn 'Abd Allāh ibn 'Abd al-Qādir. N.p.: Maktabat al-'Ulūm wa-al-Ḥikam, 1986.
———. *Ṭabaqāt al-fuqahā' al-shāfi'īyah*. Edited by al-Nawawī, al-Mizzī, & Muḥyī

al-Dīn 'Alī Najīb. 2 vols. Beirut: Dār al-Bashā'ir al-Islāmīyah, 1992.

Ibn 'Asākir (d. Damascus, 571/1176). *Tabyīn kadhib al-muftarī fī-mā nusiba ilá al-imām Abī al-Ḥasan al-Ash'arī*. Damascus: al-Qudsī, 1347.

———. *Tahdhīb "Tārīkh" Ibn 'Asākir*. Abridged by 'Abd al-Qādir Badrān. 7 vols. Damascus: Rawḍat al-Shām, 1329?-51.

Ibn Farḥūn (d. Medina, 799/1397). *Al-Dībāj al-mudhahhab fī ma'rifat a'yān 'ulamā' al-madhhab*. Edited by Muḥammad al-Aḥmadī Abū al-Nūr. 2 vols. Cairo: Dār al-Turāth, 1972, 1976.

Ibn Ḥajar (d. Cairo, 852/1449). *Lisān "al-Mīzān."* 7 vols. Hyderabad: Maṭba'at Majlis Dā'irat al-Ma'ārif, 1329-31.

———. *Raf' al-iṣr 'an quḍāt Miṣr*. Pages 501-614 in al-Kindī. *The Governors and Judges of Egypt*. Edited by Rhuvon Guest. E. J. W. Gibb Memorial Series 19. Leiden: E. J. Brill, 1912.

———. *Tabṣīr al-muntabih bi-taḥrīr "al-Mushtabih."* Edited by 'Alī Muḥammad al-Bijāwī. 4 vols. Cairo: al-Dār al-Miṣrīyah lil-Ta'līf wa-al-Tarjamah, 1967.

———. *Tahdhīb "al-Tahdhīb."* 12 vols. Hyderabad: Majlis Dā'irat al-Ma'ārif al-Niẓāmīyah, 1325-27.

———. *Taqrīb "al-Tahdhīb."* Edited by 'Abd al-Wahhāb 'Abd al-Laṭīf. 2 vols. Medina: Mūḥammad Sulṭān al-N*m*n*kānī, 1961.

Ibn Ḥazm (d. Majorca, 456/1064). *Al-Iḥkām fī uṣūl al-aḥkām*. 8 vols. in 2. Cairo: al-Khānjī, 1345.

———. *Al-Iḥkām fī uṣūl al-aḥkām*. Edited by Muḥammad Aḥmad 'Abd al-'Azīz. 2 vols. Cairo: Maktabat 'Āṭif, 1978.

———. *Al-Iḥkām fī uṣūl al-aḥkām*. 8 vols. in 2. Beirut: Dār al-Kutub al-'Ilmīyah, n.d.

Ibn Kamāl Pasha (d. Istanbul, 940/1533). *Ṭabaqāt al-mujtahidīn*. Pages 558f in Ibn Abī al-Wafā'. *Al-Jawāhir al-muḍīyah fī ṭabaqāt al-ḥanafīyah* 2. Hyderabad: Majlis Dā'irat al-Ma'ārif al-Niẓāmīyah, 1332.

Ibn Kathīr (d. Damascus, 774/1373). *Al-Bidāyah wa-al-nihāyah fī al-tārīkh*. 14 vols. Cairo: Maṭba'at al-Sa'ādah, 1932-39.

———. *Ṭabaqāt al-fuqahā' al-shāfi'īyīn*. Edited by Aḥmad 'Umar Hāshim & Muḥammad Zaynuhum Muḥammad 'Azib. 3 vols. Al-Ẓāhir, Egypt: Maktabat al-Thaqāfah al-Dīnīyah, 1993.

Ibn Khaldūn (d. Cairo, 806/1408). *Al-Muqaddimah*. Beirut: al-Maṭba'ah al-Adabīyah, 1900. Reprinted Beirut: Dār al-Qalam, 1978.

———. *Notices et extraits des manuscrits de la Bibliothèque impériale et autres bibliothèques* 16-18: *Prolégomènes d'Ebn-Khaldoun*. Edited by M. Quatremère. 3 vols. Paris: Didot Frères, Fils, &al., 1858. (*Al-Muqaddimah*.)

Ibn Khallikān (d. Damascus, 681/1282). *Wafayāt al-a'yān wa-anbā' abnā' al-zamān*. Edited by Iḥsān 'Abbās. 7 vols. + index. Beirut: Dār al-Thaqāfah, 1968, 1973.

Ibn Miskawayh (d. Rayy, 421/1030). *The Concluding Portion of the Experiences of the Nations* 1: *Reigns of Muqtadir, Qahir and Radi*. Edited by H. F. Amedroz. The Eclipse of the 'Abbasid Caliphate, Original Chronicles of the Fourth Islamic Century 1. London: Basil Blackwell, 1920. (*Tajārib al-umam*.)

———. *The Concluding Portion of the Experiences of the Nations* 2: *Reigns of Muttaqi, Mustakfi, Muti' and Ta'i'*. Edited by H. F. Amedroz. Eclipse of the 'Abbasid Caliphate 2. Oxford: Basil Blackwell, 1921. (*Tajārib al-umam*.)

——. *The Concluding Portion of the Experiences of the Nations* 1: *Reigns of Muqtadir, Qahir and Radi*. Translated by D. S. Margoliouth. The Eclipse of the 'Abbasid Caliphate, Original Chronicles of the Fourth Islamic Century 4. London: Basil Blackwell, 1920. (*Tajārib al-umam*.)

Ibn Qudāmah al-Maqdisī (d. Damascus, 620/1223). *Al-Mughnī*. Edited by Ṭāhā Muḥammad al-Zaynī. 10 vols. Cairo: Maktabat al-Qāhirah, 1388-90.

Ibn Rajab (d. Damascus, 795/1393?). *Sharḥ "'Ilal" al-Tirmidhī*. Edited by Hammām 'Abd al-Raḥīm Sa'īd. 2 vols. Al-Zarqā', Jordan: Maktabat al-Manār, 1987.

Ibn Sa'd (d. Baghdad, 230/845). *Al-Ṭabaqāt al-kubrá*. 8 vols. + index. Beirut: Dār Ṣādir, 1957-68.

Ibn Shahrāshūb (d. 588/1192-93). *Ma'ālim al-'ulamā'*. Edited by Muḥammad Ṣādiq Āl Baḥr al-'Ulūm. Najaf: al-Maṭba'ah al-Ḥaydarīyah, 1961.

Ibn Ṭāhir al-Baghdādī (d. Isfarayin, 429/1037). *Al-Farq bayna al-firaq*. Edited by Muḥyī al-Dīn 'Abd al-Ḥamīd. Cairo: Maktabat Muḥammad 'Alī Ṣabīḥ, n.d.

Al-Idrīsī (d. Samarqand, 405/1014-15). *Tārīkh Istirābādh*. Excerpts on pages 466-504 of al-Sahmī. *Tārīkh Jurjān*. Hyderabad: Maṭba'at Majlis Dā'irat al-Ma'ārif al-'Uthmānīyah, 1950.

'Iyāḍ, al-Qāḍī—*v*. al-Qāḍī 'Iyāḍ.

Kātib Çelebī (d. Istanbul, 1067/1657). *Kashf al-ẓunūn 'an asāmī al-kutub wa-al-funūn*. Edited by Şerefettin Yaltkaya & Rifat Bilge. 2 vols. Istanbul: Maarif Matbaası, 1941, 1943.

Al-Khallāl (d. Baghdad 311/923). *Al-Amr bi-al-ma'rūf wa-al-nahy 'an al-munkar*. Edited by 'Abd al-Qādir Aḥmad 'Aṭā. Nawādir al-Turāth 2. Cairo: Dār al-I'tiṣām, 1975.

——. *Al-Musnad min masā'il Abī 'Abd Allāh Aḥmad ibn Muḥammad ibn Ḥanbal*. Edited by Ẕiyā'uddīn Aḥmad. Asiatic Society of Bangladesh Publication 29. Dacca: Asiatic Society of Bangladesh, 1975.

Al-Khaṣṣāf (d. Baghdad, 261/874). *Adab al-qāḍī*. Edited by Farḥat Ziyādah. Cairo: American University in Cairo Press, 1978.

——. *Das Kitāb al-ḥiial ual-maḥāriğ*. Edited by Joseph Schacht. Beiträge zur semitischen Philologie und Linguistik, edited by G. Bergsträsser, 4. Hanover: Heinz Lafaire, 1923.

Al-Khaṭīb al-Baghdādī (d. Baghdad, 463/1071). *Kitāb al-Kifāyah fī 'ilm al-riwāyah*. Hyderabad: Dā'irat al-Ma'ārif al-'Uthmānīyah, 1938.

——. *Tārīkh Baghdād aw madīnat al-salām*. 14 vols. Cairo: Maktabat al-Khānjī, 1931.

Al-Khushanī (d. Cordoba, 371/981?). *Ṭabaqāt 'ulamā' Ifrīqiyah*. *Apud* Abū al-'Arab. *Classes des savants de l'Ifriqiya*. Edited by Mohammed ben Cheneb. Publications de la Facultée des lettres d'Alger, Bulletin de correspondance africaine 51. Paris: Leroux, 1916.

——. *Ṭabaqāt 'ulamā' Ifrīqiyah*. Pages 177-311 in Abū al-'Arab. *Quḍāt Qurṭubah wa-'Ulamā' Ifrīqīyah*. Edited by 'Izzat al-'Aṭṭār al-Ḥusaynī. Min Turāth al-Andalus 2. Cairo: Maktabat al-Khānjī, 1953.

Al-Khʷārizmī (*fl.* 365/975). *Liber Mafâtîh al-olûm*. Edited by G. van Vloten. Leiden: E. J. Brill, 1895.

Al-Khʷārizmī, Muḥammad ibn Maḥmūd (d. 665/1266-67?). *Jāmi' masānīd al-imām al-a'ẓam*. 2 vols. Hyderabad: Dā'irat al-Ma'ārif, 1332.

Al-Kindī (d. Old Cairo, 350/961). *The Governors and Judges of Egypt*. Edited by Rhuvon Guest. E. J. W. Gibb Memorial Series 19. Leiden: E. J. Brill, 1912. (*Tasmiyat wulāt Miṣr. Kitāb al-Quḍāh.*)

Al-Maqrīzī (d. Cairo, 845/1442). *Kitāb al-Mawā'iẓ wa-al-i'tibār bi-dhikr al-khiṭaṭ wa-al-āthār*. Edited by Muḥammad ibn 'Abd al-Raḥmān Quṭṭah al-'Adawī. 2 vols. Bulaq: Dār al-Ṭibā'ah al-Miṣrīyah, 1853.

———. *Kitāb al-Muqaffá al-kabīr*. Edited by Muḥammad al-Ya'lawī. 8 vols. Beirut: Dār al-Gharb al-Islāmī, 1991.

Al-Mas'ūdī (d. Old Cairo, 345/956-957?). *Murūj al-dhahab wa-ma'ādin al-jawāhir*. Edited by Charles Pellat. Manshūrāt al-Jāmi'ah al-Lubnānīyah, Qism al-dirāsāt al-tārīkhīyah, 11. 7 vols. Beirut: al-Jāmi'ah al-Lubnānīyah, 1973-74.

———. *Les Prairies d'or*. Edited by C. A. C. Barbier de Meynard & B. M. M. Pavet de Courteille. 9 vols. Paris: Imprimerie impériale, 1861-77. (*Murūj al-dhahab.*)

Al-Māwardī (d. Baghdad, 450/1058). *Adab al-qāḍī*. Edited by Muḥyī Hilāl al-Sirḥān. Iḥyā' al-Turāth al-Islāmī 4. 2 vols. Baghdad: Dīwān al-Awqāf, 1972.

Al-Muqaddasī (i.e., al-Maqdisī; *fl.* 375/985). *Descriptio imperii moslemici*. Edited by M. J. de Goeje. Bibliotheca geographorum Arabicorum 3. 2nd edn. Leiden: E. J. Brill, 1906. (*Aḥsan al-taqāsīm fī ma'rifat al-aqālīm.*)

Al-Muzanī (d. Old Cairo, 264/877?). *Al-Mukhtaṣar*. On margins of al-Shāfi'ī. *Kitāb al-Umm* 1-5. Bulaq: al-Maṭba'ah al-Kubrá al-Amīrīyah, 1902-6.

Al-Najāshī (d. 450/1058-59?). *Rijāl al-Najāshī*. Edited by Muḥammad Jawād al-Nā'īnī. 2 vols. Beirut: Dār al-Aḍwā', 1988.

Al-Nawawī (d. Nawā, 676/1271). *Al-Majmū'. Sharḥ "al-Muhadhdhab."* Edited by Zakarīyā' 'Alī Yūsuf. 9 vols. + continuations. Cairo: Maṭba'at al-'Āṣimah, 1966-, & Maṭba'at al-Imām, n.d.

———. "Introduction." *Ṣaḥīḥ Muslim bi-sharḥ al-Nawawī*. 18 vols. Cairo: al-Maṭba'ah al-Miṣrīyah, 1929.

———. *Tahdhīb al-asmā' wa-al-lughāt*. 3 vols. in 2. Cairo: Idārat al-Ṭibā'ah al-Munīrīyah, 1927.

Al-Nawbakhtī (attributed; d. Baghdad, 310/922?). *Die Sekten der Schi'a*. Edited by Helmut Ritter. Bibliotheca Islamica 4. Istanbul: Staatsdruckerei, 1931. (*Kitāb Firaq al-shī'ah.*)

Al-Nisā'ī (d. Ramlah? 303/915?). "Tasmiyat fuqahā' al-amṣār." Pages 7-10 in *Majmū'at rasā'il fī 'ulūm al-ḥadīth*. Edited by Ṣubḥī al-Badrī al-Sāmarrā'ī. Medina: Muḥammad 'Abd al-Muḥsin, 1969.

Al-Qāḍī 'Iyāḍ (d. Marrakech, 544/1149). *Tartīb al-madārik wa-taqrīb al-masālik li-ma'rifat a'lām madhhab Mālik*. Edited by Aḥmad Bakīr Maḥmūd. 5 vols. in 3. Beirut: Maktabat al-Ḥayāh, 1967, 1968.

Al-Qāḍī al-Nu'mān (d. Cairo, 363/974). *Da'ā'im al-islām wa-dhikr al-ḥalāl wa-al-ḥarām wa-al-qaḍāyā wa-al-aḥkām 'an ahl bayt rasūl Allāh*. Edited by 'Āṣif ibn 'Alī Aṣghar Fayḍī. 2 vols. Cairo: Dār al-Ma'ārif, 1951, 1952.

Al-Qāri' al-Harawī (d. Mecca, 1014/1605). *Manāqib al-imām al-a'ẓam*. Pages 450-556 in Ibn Abī al-Wafā'. *Al-Jawāhir al-muḍīyah fī ṭabaqāt al-ḥanafīyah* 2. Hyderabad: Majlis Dā'irat al-Ma'ārif al-Niẓāmīyah, 1332.

Al-Ṣafadī (d. Damascus, 764/1363). *Das biographische Lexicon des Ṣalāḥaddīn Ḫalīl ibn Aybak aṣ-Ṣafadī* 3. Edited by Sven Dedering. Bibliotheca Islamica 6. Damascus: al-Maṭba'ah al-Hāshimīyah, 1953.

——. *Das biographische Lexicon des Ṣalāḥaddīn Ḫalīl ibn Aybak aṣ-Ṣafadī* 8. Edited by Muḥammad Yūsuf Najm. Bibliotheca Islamica 6. Wiesbaden: Franz Steiner Verlag, 1971.

Al-Sahmī (d. Nishapur, 427/1035-36). *Tārīkh Jurjān aw Kitāb Ma'rifat 'ulamā' ahl Jurjān*. Hyderabad: Maṭba'at Majlis Dā'irat al-Ma'ārif al-'Uthmānīyah, 1950.

Ṣāliḥ ibn Aḥmad (d. Isfahan, 266/880?). *Sīrat al-imām Aḥmad ibn Ḥanbal*. Edited by Fu'ād 'Abd al-Mun'im Aḥmad. Alexandria: Mu'assasat Shabāb al-Jāmi'ah, 1981.

Al-Sam'ānī (d. Marv, 562/1166). *The Kitāb al-Ansāb*. E. J. W. Gibb Memorial Series 20. Leiden: E. J. Brill, 1912.

Al-Sarrāj (d. 378/988). *The Kitáb al-Luma' fī 'l-taṣawwuf*. Edited by Reynold Alleyne Nicholson. E. J. W. Gibb Memorial Series 22. Leiden: E. J. Brill, 1914. Reprinted London: Luzac & Co., 1963.

Al-Shāfi'ī (d. Old Cairo, 204/820). *Kitāb al-Umm*. 7 vols. Bulaq: al-Maṭba'ah al-Kubrá al-Amīrīyah, 1902-6.

Al-Shahrastānī (d. Shahrastan, 548/1153). *Book of Religious and Philosophical Sects*. Edited by William Cureton. 2 vols. London: Society for the Publication of Oriental Texts, 1842, 1846. (*Al-Milal wa-al-niḥal*.)

——. *Al-Milal wa-al-niḥal*. Edited by Aḥmad Fahmī Muḥammad. 2 vols. Cairo: Maktabat al-Ḥusayn al-Tijārīyah, 1948.

——. *Al-Milal wa-al-niḥal*. Edited by 'Abd al-Laṭīf Muḥammad al-'Abd. Cairo: Maktabat al-Anjilū-al-Miṣrīyah [*sic*], 1977.

——. *Muslim Sects and Divisions*. Translated by A. K. Kazi & J. G. Flynn. London: Kegan Paul, 1984. (*Al-Milal wa-al-niḥal*.)

Al-Subkī, Tāj al-Dīn (d. Damascus, 771/1370). *Ṭabaqāt al-shāfi'īyah al-kubrá*. Edited by Maḥmūd Muḥammad al-Ṭanāḥī & 'Abd al-Fattāḥ al-Ḥulw. 10 vols. Cairo: 'Īsá al-Bābī al-Ḥalabī, 1964-76.

Al-Sulamī (d. Nishapur, 412/1012). *Kitāb Ṭabaqāt al-ṣūfīyah*. Edited by Johannes Pedersen. Leiden: E. J. Brill, 1960.

Al-Suyūṭī (d. Cairo, 911/1505). *Tārīkh al-khulafā'*. Beirut: Dār al-Thaqāfah, 1970's.

Al-Ṭabarī (d. Baghdad, 310/923). *Annales*. Edited by M. J. de Goeje. 3 vols. in 15. Leiden: E. J. Brill, 1879-1901. (*Tārīkh al-rusul wa-al-mulūk*.)

——. *Hādhā mā taḥtawī 'alayhī nuskhat al-Maktabah al-khadīwīyah min Kitāb Ikhtilāf al-fuqahā'*. Edited by Frederick Kern. Cairo: Maṭba'at al-Mawsū'āt & Maktabat al-Taraqqī, 1902.

——. *Das Konstantinopler Fragment des Kitāb Iḫtilāf al-fuqahā'*. Edited by Joseph Schacht. Veröffentlichungen der "De Goeje-Stiftung" 10. Leiden: E. J. Brill, 1933.

——. *Tārīkh al-Ṭabarī*. Edited by Muḥammad Abū al-Faḍl Ibrāhīm. Dhakhā'ir al-'Arab 30. 10 vols. Cairo: Dār al-Ma'ārif, 1960-69.

Al-Ṭūsī, Shaykh al-Ṭā'ifah (d. Najaf, 460/1067?). *Al-Fihrist*. Edited by Muḥammad Ṣādiq Āl Baḥr al-'Ulūm. Nashrīyāt al-Maktabah al-Murtaḍawīyah 95. Najaf: al-Maṭba'ah al-Ḥaydarīyah, 1937.

——. *Ikhtiyār ma'rifat al-rijāl al-ma'rūf bi-"Rijāl al-Kashshī."* Edited by Ḥasan al-Muṣṭafawī. Dānishgadah-yi Ilāhīyāt va Ma'ārif-i Islāmī Mashhad: Dānish-

gāh-i Mashhad, 1348.
Al-'Uqaylī (d. Hijaz, 322/934). *Kitāb al-Ḍu'afā' al-kabīr*. Edited by 'Abd al-Mu'ṭī Amīn Qal'ajī. 4 vols. Beirut: Dār al-Kutub al-'Ilmīyah, 1984.
Wakī' (d. Baghdad, 306/918). *Akhbār al-quḍāh*. Edited by 'Abd al-'Azīz Muṣṭafá al-Marāghī. 3 vols. Cairo: Maṭba'at al-Istiqāmah, 1947-50.
Al-Yāfi'ī (d. Mecca, 768/1367). *Mir'āt al-janān wa-'ibrat al-yaqẓān*. 4 vols. Hyderabad: Dā'irat al-Ma'ārif al-Niẓāmīyah, 1337-39.
Yāqūt (d. Aleppo, 626/1229). *Irshád al-aríb ilá ma'rifat al-adíb*. Edited by D. S. Margoliouth. E. J. W. Gibb Memorial Series 6. 7 vols. Leiden: E. J. Brill, 1907-27.
———. *Irshād al-arīb ilá ma'rifat al-adīb*. Edited by Iḥsān 'Abbās. 7 vols. Beirut: Dār al-Gharb al-Islāmī, 1993.

SECONDARY SOURCES

Abū Zahrah. *Tārīkh al-madhāhib al-islāmīyah* 2: *Fī tārīkh al-madhāhib al-fiqhīyah*. Cairo: Dār al-Fikr al-'Arabī, n.d.
ALA-LC Romanization Tables. Edited by Randall K. Barry. Washington, DC: Library of Congress Cataloging Distribution Service, 1991.
Allard, Michel. *Le Problème des attributs divins dans la doctrine d'al-Aš'arī et de ses premiers grands disciples*. Recherches publiées sous la direction de l'Institut de lettres orientales de Beyrouth 28. Beirut: Imprimerie catholique, 1965.
Badrān, 'Abd al-Qādir. *Al-Madkhal ilá madhhab al-imām Aḥmad*. N.p., n.d.
Békir, Ahmed. *Histoire de l'école malikite en Orient jusqu'à la fin du Moyen Age*. Paris: Université de Paris, n.d.
Bernand, Marie. "Ḥanafī *uṣūl al-fiqh* Through a Manuscript of al-Ǧaṣṣāṣ." *Journal of the American Oriental Society* 105 (1985):623-635.
Bloch, Marc. *The Historian's Craft*. Translated by Peter Putnam. New York: Knopf, 1953.
Brunschvig, Robert. "Fiqh Fâtimide et histoire de l'Ifrîqiya." Pages 13-20 in *Mélanges d'histoire et d'archéologie de l'Occident musulman. Hommage à G. Marçais* 2. Algiers: Gouvernement général de l'Algérie, 1957.
———. "Polémiques médiévales autour du rite de Mālik." *Al-Andalus* 15 (1950): 377-435.
Bulliet, Richard W. "Conversion to Islam and the Emergence of a Muslim Society in Iran." Pages 30-51 in *Conversion to Islam*. Edited by Nehemia Levtzion. New York: Holmes & Meier, 1979.
Cahen, Claude. "La changeante portée sociale de quelques doctrines religieuses." Pages 5-22 in *L'Elaboration de l'Islam. Colloque de Strasbourg, 12-13-14-juin*. Edited by Claude Cahen. Paris: Presses universitaires de France, 1961.
———. *Les Peuples musulmanes dans l'histoire médiévale*. Damascus: Institut français de Damas, 1977.
Calder, Norman. *Studies in Early Islamic Jurisprudence*. New York: Clarendon Press, 1993.
Chabbi, Jacqueline. "Remarques sur le développement historique des mouvements ascétiques et mystiques au Khurasan, IIIe/IXe siècle-IVe/Xe siècle." *Studia Islami-*

ca, no. 46 (1977), 5-72.
Coulson, N. J. *A History of Islamic Law*. Islamic Surveys 2. Edinburgh: University Press, 1964.
Denny, Frederick Mathewson. *An Introduction to Islam*. New York: Macmillan, 1985.
Dickinson, Eerik. "Aḥmad b. al-Ṣalt and His Biography of Abū Ḥanīfa." *Journal of the American Oriental Society* 116 (1996):406-417.
Encyclopaedia of Islam. New edition. Edited by B. Lewis, &al. Leiden; E. J. Brill, 1960-. S.v. "Abū Ḥanīfa," by J. Schacht; s.v. "Abū Yūsuf," by J. Schacht; s.v. "Ahl al-Ḥadīth" by J. Schacht; s.v. "Aḥmad b. Ḥanbal" by H. Laoust; s.v. "*Aṣḥāb al-ra'y*," by J. Schacht; s.v. "al-Barbahārī," by H. Laoust; s.v. "Ghulām al-Khallāl," by H. Laoust; s.v. "Mālik," by J. Schacht; s.v. "Miḥna," by M. Hinds; s.v. "Mu'tazila," by D. Gimaret.
Endress, Gerhard. *An Introduction to Islam*. Translated by Carole Hillenbrand. New York: Columbia University Press, 1988.
Ernst, Carl W. *Words of Ecstasy in Sufism*. Albany: State University of New York Press, 1985.
Esposito, John L. *Islam: The Straight Path*. New York: Oxford University Press, 1988.
Ess, Josef van. "Ḍirār b. 'Amr und die 'Cahmiya': Biographie einer vergessenen Schule." *Der Islam* 43 (1967):241-279; 44 (1968):1-70, 318-320.
——— . *Die Gedankenwelt des Ḥāriṯ al-Muḥāsibī*. Bonner orientalische Studien, n.s., 12. Bonn: Selbstverlag des orientalischen Seminars der Universität Bonn, 1961.
——— . "Ibn Kullāb und die Miḥna." *Oriens* 18-19 (1965-1966):92-141. Translated with additional notes by Claude Gilliot. "Ibn Kullāb et la *Miḥna*." *Arabica* 37 (1990):173-233.
——— . *Theologie und Gesellschaft im 2. und 3. Jahrhundert Hidschra. Eine Geschichte des religiösen Denkens im frühen Islam*. 6 vols. Berlin: de Gruyter, 1991-95.
Finkel, Joshua. "A Risāla of al-Jāḥiẓ." *Journal of the American Oriental Society* 47 (1927):311-334.
Fück, Johann. "Neue Materialien zum Fihrist." *Zeitschrist für der deutsche morgenländische Gesellschaft* 90 (1936):298-321.
——— . "Some Hitherto Unpublished Texts on the Mu'tazilite Movement From Ibn al-Nadīm's 'Kitāb al-Fihrist.'" Pages 51-74 in *Professor Muḥammad Shafī' Presentation Volume*. Edited by S. M. Abdullah. Lahore: Majlis-e-Armughān-e-'Ilma, 1955.
Gilliot, Claude. *Exégèse, langue et théologie en islam. L'exégèse coranique de Tabarî*. Librairie philosophique. Paris: J. Vrin, 1990.
——— . "Le traitement du *ḥadīṯ* dans le *Tahḏīb al-āṯār* de Tabari." *Arabica* 41 (1994):309-351.
——— . "Quand la théologie s'allie à l'histoire. Triomphe et échec de rationalisme musulman à travers l'œvre d'al-Ǧuwaynī." *Arabica* 39 (1992):241-260.
Gimaret, Daniel. "Cet autre théologien sunnite: Abū l-'Abbās al-Qalānisī." *Journal asiatique* 277 (1989):227-261.
——— . "Un document majeur pour l'histoire du kalām: Le *Muǧarrad maqālāt al-*

Aš'arī d'Ibn Fūrak." *Arabica* 32 (1985):185-218.
Goldziher, Ignaz. *Introduction to Islamic Theology and Law*. Translated by Andras & Ruth Hamori. Modern Classics in Near Eastern Studies. Princeton: University Press, 1981.
——. "Zur Geschichte der hanbalitischen Bewegungen." *Zeitschrift für der deutsche morgenländische Gesellschaft* 62 (1908):1-28.
Graham, William A. "Traditionalism in Islam." *Journal of Interdisciplinary History* 23 (1992-93):495-522.
Halkin, A. S. "The Ḥashwiyya." *Journal of the American Oriental Society* 54 (1934):1-28.
Hallaq, Wael B. "On the Origins of the Controversy About the Existence of Mujtahids and the Gate of Ijtihad." *Studia Islamica*, no. 63 (1986), 129-141.
——. "Was al-Shafi'i the Master Architect of Islamic Jurisprudence?" *International Journal of Middle East Studies* 25 (1993):587-605.
——. "Was the Gate of Ijtihad Closed?" *International Journal of Middle East Studies* 16 (1984):3-41.
Halm, Heinz. *Die Ausbreitung der šāfi'itischen Rechtsschule*. Beihefte zum tübinger Atlas des vorderen Orients, B (Geisteswissenschaften), 4. Wiesbaden: Ludwig Reichert, 1974.
Hodgson, Marshall G. S. *The Venture of Islam. Conscience and History in a World Civilization*. 3 vols. Chicago: University of Chicago Press, 1973.
Idris, Roger. "Réflexions sur le Mālikisme sous les umayyades d'Espagne." Pages 397-414 in *Atti del terzo congresso di studi arabi e islamici, Ravello, 1-6 settembre 1966*. Naples: Istituto universitario orientale, 1967.
Jackson, Sherman A. *Islamic Law and the State. The Constitutional Jurisprudence of Shihāb al-Dīn al-Qarāfī*. Studies in Islamic Law and Society, edited by Ruud Peters & Bernard Weiss, 1. Leiden: E. J. Brill, 1996.
Juynboll, G. H. A. *Muslim Tradition: Studies in Chronology, Provenance and Authorship of Early* ḥadīth. Cambridge: University Press, 1983.
——. "Some Notes on Islam's First *fuqahā'* Distilled From Early *ḥadīṯ* Literature." *Arabica* 39 (1992):287-314.
Khoury, Raif Georges. *'Abd Allāh ibn Lahī'a (97-174/715-790): Juge et grand maître de l'école égyptienne*. Codices arabici antiqui 4. Wiesbaden: Harrasowitz, 1986.
Landau-Tasseron, Ella. "The 'Cyclical Reform': A Study of the Mudjaddid Tradition." *Studia Islamica*, no. 70 (1989), 79-117.
Laoust, Henri. *La profession de foi d'Ibn Baṭṭa, traditioniste et jurisconsulte musulman d'école hanbalite, mort en Irak à 'Ukbarâ en 387/997*. Damascus: Institut français de Damas, 1958.
Lecomte, Gérard. "Un exemple d'évolution de la controverse en Islam: de l'*Iḫtilāf al-ḥadīṯ* d'al-Šāfi'ī au *Muḫtalif al-ḥadīṯ* d'Ibn Qutayba." *Studia Islamica*, no. 27 (1967), 5-40.
Librande, Leonard. "The Supposed Homogeneity of Technical Terms in Ḥadīth Study." *Muslim World* 72 (1982):34-50.
Macdonald, Duncan Black. *Development of Muslim Theology, Jurisprudence and Constitutional Theory*. New York: C. Scribner's Sons, 1903.
Madelung, Wilferd. "The Early Murji'a in Khurāsān and Transoxania and the

Spread of Hanafism." *Der Islam* 59 (1982):32-39.

———. "Imāmism and Mu'tazilite Theology." Pages 13-29 in *Le Shî'isme imâmite*. Edited by T. Fahd. Paris: Presses universitaires de France, 1979.

———. "The Origins of the Controversy Concerning the Creation of the Koran." Pages 504-525 in *Orientalia hispanica: sive studia F. M. Pareja octogenaria dicata* 1: *Arabica Islamica*. Edited by J. M. Barral. Leiden: E. J. Brill, 1974.

Al-Maghribī, 'Alī 'Abd al-Fattāḥ *Al-Firaq al-kalāmīyah al-islāmīyah: Madkhal wa-dirāsah*. Silsilat dirāsāt kalāmīyah. Cairo: Maktabat Wahbah, 1986.

Makdisi, George. "Ash'arī and the Ash'arites in Islamic Religious History." *Studia Islamica*, no. 17 (1962), 37-80, 18 (1963), 19-39.

———. "La Corporation à l'époque classique de l'Islam." Pages 35-49 in *Présence de Louis Massignon: Hommages et témoignages*. Paris: Maisonneuve & Larose, 1987.

———. "The Guilds of Law in Medieval Legal History: An Inquiry Into the Origins of the Inns of Court." Pages 233-252 in *Zeitschrift für Geschichte der arabisch-islamischen Wissenschaften* 1. Edited by Fuat Sezgin. Frankfurt: Institut für Geschichte der arabisch-islamischen Wissenschaften, 1984.

———. "Hanbalite Islam." Pages 216-274 in *Studies on Islam*. Translated & edited by Merlin L. Swartz. New York: Oxford University Press, 1981.

———. *Ibn 'Aqīl et la résurgence de l'Islam traditionaliste au XIe siècle (Ve siècle de l'Hégire)*. Damascus: Institut français de Damas, 1963.

———. "Muslim Institutions of Learning in Eleventh-Century Baghdad." *Bulletin of the School of Oriental and African Studies* 24 (1961):1-56.

———. *The Rise of Colleges: Institutions of Learning in Islam and the West*. Edinburgh: Edinburgh University Press, 1981.

———. *The Rise of Humanism in Classical Islam and the Christian West, With Special Reference to Classicism*. Edinburgh: Edinburgh University Press, 1990.

———. "*Ṭabaqāt*-Biography: Law and Orthodoxy in Classical Islam." *Islamic Studies* (Islamabad) 32 (1993):371-396.

Mansour, Mansour Hasan. "The Spread and the Domination of the Maliki School of Law in North and West Africa, Eighth-Fourteenth Century." Ph.D. dissertation. University of Illinois at Chicago Circle, 1981.

Marçais, Georges. *La Berbérie musulmane et l'Orient au moyen âge*. Les Grandes crises de l'histoire. Paris: Aubier, Editions Montaigne, 1946.

Massignon, Louis. "Cadis et naqibs baghdadiens." Pages 258-265 in *Opera minora* 1. Edited by Y. Moubarac. Recherches et documents. Beirut: Dar al-maaref, 1963.

———. *The Passion of al-Hallāj, Mystic and Martyr of Islam*. Translated by Herbert Mason. Bollingen Series 98. 4 vols. Princeton: University Press, 1982.

Melchert, Christopher. "The Formation of the Sunni Schools of Law, Ninth-Tenth Centuries C.E." Ph.D. dissertation. University of Pennsylvania, 1992.

———. "The Proto-Imāmīyah Between Rationalism and Traditionalism." Forthcoming in *Shī'ī Islam: Faith, Experience, and Worldview*. Edited by Lynda S. Clarke with Mahmoud Ayoub.

———. "The Transition From Asceticism to Mysticism at the Middle of the Ninth Century C.E." *Studia Islamica* 83 (1996):51-70.

Meron, Ya'akov. "The Development of Legal Thought in Hanafi Texts." *Studia Is-*

lamica, no. 30 (1969), 73-118.
Mez, Adam. *The Renaissance of Islam*. Translated by Salahuddin Khuda Bukhsh & D. S. Margoliouth. London: Luzac, 1937.
Monès, H. "Le Malékisme et l'échec des Fatimides en Ifriqiya." Pages 197-220 in *Etudes d'Orientalisme dédiées à la mémoire de Lévi-Provençal* 1. Paris: G.-P. Maisonneuve & Larose, 1962.
Mottahedeh, Roy P. *Loyalty and Leadership in an Early Islamic Society*. Princeton Studies on the Near East. Princeton: University Press, 1980.
Mudarris, Muḥammad Maḥrūs 'Abd al-Laṭīf. *Mashāyikh Balkh min al-Ḥanafīyah wa-mā infaradū bihi min al-masā'il al-fiqhīyah*. Iḥyā' al-turāth al-islāmī. 2 vols. Baghdad: Wizārat al-Awqāf, 1978, 1979.
Nagel, Tilman. *Die Festung des Glaubens. Triumph und Scheitern des islamischen Rationalismus in 11. Jahrhundert*. Munich: C. H. Beck, 1988.
Patton, Walter M. *Aḥmed ibn Ḥanbal and the Miḥna*. Leiden: E. J. Brill, 1897.
Pessagno, J. Merie. "The Murji'a, Īmān, and Abū 'Ubayd." *Journal of the American Oriental Society* 95 (1975):382-394.
Peters, F. E. *Allāh's Commonwealth: A History of Islam in the Near East, 600-1100 A.D.* New York: Simon & Schuster, 1973.
Reinhart, A. Kevin. *Before Revelation: The Boundaries of Muslim Moral Thought*. SUNY Series in Middle Eastern Studies. Albany: State University of New York Press, 1995.
Rippin, Andrew. *Muslims. Their Religious Beliefs and Practices* 1: *The Formative Period*. London: Routledge, 1990.
Robson, James. "Standards Applied by Muslim Traditionists." *Bulletin of the John Rylands Library Manchester* 43 (1960-61):459-479.
Rosenthal, Franz. "General Introduction." Pages 3-154 in *The History of al-Ṭabarī* 1: *General Introduction and From the Creation to the Flood*. SUNY Series in Near Eastern Studies & Bibliotheca Persica. Albany: State University of New York Press, 1989.
Sabari, Simha. *Mouvements populaires à Bagdad à l'époque "abbaside," IXᵉ-XIᵉ siècles*. Centre "Shiloah" des études du Moyen-Orient et de l'Afrique, Université de Tel Aviv, Etudes de civilisation et d'Histoire Islamiques. Paris: Adrien Maisonneuve, 1981.
Ṣabrī, 'Āmir Ḥasan. *Zawā'id 'Abd Allāh ibn Aḥmad ibn Ḥanbal fī "al-Musnad."* Beirut: Dār al-Bashā'ir al-Islāmīyah, 1990.
Schacht, Joseph. "Early Doctrines on Waqf." Pages 443-452 in *Altmışıncı doğum yılı münasebetiyle Fuad Köprülü armağanı Mélanges Fuad Köprülü*. Istanbul: Osman Yalçın Matbaası, 1953.
———. "Modernism and Traditionalism in a History of Islamic Law." *Middle Eastern Studies* 1 (1965):388-400.
———. *The Origins of Muhammadan Jurisprudence*. Oxford: Clarendon Press, 1950.
———. "The Schools of Law and Later Developments of Jurisprudence." Pages 57-84 in *Law in the Middle East* 1: *Origin and Development of Islamic Law*. Edited by Majid Khadduri & Herbert J. Liebesny. Washington, DC: Middle East Institute, 1955.
———. "Sur la transmission de la doctrine dans les écoles juridiques de l'Islam."

Annales de l'Institut des études orientales (Algiers) 10 (1952):399-419.
——. "Sur quelques manuscrits de la bibliothèque de la mosquée d'al-Qarawiyyīn à Fès." Pages 271-284 in *Etudes d'orientalisme dédiées à la mémoire de Lévi-Provençal* 1. Paris: G.-P. Maisonneuve & Larose, 1962.

Şeşen, Ramazan, Cevat İzgi, & Cemil Akpınar. *Catalogue of Manuscripts in the Köprülü Library*. 3 vols. Istanbul: Research Centre for Islamic History, Art & Culture, 1986.

Sezgin, Fuat. *Geschichte des arabischen Schrifttums*. 9 vols. to date. Leiden: E. J. Brill, 1967-.

Smith, Wilfred Cantwell. "The Concept of *Shari'a* Among Some *Mutakallimūn*." Pages 581-602 in *Arabic and Islamic Studies in Honor of Hamilton A. R. Gibb*. Edited by George Makdisi. Leiden: E. J. Brill, 1965.

Snouck Hurgronje, Christiaan. *Selected Works*. Edited by G.-H. Bousquet & Joseph Schacht. Leiden: E. J. Brill, 1957.

Sourdel, Dominique. "Une Profession de foi de l'historien al-Ṭabarī." *Revue des études islamiques* 36 (1968):177-199.

Spectorsky, Susan A. "Aḥmad Ibn Ḥanbal's *Fiqh*." *Journal of the American Oriental Society* 102 (1982):461-465.

——. *Chapters on Marriage and Divorce. Responses of Ibn Ḥanbal and Ibn Rāhwayh*. Austin: University of Texas Press, 1993.

Strothmann, Rudolf. "Recht der Ismailiten." *Der Islam* 31 (1954):131-146.

Talbi, M. "Kairouan et le mālikisme espagnol." Pages 317-337 in *Etudes d'orientalisme dédiées à la mémoire de Lévi-Provençal* 1. Paris: G.-P. Maisonneuve & Larose, 1957.

Tritton, A. S. *Islam: Belief and Practices*. London: Hutchinson Library, 1951.

Vesey-Fitzgerald, S. G. *Muhammadan Law. An Abridgement According to Its Various Schools*. London: Clarendon Press, 1931.

Watt, W. Montgomery. "The Closing of the Door of *Iǧtihād*." Pages 675-678 in *Orientalia hispanica: sive studia F. M. Pareja octogenario dicata* 1: *Arabica Islamica*. Edited by J. M. Barral. Leiden: E. J. Brill, 1974.

——. *The Formative Period of Islamic Thought*. Edinburgh: Edinburgh University Press, 1973.

——. *Islam and the Integration of Society*. International Library of Sociology & Social Reconstruction. London: Routledge & Kegan Paul, 1961.

Weber, Max. *Economy and Society: An Outline of Interpretive Sociology*. Edited by Guenther Roth & Claus Wittich. 2 vols. Berkeley: University of California Press, 1978.

Weiss, Bernard. *The Search for God's Law. Islamic Jurisprudence in the Writings of Sayf al-Dīn al-Āmidī*. Salt Lake City: University of Utah Press, 1992.

INDEX

"Al-" and "the" omitted from beginnings of entries. "20f" indicates pages 20 and 21, "20n" a footnote on 20. "'A." = 'Alī. "AB" = Abū Bakr. "AD" = Abū Dāwūd. "AJ" = Abū Ja'far. "'Al." = 'Abd Allāh. "AM" = Abū Muḥammad. "AQ" = Abū al-Qāsim. "'Ar." = 'Abd al-Raḥmān. "AS" = Abū Sulaymān. "'Az." = 'Abd al-'Azīz. "Attr." = attributed to. "Ca." = circa. "Cent." = century. "Ch." = "chapter." "D." = Dāwūd, died. "*Fl.*" = *floruit*. "H." = Hārūn. "Ḥ." = Ḥasan. "Ḥu." = Ḥusayn. "Ibr." = Ibrāhīm. "Isḥ" = Isḥāq. "*K.*" = *Kitāb*. "M." = Muḥammad. "N." = "note." "Q." = Qāsim. "Sul." = Sulaymān. "*V.*" = *vide*.

STUDIES IN ISLAMIC LAW AND SOCIETY

Edited by

RUUD PETERS AND BERNARD WEISS

Studies in Islamic Law and Society accomodates monographs, collections of essays, critical editions of texts with annotated translation, and reference works whose subject-matter lies within the field of classical and modern Islamic law. Both the study of legal texts and legal discourse and the study of the social circumstances in which law has been and is being shaped—the reciprocity of influence of law on society and society on law—are integral to the series, and works representing either type of study or both will be considered for inclusion. *Studies in Islamic Law and Society* will provide a focal point for scholars researching Islamic law both as a medium in its own right and as a phenomenon inviting historical and social analysis.

1. JACKSON, S.A. *Islamic Law and the State.* The Constitutional Jurisprudence of Shihāb al-Dīn al-Qarāfī. 1996. ISBN 90 04 10458 5
2. SAEED, A. *Islamic Banking and Interest.* A Study of the Prohibition of Riba and its Contemporary Interpretation. 1996. ISBN 90 04 10565 4
3. SHAHAM, R. *Family and the Courts in Modern Egypt.* A Study Based on Decisions by the Sharīʿa Courts 1990-1955. 1997. ISBN 90 04 10742 8
4. MELCHERT, C. *The Formation of the Sunni Schools of Law, 9th-10th Centuries C.E.* 1997. ISBN 90 04 10952 8

ISSN 1384–1130